Teach Yourself®
Microsoft® Project 2000

Teach Yourself® Microsoft® Project 2000

Vickey L. Quinn

IDG Books Worldwide, Inc.
An International Data Group Company

Foster City, CA • Chicago, IL • Indianapolis, IN • New York, NY

Teach Yourself® Microsoft® Project 2000

Published by
IDG Books Worldwide, Inc.
An International Data Group Company
919 E. Hillsdale Blvd., Suite 400
Foster City, CA 94404
`www.idgbooks.com` (IDG Books Worldwide Web site)

ISBN: 0-7645-3400-9

Printed in the United States of America

10 9 8 7 6 5 4 3 2 1

1VH/RT/QT/QQ/IN

Distributed in the United States by IDG Books Worldwide, Inc.

Distributed by CDG Books Canada Inc. for Canada; by Transworld Publishers Limited in the United Kingdom; by IDG Norge Books for Norway; by IDG Sweden Books for Sweden; by IDG Books Australia Publishing Corporation Pty. Ltd. for Australia and New Zealand; by TransQuest Publishers Pte Ltd. for Singapore, Malaysia, Thailand, Indonesia, and Hong Kong; by Gotop Information Inc. for Taiwan; by ICG Muse, Inc. for Japan; by Intersoft for South Africa; by Eyrolles for France; by International Thomson Publishing for Germany, Austria and Switzerland; by Distribuidora Cuspide for Argentina; by LR International for Brazil; by Galileo Libros for Chile; by Ediciones ZETA S.C.R. Ltda. for Peru; by WS Computer Publishing Corporation, Inc., for the Philippines; by Contemporanea de Ediciones for Venezuela; by Express Computer Distributors for the Caribbean and West Indies; by Micronesia Media Distributor, Inc. for Micronesia; by Chips Computadoras S.A. de C.V. for Mexico; by Editorial Norma de Panama S.A. for Panama; by American Bookshops for Finland.

For general information on IDG Books Worldwide's books in the U.S., please call our Consumer Customer Service department at 800-762-2974. For reseller information, including discounts and premium sales, please call our Reseller Customer Service department at 800-434-3422.

For information on where to purchase IDG Books Worldwide's books outside the U.S., please contact our International Sales department at 317-596-5530 or fax 317-572-4002.

For consumer information on foreign language translations, please contact our Customer Service department at 800-434-3422, fax 317-572-4002, or e-mail rights@idgbooks.com.

For information on licensing foreign or domestic rights, please phone +1-650-653-7098.

For sales inquiries and special prices for bulk quantities, please contact our Sales department at 800-762-2974 or write to the address above.

For information on using IDG Books Worldwide's books in the classroom or for ordering examination copies, please contact our Educational Sales department at 800-434-2086 or fax 317-572-4005.

For press review copies, author interviews, or other publicity information, please contact our Public Relations department at 650-653-7000 or fax 650-653-7500.

For authorization to photocopy items for corporate, personal, or educational use, please contact Copyright Clearance Center, 222 Rosewood Drive, Danvers, MA 01923, or fax 978-750-4470.

Library of Congress Cataloging-in-Publication Data

Quinn, Vickey L., 1955-
    Teach Yourself Microsoft Project 2000 / Vickey L. Quinn.
      p.   cm.
    Includes index.
    ISBN 0-7645-3400-9 (alk. paper)
    1. Microsoft Project 2000. 2. Industrial project management--Computer programs. I. Title.
HD69.P75 Q56 2000
658.4'04'02855369--dc21
                            99–049484
                            CIP

ABOUT IDG BOOKS WORLDWIDE

Welcome to the world of IDG Books Worldwide.

IDG Books Worldwide, Inc., is a subsidiary of International Data Group, the world's largest publisher of computer-related information and the leading global provider of information services on information technology. IDG was founded more than 30 years ago by Patrick J. McGovern and now employs more than 9,000 people worldwide. IDG publishes more than 290 computer publications in over 75 countries. More than 90 million people read one or more IDG publications each month.

Launched in 1990, IDG Books Worldwide is today the #1 publisher of best-selling computer books in the United States. We are proud to have received eight awards from the Computer Press Association in recognition of editorial excellence and three from Computer Currents' First Annual Readers' Choice Awards. Our best-selling ...For Dummies® series has more than 50 million copies in print with translations in 31 languages. IDG Books Worldwide, through a joint venture with IDG's Hi-Tech Beijing, became the first U.S. publisher to publish a computer book in the People's Republic of China. In record time, IDG Books Worldwide has become the first choice for millions of readers around the world who want to learn how to better manage their businesses.

Our mission is simple: Every one of our books is designed to bring extra value and skill-building instructions to the reader. Our books are written by experts who understand and care about our readers. The knowledge base of our editorial staff comes from years of experience in publishing, education, and journalism — experience we use to produce books to carry us into the new millennium. In short, we care about books, so we attract the best people. We devote special attention to details such as audience, interior design, use of icons, and illustrations. And because we use an efficient process of authoring, editing, and desktop publishing our books electronically, we can spend more time ensuring superior content and less time on the technicalities of making books.

You can count on our commitment to deliver high-quality books at competitive prices on topics you want to read about. At IDG Books Worldwide, we continue in the IDG tradition of delivering quality for more than 30 years. You'll find no better book on a subject than one from IDG Books Worldwide.

John J. Kilcullen
John Kilcullen
Chairman and CEO
IDG Books Worldwide, Inc.

Eighth Annual Computer Press Awards ≥1992

Ninth Annual Computer Press Awards ≥1993

Tenth Annual Computer Press Awards ≥1994

Eleventh Annual Computer Press Awards ≥1995

IDG is the world's leading IT media, research and exposition company. Founded in 1964, IDG had 1997 revenues of $2.05 billion and has more than 9,000 employees worldwide. IDG offers the widest range of media options that reach IT buyers in 75 countries representing 95% of worldwide IT spending. IDG's diverse product and services portfolio spans six key areas including print publishing, online publishing, expositions and conferences, market research, education and training, and global marketing services. More than 90 million people read one or more of IDG's 290 magazines and newspapers, including IDG's leading global brands — Computerworld, PC World, Network World, Macworld and the Channel World family of publications. IDG Books Worldwide is one of the fastest-growing computer book publishers in the world, with more than 700 titles in 36 languages. The "...For Dummies®" series alone has more than 50 million copies in print. IDG offers online users the largest network of technology-specific Web sites around the world through IDG.net (http://www.idg.net), which comprises more than 225 targeted Web sites in 55 countries worldwide. International Data Corporation (IDC) is the world's largest provider of information technology data, analysis and consulting, with research centers in over 41 countries and more than 400 research analysts worldwide. IDG World Expo is a leading producer of more than 168 globally branded conferences and expositions in 35 countries including E3 (Electronic Entertainment Expo), Macworld Expo, ComNet, Windows World Expo, ICE (Internet Commerce Expo), Agenda, DEMO, and Spotlight. IDG's training subsidiary, ExecuTrain, is the world's largest computer training company, with more than 230 locations worldwide and 785 training courses. IDG Marketing Services helps industry-leading IT companies build international brand recognition by developing global integrated marketing programs via IDG's print, online and exposition products worldwide. Further information about the company can be found at www.idg.com.

1/26/00

Credits

Acquisitions Editor
Laura Moss

Project Editors
Valerie Perry
Katharine Dvorak

Technical Editor
Dennis Cohen

Copy Editors
Nancy Rapoport
Marti Paul

Project Coordinator
Emily Perkins

Graphics and Production Specialists
Karl Brandt
Mary Jo Weis
Jacque Schneider
Amy Adrian

Quality Control Specialist
Chris Weisbart
Laura Albert

Book Designers
Daniel Ziegler Design
Cátálin Dulfu
Kurt Krames

Proofreading and Indexing
York Production Services

About the Author

Vickey Quinn has over 15 years experience in the field of project management. After serving as a project manager in an MIS environment, she trained and consulted over 4,500 project management software users throughout North America. In addition, Vickey continues to add to her comprehensive view of project management through her work with many Fortune 1000 companies and governmental agencies across the country. Currently, she provides client-oriented project management consulting support, methodology, and software tool training and support, and designs and develops project management courseware.

As Dr. Kichiro Hayashi told me recently, "I cannot teach you anything. I can only create opportunities in which you can learn." With that thought in mind, I want to dedicate this Teach Yourself book to the people who create learning opportunities for me. My sincerest affection, love, and gratitude to all of you.

Welcome to
Teach Yourself

Welcome to *Teach Yourself*, a series read and trusted by millions for a decade. Although you may have seen the *Teach Yourself* name on other books, ours is the original. In addition, no *Teach Yourself* series has ever delivered more on the promise of its name than this series. That's because IDG Books Worldwide has transformed *Teach Yourself* into a new cutting-edge format that gives you all the information you need to learn quickly and easily.

Readers have told us that they want to learn by doing and that they want to learn as much as they can in as short a time as possible. We listened to you and believe that our new task-by-task format and suite of learning tools deliver the book you need to successfully teach yourself any technology topic. Features such as our Personal Workbook, which lets you practice and reinforce the skills you've just learned, help ensure that you get full value out of the time you invest in your learning. Handy cross-references to related topics and online sites broaden your knowledge and give you control over the kind of information you want, when you want it.

More Answers . . .

In designing the latest incarnation of this series, we started with the premise that people like you, who are beginning to intermediate computer users, want to take control of your own learning. To do this, you need the proper tools to find answers to questions so you can solve problems now.

In designing a series of books that provide such tools, we created a unique and concise visual format. The added bonus: *Teach Yourself* books actually pack more information into their pages than other books written on the same subjects. Skill for skill, you typically get much more information in a *Teach Yourself* book. In fact, *Teach Yourself* books, on average, cover twice the skills covered by other computer books — as many as 125 skills per book — so they're more likely to address your specific needs.

Welcome to Teach Yourself

...In Less Time

We know you don't want to spend twice the time to get all this great information, so we provide lots of time-saving features:

▶ A modular task-by-task organization of information: any task you want to perform is easy to find and includes simple-to-follow steps

▶ A larger size than standard makes the book easy to read and convenient to use at a computer workstation. The large format also enables us to include many more illustrations — 500 screen illustrations show you how to get everything done!

▶ A Personal Workbook at the end of each chapter reinforces learning with extra practice, real-world applications for your learning, and questions and answers to test your knowledge

▶ Cross-references appearing at the bottom of each task page refer you to related information, providing a path through the book for learning particular aspects of the software thoroughly

▶ A Find It Online feature offers valuable ideas on where to go on the Internet to get more information or to download useful files

▶ Take Note sidebars provide added-value information from our expert authors for more in-depth learning

▶ An attractive, consistent organization of information helps you quickly find and learn the skills you need

These *Teach Yourself* features are designed to help you learn the essential skills about a technology in the least amount of time, with the most benefit. We've placed these features consistently throughout the book, so you quickly learn where to go to find just the information you need — whether you work through the book from cover to cover or use it later to solve a new problem.

You will find a *Teach Yourself* book on almost any technology subject — from the Internet to Windows to Microsoft Office. Take control of your learning today, with IDG Books Worldwide's *Teach Yourself* series.

Teach Yourself
More Answers in Less Time

Search through the task headings to find the topic you want right away. To learn a new skill, search the contents, chapter opener, or the extensive index to find what you need. Then find — at a glance — the clear task heading that matches it.

Learn the concepts behind the task at hand and, more important, learn how the task is relevant in the real world. Time-saving suggestions and advice show you how to make the most of each skill.

After you learn the task at hand, you may have more questions, or you may want to read about other tasks related to the topic. Use the cross-references to find different tasks to make your learning more efficient.

Creating a New Project

Creating a new project involves three basic steps: starting a new file, establishing general project information, and selecting file properties.

Starting a new project file involves a simple menu choice, or you can click the New Project button on the Standard toolbar. Both techniques open the New dialog box with the Blank Project option highlighted. When you select the Blank Project option, the Project Information dialog box opens.

The Project Information dialog box houses important pieces of project data. The Schedule from field should be completed first. You can create your schedule from either the project Start or Finish date. Scheduling from the project start date enables you to enter or choose the project start date; Project 2000 calculates a finish date. Similarly, scheduling from the project finish date allows you to enter a finish date for the project; Project 2000 calculates the start date.

Next, review and modify, if necessary, both the Current and Status date fields. The current date should represent today's date as a reference point for Project 2000 calculations. Also, many progress tracking calculations in Project 2000, like earned value, complete-through dates, and progress lines rely on the Status date. A status date allows you to accurately report through a "frozen" date rather than allowing recalculations to occur on an automatic basis every day.

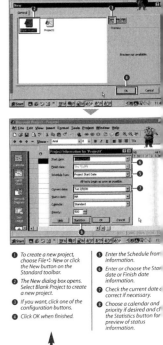

① To create a new project, choose File ⌐ New or click the New button on the Standard toolbar.

② The New dialog box opens. Select Blank Project to create a new project.

③ If you want, click one of the configuration buttons.

④ Click OK when finished.

⑤ Enter the Schedule from information.

⑥ Enter or choose the Start date or Finish date information.

⑦ Check the current date and correct if necessary.

⑧ Choose a calendar and priority if desired and click the Statistics button for preview of status information.

CROSS-REFERENCE

See Chapter 14, "Tracking Progress," for more information about using the Status line.

44

Ultimately, people learn by doing. Follow the clear, illustrated steps presented with every task to complete a procedure. The detailed callouts for each step show you exactly where to go and what to do to complete the task.

Welcome to Teach Yourself

Go to this area if you want special tips, cautions, and notes that provide added insight into the current task.

The current chapter name and number always appear in the top right-hand corner of every task spread, so you always know exactly where you are in the book.

Defining a New Project

CHAPTER 3

Use the Calendar field in the Project Information dialog box to choose which calendar to use as the master calendar for the project. Project 2000 references this calendar when scheduling tasks.

The Priority field lets you set a resource leveling priority at the project level (1–1000). This field is useful when sharing resources across projects.

Clicking the Statistics button provides progress summary information. Like the Status date mentioned earlier in this task, this information is more valuable after the project is under way.

Next, let's consider file properties, the third step. The File Properties dialog box contains five tabs. The General tab contains fields for information such as type, location, and size of file as well as file attributes. The entries on the Summary tab, like Title, Manager, and Company might appear on report headers. The Statistics tab contains dates for project creation, modification, or printing. The Contents tab gives a summary of project information. The final tab, Custom, allows you to establish custom properties for search purposes.

TAKE NOTE

▶ **PROJECT INFORMATION**

To return to the Project Information dialog box after the initial entries, choose Project ⇨ Project Information.

w the information on the Project cs screen.

he Close button when d.

⓫ *To change or add information, choose File ⇨ Properties.*

⓬ *Choose one of the five tabs and enter the appropriate data.*

⓭ *Click OK when finished.*

FIND IT ONLINE

For Project 2000 technical tips, see
http://www.mshk.com/MSClub/techtip.htm.

45

Who This Book Is For

This book is written for you, a beginning to intermediate PC user who isn't afraid to take charge of his or her own learning experience. You don't want a lot of technical jargon; you *do* want to learn as much about PC technology as you can in a limited amount of time. You need a book that is straightforward, easy to follow, and logically organized, so you can find answers to your questions easily. And, you appreciate simple-to-use tools such as handy cross-references and visual step-by-step procedures that help you make the most of your learning. We have created the unique *Teach Yourself* format specifically to meet your needs.

Use the Find It Online element to locate Internet resources that provide more background, take you on interesting side trips, and offer additional tools for mastering and using the skills you need. (Occasionally you'll find a handy shortcut here.)

Personal Workbook

It's a well-known fact that much of what we learn is lost soon after we learn it if we don't reinforce our newly acquired skills with practice and repetition. That's why each *Teach Yourself* chapter ends with your own Personal Workbook. Here's where you can get extra practice, test your knowledge, and discover ideas for using what you've learned in the real world. There's even a Visual Quiz to help you remember your way around the topic's software environment.

Feedback

Please let us know what you think about this book, and whether you have any suggestions for improvements. You can send questions and comments to the *Teach Yourself* editors on the IDG Books Worldwide Web site at **www.idgbooks.com**.

Personal Workbook

Q&A

❶ Describe two techniques to create a new project file.

_____

_____

_____

❷ Under what conditions or constraints would you schedule the project from the finish date rather than from the start date?

_____

_____

_____

❸ When is it reasonable for the Status Date to be different from the Current Date?

_____

_____

_____

❹ On which Options tab is the date format choice found?

_____

_____

_____

❺ When would you use manual rather than automat recalculation?

_____

_____

_____

❻ What technique can you use to copy a calendar f one project to another?

_____

_____

_____

❼ Describe the function of a project calendar.

_____

_____

_____

❽ Describe what is meant by the calendar term "N default working hours."

_____

_____

_____

ANSWERS: PAG

> After working through the tasks in each chapter, you can test your progress and reinforce your learning by answering the questions in the Q&A section. Then check your answers in the Personal Workbook Answers appendix at the back of the book.

Welcome to Teach Yourself

Another practical way to reinforce your skills is to do additional exercises on the same skills you just learned without the benefit of the chapter's visual steps. If you struggle with any of these exercises, it's a good idea to refer to the chapter's tasks to be sure you've mastered them.

Defining a New Project

Read the list of Real-World Applications to get ideas on how you can use the skills you've just learned in your everyday life. Understanding a process can be simple; knowing how to use that process to make you more productive is the key to successful learning.

EXTRA PRACTICE

Create a new project using the menu choice as well as the toolbar button.

In the Project Information dialog box, instruct Project 2000 to schedule your project from the finish date, and then enter a desired finish date.

Give your project a title and assign yourself as Manager using the Project Properties dialog box.

Look at the Standard default calendar.

Create a new calendar using the Standard calendar as the base.

Copy a custom calendar from one project to another.

REAL-WORLD APPLICATIONS

✔ You've been given a new project assignment so you use the File ➪ New command to create a new project file.

✔ Management has established a deadline (constraint) for this project so you choose to schedule from the project finish date and ask Microsoft Project 2000 to schedule backwards toward the project start date.

✔ Your company's standard hours include extended days with every other Friday off so you create a new calendar to reflect this.

✔ You are managing one piece of a large project so you copy the project calendar from the master project file into your project before adding tasks.

Visual Quiz

How do you select this noncontiguous group of dates in 2000?

Take the Visual Quiz to see how well you're learning your way around the technology. Learning about computers is often as much about how to find a button or menu as it is about memorizing definitions. Our Visual Quiz helps you find your way.

Acknowledgments

I would like to thank the following people for the roles they've played in the creation of this book: Martine Edwards and Laura Moss for giving me this opportunity; Valerie Haynes Perry and Katharine Dvorak for their cheerful expressions of patience, support, and guidance, and for their helpful suggestions to this first-time author; Dennis Cohen for the unenviable task of trying to keep me "on the straight and narrow;" Jason Luster and Jake Mason for their valuable assistance in creating a test environment; Adrian Jenkins of Microsoft Corporation for returning all my phone calls in a very timely manner; my friend and colleague, Eric Spanitz, for the client-server technical assistance and general support; and Ken Mosteller and Joan Knutson for supporting my "moonlighting" efforts.

A professor once told me "I can't teach you anything . . . I can only provide the opportunity in which you can learn." I would like to acknowledge the following for the learning opportunities they provide.

Special thanks go to Don Quinn, my Dad, for the opportunities to learn to be confident and passionate through sports competition; my Mom, Clara Quinn, for the opportunities to learn to be gentle with all living creatures, even myself; my sister, Dr. Donna Quinn-Butler, for allowing me to learn that asking for help is not a sign of weakness; my brother, Terry Quinn, for the many opportunities to learn that seeking adventure is what makes the heart remain young; my first boss at age 16 and my brother-in-law for many years, Robert Butler, for allowing me to learn the value of networking; Robert Lucero for the opportunities to see that the girl inside me still needs far more attention than the woman I have become; and my dogs, Brutus, Gabby, J.B., and Noel, for the daily lessons about unconditional love.

Contents

Contents

Contents

Contents

Contents

Teach Yourself®
Microsoft® Project 2000

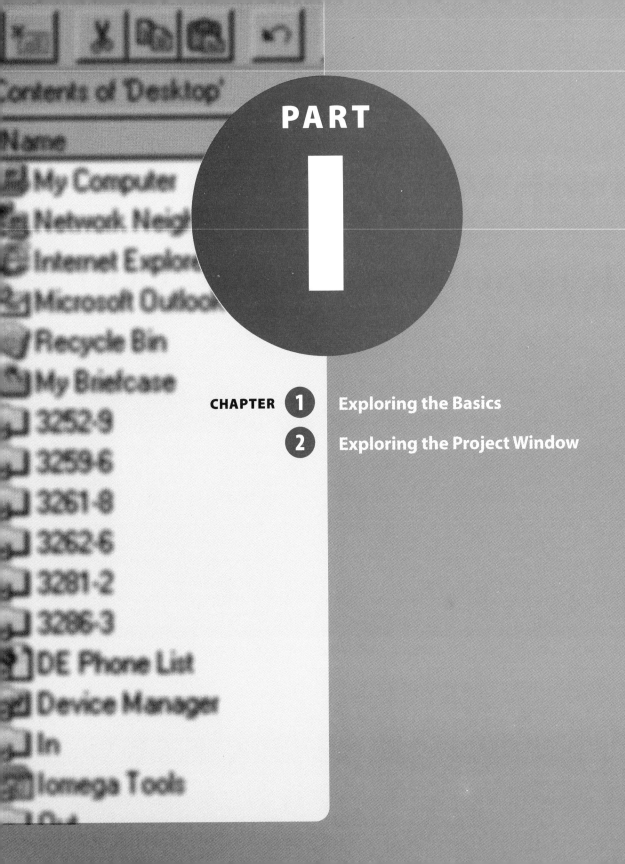

PART

I

Exploring the Basics

What do the building of the pyramids, the launching of the first space flight, the development of Microsoft Project 2000, moving an office, publishing a manuscript, and planning a wedding or reunion all have in common? They are all examples of projects.

Projects range in size and complexity from publishing a marketing brochure to launching a telecommunications satellite. Effective use of Microsoft Project 2000 requires a basic knowledge of the discipline of project management.

It falls to the leadership of the project manager to achieve results while balancing constraints and managing risks that can derail project efforts. As an integral part of the success of any project, the project manager spends time clarifying questions and issues surrounding the project, communicating about project work and issues, coordinating the work efforts, managing project progress, and closing out the project.

To lay the foundation for teaching yourself about Microsoft Project 2000, Part I covers the basics of a project life cycle as well as Microsoft Project basics such as starting and exiting the application and using the new HTML-based Help. You will also explore the basic Project 2000 window, including its menu, toolbars, project views, and tables.

CHAPTER 1

MASTER THESE SKILLS

▶ Examining a Project Life Cycle

▶ Starting and Exiting Microsoft Project 2000

▶ Using the Help Home Page

▶ Using the Project Map

▶ Working with the Office Assistant

▶ Using the Menu Bar

▶ Exploring Toolbars

▶ Setting Up an Electronic Project Binder

Exploring the Basics

Learning the basics of Microsoft Project 2000 includes starting and exiting the program, becoming familiar with the online help systems as well as the major window components like the menu, toolbars, and View Bar. Any attempts to teach yourself how to use Project 2000 should be coupled with a thorough understanding of the various forms of help available to you online. Few users today read (or even have) a hard copy of a traditional user's manual. Once you understand where to get help and how to use the menu, toolbars, and View Bar, navigating around and using Microsoft Project 2000 becomes easy and painless.

Microsoft Project 2000 continues the Microsoft Office 2000 family member (Excel, Access, Word, Outlook, Publisher, FrontPage, PhotoDraw, and PowerPoint) tradition of providing valuable online assistance and support for users. If you are already familiar with any of these products, you will recognize the new HTML-based Help in Project 2000. The content coverage of Help in Project 2000 is equal to or greater than the Help options available in Project 98. When you launch Project 2000, a Help home page displays. All forms of available help are accessible from the home page.

You'll find it easy to get acquainted with Project 2000 with What's New, Quick Preview, and the Tutorial forms of help. What's New lists features new to Project 2000, while the Quick Preview is a product tour of features and functionality. The Tutorial provides a series of lessons for first-time users. Technical information and answers usually found in a hard-copy user's manual are found under Reference. A configurable Office Assistant responds to requests typed in your own words. Microsoft Project 2000 also supplies a chronological Project Map to guide you through typical project management activities.

As is typical of other Windows applications, menus and toolbars provide access to software features and functionality. Project 2000 offers a complete menu of options as well as ten selectable toolbars. You'll explore both in this chapter.

As an added convenience, Microsoft Project 2000 includes a side View Bar that provides quick access to views frequently in demand such as Gantt Chart, Network Diagram, and Calendar.

So relax. With this book in hand as well as the numerous sources of help available in Microsoft Project 2000, you'll be navigating around and working on projects in a short while.

Examining a Project Life Cycle

Projects often seem to develop lives of their own as a result of their dynamic nature. It is important to recognize that projects have a typical pattern to their lives — called a life cycle. A project *life cycle* identifies the process of managing projects from concept to close-out.

A typical project life cycle attempts to define the beginning and end of a project and usually includes several phases. Each phase is marked by the completion of one or more deliverables, or tangible work products. Furthermore, each phase typically ends in a phase-end review to determine if the project should continue, to turn over the deliverable to the next phase participants, and to review quality. These reviews are called *phase exits*, *stage gates*, *kill points*, or *Go/No Go Points*. Although these phases are typically presented as sequential, a significant amount of overlap occurs.

Although product-oriented industries, such as software development, construction, and pharmaceutical development, create proprietary life cycles that describe in great detail how product-centered projects are created, they share common characteristics with project life cycles that aren't product-oriented. The following descriptions are representative of a generic five-phase project life cycle:

▶ *Selecting and approving* is the first phase in the life cycle. It takes the project from concept to the naming of a project manager. It is common in complex projects to write a *business case* outlining the business need and rationale for the project concept. Many organizations adopt project prioritization schemes to slot projects into *active project queues*.

▶ *Defining* is the next life-cycle phase. During this phase, the tangible results of the project are clarified, agreed to, and documented. This process usually

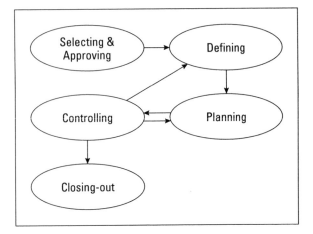

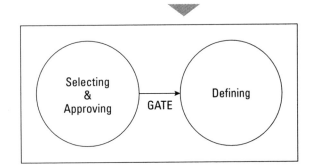

▶ A typical project life cycle contains numerous overlapping phases.

▶ Selecting and Approving combined with Defining ta a project from concept to definition of the end result

CROSS-REFERENCE

See "Customizing Toolbars" in Chapter 17 for information about creating your own toolbars.

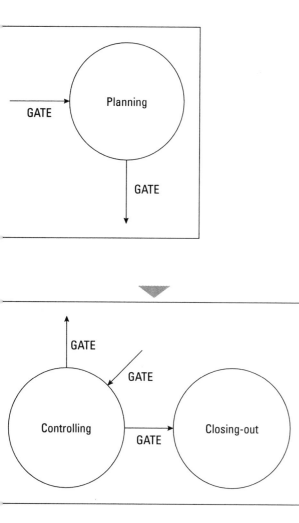

involves dialogue between the project stakeholders to gain understanding about project scope. A *definition document* is produced.

▶ *Planning* involves the identification of project tasks and the development of estimates, sequencing information, and perhaps resource allocation information, budgeting, and risk assessment data. During the planning phase, the definition document is used as the basis for schedule development. Often, technical requirements are further clarified and documented during this phase.

▶ *Controlling* includes managing, reforecasting, and replanning project activities. It is during the controlling phase that the execution of all project tasks occurs. This phase also includes managing the quality of the deliverables created during the project, managing risk, and meeting stakeholder expectations. Effective control of changes in scope is vital to the success of the project and must be monitored here.

▶ *Closing-out* a project includes collecting data for the last project tasks, turning the deliverables over to the client, conducting a close-out meeting, and archiving project information. Discussions of lessons learned can lead to continuous improvement in the project management process.

▸ Planning involves setting expectations and analyzing risks.

▶ Controlling the project involves managing the work in progress as well as the people working on the project.

▶ Closing-out captures lessons learned and archives project data. The deliverables are turned over to the customer.

FIND IT ONLINE

For the latest project management books, see
http:\\www.pmibooks.org.

Starting and Exiting Microsoft Project 2000

Starting Microsoft Project 2000 from the Windows desktop is the same as starting any other Windows application. The Windows desktop contains three convenient methods for launching Microsoft Project 2000: the Start button, the Microsoft Project 2000 icon, and the Quick Launch Toolbar.

Clicking the Start button at the lower-left corner of your Windows desktop pops up the Start menu, which is a list of options. If you move the mouse cursor to the Programs selection, a cascaded menu appears. Moving the cursor to Microsoft Project 2000 and clicking the mouse starts the program.

Installing Microsoft Project 2000 automatically places an icon on your desktop. Frequent users of Microsoft Project 2000 will want to leave this icon on the desktop because you can launch the program simply by double-clicking the icon. To keep your desktop neat, you can right-click the desktop and select Arrange Icons ⇨ Auto Arrange. This command arranges all desktop icons in rows and columns.

The Quick Launch toolbar is the toolbar to the right of the Start button on the Windows desktop. Clicking a Quick Launch toolbar button starts an application. You can customize the Quick Launch toolbar to add Project 2000 as a button.

Closing Project 2000 is as easy as starting it up. Of course, you'll want to exit the program using an acceptable procedure. Applications typically store information in the Windows Registry, and when you terminate the program in an appropriate manner, the information is stored. If the program isn't terminated correctly, your data could be lost.

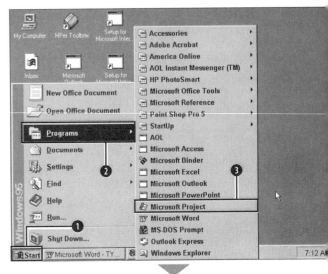

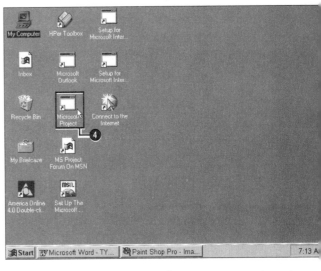

❶ Click the Start button to open the Start menu.

❷ Select Programs to open the Programs menu.

❸ Select Microsoft Project 2000 to start the application.

❹ Alternatively, from the desktop, double-click the Microsoft Project 2000 icon to start the application.

CROSS-REFERENCE

See "Saving and Password Protecting Files" in Chapter 4 for information about save options.

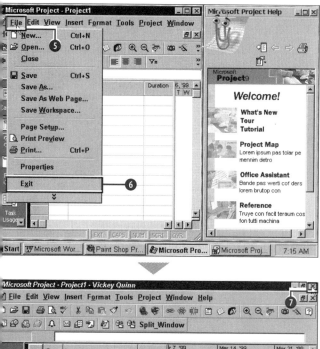

You can close Microsoft Project 2000 using any of the following three methods. You can choose Exit from the File menu, or you can click the Close button (the small box with an X) at the right end of the Title bar at the top of the main window. Another alternative is to use Alt+F4 to close the application. When you close Project 2000 you will be prompted to save all unsaved project files.

TAKE NOTE

▶ **LEFT-HANDED USE OF THE MOUSE**

References in this book refer to a mouse configured for "right-handed" use, which means that the left button chooses, selects, and drags while the right button opens shortcut menus. The right and left buttons switch roles when you configure the mouse for "left-handed use."

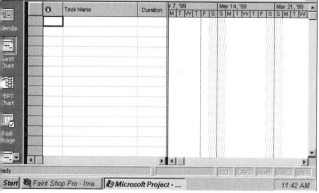

● To close the program, click File from the main menu to list menu options.

● Click Exit to close the program.

❼ Or, click the Close button on the Title bar.

FIND IT ONLINE

For a Start menu troubleshooting tip, see **http://www.worldowindows.com/w98t-tech.html**.

Using the Help Home Page

To take advantage of the latest in online help technology, Project 2000 uses an HTML-based help system. Online help means that help is always available with the click of a mouse. The online sources for help replace the hard-copy user manuals of old. Due to the new HTML-based technology, volumes of help are available online. HTML-based help enables you to view specific help information and click Home to go back to the home page or click any of the Web links to go to a different location.

The new Help Home Page lists the various sources of help available. Which source of help you select depends partly on your current needs and partly on personal preference. Becoming familiar with the various forms of help and how to access them is an important asset as you teach yourself Microsoft Project 2000. So, let's preview all the help sources listed on the home page here, and look at three of them — the Project Map, the Office Assistant, and Reference — in more detail on succeeding pages.

At startup, the Help Home Page button automatically displays on the Windows Task Bar at the bottom of the project window. You can resize the home page pane by dragging the pane divider to the right. You can also choose to no longer have the Help Home Page option automatically display at startup by deselecting the checkbox located at the bottom of the home page. To display the home page again after deselecting the box, choose Help ➪ Contents and Index.

You can get a list of the powerful new features found in Project 2000 by selecting the What's New choice.

Quick Preview gives high-level preview information about building a plan, managing a project, communicating project information to others, and getting assistance while you work.

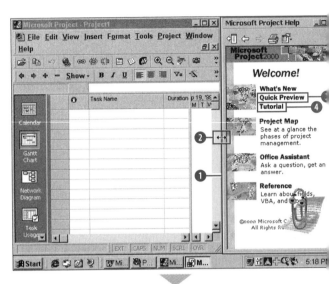

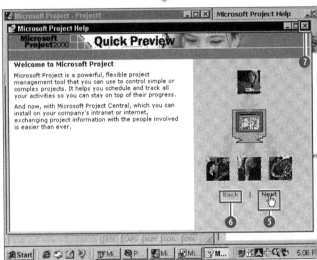

1. The Help Home Page.

2. Drag the pane divider to resize the Help window.

3. Click Quick Preview for a functionality tour.

4. Click Tutorial to begin lessons.

5. Click Next to move forward through the high-level preview screens.

6. Click Back to move back through the preview screens.

7. Click the Close button to return to the Help Home Page.

CROSS-REFERENCE

See "Working with the Office Assistant" later in this chapter for information on HTML-based help.

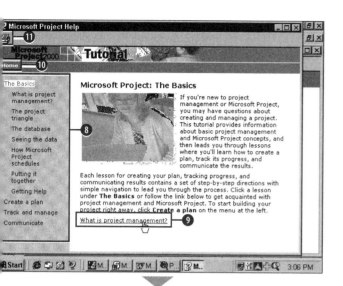

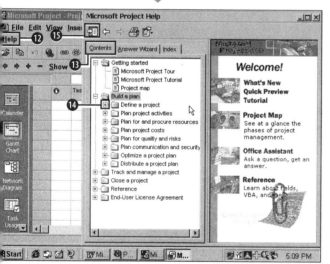

The Tutorial is a series of lessons with step-by-step instructions intended to give the first-time user assistance in getting started using Project 2000. Lessons available include Getting Around, Creating a Plan, Tracking and Managing, and Communicating.

The Project Map identifies and describes typical project management activities along with Microsoft Project 2000 corresponding instructions.

The Office Assistant is always eager to answer your questions typed in your own words.

The Reference choice is a convenient substitute to a hard copy user manual. Reference supplies technical information such as field descriptions, troubleshooting tips, product specifications, and a glossary.

TAKE NOTE

USING THE HELP MENU

The Help menu offers choices not found on the Help Home Page or shortcuts to home page help topics. For example, the Contents and Index choice opens an additional "page" to the Help Home Page that is similar to Contents and Index help from previous versions of Microsoft Project. Choosing Getting Started offers quick access to the Quick Preview, Tutorial, or Project Map. About Microsoft Project offers system information, technical support options, and your product identification number.

- Click a topic along the left-hand margin for more information.

- Click HTML links for quick access to help.

- To return to the home page, click Home.

- To print the current help page, click the printer icon.

- ⑫ To access Contents and Index help, choose Help ⇨ Contents and Index.

- ⑬ Choose the Contents tab.

- ⑭ Click a plus sign (+) to expand the list of choices.

- ⑮ Click the Hide button to hide the Contents and Index "page."

FIND IT ONLINE

For information about configuring a three-button mouse, see **http://www.digconsys.com/**.

11

Using the Project Map

The Project Map, found on the Help Home Page, offers brief explanations for many project management activities, practices, and procedures. The Project Map serves as a project management primer of high-level activities and terms. If you are new to project management, it is worthwhile reading elements of the Project Map prior to defining and planning a project using Project 2000.

The Project Map consists of three main project management topic sections: Build a plan, Track and manage a project, and Close a project. Although grouped differently, these sections are similar in content to the project management life cycle phases discussed previously in this chapter. Each section of the Project Map is divided into typical project management activities. Click any of these activities for an HTML-based list of subactivities. Even the subactivities include HTML-based links to definitions of project management terms. For example, the activity "Define a project" appears under the first section, "Build a plan." "Define a project" is further divided into numerous HTML-based subtopics including Initiate a project, Start a project file, Define project deliverables, and Organize a project into master and subproject files. Even "Initiate a project" includes HTML-based links to definitions of objectives, deliverables, milestones, stakeholders, assumptions, and constraints. Remember to access the Project Map at any time to check the definition of a project management term prior to use.

HTML links provide information about specific how-to's of project management. Section 1, "Build a plan," includes help to define a project, plan project activities, plan for and procure resources, plan project costs, plan

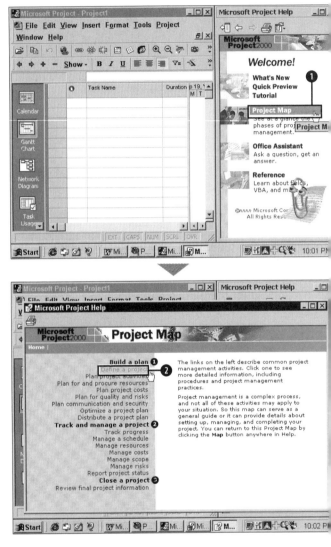

① Click Project Map from the Help Home Page to display the Project Map HTML-based project management guide.

▶ The Project Map displays three section headings with HTML links for more specific information.

② Click "Define a project" for topics concerning setting up a project.

CROSS-REFERENCE

See Chapter 6 for more information about creating a schedule.

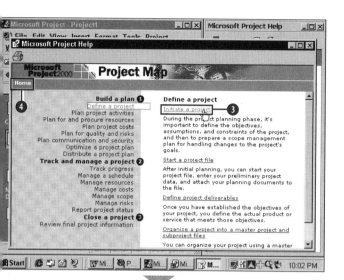

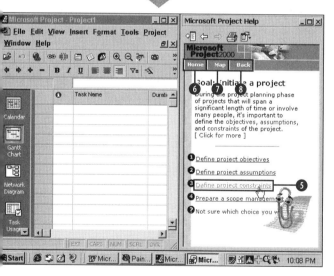

for quality and risks, plan communication and security, optimize a project plan, and distribute a project plan. Section 2, "Track and manage a project," suggests ways to track progress, manage a schedule, manage resources, manage costs, manage scope, manage risks, and report project status. Lastly, Section 3, "Close a project," provides information on how to review final project information. As you can see, these topics and more are covered in greater application detail in the remaining chapters of this book.

Remember that the Map is a general guide and all activities may not be appropriate for all projects.

TAKE NOTE

▶ FINDING THE MAP

You can also find quick access to the Project Map from Getting Started on the Help menu.

▶ PRINTING THE MAP

For a checklist or visual reference for your office wall, consider printing the Project Map. You can then follow your progress through the various project steps and phases. To print the Map, click the printer icon located at the top of the help page when the Map displays on the screen.

The "Define a project" site offers more detailed subtopic choices.

Click the "Initiate a project" link for information about scope documents and other project initiation documents.

From within the Project Map, click Home to return to the Help Home Page.

5 *From the "Initiate a project" subtopic, click "Define project constraints" for more information about project constraints.*

6 *Click Home to return to the Help Home Page.*

7 *Click Map to return to the Project Map main page.*

8 *Click Back to go back a page.*

FIND IT ONLINE

For Web-based tools to help capture enterprise-wide project information see **www.projcontrol.com**.

Working with the Office Assistant

The Office Assistant is the most intuitive form of help available in Microsoft Project 2000. Whereas the other forms of help require the use of lists or categories of predetermined topics, the Assistant allows you to type your help request in your own words. Click Search and, like any good assistant, the Office Assistant will then ask for clarification about your request or present potential answers to your question.

When making a request, use specific sentences rather than one or two words. For example, asking "How do I print a legend on a chart?" will come closer to giving you what you are looking for as opposed to merely typing "printing options." Other examples of specific requests include: What is a critical path? How do I filter for milestone tasks? or Show me the Calendar view.

The default assistant's name is Clippit, a paperclip-like character. To configure your assistant or choose a different assistant, right-click on the character that "floats" on the Help Home Page. Right-clicking shows a drop-down menu with four choices: Hide, Options, Choose Assistant, and Animate!.

The Hide command removes the character from your screen. To retrieve the Assistant again, click the Help button on the Standard Toolbar. You can also access the Office Assistant by choosing Help ⇨ Microsoft Project Help or pressing the F1 key.

The Options or Choose Assistant choices display a dialog box with two tabs. The Options tab allows for configuring the capabilities of your assistant. You can direct your assistant to respond to the F1 key, move when in the way, make sounds, and show usage tips.

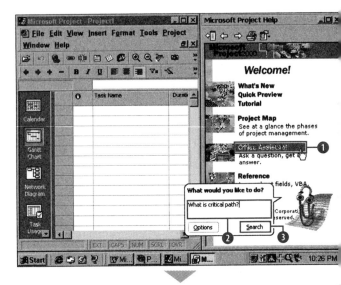

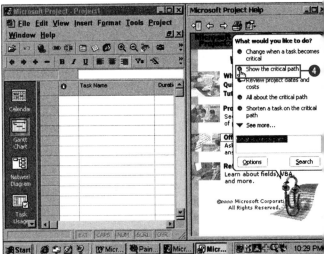

❶ To activate the Office Assistant, click Office Assistant from the Help Home Page.

▶ The Office Assistant (Clippit) awaits a request.

❷ Type your request in the test box. For this example, type **What is critical path?**

❸ Click Search to activate the Assistant.

▶ Numerous choices are presented for selection.

❹ Click "Show the critical path" for additional information.

CROSS-REFERENCE

See "Selecting Default Options" in Chapter 3 for more information about setting Help display default options.

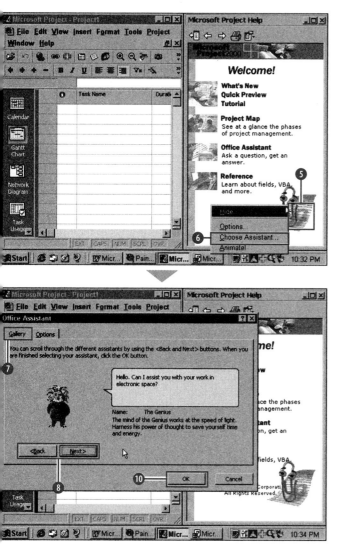

The Gallery tab displays a collection of eight different Assistant personalities. You can choose from such characters as Clippit (a paperclip), The Dot (a dot with character), F1 (a robot), The Genius (an intelligent-looking character), Office Logo (logo of Office products), Mother Nature (the earth), Links (a cat), or Rocky (a dog). The Genius is the assistant shown in the figure on the opposite page.

The Animate! menu choice allows the personality of your assistant to show through animated antics.

TAKE NOTE

▶ MOVING THE OFFICE ASSISTANT

To move the Office Assistant manually, click and drag the assistant to another location.

If you check the "Move when in the way" box in the Options dialog box, the Office Assistant automatically changes from the large to the small size after five minutes of non-use.

▶ SHARING THE ASSISTANT

Remember that the Assistant is shared by all Microsoft Office Family Member programs. Changing the Assistant in Project 2000 affects the Assistant in all Office programs.

⑤ To configure your assistant, right-click anywhere on the figure. Or, click Options in the Search dialog box.

⑥ From the drop-down menu select Choose Assistant.

▶ The same dialog box opens whether you select Options or Choose Assistant. The menu choice informs Project 2000 which tab to show on top in the dialog box.

⑦ To select an Assistant, click the Gallery tab.

⑧ Click the Next or Back buttons to scroll through the Assistant choices.

⑨ Scroll until you locate The Genius character.

⑩ Click OK to select The Genius as your new assistant.

FIND IT ONLINE

For the Microsoft Home Page see
http://www.microsoft.com.

Using the Menu Bar

The Microsoft Project 2000 menu architecture is consistent with other Windows programs so you can launch rapidly into using the application. The menu bar, which contains titles for pull-down menus, is found at the top of the window just under the Title bar.

Operating the menu is also consistent across Windows applications. For example, the use of an ellipsis, or three dots (. . .), after a menu option indicates that choosing this selection, or command, opens a dialog box. For a sample, look at the Open command under the File menu.

Underlined letters and hotkeys, called *accelerator keys*, are common as well. Underlined letters (like the M in More Views in the View menu) show that you can press the underlined character to activate the selection instead of clicking with the mouse.

Hotkeys are shortcut commands that also substitute for mouse clicks as an alternative method of selection (the hotkey combination for Copy Cell on the Edit menu is Ctrl+C).

Chevrons, those downward pointing arrows, like those at the bottom of the File menu, indicate additional options. When your cursor passes over these arrows, the additional cascading downward menu displays.

A right arrow to the right of a menu selection indicates that that selection offers a cascading menu of additional choices, like the cascading menu for View ⇨ Table.

Now, for a tour of menu highlights. The most frequently used menu commands, or choices, are also found as buttons on toolbars, which are covered in the next task.

The *File menu* contains commands for file operations, workgroup commands, and printing commands. The *Edit menu* displays commands for task operations

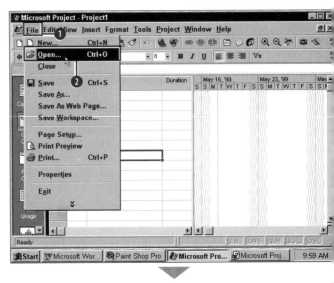

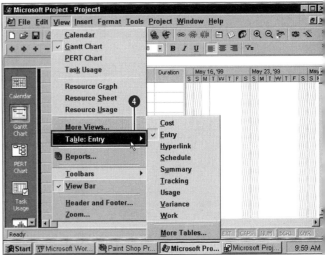

❶ Click any main menu option for a pull-down menu.

❷ Choosing an option with an ellipsis, such as Open from the File menu, opens the associated dialog box.

❸ Press the letter O, the underlined letter in Open on the File menu, as an alternate way to make that selection.

❹ For an example of a cascading menu, choose View ⇨ Table: Entry.

▶ The cascading menu appears as you highlight the word "Table" in the View menu.

CROSS-REFERENCE

See "Customizing the Menu" in Chapter 17 for tips on creating your own custom menu.

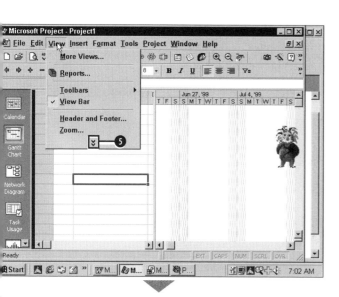

as well as choices for deleting tasks, linking and unlinking tasks, splitting tasks, and finding tasks.

The *View menu* displays numerous view titles as well as a listing of all views (More Views), tables, reports, toolbars, and the View Bar.

Insert offers choices for putting information into the existing project or window such as new or recurring tasks, columns, or objects.

The *Format menu* allows for configuring fonts, the timescale, task bars, gridlines, the GanttChartWizard, text styles, and bar styles.

To access the project calendar, perform resource leveling, or reach Options or the Organizer, choose *Tools.*

The *Project menu* allows you to sort or filter project information or reach the Project Information dialog box.

Window presents choices for arranging, hiding, or splitting the project window.

Lastly, the *Help menu* displays the numerous help options available.

TAKE NOTE

CASCADING ENUS

When you highlight a menu selection that shows a right arrow, a cascading menu automatically displays. Cascading menus allow you to automatically walk deeper and deeper into the menu structure to locate your choice. If you think of the menu as a tree diagram, the cascading menus allow you to view one branch at a time rather than deal with the confusion and complexity of the entire menu structure.

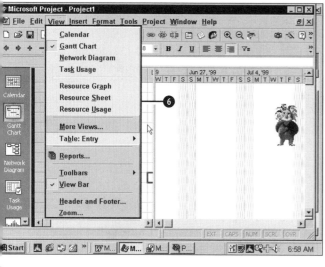

⑤ Move your pointer over the chevrons in the View menu to display the full menu.

⑥ Highlighting the chevrons displays the full menu.

FIND IT ONLINE

For information about Windows 98, see **http://www. microsoft.com/windows98/default.asp**.

Exploring Toolbars

Toolbars greatly simplify the everyday use of Microsoft Project 2000. Without them, users would need to use exhaustive menus or remember long lists of hotkeys. "Out-of-the-box" Microsoft Project 2000 offers ten toolbars for standard and specialty commands as well as the capability to create custom toolbars.

You decide how many, if any, toolbars to display in your project window. These toolbars stay on the window for all project files opened. It is common to keep the Standard toolbar showing at all times and to display the specialty toolbars as needed. Remember that showing more toolbars reduces the available screen space for viewing project information.

From the toolbars cascading menu, (View ⇨ Toolbars) a toolbar list appears with checkboxes for selecting and deselecting toolbars. Or, simply right-click in a toolbar area to display the same selection list. The following list provides brief descriptions of each of the ten default toolbars.

The *Standard toolbar* contains the most commonly used commands for saving, printing, finding a task, zooming, cutting, copying, and pasting.

The *Formatting toolbar* contains commands — such as Font, Font Size, Bold, and Underline — to change the appearance of text in views.

The *Custom Forms toolbar* displays buttons for entering task or resource information in a convenient form format — for example, the Cost Tracking and Work Tracking forms.

The *Drawings toolbar* displays commands for adding graphics and text, such as text boxes or arrows, to Gantt Charts.

For convenient methods of assigning resources and resolving resource overallocation conflicts, use the *Resource Management toolbar*.

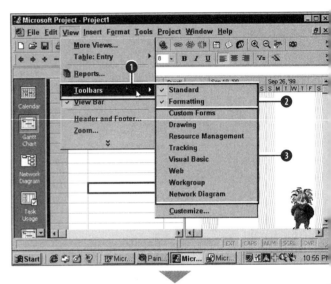

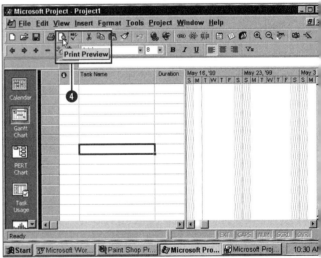

❶ Select View ⇨ Toolbars for a cascading menu of available toolbars.

❷ Clicking a toolbar name selects it for display. Standard and Formatting are selected in this example.

❸ Uncheck a selection so it does not display. The other selections are unchecked in the example.

❹ Position the mouse pointer over any button for a pop-up tooltip. The example shows the tooltip for Print Preview

CROSS-REFERENCE

See "Customizing Toolbars" in Chapter 17 for information about adding buttons to toolbars.

18

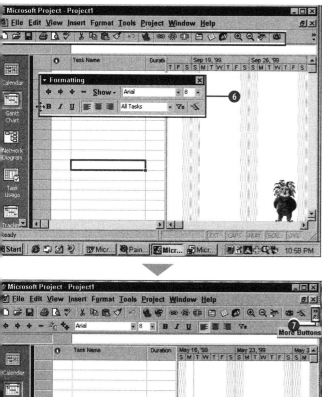

The *Tracking toolbar* displays buttons for viewing project progress information as well as updating the schedule.

For easy access to tools for recording, running, and editing macros, display the *Visual Basic toolbar*.

To activate a Web browser quickly, display the *Web toolbar*.

The *Workgroup toolbar* shows tools to exchange information with other members of a workgroup.

The *Network Diagram toolbar*, new to Project 2000, offers choices for configuring the Network Diagram (also known as the PERT Diagram).

TAKE NOTE

BUTTON FUNCTIONS

To discover the function of a specific button, click What's This? on the Help menu, and then click the button.

TOOLTIPS

Position the mouse pointer over any button on the toolbar for a pop-up tooltip.

TOOLBAR PREVIEW

The toolbar selection available through Reference help displays all toolbar buttons with descriptions. Use this information when deciding which toolbars to display or when developing custom toolbars.

TOOLBAR CHEVRONS

Chevrons, two right-pointing arrows, at the end of a toolbar indicate that more buttons exist for that toolbar. Click the chevrons to display the additional buttons.

➍ To move a toolbar, position the mouse pointer over the thick line at the left toolbar margin until the four-sided arrow appears. Drag the toolbar to the desired location.

➎ Drag the toolbar back above the project window to restore it to the default position.

➐ Click the chevrons at the right end of a toolbar for additional button commands.

FIND IT ONLINE

Find clip art for custom toolbar buttons at
http://www.bizart.com/.

Setting Up an Electronic Project Binder

For Microsoft Office users, the Office Binder command is a terrific asset in report production. The Office Binder keeps related files together and acts as an electronic version of a paperclip, binder tab, or manila folder. Because these files are together in the Office Binder, you can apply a consistent style, consecutive page numbers, and consistent headers and footers to all. You can also perform a spell check on the files. These techniques help ensure a professional-looking final report rather than a report that looks like it was slapped together from various documents. Because of features like these, the Office Binder is far more convenient and offers more functionality and sophistication than merely attaching documents to project schedules. Binder options enable you to create a truly cohesive project notebook.

As an individual project manager, consider using a binder to keep all of the project information and documents together for easy reference and report generation for team members, sponsors, and customers. If appropriate, you may make the binder available to many using a shared network drive or posting it to the Web. You can create the binder anytime that seems appropriate. You can generate the blank binder and add contents as you go or create the contents first and then "gather" your files together into the notebook.

Electronic Binders allow you to create a library of current information as well as historical information from which you can create new summary binders or report on individual projects. This library can remain electronic or can be printed in hard-copy form. Using Binder Send To features, you can send binder contents to mail recipients, routing recipients, or Exchange folders — all electronically! For the virtual project office or an office that is short on storage space, the electronic notebook is an ideal solution.

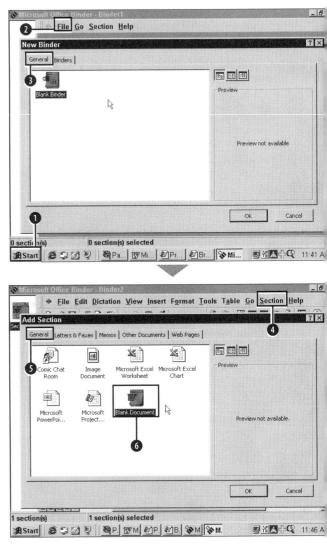

CROSS-REFERENCE

See Chapter 13 for more information about posting your binder on the Web.

❶ To create a new binder, choose Start ➪ Programs ➪ Microsoft Binder or Start ➪ Programs ➪ Office Tools ➪ Microsoft Binder.

❷ Choose File ➪ New Binder to display this dialog box.

❸ On the General tab, choose Blank Binder and click OK.

❹ To create Binders sections a you work, choose Section ➪ Add to display this dialog box.

❺ In the Add Section dialog box, click any tab to create binder contents or sections

❻ For example, on the Genera tab, click Blank Document and click OK to launch MS Word to a blank new document.

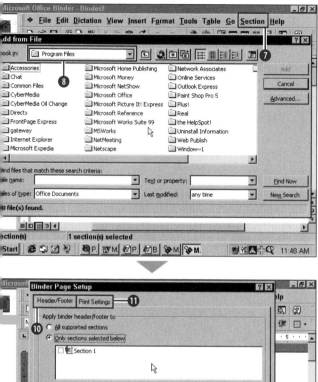

When creating a new blank or report (template) binder, think of the sections as separate schedules, documents, spreadsheets, or slide presentations you bring together into one manual binder. You add these sections as new creations or import them from an existing file, delete them, or rename, rearrange, or hide them in the binder.

Binder page setup options include page numbering, defining headers and footers, and various printing options. Binder Options offer features for printing the binder contents as single jobs or separate sections. You also establish default binder locations.

TAKE NOTE

► LOCATING THE OFFICE BINDER

Microsoft Binder is included as part of the Microsoft Office suite of products. Microsoft Binder installs automatically with Office 97 but not with Office 2000. If the Binder doesn't appear after installing Office 2000, look for it on the Microsoft Office 2000 CD-ROM under Office Tools. To install Binder from the CD, choose Start ⇨ Settings ⇨ Control Panel and double-click Add/Remove Programs. For Office 97 versions, the typical location to launch the binder is Start ⇨ Programs ⇨ Microsoft Binder. For Office 2000 versions, the typical launch location is Start ⇨ Programs ⇨ Office Tools ⇨ Microsoft Binder.

- To add already created section contents, choose Section ⇨ Add from File to display this dialog box.

- From the Add from File dialog box, choose the folder and file to add to the Binder.

  Repeat for remaining contents.

⑨ To set up the Binder for transmission or printing, choose File ⇨ Binder Page Setup to display this dialog box.

⑩ Click the Header/Footer tab to customize.

⑪ Click the Print Settings tab to change those options.

FIND IT ONLINE

For more about managing project communications, see **http://www.eniac.com/whitepap/projec10.htm**.

Personal Workbook

Q&A

1 What are two ways to exit Project 2000?

_____

_____

_____

2 What is the Help Home Page?

_____

_____

_____

3 What is the purpose of a project binder?

_____

_____

_____

4 What is a *hotkey?*

_____

_____

_____

5 In Project 2000, what is an *Office Assistant?*

_____

_____

_____

6 What are three ways to start Project 2000?

_____

_____

_____

7 What does an arrow to the right of a menu command indicate?

_____

_____

_____

8 What are four toolbars available for display in Project 2000?

_____

_____

_____

ANSWERS: PAGE 317

22

EXTRA PRACTICE

1. Start Project 2000 using the three techniques mentioned in this chapter.

2. Create a practice project binder and include two existing documents.

3. Try using the different forms of help described in this chapter.

4. Choose a different personality for your Office Assistant.

5. Use Reference Help for descriptions of the different toolbars available.

6. Explore displaying and hiding toolbars from your window.

REAL-WORLD APPLICATIONS

✔ You create a binder to serve as your project notebook.

✔ As you are using Microsoft Project 2000, you can't quite remember what planning step comes next. For a quick reminder you display the Project Map from the Help section.

✔ To quickly navigate between the various forms of help available, you use the Help Home Page.

✔ To switch tables on your Gantt Chart you use the cascading menu list of all tables.

Visual Quiz

How do you change the appearance of the Office Assistant from Clippit (the paperclip) to The Genius?

_____

_____

_____

_____

_____

_____

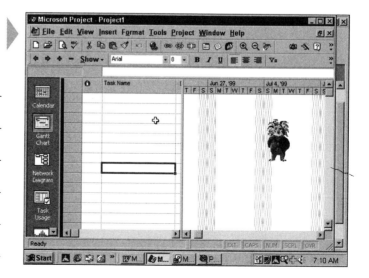

CHAPTER 2

Exploring the Project Window

The project window serves as the main interface between Project 2000 features and functions and project database information. For example, the project window may display a Gantt Chart or Network Diagram (also known as a PERT Chart) with task information, or it may show current information about project resources. In addition, various forms and tables provide easy access to data entry screens. Because of the architecture of Microsoft Project 2000, there is no need to enter the same data more than once as any information entered in a form or table is available for use in any other table, form, or view containing that same data field. It may help to think of project data as residing in a database; you decide how to view the data by selecting various views and tables.

Because the project window plays such an important part in using Microsoft Project 2000, it's wise for those wishing to be efficient users to invest the time to become comfortable with it. This chapter covers the main features of the project window with the goal of helping you feel comfortable.

Not all project views contain the same window features. However, if a feature is contained in a view, it will work the same as in any other view. For example, scroll bars and buttons perform in the same way in any view that contains them. Common window components include scroll buttons and bars, tables, spreadsheet-like cells, zoom buttons, an entry bar, and pane dividers. These components also behave the same as in other Microsoft Office products (Excel, Outlook, PowerPoint, Access, Word, Publisher, PhotoDraw, FrontPage) so frequent users of Microsoft Office applications will already be familiar with these components.

In this chapter you learn how to view project data easily by using scroll buttons and bars, using the pane divider, and splitting the viewing window to see two views simultaneously. You will also explore how to view different types of charts by using the View Bar, change views and tables, adjust the width of columns to accommodate varying data character lengths, and adjust the timescale for various perspectives. You'll use Zoom In and Zoom Out as shortcuts for altering the timescale and you will also preview a very useful column, the Indicators column.

Understanding the Project Window

When you launch Microsoft Project 2000 for the first time, you see a blank Gantt Chart template in the left-hand window with the Help Home Page on the right. The Gantt Chart is probably the most recognized chart of project management. Before entering project data into this template, let's explore the window components so that you feel comfortable handling your data.

The default screen displays an unpopulated window pane. In software terms, a *pane* is a section of a window that contains a view.

A *view* is a tool for holding and displaying data. Accountants use common tools like spreadsheets, bar charts, and pie charts to manipulate information. Likewise, project managers use common tools like Gantt Charts, Network Diagrams, Calendars, and histograms to work with project data.

The Gantt Chart view is designed using two main components. The left side of the Gantt Chart usually displays a spreadsheet-like table, while the right side displays bars representing tasks beneath a timescale. A moveable, vertical split bar enables you to decide how much space is available for each side. Dragging the bar to the right allows more table columns to show, while dragging the bar to the left allows more display room for the task bars.

In contrast, *combination views* have two panes, showing a view at the top and another view on the bottom of the window. A moveable horizontal split bar enables you to determine the height of each view. Split windows offer the opportunity to view different combinations of forms, views, and charts on the top and bottom portions

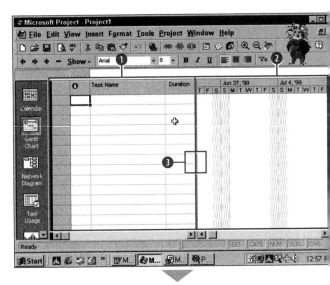

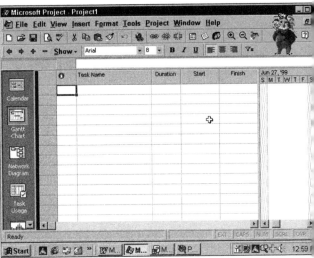

❶ Click the spreadsheet side of the Gantt Chart.

❷ Click the timescale side of the chart.

❸ Drag the pane divider to the right to display more columns.

▶ Results of dragging the pa[ne] divider to the right.

CROSS-REFERENCE

See "Applying Standard Tables" in this chapter for displaying different columns for the Gantt Chart.

Exploring the Project Window

CHAPTER
2

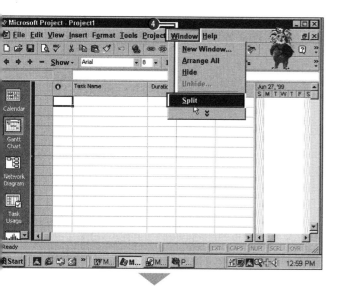

To split the window for a combination view, choose Window ➪ Split.

▶ A sample of a split window.

of the window. For example, you might display a Gantt Chart at the top and a Task Form on the bottom for ease of entering project details task by task. Or, you might show a Resource Usage view in the top pane and a Resource Graph in the bottom pane as you assign and analyze resource allocations. Keep in mind that the bottom view always displays more detailed information about the task or resource selected in the top pane. To show combination views, choose Window ➪ Split Window.

To switch between the top and bottom views in a split window, click anywhere in the desired pane. A bar appears in color or black along the left margin of the pane to indicate the active view.

TAKE NOTE

WHO WAS HENRY GANTT?

Although Henry Gantt died in 1919, it wasn't until some years later that the chart that bears his name became widely used in the field of project management. After receiving an advanced degree from the Stevens Institute of Technology, he began a long career as a consulting engineer in the field of industrial operations. Gantt published what was a rather controversial paper for his time, "Training Workers," in which he made the assertion that workers are human beings, not machines, and should therefore not be driven, but led.

For the Microsoft Project 2000 Home Page, see http:// www.microsoft.com/office/project/default.htm.

27

Working with the Project Window

It is often necessary to adjust various window components in order to see all relevant project data. For example, typical screen adjustment features include the pane divider, scroll buttons and bars, zoom in and out, column width, and the timescale. In this task, you will work with the main data display, the Gantt Chart. Later tasks cover working with the other major views.

Vertical and horizontal scroll bars, located at the right side and bottom edge of scrollable panes, provide access to the contents of a view. Arrows, located on the scroll bars, scroll one row, column, or time period at a time. Drag the scroll box (also found on the scroll bar) to scroll more quickly. If you click and hold the scroll button, a pop-up box describing the timeframe highlighted or the task selected appears. In the Gantt Chart view, for example, three scroll bars are available. Click the vertical scroll bar on the right edge of the pane to scroll through your tasks, one row at a time. Click and hold the scroll button found on the bottom under the task bar section to display the timeframe highlighted under the timescale. Scroll the bar under the column section to move left and right through columns that may be too numerous to display all at once.

Click the Zoom In and Zoom Out buttons on the Standard toolbar, and the timescale cycles through predetermined time periods to show a close-up to long-range view of your project schedule. Click the Zoom In button to cycle through a day, half-day, hours, and minutes. Conversely, click the Zoom Out button to cycle through three days, a week, a month, a quarter, and a half-year. A fiscal year timescale setting is now available

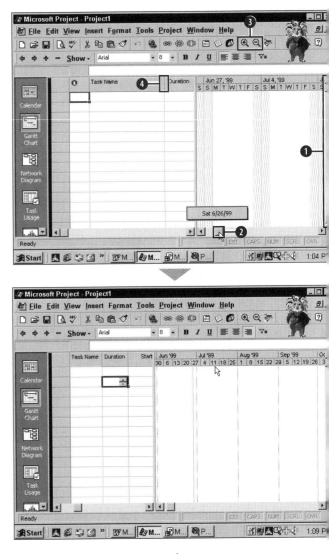

❶ Click the vertical scroll arrows or drag the scroll box to scroll through task rows.

❷ Click the horizontal scroll arrows or drag the scroll box to scroll through time.

❸ Click the Zoom In or Zoom Out buttons to cycle through the timescale choices.

❹ Drag the column name borders to change the column width.

▶ Results of clicking the Zoom Out button.

CROSS-REFERENCE

The task "Exploring Formatting Options" in Chapter 12 covers more precise adjustments to the timescale.

in Project 2000. Hovering your mouse pointer over the timescale header causes a pop-up box to open displaying the corresponding specific date or date range of the timescale.

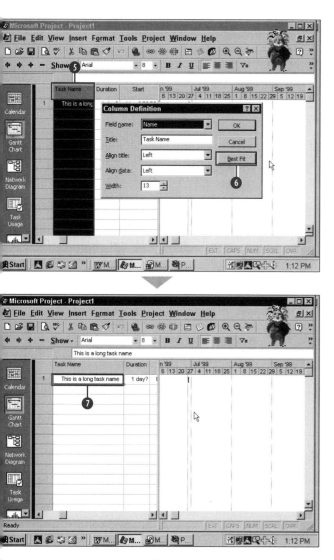

CHANGING PANE SIZE

To change the size of all panes simultaneously, drag the split bar intersection (the place where the vertical and horizontal split bars intersect) either up, down, left, or right.

ADJUSTING COLUMN WIDTH

To adjust the width of a table column, follow one of these three methods.

Manually, grab the right-hand column separator line in the column header area until the pointer is a two-sided arrow. Now, drag the column separator line to the right or left to increase or decrease the width of the column.

Alternatively, double-click the name of a column to adjust. In the Column Definition dialog box, adjust the width or choose the Best Fit button.

As a third method, move your mouse pointer over the separator line to the right of the column header of the column you want to alter. When the pointer displays a two-sided arrow, double-click the separator line. The column width automatically adjusts for the longest entry in the column.

⑤ To use the Best Fit for column width, double-click the Task Name column header.

⑥ The Column Definition dialog box opens. Click the Best Fit button.

⑦ Best Fit adjusts the column width to accommodate all entries you have entered in the field.

FIND IT ONLINE

For project management books, events, and discussion forums, see **http://www.allpm.com/index.htm**.

Using the View Bar

The *View Bar* is a vertical list of commonly used views that resides along the left-hand side of the project window. Using View Bar icons is a convenient way to select and switch between project views with the click of the mouse. The standard View Bar contains seven view icons with an eighth icon for More Views. Remember, views are formats for displaying project information. The standard views available in Project 2000 use formats that are familiar to most project managers.

Views can be categorized first by whether they focus on tasks or resources. Within that grouping, views fall into one of three main categories: graphical views like Gantt Charts, Network Diagrams, Calendars, or Resource Graphs; sheet views with rows and columns like the Task Sheet or Resource Sheet; or a Form view, like a Task Form, which contains fields for data entry and looks much like a paper form.

A brief description of each view found on the View Bar is provided here as an introduction. Later chapters deal in depth with all the standard views. Look at each view on the View Bar to get a feel for the presentation format of information residing in a project database.

▶ *Calendar view* is a monthly calendar showing tasks and task duration estimates. Each task is shown as a bar that spans the timeframe on the calendar for which it is scheduled.

▶ *Gantt Chart view* depicts a list of tasks with task information. The Gantt Chart is probably the most commonly used project management chart for presentation purposes.

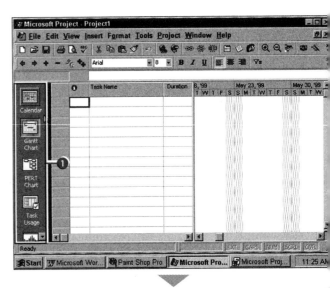

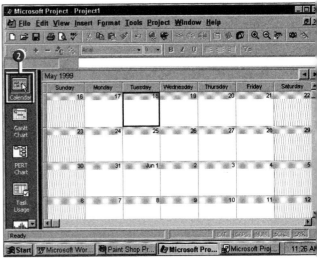

❶ Click any icon found on the View Bar to switch to that view.

❷ Click the Calendar icon to display the Calendar view.

CROSS-REFERENCE

See "Changing Standard Views" later in this chapter for a complete list of the standard views.

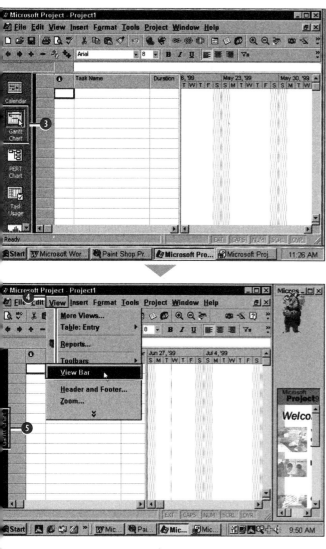

▶ *Network Diagram view* is a sequence or logic diagram showing task dependencies.

▶ *Task Usage view* shows assigned resources grouped under each task.

▶ *Resource Graph view* is a bar chart or histogram displaying resource allocations, costs, or work.

▶ *Resource Sheet view* gives general resource information using rows and columns.

▶ *Resource Usage view* displays assigned tasks grouped under each resource.

▶ *More Views* selection takes you to a list of all views (custom as well as standard).

TAKE NOTE

▶ **TO SHOW OR NOT TO SHOW THE VIEW BAR**

The View Bar is similar to other toolbars in that you can choose to display it or hide it. To hide it, remove the checkmark for the View Bar from the View menu. To display it again, simply check the View Bar option again. Even if you are not displaying the View Bar, you can still see the active view you are using by looking at the active split bar indicator. This indicator is a vertical black bar (or colored bar) located along the left-hand side of the window. The name of the active view will appear in this bar.

---

③ *Click the Gantt Chart icon to display the Gantt Chart.*

④ *Deselect the View Bar from the View menu by unchecking the selection.*

⑤ *The view name is shown on the active split bar. This example shows a Gantt Chart format.*

FIND IT ONLINE

To read an online Microsoft Project 2000 newsletter, see **http://www.pmsolutionsinc.com/micropn.htm.**

31

Changing Standard Views

Remember, views are windows that allow you to see project information. Standard and custom views can be selected from the View Bar, located along the left side of the window, or from the View menu. For split windows, activate the top or bottom pane by clicking anywhere in the pane; then choose which view to place in that pane.

Microsoft Project 2000 provides a choice of default views as well as the ability to create your own views. You can even add your favorite custom views to the View menu. Table 2.1 shows a partial list of the standard views.

With this multitude of choices comes the added complexity for inexperienced users of remembering from work session to work session which forms, sheets, charts, or graphs they like. Split windows add more complexity as you try to remember which combination of these views you prefer. Many users write the names of favorite views on post-it notes to place around their monitors. An alternative is to customize views with names that describe their use, like Vickey's Tracking Gantt, and place these on the View menu for easy selection. (In Chapter 17 you learn how to customize views.)

Another example is to change your default startup view. The Gantt Chart view is the default view that displays when you launch Microsoft Project 2000. To change the default view, select Tools ⇨ Options, and then click the View tab. In the Default view box, click the view that you want to display at startup.

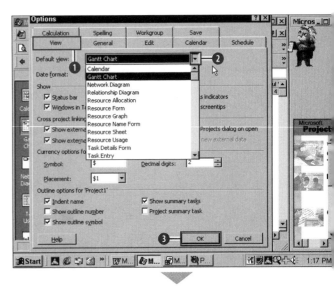

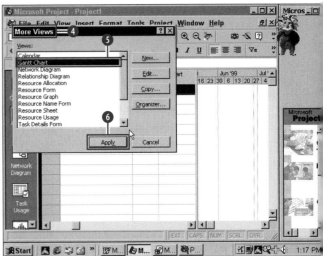

❶ To change the default view that appears at startup, choose Tools ⇨ Options ⇨ View tab.

❷ Click the down arrow in the Default view field for a drop-down list of choices.

❸ Select a different default view and click OK.

❹ To select a different view for display, choose View ⇨ More Views or click the More Views button on the View Bar.

❺ Select a view from the list.

❻ Click Apply to display your selection.

CROSS-REFERENCE

For information about creating new views, see "Creating New Views" in Chapter 17.

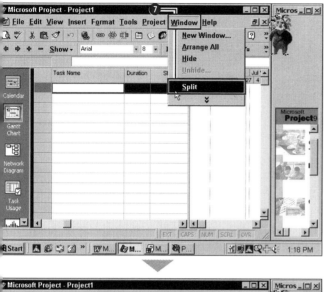

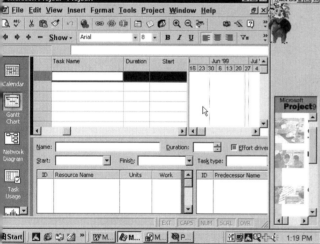

To split the window in order to choose two different views, choose Window ➪ Split.

▶ A split window displays a view on the top and a view on the bottom.

Table 2.1: STANDARD VIEWS

View Name	Description
Bar Rollup	Gantt Chart with a Rollup Table
Calendar	Familiar calendar format
Descriptive Network Diagram	Logic diagram
Detail Gantt	Gantt Chart with task details
Gantt Chart	Task Sheet plus task bars shown under a timescale
Leveling Gantt	Gantt Chart with the Delay Table
Resource Allocation	Resource Usage: top pane Leveling Gantt: bottom pane
Resource Graph	Displays resource allocation information over time (histogram)
Resource Sheet	List of resource information with columns and rows
Resource Usage	Lists resources with task assignments and a distribution chart
Task Details Form	Similar to Task Form with more details
Task Entry	Gantt Chart: top pane Task Form: bottom pane
Task Form	Information about a single task
Task Sheet	Spreadsheet of task information
Task Usage	Lists tasks with resource assignments and a distribution chart

FIND IT ONLINE

For the latest Project 2000 news, go to **http://www. microsoft.com/office/project/projnews.htm**.

Applying Standard Tables

To further enhance the usability of the view you display, apply a table to that portion of the view that contains columns of data or a sheet. A table is a predetermined set of columns typically chosen for a particular project management purpose. For example, the *Entry* table is convenient when entering initial data, the *Cost* table when working with the budget, or the *Schedule* table when analyzing the critical path.

Tables enhance the adaptability and functionality of views and, as such, task tables apply exclusively to task views and resource tables apply exclusively to resource views. A Network Diagram, for example, contains only a graphical depiction of tasks and no columns, so a table cannot be applied. However, the Gantt Chart is also a graphical chart but the left side contains columns and rows of information so it is eligible to display a table.

Tables have names that correspond to their functions, like Entry, Cost, or Baseline and are simply a collection of specific columns. Like views, tables can be customized and new tables can also be created. Microsoft Project 2000 supplies fourteen task tables and ten resource tables as defaults.

Table 2.2 lists the default task tables and their typical purposes.

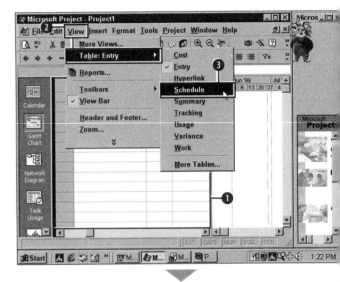

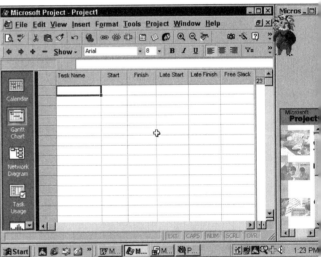

❶ To apply a different table to a Gantt Chart, click (to activate) anywhere in the spreadsheet side of the chart.

❷ Choose View ⇨ Table.

❸ Select the Schedule table from the cascading menu.

▶ Note the columns on the Schedule table: Start, Finish, Late Start, Late Finish, and Free Slack. All of them are needed to manage the schedule.

CROSS-REFERENCE

For information about creating new tables, see "Creating New Tables" in Chapter 17.

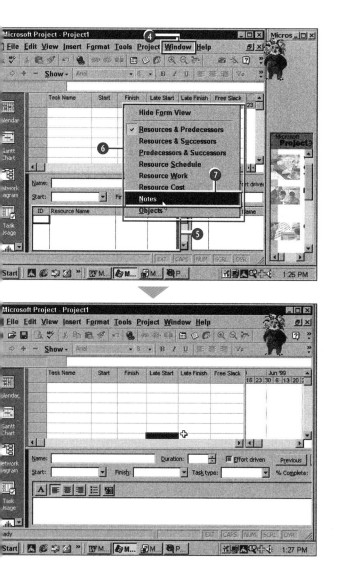

Table 2.2: DEFAULT TASK TABLES

Task Table	Purpose
Baseline	To compare planned versus actual data
Constraint Dates	To view tasks whose dates are controlled by a user-entered date
Cost	To see typical budget information
Delay	To view the delay amounts associated with each task
Earned Value	To view standard earned value calculations during project tracking
Entry	Default table for initial data entry
Export	Typical data to export
Hyperlink	Allows you to create a hyperlink to a file on your computer, on the network, or on the World Wide Web.
Rollup Table	Shows rollup task data
Schedule	Displays scheduling information
Summary	Shows basic task information
Tracking	Place to record actual task information as the project progresses
Usage	Contains hours of work expended
Variance	Summarizes what was planned and what has actually occurred
Work	Contains fields for hours planned and worked

● To display different information in a form view, choose Window ⇨ Split.

● Activate (click) anywhere in the bottom pane (the Task Form).

With the mouse, right-click to display a list of options. The checkmark indicates the current choice.

● Choose Notes as the display option.

▶ The Task Form is still shown but the details are different. Now a field is available to enter task notes such as a task description or possible risk considerations.

FIND IT ONLINE

Find the Center for International Project and Program Management at **http://www.ioi.ie/~mattewar/CIPPM.**

Using the Indicators Column

Indicators are icons that appear in the Indicators column. The Indicators column supplies valuable notes, warnings, and reminders about tasks and resources that currently display on the screen.

In both task and resource views, the Indicators column appears by default on the Entry, Hyperlink, and Usage tables. The column appears between the ID column and the Task Name column. Of course, you can add the Indicators column to any other predefined or custom table.

Here is a brief summary of task indicators:

▶ The *Task Note Indicator* displays if you type notes about the task.

▶ *Constraint Indicators* indicate the constraint (other than ASAP) set for the task. Typical constraints are Finish No Later Than, Must Start On, Finish No Earlier Than, Must Finish On, Start No Earlier Than, Start No Later Than, and As Late As Possible.

▶ *Recurring Task Indicators* remind you of recurring or repeating tasks.

▶ *Completed Task Indicators* appear when the tasks are 100 percent complete.

▶ Task Usage view displays a *Resource Contour Indicator* when you assign an assignment contour other than "flat" to a resource.

❶ The Notes Indicator.

❷ The Constraint Indicator.

❸ The Completed Task Indicator.

❹ The Recurring Task Indicator.

❺ Hover your mouse pointer over an indicator icon for a description.

CROSS-REFERENCE

See "Identifying Resource Overallocation Conflicts" in Chapter 11 for more on managing resources.

▶ *Workgroup Indicators* show at various times to provide information about workgroup features. For example, an icon displays to indicate that an assignment is made but the assigned resource has not yet confirmed the assignment.

▶ *Hyperlink Indicators* show that the task contains a hyperlink to a Web location.

Indicators display information about the task or resource for a particular row. As you point your mouse pointer to the Indicator icon, a small box appears giving additional information. Watch for these icons to appear as you continue teaching yourself throughout the remainder of this book.

TAKE NOTE

▶ RESOURCE VIEW INDICATORS

The two primary indicators for resource views are the Overallocated Indicator and the Notes Indicator. The Overallocated Indicator displays if the resource is currently scheduled for work that exceeds the total amount of available time. The Notes Indicator displays if you type information into the Resource Notes field.

The Resource Contour Indicator.

7 *The Resource Note Indicator.*

FIND IT ONLINE

For answers to questions about MS Project, see **www. coe.unce.edu/project_mosaic/PC/project/faq.html.**

Personal Workbook

Q&A

1 What are the two main components that display as part of a Gantt Chart window?

_____

_____

_____

2 What is a *combination view?*

_____

_____

_____

3 Name one icon that displays in an Indicators column.

_____

_____

_____

4 What are the three main types of views available in Microsoft Project 2000?

_____

_____

_____

5 What is the purpose of a table in a view?

_____

_____

_____

6 How do you change the default startup view?

_____

_____

_____

_____

7 What are two ways to adjust the width of a column?

_____

_____

_____

8 What is the purpose of the View Bar?

_____

_____

_____

ANSWERS: PAGE 318

EXTRA PRACTICE

1. Change the default startup view from the Gantt Chart to the Task Usage view.

2. Display a split window onscreen with a Gantt Chart in the top pane and a Task Details view in the bottom pane.

3. On the Gantt Chart, change the table from the Entry table to the Schedule table and then change it back again.

4. Use the Best Fit option to adjust column width.

5. Use the Zoom In and Zoom Out buttons to cycle through various timescale options.

6. Drag the pane divider to show only one column and more timescale.

REAL-WORLD APPLICATIONS

✔ You are assigning resources to tasks so you split the window and display the Gantt Chart in the top pane and the Resource Usage view in the bottom pane.

✔ As you put together your project budget, you switch to the Cost table because it contains the columns you want to use.

✔ To discuss the logical flow of deliverables through your project, you print the Network Diagram for use at a team planning session.

✔ You use the Indicators column to quickly locate tasks with constraints.

Visual Quiz

How can you re-create this split window? (Hint: Use a Gantt Chart with the Schedule table on the top and a Task Form on the bottom pane.)

_____

_____

_____

_____

_____

PART

II

Contents of 'Desktop'

Name

My Computer

Network Neigh

Internet Explore

Microsoft Outloo

Recycle Bin

My Briefcase

3252-9

3259-6

3261-8

3262-6

3281-2

3286-3

DE Phone List

Device Manager

In

Iomega Tools

Getting Started

Getting started is often the biggest hurdle to overcome in planning a strategy for accomplishing project goals. This book is designed to lead you through a typical sequence of steps that project managers use to plan and execute a project.

The first two chapters of this book helped lay the foundation for using Project 2000 by introducing you to the Help system and the project window. This section covers defining a new project in Project 2000 and getting your files organized for better data control. After defining a new project, you will begin the real work of planning.

Specifically, you will explore techniques for creating new project files and setting up those files by establishing task default options and project calendars. You will also practice using password protection for project files as well as file maintenance techniques. Finally, you will investigate sharing project information with other projects and applications through the use of file types and the Global.mpt file.

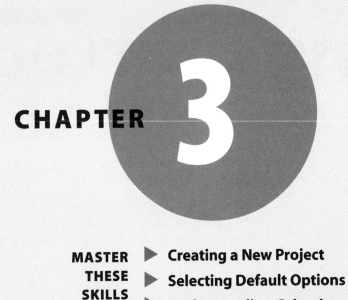

CHAPTER 3

Defining a New Project

I t isn't always easy to determine whether you have a project or simply "an assignment." Nor is it easy to determine whether scheduling and tracking software will help manage the project or add more overhead. Let's tackle the question of whether you have a project first.

Most organizations define work as either project or non-project work so check your company definition first. Does your assignment fit this definition? If your organization does not have a standard definition, ask yourself whether this work has an objective, start and finish points, and deliverables? If the answers are "yes," then consider your work to be a project.

Now, on to the question of whether your project is complex enough to use scheduling software. Most simply, any time a to-do list won't suffice, you can benefit from using Project 2000. For example, even in a short to-do list of twenty-five items, better schedule-management decisions can be made if you use Project 2000 often to calculate the critical path. Of course, you can manually calculate the critical path every day, but do you really want to? In addition, most project customers or sponsors want reports, which are much easier to generate if all the project data resides in a project file. If you spend the time up front to become an efficient Project 2000 user, you will probably use paper and pencil project management tools less frequently and software tools more often.

Before you create a new project, decide the overall organization for the project. Do you have a single project or do you actually have a *program* — a collection of related projects? Or do you have a large project that you wish to divide into subprojects? Or, will you store all project tasks in one file? Answering these questions before you begin will lead to a more solid organizational foundation for your efforts. Remember that you can consolidate or bring project pieces together into one file at a later date.

For large projects managed by different project managers, consider starting each manager out with a template containing a project calendar. After the project information is entered, the individual project pieces can then be brought together for that cohesive project look.

In this chapter, you will learn how to define a new project as well as set up the basic project structure. Defining a new project typically includes naming the project, establishing high-level project information and project properties, and establishing a project calendar.

Creating a New Project

Creating a new project involves three basic steps: starting a new file, establishing general project information, and selecting file properties.

Starting a new project file involves a simple menu choice, or you can click the New Project button on the Standard toolbar. Both techniques open the New dialog box with the Blank Project option highlighted. When you select the Blank Project option, the Project Information dialog box opens.

The Project Information dialog box houses important pieces of project data. The Schedule from field should be completed first. You can create your schedule from either the project Start or Finish date. Scheduling from the project start date enables you to enter or choose the project start date; Project 2000 calculates a finish date. Similarly, scheduling from the project finish date allows you to enter a finish date for the project; Project 2000 calculates the start date.

Next, review and modify, if necessary, both the Current and Status date fields. The current date should represent today's date as a reference point for Project 2000 calculations. Also, many progress tracking calculations in Project 2000, like earned value, complete-through dates, and progress lines rely on the Status date. A status date allows you to accurately report through a "frozen" date rather than allowing recalculations to occur on an automatic basis every day.

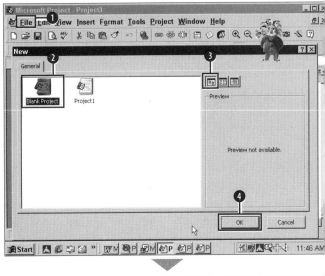

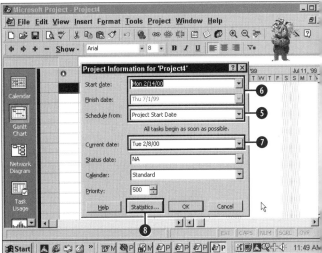

❶ To create a new project, choose File ➪ New or click the New button on the Standard toolbar.

❷ The New dialog box opens. Select Blank Project to create a new project.

❸ If you want, click one of the configuration buttons.

❹ Click OK when finished.

❺ Enter the Schedule from information.

❻ Enter or choose the Start date or Finish date information.

❼ Check the current date and correct if necessary.

❽ Choose a calendar and priority if desired and click the Statistics button for a preview of status information.

CROSS-REFERENCE

See Chapter 14, "Tracking Progress," for more information about using the Status line.

Use the Calendar field in the Project Information dialog box to choose which calendar to use as the master calendar for the project. Project 2000 references this calendar when scheduling tasks.

The Priority field lets you set a resource leveling priority at the project level (1–1000). This field is useful when sharing resources across projects.

Clicking the Statistics button provides progress summary information. Like the Status date mentioned earlier in this task, this information is more valuable after the project is under way.

Next, let's consider file properties, the third step. The File Properties dialog box contains five tabs. The General tab contains fields for information such as type, location, and size of file as well as file attributes. The entries on the Summary tab, like Title, Manager, and Company might appear on report headers. The Statistics tab contains dates for project creation, modification, or printing. The Contents tab gives a summary of project information. The final tab, Custom, allows you to establish custom properties for search purposes.

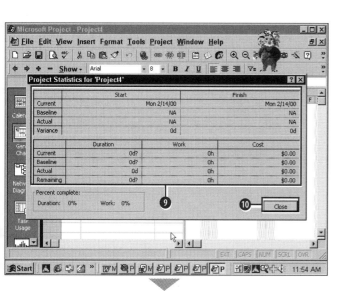

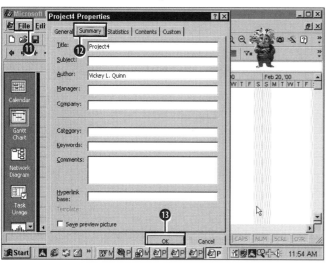

TAKE NOTE

▶ **PROJECT INFORMATION**

To return to the Project Information dialog box after the initial entries, choose Project ➪ Project Information.

⑨ Preview the information found on the Project Statistics screen.

⑩ Click the Close button when finished.

⑪ To change or add information, choose File ➪ Properties.

⑫ Choose one of the five tabs and enter the appropriate data.

⑬ Click OK when finished.

FIND IT ONLINE

For Project 2000 technical tips, see
http://www.mshk.com/MSClub/techtip.htm.

Selecting Default Options

Before entering project tasks, consider selecting default options that make data entry more efficient. In this task you can review those options by choosing Tools ➪ Options from the main menu. Although there are nine option tabs available at this time, I'll limit the discussion to those choices that assist with data entry and save the other choices for later discussions.

On the View tab, notice that some selections are available for all projects while others are available for the active project only. Those for the active project are enclosed by a border with the name of the project listed.

On the View tab change selections for default view and date format. The *default* view is the view displayed when you create a new project. Also, remember that some of the date formats are rather lengthy and require significant column space when shown in a table.

Several choices on the Schedule tab are useful when entering new tasks. For example, the New tasks field has two choices: Start On Project Start Date or Start On Current Date. The usual choice is to have new tasks begin on the project start date as shown in the Project Information dialog box. In addition, to save time during task entry, determine the most common unit for the task duration and work that will be entered as well as the most common type of task. Lastly, clear the checkmark from the "Autolink inserted or moved tasks" box. By clearing this field, you can enter tasks in any order, rearrange them, and then establish task links as opposed to having links set automatically as you enter tasks.

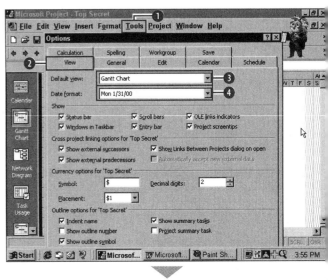

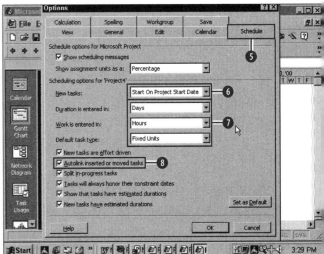

❶ To choose options discussed in this task, choose Tools ➪ Options.

❷ Click the View tab.

▶ Note the options are just for this project.

❸ Select a default view of your choice.

❹ Select a default date format.

❺ Click the Schedule tab.

❻ Select a scheduling option for New tasks.

❼ Select default units for Duration and Work as well as Default task type.

❽ Uncheck the "Autolink inserted or moved tasks" box

CROSS-REFERENCE

See "Understanding the Task Type" in Chapter 6 for more information about setting that default.

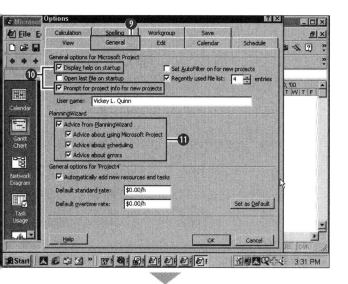

For ease of use, set calculation to automatic on the Calculation tab. Then, whenever you enter or edit information, Project 2000 will perform all calculations. However, manual calculation is more convenient if you are entering large amounts of data at one time, and you want to wait to recalculate at the conclusion of entering the data rather than waiting for the recalculation between each entry. However, seeing the results of each entry can help flag input errors or raise red flags.

The General tab contains startup options. For example, you can set Microsoft Project to show help at startup or open the last file at startup.

In the Calendar tab, you can set high-level project information such as the fiscal year, default calendar start and end times, and the number of hours per day and week.

TAKE NOTE

USING DIALOG BOXES

After clicking the question mark button on a dialog box, position the pointer over a field in the dialog box and click for help about the topic. Clicking the X (the close button) closes the dialog box. Choosing OK closes the box and accepts all changes made while clicking. Cancel closes the box without accepting changes.

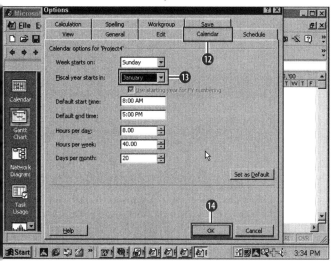

⑨ Click the General tab.

⑩ For practice, check Display help on startup and Prompt for project info for new projects.

⑪ Also for practice, accept all the advice available from the Planning Wizard.

⑫ Click the Calendar tab.

⑬ Set the start of your company's fiscal year.

⑭ Click OK when finished.

FIND IT ONLINE

To share a preview version with a friend, see
www.microsoft.com/office/98/project/trial/info.htm.

Understanding Calendars

A project calendar provides the basis for all task scheduling. As Project 2000 calculates start and finish dates for each task, the calendar is checked for workdays and work hours. In this way company holidays, government holidays, and weekends can be treated as work time or non-work time.

Each project may only have one project calendar serve as the master calendar for scheduling purposes, but further scheduling restrictions exist with the use of resource calendars and task calendars. These three calendar types are all created in the same way, just applied differently.

If you plan to consolidate multiple separate projects into one project at a later date, make sure all the component projects use the same project calendar. Otherwise, some dates will be changed during *consolidation,* which brings the component projects together into one project. This occurs because all tasks coming in to the consolidated version will be forced to fit schedule-wise into that master project calendar.

Calendars are modified or defined using the Project Information dialog box. The top field is a drop-down list of calendars to choose from for modification. A default Standard Project Calendar appears on your list. Rather than modify the Standard Calendar, consider copying it and modifying the calendar copy. Using this technique, you can experiment with calendars before selecting the best one. Otherwise, you might change the standard or default items that ship with Project 2000, and then wish you had them back again.

Later, as you enter resources, a calendar will be created automatically for each person by Project 2000. All

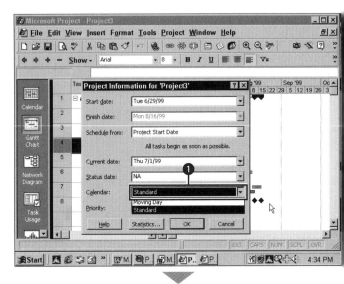

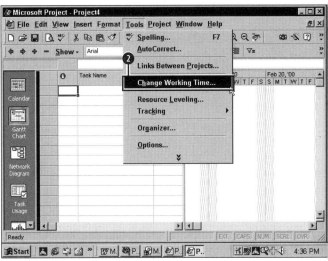

① To select a different project calendar prior to entering tasks, select Project ➪ Project Information.

② To view the current calendar information, click Tools ➪ Change Working Time.

CROSS-REFERENCE

See "Exploring the Global.mpt File" in Chapter 4 for more on including calendars in a template.

other calendars must be created. Resource calendars define days off (other than standard days) like vacations, training, or conferences. Task calendars handle task scheduling that doesn't fit into the standard calendar. For example, in my home spa installation project, the task *Lay Foundation Pad* didn't stop work on Friday at 5:00 like I did. The concrete pad continued to cure or dry after 5:00 so I developed a 24-hour 7-day/week calendar for that task.

As you look at the calendar display in the Project Information dialog box notice the scroll arrows. Scroll arrows move the calendar month display backwards and forwards in time from January 1984 until December 2049. The legend at the left of the dialog box indicates the work status of each individual date.

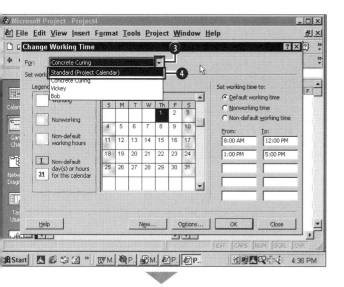

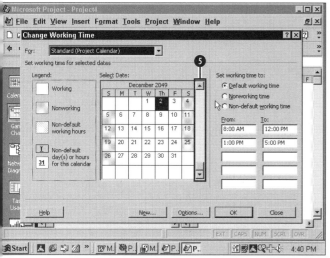

③ Click the drop-down arrow for a list of calendars.

④ Select a calendar to use as the project calendar.

▶ Note the two resource calendars for Vickey and Bob and the task-specific calendar, Concrete Curing.

⑤ To watch time fly, use the arrows or scroll box to scroll from January 1984 to December 2049.

TAKE NOTE

▶ USING COMMON CALENDARS

Three convenient ways exist to ensure consistency among calendars. Either ask developers of individual project pieces to start with a template project file that contains the calendar for common use. Or, ask developers to copy a calendar from one project to another so that all can start with the same calendar (more information later in this task about copying calendars to other projects). Or, copy the calendar to the Global.mpt file so that it is available to all projects.

FIND IT ONLINE

For a list of Microsoft Project 2000 features, see **http://microsoft.com/hk/product/prodref/576_newf.htm**.

Creating and Modifying Calendars

Using the same dialog box as discussed in the last task, you can create and modify calendars. To define a new calendar, click the New button, and a Create New Base Calendar dialog box appears. Give the new calendar a descriptive name for easy recognition and decide whether to create a completely new calendar or make a copy from an existing calendar (like the Standard) to use as a base. Creating a new calendar is easier if you copy an existing calendar that already contains most of your basic choices. Now you are ready to define a new calendar. These custom calendars are then available for use in the drop-down list for project calendar selection in the Project Information dialog box.

The following are hints for modifying calendar selections.

For non-contiguous (non-touching) date selections, click the first date, and then use Ctrl+click for each subsequent date. To select all dates that fall between two date selections, click the first date choice followed by Shift+click on the second date. Finally, to select a day of the week, such as all Friday dates, click the day header, which in this case is F. Note that choosing Fridays will select all Fridays from 1984 through 2049 whether or not your project spans that length of time.

After selecting a date or dates, look to the right side of the dialog box at the radio buttons listed in the "Set working time to" box. The "Default working time"

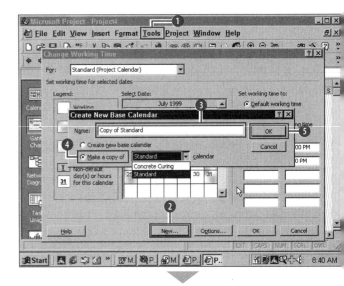

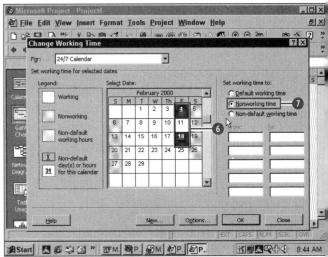

❶ To create a new calendar, select Tools ➪ Change Working Time.

❷ Click New.

❸ Type a name for the new calendar.

❹ Click to create a new base calendar from the defaults or choose a calendar to make a copy from.

❺ Click OK when complete.

❻ To modify new or existing calendars, first select the dates to modify, February 4 and 18, 2000 in this example

❼ Click the Nonworking time radio button. (I'm giving you those dates off!) Notice the legend symbol for this exception.

CROSS-REFERENCE

See "Exploring the Global.mpt file" in Chapter 4 for more on working with calendars.

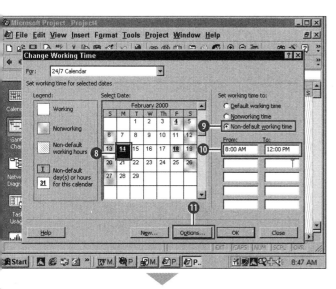

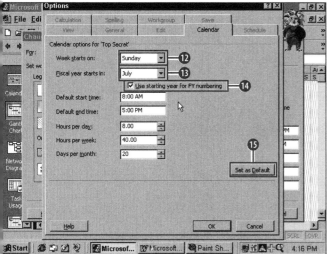

choice resets the dates to the choices from the Calendar tab of the Options dialog box. The "Nonworking time" choice marks the date so that no work can take place on that day. The "Non-default working time" selection marks the date as available for work and requires you to enter working times for the selected date(s).

Each calendar date will display one or more of the legend options to indicate the availability of the date for work. For example, if you change the working hours for a Friday so that the new hours are from 8:00 a.m. until noon rather the standard 8:00 a.m. until 5:00 p.m. time, the date shading indicates Non-default working hours. This change will also show as an exception (with a different legend symbol), which means the date was edited within this calendar.

Remember to check or change the work hours (From and To) to indicate the default or non-default hours for the selected dates.

TAKE NOTE

▶ **NAMING CALENDARS**

Calendar names should be descriptive such as 24 Hours or Night Shift. It is very difficult to remember differences between Standard 1, Standard 2, and Standard 3.

---

⑧ Select February 14, 2000.

⑨ Click Non-default working time to adjust the hours.

⑩ In the From and To boxes, set the work time from 8:00 AM to 12:00 PM only. (Delete entries for 1:00 PM and 5:00 PM.)

⑪ Click the Options button to immediately view or change calendar settings on the Calendar tab of the Options dialog box.

⑫ Use the drop-down list to revise the "Week starts on" setting.

⑬ To switch from calendar year to fiscal year, use the drop-down list to select a month other than January as the start of the year.

⑭ Check to have your timescale reflect the fiscal year numbering.

⑮ Click Set as Default.

FIND IT ONLINE

For online magazine articles and product tips, go to
http://microsoft.com/magazine/.

Sharing Calendars

The project calendar serves as the cornerstone for project scheduling. All tasks schedule according to the selected project calendar with task calendar exceptions and resource calendar exceptions factored in later. It becomes easy to see that if you plan to combine separate projects or project pieces together at a later time it is very important that all tasks schedule using the same calendar.

For example, suppose you are one of three project managers planning a rather large or complex project. You schedule tasks based on a very precise calendar to match company standards and holidays. One comanager creates a 24/7 calendar because his staff has flexible hours. The third comanager designates every other Friday as nonwork because team members are unavailable for project work on those days. As you and the other managers combine your pieces together to look at overlapping resources and tasks, you must choose which calendar serves as the project calendar. This reschedules the other two project pieces to the dismay of the other project managers. Now they find that tasks are scheduled when no one is available to work on them or resources are available but there is no work to do! In addition, task deadline dates differ depending on whose schedule you look at! The simple solution to this calendar dilemma is either to start from the same template that contains a calendar or to share calendars. In this task, you'll explore sharing calendars using the Organizer and the Global.mpt file.

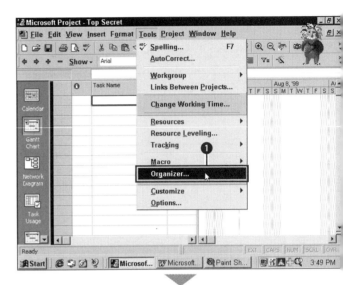

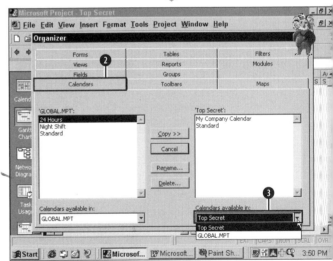

❶ To copy calendars from one file to another using the Organizer, choose Tools ➪ Organizer.

❷ Select the Calendars tab.

❸ Click the "Calendars available in" drop-down arrow (right-hand side) and select the source file.

CROSS-REFERENCE

See "Combining Projects" in Chapter 16 for more information about multiple project considerations.

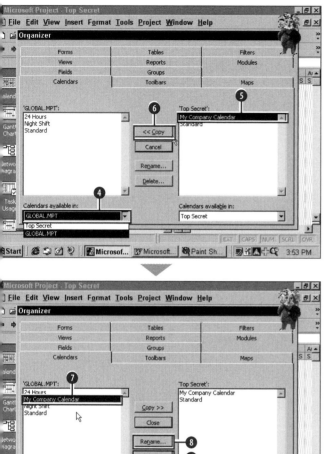

The Organizer (Tools ⇨ Organizer) is a Project 2000 dialog box that enables easy swapping of project components, like calendars, between projects. For example, in the Organizer dialog box on the Calendars tab, notice the two drop-down lists at the bottom of this box showing calendars available in various project files. In one box, select the project you want to copy the calendar from and in the other box select the project you want to copy the calendar into. After selecting the calendar by name in the "from" list, click the Copy>> button (notice the arrow points in the "to" direction). You can also rename calendars here or delete unwanted calendars.

To ensure a calendar's availability for all projects, copy it into the file named Global.mpt. The Global.mpt file stores all standard and custom items like tables, views, calendars, toolbars, fields, forms, groups, filters, and reports and opens each time you launch Project 2000.

TAKE NOTE

SHIFT SCHEDULING

Shift scheduling was rather difficult in previous versions of Microsoft Project. With the addition of task calendars you can now accurately schedule tasks when you want them to occur. Choose one shift, perhaps the day shift, to use the project calendar. Create and assign different task calendars to both the evening and night shifts.

● *Click the "Calendars available in" drop-down arrow (left-hand side) and choose the destination file, Global.mpt, to make the calendar available to all projects.*

● *Select the source calendar to copy.*

● *Click the Copy button.*

⑦ *Locate the newly copied calendar in the Global.mpt list of calendars.*

⑧ *For calendar maintenance, click the Rename button to develop more descriptive names.*

⑨ *Click the Delete button to erase a calendar.*

FIND IT ONLINE

For interesting ways to share data between Microsoft Office products, see the Microsoft Office Home Page at http://www.microsoft.com/office/.

Personal Workbook

Q&A

1 Describe two techniques to create a new project file.

_____

_____

_____

2 Under what conditions or constraints would you schedule the project from the finish date rather than from the start date?

_____

_____

_____

3 When is it reasonable for the Status Date to be different from the Current Date?

_____

_____

_____

4 On which Options tab is the date format choice found?

_____

_____

5 When would you use manual rather than automatic recalculation?

_____

_____

_____

6 What technique can you use to copy a calendar from one project to another?

_____

_____

_____

7 Describe the function of a project calendar.

_____

_____

_____

8 Describe what is meant by the calendar term "Non-default working hours."

_____

_____

_____

ANSWERS: PAGE 318

EXTRA PRACTICE

1 Create a new project using the menu choice as well as the toolbar button.

2 In the Project Information dialog box, instruct Project 2000 to schedule your project from the finish date, and then enter a desired finish date.

3 Give your project a title and assign yourself as Manager using the Project Properties dialog box.

4 Look at the Standard default calendar.

5 Create a new calendar using the Standard calendar as the base.

6 Copy a custom calendar from one project to another.

REAL-WORLD APPLICATIONS

✔ You've been given a new project assignment so you use the File ⇨ New command to create a new project file.

✔ Management has established a deadline (constraint) for this project so you choose to schedule from the project finish date and ask Microsoft Project 2000 to schedule backwards toward the project start date.

✔ Your company's standard hours include extended days with every other Friday off so you create a new calendar to reflect this.

✔ You are managing one piece of a large project so you copy the project calendar from the master project file into your project before adding tasks.

Visual Quiz

How do you select this noncontiguous group of dates in May, 2000?

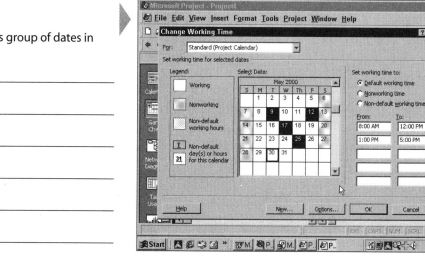

CHAPTER 4

MASTER
THESE
SKILLS

▶ **Understanding File Types**

▶ **Saving and Password Protecting Files**

▶ **Closing and Opening Files**

▶ **Using File Maintenance Extras**

▶ **Exploring the Global.mpt File**

Organizing Project Files

Sharing project data from a variety of software applications is an everyday occurrence for many teams, workgroups, and organizations. For example, you may want to create a project schedule in Microsoft Project 2000, use Excel (a Microsoft spreadsheet) for project budget analysis, conduct project risk assessment using Risk+ (ProjectGear, Inc.), and use Access (a Microsoft database application) for report generation. If that isn't enough, you may then decide to use one of the numerous enterprise data management and reporting tools that utilizes project information for the entire organization. Although this may sound complex, software developers write programs using standard protocols so that data can be shared rather easily.

Not all readers of this book have an immediate need to share data, but as you become a more skilled Project 2000 user, you may start to see opportunities and benefits to sharing rather than re-entering data. Even if you never share Project data, file maintenance and organization is still an important aspect of software use. By creating meaningful directories and filenames, you can organize your information so that it is readily accessible.

The goal of file organization is to have project data available at our fingertips, like looking into a well-organized file cabinet as opposed to opening the drawer and seeing files thrown in haphazardly.

This chapter familiarizes you with different file types and their uses, and also covers how to best utilize routine file functions like Open, Save, Close, and the new automatic File Save feature. You will also cover file maintenance functions like deleting, copying, and renaming files.

In addition to file functions, you will examine security features available in Project 2000. Workgroups often establish different levels of project information accessibility. Security features enable you to create a file that is read-only, read-only recommended, write accessible, or password protected.

The Global.mpt file is a special template that allows you to customize Project 2000 in minor or very substantial ways. Using the Global.mpt file, you can provide custom items like tables, views, and toolbars available to every member of your workgroup or organization. In this chapter you will view the Organizer as a means of altering the Global.mpt file.

Understanding File Types

Although novice users, looking only to use the basic features of Microsoft Project 2000, may not yet be concerned with file types, they should keep them in mind for future needs and opportunities. For more experienced users, file types make information sharing possible.

In this task, you'll review the file types available when saving files in Project 2000 in order to understand the many data sharing options. The file types determine whether you can share entire project files, or a table (like the entry table of data in a Gantt Chart), or selected data fields.

It is an acceptable practice to use the standard project format, MPP extension, at all times when saving Project 2000 files until the need arises to share data. When this occurs, simply save the file as a different type and the extension will automatically be added. Software applications developed as add-ins to Microsoft Project 2000 can usually read this format.

The template format (MPT extension) represents template files. Templates allow you to save boilerplate information for reuse. The Global.mpt, for example, is a master template for Project 2000, and I'll review it in more detail later in this chapter. You can also create template files of your own which I'll also discuss later in this chapter.

The CSV (comma-separated values) and Text (tab-delimited) formats allow you to export, in a text format, data from a single Project 2000 table. Both of these formats are typically for sharing project information with a word processing application for reports or documentation.

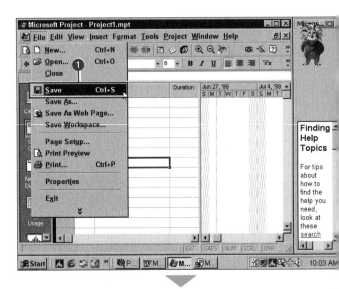

① Select File ➪ Save on a new project or Save As to save the file using an alternative format, and the Save As dialog box opens.

② Click the "Save as type" drop down arrow for a list of format options.

CROSS-REFERENCE

See Chapter 15, "Using Microsoft Project 2000 in Workgroups," for more about information sharing.

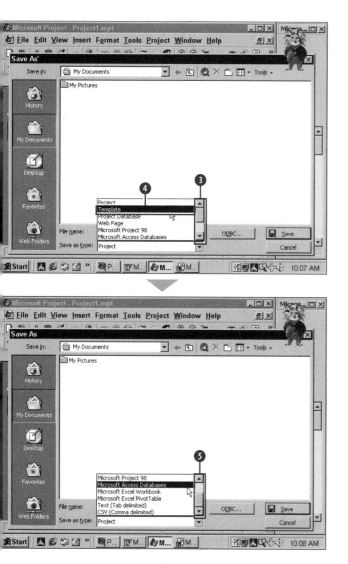

The Microsoft Access Databases format allows the storing of entire projects for use in Microsoft Access. The Project Database format is similar in that you can save all or part of a project but specifically for databases other than Access.

Microsoft Excel spreadsheet users will recognize the XLS extension for Microsoft Excel Workbooks. This format allows you to export field data, not entire projects. There is also an extension to export to a Microsoft Excel Pivot Table.

Web Page is a format used by browser programs on the World Wide Web and intranets. It offers exciting avenues for information sharing, especially for distributed teams or workgroups.

The Microsoft Project 98 format allows you to save a project developed in Project 2000 and open it in Project 98. Remember, some information will be lost or unavailable due to differences in architecture and functionality between the two versions.

TAKE NOTE

▶ PREPARING TO SHARE

A little time spent up front discussing with your LAN administrator common or shared directories and the other "physical" requirements can save much time later.

③ Using the arrows or scroll box, view all format options.

④ Choose a format from the list by clicking the name.

⑤ Scroll the list until you find the desired format.

FIND IT ONLINE

See **http://stekt.oulu.fi/~jon/jouninfo/filex** for a list of file extensions and what they mean.

59

Saving and Password Protecting Files

Assume you have a new project file open in Microsoft Project 2000. Let's review the options in the same order you will probably need to use them: file saving options, file closing options, and file opening options.

First, the file save options. From the File menu, choose Save (or Save As) to open the Save dialog box. Name the file in the File name field and decide the type of file format using the drop-down list. Remember to name the file with descriptive words; Office_Move is easier to remember than Project_1A.

Decide where to store your file in the Save in: section. Again, organize your files in directories that make sense to you. Probably every Windows user has forgotten where a particular project file is located. (I know I have!) Fortunately, you can search all drives and directories for "missing" files.

Select General Options from the Tools drop-down menu for several valuable safety choices. For example, the "Always create backup" option, if checked, will make a backup copy of your project file each time you save the file. Likewise, the file sharing options offer three levels of protection to guard against unauthorized access.

The most restrictive option, Protection password, requires each user to enter the correct case-sensitive password to open the file. Caution: write the password down and store it! Your trouble in locating "missing" files will seem minor compared to your trouble in dealing with a forgotten password! (I have done that, too!)

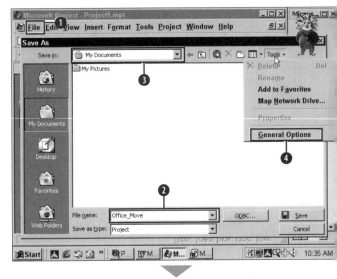

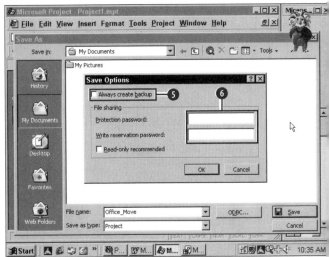

❶ To save a file, choose File ➪ Save (or Save As) to open the Save As dialog box.

❷ Name the file in the File name field and choose the file format type.

❸ Decide where to store your file in the "Save in" field.

❹ Click Tools ➪ General Options to set file security precautions.

❺ Check the "Always create backup" option for a backup copy with each save.

❻ Enter a password for either the Protection password or Write Reservation password if desired. Or, check the box for Read-only recommended if desired.

CROSS-REFERENCE

For more information and other examples of data sharing, see Chapter 13.

Organizing Project Files

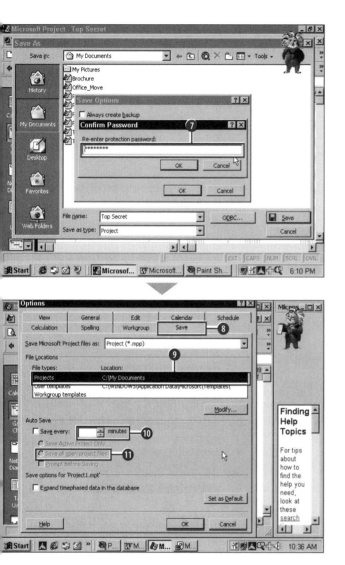

The Write reservation password is also a case-sensitive password that limits those who can make changes to the project plan. Without the correct password, the file is opened as read-only.

The least restrictive applied option, the Read-only recommended, causes a screen prompt to appear suggesting that the file be opened as read-only, but this is merely a suggestion and can be overridden. If overridden, the user has complete read and write access. This file sharing option is the least restrictive of the three.

> **TAKE NOTE**
>
> ### USING AUTOMATIC FILE SAVE
>
> New to Project 2000 is a timed save feature. A timed save means you can automatically save a project file every few minutes. Users can customize Auto Save to choose the save time interval as well as the option to save only the active project or save all open project files. The Auto Save dialog box is found through the Tools menu under Options on the new Save tab.
>
> The new Save tab also enables you to specify the default directory to use when saving your files as well as the default format for project files. You can specify different default directories for project files, user templates, and workgroup templates.

⑦ If you set a password in the previous step, you need to retype the password to confirm the entry.

⑧ To access the Auto Save dialog box, choose Tools ⇨ Options and select the Save tab.

⑨ Choose the default directory for file storage of each file type.

⑩ Set the desired time interval between automatic saves.

⑪ Choose to Auto Save the active project or all open projects.

FIND IT ONLINE

For Windows 98 tips, visit the IDG Web site at
http://www.idg.net.

Closing and Opening Files

To close a file, simply click the Close (X) button located in the upper-right corner of your project window, or from the File menu choose Close. If you have made changes without saving the file, either of these commands generates a prompt asking if you want to save changes before closing. A "yes" response opens the File Save dialog box if the file is "new" and hasn't been saved previously; otherwise, a save occurs using information you have previously supplied.

It is not necessary to close a project file before opening another project file. In fact, many of the workgroup techniques and multiple-project features work only because you have numerous files open at the same time. I explore these ideas in greater detail in later chapters. If your computer is memory constrained or a bit on the slow side, leaving numerous files open is probably not a good idea. Even though you may be viewing only one file currently, all the open ones are held in active memory.

To open a file simply click the Open button on the Standard toolbar or choose File ⇨ Open from the menu. Remember to specify the correct directory and file type when locating files.

Saving and opening Project 98 files in Project 2000 require special consideration. In Project 2000, you can save a project file in the native Project 98 file format to exchange project information with users who have not yet upgraded. Keep in mind, however, that Project 98 does not contain all the features found in Project 2000.

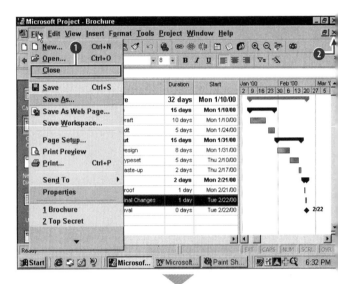

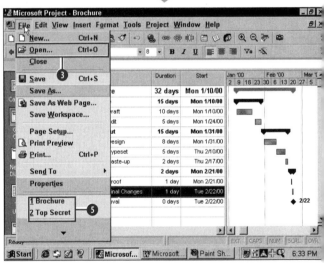

❶ To close a project, choose File ⇨ Close.

❷ Or, click the Close Window button.

❸ To open a file choose File ⇨ Open.

❹ Or, click the Open button on the Standard toolbar.

❺ Or, click one of the most recently used files.

CROSS-REFERENCE
See "Working with Shared Resources" in Chapter 16 for more on working in a multiple project environment.

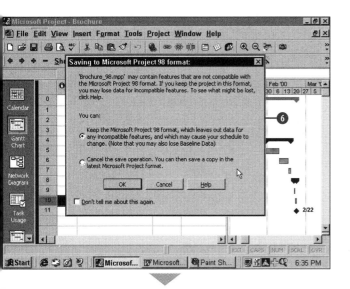

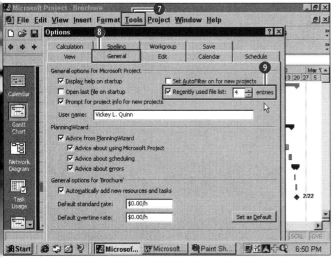

If you save a Project 2000 file in the Project 98 format some information may be lost, but you will receive a reminder about this potential data loss when you save to this format. Typical data loss occurs in saving baseline information, Network Diagram (a.k.a. PERT Chart) information, task calendars, and material resources.

Although no warning appears, intermingling Project 2000 and Project 98 files is discouraged since such intermingling can lead to surprising results. For example, data loss or corruption can occur if you develop a master project file containing inserted projects of both file formats. Additionally, you should not use a Project 98 resource list as the resource pool for your Project 2000 projects. Nor should you combine projects using both file formats, make project changes, and break the projects apart again.

TAKE NOTE

LISTING MOST RECENTLY USED FILES

A list of your four most recently used files appears at the bottom of the File menu. You can click one of these to open the file. The default number of files to display is four, but you can actually select from zero to nine recently used files to display at the bottom of the file menu. This option is found on the General tab under Tools ⇨ Options.

⑥ When saving a Project 2000 file into a Project 98 format, you see this warning.

⑦ To adjust the number of most recently open files that appear on the File list, choose Tools ⇨ Options.

⑧ Click the General tab.

⑨ Change to the number of files you want to display.

FIND IT ONLINE

For Windows file utilities, visit **http://home.cdarchive. com/ftp/shareware/05A.htm.**

Using File Maintenance Extras

Numerous file management extras make working with files more productive. "Extras" include file search capabilities and file copying, deleting, moving, and renaming.

Even the most organized person occasionally needs to search for a "difficult to locate" project file. Using the Open dialog box enables you to look in different directories to locate the file or use various search criteria to locate the file. For example, you can search by filename, file type, or the date the file was last modified. You can also add property values to the search criteria. Properties include items like application name, author, category, comments, company name, creation date, keywords, and numerous others found on a drop-down list.

Here are a few tips for searching for files. Searching for long filenames with spaces can be very complicated. Instead of using spaces consider using an underscore (_) between words to aid in searching later.

Be sure to verify that the correct location appears in the "Look in" box. Sometimes Windows 98 modifies this without warning and you may overlook the simple solution to your search problems.

Unless you are absolutely sure of the filename (without a hint of doubt), don't use the *Match exactly* choice.

If you thought the criteria search of "File name includes" sounds easy and too good to be true, it probably is. When files are stored on your hard disk, they are layered with internal (Windows) locator names assigned, thus making it difficult or impossible to locate the actual text you typed as the filename.

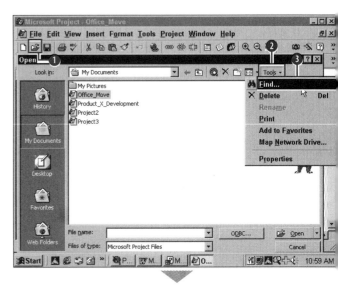

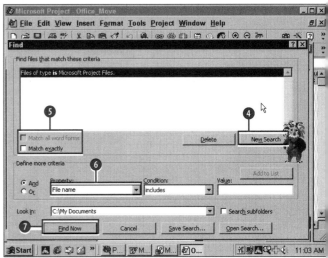

❶ To enter search criteria, first click the Open button on the Standard toolbar.

❷ The Open dialog box appears. Click Tools from the menu.

❸ Click Find from the resulting drop-down menu

❹ Click the New Search button to start a new search.

❺ Click one of the checkboxes to determine matching restrictions.

❻ Choose a desired file Property and select or enter corresponding condition and value.

❼ Click the Find Now button to start the search.

CROSS-REFERENCE

See Chapter 3 for information about setting project information that can be used during a file search.

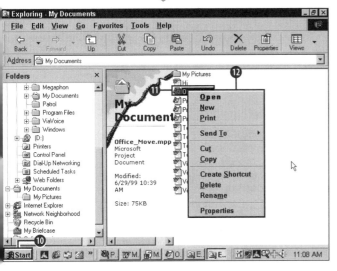

Beware of the property search criteria "Files of type" based on searching Project 2000 for specific file types (like project files). One of the choices on the list is to search for All files. Be warned that some of the files that appear may not be intended to be run manually. Attempting to run some of them can lock up your computer or result in loss of data. As a safety precaution, if you use this option, right-click the filename in question and choose Properties.

TAKE NOTE

▶ FILE MANAGEMENT "EXTRAS" USING THE OPEN DIALOG BOX

To practice the file management techniques above, choose File ➪ Open or click the Open button on the Standard toolbar. Highlight the file of interest and right-click on the filename. A shortcut menu appears showing a wide array of file maintenance options such as Open, Open Read-Only, Print, Send To (a floppy drive, or CD-ROM drive, or a mail recipient), Cut, Copy, Delete, Rename, or Properties.

▶ FILE MAINTENANCE USING WINDOWS EXPLORER

Some may find it easier to perform file operations from Windows Explorer since you can view many directories and files at once. Right-clicking on a filename in Windows Explorer also pops up the shortcut menu.

---

⑧ *From the Open dialog box right-click any filename to activate a shortcut menu.*

⑨ *Choose one of the resulting file maintenance options.*

▶ *As an alternative to the previous technique, use Windows Explorer to perform file maintenance functions.*

⑩ *Choose Start ➪ Programs ➪ Windows Explorer.*

⑪ *Select the appropriate folder and file for maintenance.*

⑫ *Right-click the filename for the shortcut menu.*

FIND IT ONLINE

Learn about Anywhere 98, a file copying and moving shareware program, at **http://www.liquidmirror.com**.

Exploring the Global.mpt File

The Global.mpt file is a master template file that opens each time you launch Project 2000. Rather than contain tasks or resources, this template contains all the default items available for use in all your projects. Items such as views, calendars, forms, reports, tables, filters, toolbars, and custom fields all reside in the Global.mpt file.

It is absolutely imperative for those wishing to standardize a workgroup or for an entire corporation using custom project formats to know how to use the Global.mpt file. Imagine, for example, that you create a custom calendar, two custom toolbars, custom filters, a custom menu, and numerous custom fields that you want to be available to all members of your department. You could, of course, ask each member of the department to always open a regular template file (one with an mpt extension) first so that the custom items show, and then save this file with a new project name. Many department members will do exactly as outlined above while others will forget to open the template first and confusion will reign as they are unable to locate and use the custom items.

Instead, adding these custom items to the Global.mpt file will ensure their availability in every project automatically, as if these custom features came "out of the box." At the advanced end of the scale, you can create complete selections of custom items, perhaps even replace the items shipped with Project 2000 with your custom choices and develop an application that is cosmetically and functionally very different from the standard version.

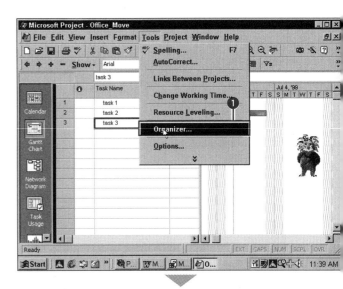

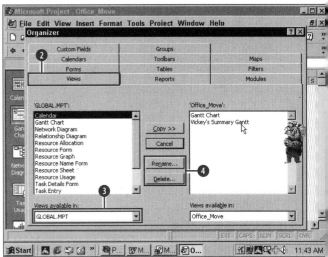

❶ Choose Tools ➪ Organizer to access the Global.mpt file.

❷ Choose one of the eleven tabs, Views for example.

❸ Locate the "Views available in" fields on the bottom left and right.

❹ Notice the other buttons for renaming or deleting an element.

CROSS-REFERENCE

See Chapter 17 for information on customizing Project 2000.

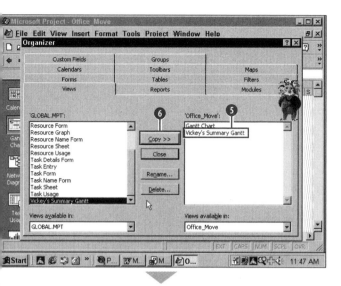

To view the information stored in the Global.mpt file, choose Tools ➪ Organizer. Check to see that GLOBAL.MPT is listed in the "Look in" field for either the left- or right-hand box located at the bottom of the dialog box. If not, select GLOBAL.MPT from the drop-down list for either side. As you examine each of the eleven tabs that make up the Organizer, the various default components that are available in Project 2000 display. On the Views tab, look for Gantt Chart, Network Diagram, and Calendar. Additionally, on the Toolbars tab find Standard, Tracking, and Formatting.

To make custom items available to all projects, copy from the file that contains the custom item to the Global.mpt file. Check for duplicate names before copying. If not, you might replace a default item unintentionally.

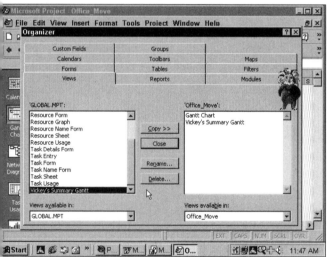

5 To copy a custom Gantt Chart view (Vickey's Summary Gantt) from a working project into the Global.mpt file, click that view.

6 Next, click the Copy button located between the two selection boxes. Notice the arrows point to the destination file.

▶ Notice the custom view, Vickey's Summary Gantt, is now listed as an available view in the Global.mpt file.

TAKE NOTE

▶ **THE VALUE OF TEMPLATES**

It is probably not possible to overemphasize the value of templates as a timesaving device. Projects that involve a life cycle, like software development or product development, are perfect candidates for a predefined template. Think of the template as a boilerplate for the information that all these similar projects share. In the template file, include common tasks, estimates, task links, resource skill information (like programmer or technician), calendars, custom tables, and reports.

FIND IT ONLINE

For information about a customized, process-driven add-in to Project 2000, see **http://www.projectdirect.com**.

Personal Workbook

Q&A

1 What is the file extension for a standard Microsoft Project 2000 file?

_____

_____

_____

2 The mpt file extension is for what file type?

_____

_____

_____

3 What is the function of a write reservation password when working with project files?

_____

_____

_____

4 Where can you see a list of your four most recently used files?

_____

_____

_____

5 How do you access the shortcut menu to rename a file?

_____

_____

_____

6 What is the function of the Global.mpt file?

_____

_____

_____

7 What are four types of information found in the Global.mpt file?

_____

_____

_____

8 What format should you use when sharing data with Microsoft Access?

_____

_____

_____

ANSWERS: PAGE 319

EXTRA PRACTICE

1. Save a project file three times — with a different file extension each time.

2. Use search criteria other than the filename to locate a project file.

3. Assign password protection to a test or practice project. Then open the file using the password.

4. Use toolbar buttons to open and save a file.

5. Using the Organizer, review the elements contained in the Global.mpt file.

6. Assign "Read-only recommended" protection to a practice project. Then open the project.

REAL-WORLD APPLICATIONS

✓ You need to generate a detailed budget based on the task list (from Project 2000) so you save the Entry table with an XLS extension and export the data to Excel.

✓ To give your report that professional look, you use the Office Binder to provide consistency in style, page numbers, and headers.

✓ You have three common project types in your organization. You lead the effort to develop template files for the three types to save planning time.

✓ You forget where you saved your project file, so instead of panicking you use search criteria for the date last modified to locate it.

Visual Quiz

How do you establish password protection for a project file?

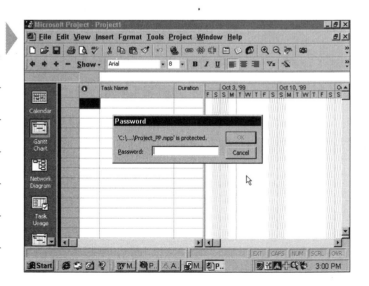

PART

III

Creating a Project Plan

Creating a project plan requires the project manager and planning team to be creative, to think "outside the box" and devise a strategy to handle whatever comes their way during the actual execution of the project.

In Part III you will use Project 2000 to record your project strategy. You will begin by developing a list of all the tasks or activities that must be completed throughout the project. Then, you will estimate how long it takes to accomplish each task and determine the dependency links or relationships between tasks.

While analyzing the schedule, you will explore the concepts of critical path and task constraints.

Additionally, you will define resources and costs and, for those wishing to use Project 2000 to manage staff and budget allocations, you will learn how to assign them to tasks.

You will also practice techniques to manipulate and view data, including filtering data to show subsets of data onscreen, sorting data, and a new feature called *Grouping*.

Finally, you will try various techniques for analyzing and reviewing your project plan prior to seeking plan approval. These techniques include checking for overallocated resources and resolving those overallocation conflicts.

CHAPTER 5

MASTER THESE SKILLS

- ▶ **Entering and Editing a Task List**
- ▶ **Copying, Deleting, and Moving Tasks**
- ▶ **Creating a Task Outline**
- ▶ **Completing the Outline**
- ▶ **Creating Milestone and Recurring Tasks**
- ▶ **Developing Custom WBS and Outline Codes**

Developing a Task Outline

The foundation for any good project schedule is a comprehensive list of tasks. You could brainstorm tasks that you think will be necessary (but you might forget some important ones), use a template of tasks if one exists, or create the list yourself.

A common technique that project managers use to create a task list is a *Work Breakdown Structure* chart (WBS). A WBS chart is a hierarchical chart, like an organizational chart or tree chart, whose purpose is to assist in the organization of the project from a conceptual level down to the task level. The WBS is generated from the top down to give your project a structure and organization because all the details flow down from the top.

Many project managers and subject matter experts jump too quickly to the detail task level without gaining the appropriate global view of the project. The WBS technique prevents that from happening with the top-down approach.

The project manager usually develops the first overall level of the WBS as the project structure. Then it is typical to invite *subject matter experts* (SMEs) in to help plan the remainder of the tasks. Inviting SMEs to help serves two purposes. First, the majority of project managers do not know task details for every aspect of the project. Second, you can better gain the support and buy-in of SMEs if you've asked them to suggest the required tasks. As a planning tool, the WBS helps you locate gaps or overlaps in task responsibility as SMEs compare notes.

Suppose you wish to create a WBS chart of all project tasks. First you decide the overall structure: maybe you will divide the project up into phases or deliverables, or components, or geographical areas. You can break a project down into the level of detail and level of management control that seem appropriate given the familiarity of the team members with similar projects.

For this example, let's choose Phases as the highest level (Level 1). Then you take each phase in turn and list the deliverables to be produced as part of that phase (Level 2). Next, take each deliverable and break it down into all the tasks necessary to complete that deliverable (Level 3). There is no preset limit to the number of levels required for a project. The key is to break the project into tasks that can be accomplished.

In Microsoft Project 2000 the WBS is represented by an outline structure, with each level shown as an indentation level, as opposed to the standard WBS chart, which is a tree diagram that looks similar to an organizational chart. In this chapter you will explore the steps necessary to create the outline of tasks.

Entering and Editing a Task List

Before entering task names, double-check to make sure that you are not establishing task dependency links automatically as you insert or move task names. Let's assume that for now you are brainstorming tasks or that your tasks don't follow each other in strict sequential order. Allowing Project 2000 to automatically create dependency links now can lead to problems later; you could end up with unwanted links that are difficult to find or time-consuming to remove. We will establish task dependency links later in a very deliberate manner. To check the default choose Tools ⇨ Options and select the Schedule tab. Uncheck the box for "Autolink inserted or moved tasks."

Entering task names into a table on the Gantt Chart is probably the most straightforward approach. To enter a task name, click an empty cell in the Task Name column on any table and begin typing. Project 2000 now supports in-cell editing, which means you are entering and changing information directly in the cell in which you are typing. Pressing the Enter key after each entry accepts the entry and moves the active cursor down to the next cell in the same column.

As an alternative to in-cell editing, use the Entry Bar located above the Gantt Chart window. The Entry Bar allows you to change cell contents and is especially useful if the contents are lengthy. When you finish typing the task name, click the checkmark to the left of the entry to accept your response. If after typing you decide not to keep the entry, click the X on the Entry Bar to cancel the entry.

To edit a task, simply click the name of the task in the Task Name column. Notice the cell's content now displays in the Entry Bar where it is available for editing, or you may modify it directly in the cell.

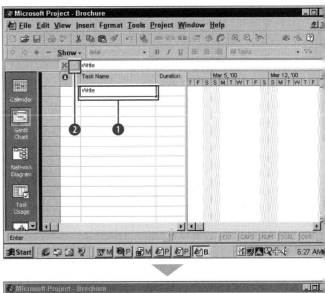

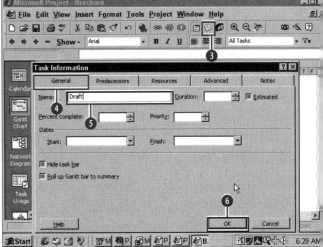

❶ To enter task names, click in an empty cell and type the name.

❷ Press Enter to continue to the next line or click the checkmark on the Entry Bar.

❸ To enter task names using forms, click the Task Information button.

❹ Select the General tab.

❺ Type the task name in the name field.

❻ Click OK.

CROSS-REFERENCE

See "Grouping Tasks" in Chapter 10 as an alternative to using a WBS structure for tasks.

If you prefer forms to spreadsheets, double-click the task name to open the Task Information dialog box with the Name field already displayed.

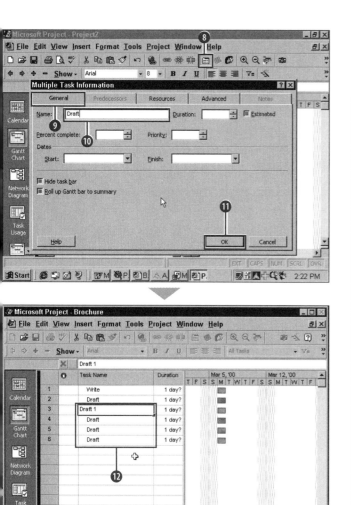

TAKE NOTE

▶ EDITING MULTIPLE TASKS

Although editing Task Names is usually a task-by-task effort, you may edit multiple task names if needed. First, select the multiple tasks either by clicking and dragging down or up for multiple selections or by clicking the first selection followed by Ctrl+click for subsequent noncontiguous (non-touching) tasks. Now, by clicking the Task Information button on the Standard toolbar, the Multiple Task Information dialog box appears for edits to the selected tasks.

▶ USING THE TASK INFORMATION DIALOG BOX TO CREATE NEW TASKS

The technique for editing multiple tasks also works for creating new tasks with similar names. For example, select four blank task name cells. Click the Task Information button to open the Multiple Task Information dialog box. Enter the common part of the four names, like Test. After clicking OK to close the box, you can edit each task individually to add the non-common part of the name.

7 To enter multiple similar task names, select multiple rows.

8 Click the Task Information button, and the Multiple Task Information dialog box opens.

9 Select the General tab.

10 Type the common part of each name.

11 Click OK when you finish.

12 In the resulting task list, add the dissimilar part to each task name.

FIND IT ONLINE

For information about a front-end tool to create WBS charts, see **http://www.criticaltools.com**.

Copying, Deleting, and Moving Tasks

To complete your task list, you may need to insert, delete, or move tasks to other locations. In addition, copying and pasting repeatable tasks from this or another list reduces your data entry time. You'll review these techniques in this task.

Before inserting tasks into the current list, consider task placement. An empty row for inserted tasks is placed above the selected task on the list. To insert a task, click the task that will appear below the inserted new task. From the Insert menu, choose New Task. A blank row displays for the new task information. To insert five new rows at once, for example, select five current tasks and from the Insert menu choose New Task. Five blank rows now display.

Deleting unwanted tasks is as easy as selecting the task and choosing Delete Task from the Edit menu. The Delete command removes the entire task row from the list, not just the cell contents, so use this command with caution. The Delete Task command does not yield a prompt as a double-check; it simply deletes the task. However if you delete a task accidentally and notice it before making other changes, choose Undo Delete from the Edit menu. The Delete key on your keyboard works the same as the Delete Task command from the Edit menu.

The cut, copy, and paste features work here just as they work in any other Windows application, and they have shortcut buttons on the Standard toolbar. The Edit menu also contains commands for Cut, Copy, and Paste.

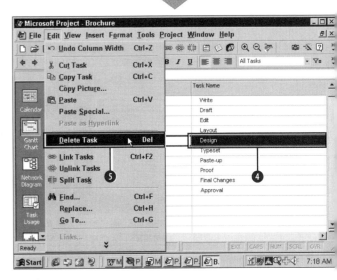

➊ To insert a task between two other tasks, select the task that will appear below the new task in the task list.

➋ Choose Insert ➪ New Task.

➌ Type the task name into the empty cell.

➍ Select the task(s) to be deleted.

➎ Choose Edit ➪ Delete Task.

CROSS-REFERENCE

See "Using Reference Help" in Chapter 1 for more information about using the Windows Clipboard.

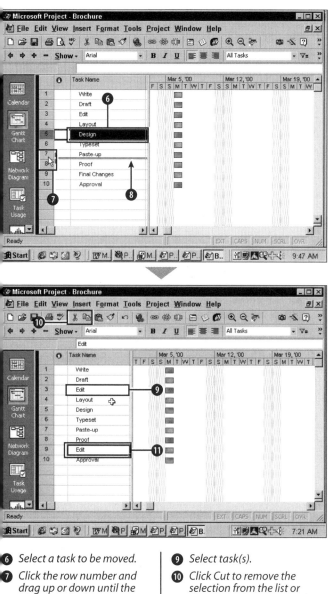

Remember, Cut removes the task name from the current location to the Clipboard (a temporary storage bin), and Copy makes a copy of the task name to place on the Clipboard. Send task names to the Clipboard using Cut or Copy, and use Paste to paste task names from the Clipboard into the destination location.

To cut or copy tasks found in another project, simply open that project file, select the tasks, and click the Cut or Copy button. These tasks are copied to the Windows Clipboard and are available for pasting into the destination project.

TAKE NOTE

▶ USING CUT AND PASTE TO MOVE A TASK

Cut and paste is one method for moving a task to a new location. In addition, you can move a task using the mouse, but this technique requires more manual dexterity. To move a task using the mouse, first select the entire task row (click the row number to select the entire row), then position the pointer over the row heading (top or bottom line that separates task rows), and click and drag the task to the new destination. A Move bar appears showing the new location. Use this as a guide before releasing the drag.

---

⑥ Select a task to be moved.

⑦ Click the row number and drag up or down until the Move bar displays.

⑧ Drag the Move bar to the desired location for the moved task and release.

⑨ Select task(s).

⑩ Click Cut to remove the selection from the list or Copy to make a copy to the Clipboard.

⑪ For the Copy option, move to the new empty location and click Paste.

FIND IT ONLINE

For tips on using the Clipboard efficiently, see **http://malektips.envprogramming.com/98w0026.html.**

Creating a Task Outline

Turning a task list into a task outline is a matter of organization. The task outline matches the Work Breakdown Structure in that each subsequent level of the WBS becomes an indentation level on the outline. The outline numbering that you'll see later in this chapter is reminiscent of outlining techniques for term papers. The term paper topics might be organized into I, II, III, and IV. Topic I breaks down into A, B, C, D, and E. Subsequently, topic A breaks down into 1, 2, 3, and 4. If complex enough, topic 1 then breaks down into a, b, and c and so on. You'll apply this same organizational technique in this section as you turn the task list into a task outline.

In Project 2000 the main topics or tasks, called *summary tasks,* are bold by default. Subtasks are the tasks indented under the summary tasks. Summary tasks, as the name indicates, summarize information for all the tasks indented underneath it, such as duration, work, and cost. This feature becomes important later as you report on larger sections of the project, like phases or deliverables.

To create the outline, select a task or contiguous tasks to indent, and click the right arrow (Indent) button on the Formatting toolbar. The summary task shows in bold by default and the indented tasks are subtasks. The left arrow (Outdent) button shifts the task back to the left.

Creating an outline, as opposed to a list of tasks, offers several advantages. First, data is automatically summarized for all indented tasks to give a higher-level view of project details. You can also display or hide the indented

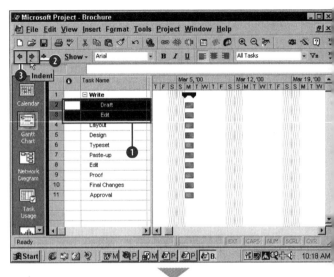

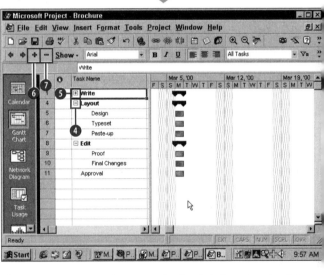

1. Select the task(s) to be indented or outdented.
2. Click the right arrow to indent.
3. Or click the left arrow to outdent.
4. Click the minus sign (−) to collapse the summary task.
5. Click the plus sign (+) to show the subtasks.
6. Click the Show Subtasks button to expand the outline.
7. Click the Hide Subtasks button to collapse the outline.

CROSS-REFERENCE

See "Exploring Formatting Options" in Chapter 12 for more about preparing summary reports.

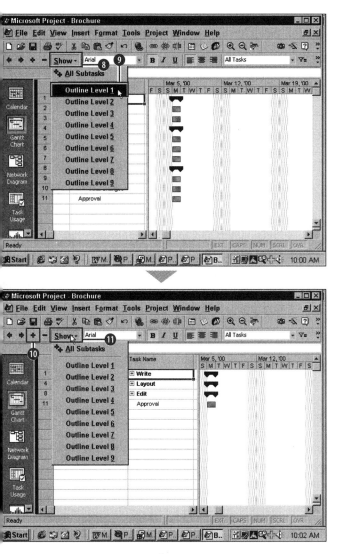

subtasks for reporting purposes. For example, before printing a high-level project summary report, you hide the subtasks so that only the summary tasks show. To collapse the outline (hide the subtasks), select the summary task containing the subtasks to hide and click the Hide Subtasks button (the minus sign) on the Formatting toolbar. To again show the subtasks, select the summary task and click the Show Subtasks button (the plus sign). To display all subtasks for multiple collapsed summary tasks, or to choose an indentation level for display, click the Show button for a drop-down list of options.

TAKE NOTE

INDENTING OR OUTDENTING A TASK USING THE MOUSE

The mouse provides a quick way to indent or outdent a task. First, position your pointer over the first letter of the task name. The pointer changes to a two-way arrow. Now, drag to the right to indent and to the left to outdent.

COLLAPSING THE ENTIRE OUTLINE

To collapse the entire outline, select all table rows and columns by clicking the blank button at the intersection of the column headers and rows. Then click the Hide Subtasks button. Now, only the summary tasks display.

---

⑧ Click the Show button for a drop-down menu.

⑨ Choose Outline Level 1 to display just that level of tasks.

⑩ On the resulting task list, click the Show Subtasks button to expand each collapsed summary task.

⑪ Alternatively, choose Show ➪ All Subtasks.

FIND IT ONLINE

For free project management tools, articles, and project templates see **http://www.4pm.com/**.

Completing the Outline

For organizational or reporting purposes you may want to use various outline display options or create custom WBS codes.

Outline display options make working with the project details easier. Outline options help you see which summary tasks are collapsed, view a project-level summary task quickly, or see WBS numbers for analysis of the project's organization. To view the available outline options, choose Tools ➪ Options and select the View tab.

Outline options for this project show at the bottom right of this tab. The Show summary tasks checkbox, if cleared, hides all summary tasks. Outlining commands are unavailable if summary tasks are hidden.

Select the Project summary task checkbox to have Project 2000 automatically display a project-level summary task. Project 2000 uses the Title field information in the Properties dialog box as the name of the project-level summary task.

Unchecking the Indent name checkbox removes the indentation of subtasks. The outlined appearance of your task list disappears but summary task names still appear in bold.

The Show outline number checkbox displays the WBS number next to each task name. Similarly, the Show outline symbol checkbox displays outline symbols next to each task name. A plus sign next to a summary task indicates a rolled-up or collapsed task while a minus sign indicates an expanded task, that is, a summary task showing its subtasks.

Project 2000 allows you to create custom WBS codes tied to individual tasks. Particularly, the codes you create adhere to the outline structure and format you specify,

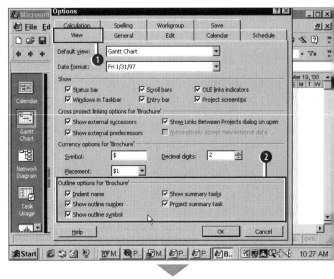

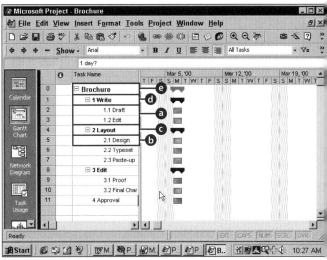

① To change outline display options, choose Tools ➪ Options and then the View tab.

② In the Outline options section, click all boxes for maximum display options.

The result:

a Indent name

b Show outline number

c Show outline symbol

d Show summary task

e Project summary task

CROSS-REFERENCE

See "Grouping Tasks" in Chapter 10 for information about grouping tasks based on codes other than WBS.

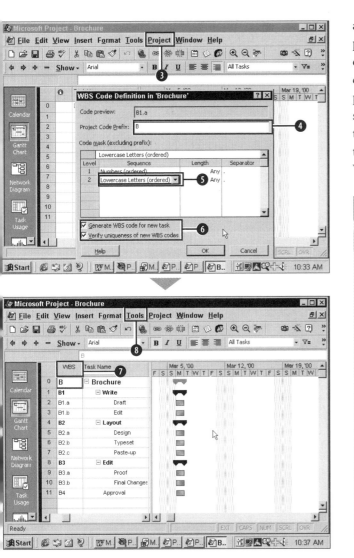

allow for renumbering of codes based on the outline placement of the tasks, maintain the uniqueness of each code, and allow you to verify the uniqueness of each code. In other words, if WBS codes represent a task's place within a WBS structure and if you change that structure, you want the WBS number associated with that task to change as well. The figures on this page and the next walk you through establishing your own unique WBS codes.

TAKE NOTE

TASK NOTES

Consider documenting important aspects of a task using the task notes field. Access task notes by clicking the Task Notes button. Typical information includes task description, estimating assumptions, task constraints, risks, performance criteria, task leader, and deliverable description.

USING THE TASK INFORMATION DIALOG BOX TO CREATE NEW TASKS

You can also create new tasks with similar names. Select four blank task name cells. Click the Task Information button to open the Multiple Task Information dialog box. Enter the common part of the four names, such as Test. After clicking OK to close the box, you can edit each task individually to add the noncommon part of the name.

---

❸ To create custom WBS codes, choose Project ➪ WBS ➪ Define Code.

❹ Enter a project code prefix if desired, such as B for the Brochure project.

❺ Choose sequence information from the drop-down list for each level.

❻ To ensure code uniqueness, click both checkboxes at the bottom of the dialog box.

▶ The resulting WBS codes are a combination of letters and numbers shown in the preceding figure.

❼ Insert a WBS column to the left of the Task Name column.

❽ Turn off outline numbers at Tools ➪ Options, and select the View tab.

FIND IT ONLINE

For an online publication for professional project management practitioners see **http://www.cpminc.org**.

Creating Milestone and Recurring Tasks

Two special types of tasks may be needed for your task list: *milestones* and *recurring* tasks. *Milestone tasks* are usually zero duration tasks that represent points in time. They serve as checkpoints for progress or signal closure of a project phase or deliverable.

Frequent milestone tasks are important because they give the team a sense of accomplishment as milestones are met. Sample milestone tasks are Design Complete, Approval Obtained, Project Complete, or Contract Signed. Include frequent milestone tasks, perhaps at least one per summary and subtask grouping, for better monitoring and control of the project.

To create a milestone task, simply create a task and enter a duration of zero. Project 2000 will automatically display a different symbol for this task. Some project managers broaden the definition of milestone tasks to include any flag or checkpoint, even if the task has a duration other than zero. Project 2000 accommodates this preference by allowing you to manually choose to make a task a milestone even if it has a duration.

To manually designate a task a milestone with a milestone symbol, choose the Advanced tab of the Task Information dialog box and check the box labeled "Mark task as milestone." The date that displays on the Gantt Chart next to the milestone symbol is the task start date.

Periodic customer meetings, quality reviews, or status meetings are good examples of *recurring tasks.* Rather than creating all the tasks yourself, let Project 2000

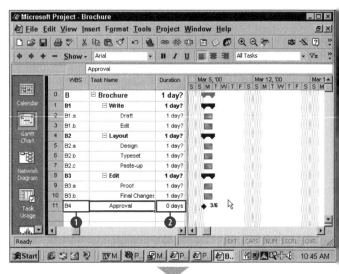

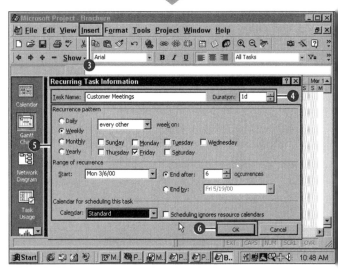

❶ Select a task to become a milestone.

❷ Enter 0 as the duration in the duration column. Note the changed task bar symbol.

❸ Click Insert ➪ Recurring Task.

❹ Complete the name and duration for the recurring event.

❺ Choose how frequently, for how long, and the scheduling calendar for these tasks.

❻ Click OK to create new tasks.

CROSS-REFERENCE

See "Estimating Duration" in Chapter 6 for information on entering zero duration milestone tasks.

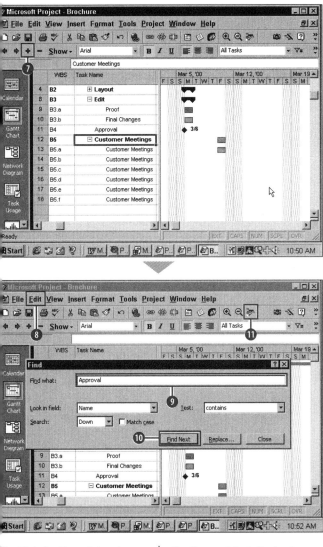

sprinkle them throughout the project at the appropriate intervals. To add recurring tasks, select a location on the task list for the group of recurring tasks to be inserted and choose Insert ➪ Recurring Task. Name the recurring task — Customer review, for example. Enter the length of the event in the Duration field. As you select an option from the *Recurrence pattern* section, the options within the box to the immediate right change to match the type of data needed. For example, you might choose Daily for every Workday; or Weekly, every week on Friday; or Monthly, the first Friday of every month. Next, either assign these events for a set period of time or select the number of occurrences. Finally, choose a calendar for scheduling these tasks. On the task list, the summary task is collapsed so you can't see the detail events until you click the Show Subtasks button.

TAKE NOTE

▶ LOCATING TASKS

To quickly locate a specific task by name, choose Edit ➪ Find and use the resulting search box to find the task. This command works in any view that contains task names in a spreadsheet format.

To easily locate a task bar on the timescale portion of a Gantt Chart without manually scrolling through time, click the Go To Selected Task button on the Standard toolbar.

⑦ Click the Show Subtasks button to view all instances of the recurring tasks.

⑧ Choose Edit ➪ Find to locate a task quickly.

⑨ Type the task name you want to find: "Approval," for example.

⑩ Click the Find Next button to locate the task.

⑪ To locate the task bar, click the Go To Selected Task button.

FIND IT ONLINE

For a tool to help you brainstorm all your project tasks visit **http://www.projectkickstart.com**.

Developing Custom WBS and Outline Codes

In previous versions of Microsoft Project, the basic structure of any project was the outline structure which includes summary tasks and subtasks. You could apply a predetermined format for WBS numbering to these tasks whose numbering also followed the outline structure.

Project 2000 offers a significant increase in the number of options available for structuring projects. The three structural options are user-defined WBS numbering based on the outline, user-defined outline codes, and user-defined grouping codes. In this chapter you'll explore both WBS and outline codes.

This page and the facing page describe the steps involved in generating WBS codes for your tasks. Using the WBS Code Definition dialog box allows you to preview the code structure as you build it. Entering a project code prefix repeats this prefix, both letters and/or numbers, for all tasks in the project.

Let's consider some basic features of using Work Breakdown Structure codes. These codes adhere to the user-defined outline structure and format as specified in the code mask (discussed next). You can renumber the WBS codes based on both the outline structure and the mask as new tasks are added or removed. In addition, you can maintain the uniqueness of any WBS number in the project.

The *code mask* is the basic structure of the WBS code. When defining a code mask, you establish the lettering or numbering sequence scheme for each indentation level of your outline. You can choose between ordered Numbers, Uppercase Letters, or Lowercase Letters, or unordered Characters.

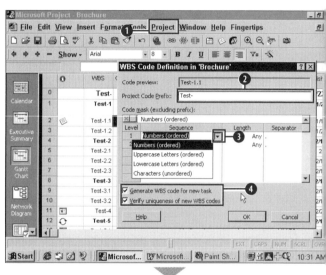

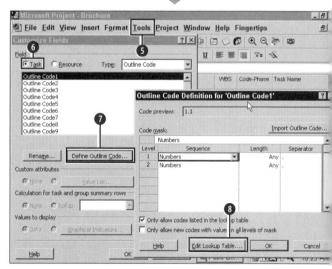

❶ For custom WBS codes, choose Project ➪ WBS ➪ Define Code.

❷ In the WBS Code Definition dialog box, enter prefix Test-.

❸ Use the drop-down arrow for Level 1 to select Numbers. Repeat for other levels.

❹ Accept Any for length; period as separator. Check these boxes to Generate WBS codes and verify uniqueness.

❺ To create custom outline codes, choose Tools ➪ Customize ➪ Fields.

❻ Click the Task radio button. Select Outline Code as the type.

❼ Click Define Outline Code and complete the code definition.

❽ Click the Edit Lookup Table button to create a list of acceptable values.

CROSS-REFERENCE

See Chapter 10 for more information about grouping codes and tasks.

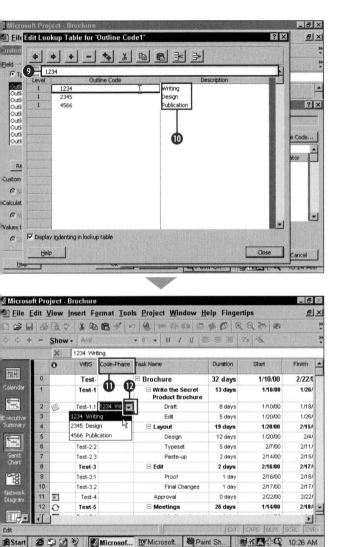

Furthermore, you define the length of each WBS section. Choosing "Any" length gives flexibility to vary with the number of tasks in the project, or you can choose a length from one to ten characters. For example, a task uses a WBS code of A1.1 if the length is Any, but uses A1.01 when the length is two characters long.

You may also decide what character separates each section of the WBS codes. Choose between a period, dash, plus sign, or slash.

You can generate the WBS codes for each task and verify their uniqueness at the same time. When you renumber tasks you can generate new codes for selected tasks or for the entire project.

TAKE NOTE

USING OUTLINE CODES

Outline codes are similar to WBS codes in function except that they are completely user-defined and are not tied to the project outline structure. Using outline codes you could, for example, create an outline hierarchy tied to company cost codes. You can then group, filter, or sort using these outline codes.

You enter outline codes manually or choose from a drop-down list. Creating a look-up table aids in guaranteeing only authorized, recognized codes are used.

You can create up to ten different outline code schemes.

9 For each task from a pick-list, type a numeric code to select. This example is for project phases.

10 Type a description for the code. Again, this example lists project phases.

11 Insert the Outline Code-1 column into the table on the Gantt Chart. The example uses Code-Phase as the title for the column.

12 Using the drop-down arrow automatically provided for the pick-list, choose the correct phase (number) for the selected task.

FIND IT ONLINE

Find international project management careers at
http://www.iscworld.com/pmpage.htm.

Personal Workbook

Q&A

1 What are two ways to open the Task Information dialog box?

_____

_____

_____

2 What is the procedure for inserting a task between two other tasks?

_____

_____

_____

3 Which dialog box is used to edit several tasks at once?

_____

_____

_____

4 What is the difference between cutting a task from the list and copying the task?

_____

_____

_____

5 What does the minus button on the Formatting toolbar do?

_____

_____

_____

6 What benefits can be gained from using custom WBS codes?

_____

_____

_____

7 What is the purpose of a milestone task?

_____

_____

_____

8 Where (on the menu) is the Recurring Task dialog box found?

_____

_____

_____

ANSWERS: PAGE 320

EXTRA PRACTICE

1 Use the Entry Bar, in-cell editing, and the Task Information dialog box to enter task names.

2 After entry, move a task down the list to a new location using the mouse.

3 Create a task outline and display outline numbers.

4 Define a recurring status meeting for every Friday for the duration of your project.

5 Copy a task and paste it three times throughout the task list.

6 Check the box to create a project-level summary task.

REAL-WORLD APPLICATIONS

✔ Your project is broken into phases so you use the outlining commands to organize the task list to match.

✔ You want to schedule a customer review each month during the project so you use the Recurring Task dialog box to define the meetings.

✔ An old project contains a number of tasks you would like to reuse so you copy and paste those tasks into your project outline.

✔ You create milestone tasks for all approvals, deliverable completions, and signoffs for the project.

Visual Quiz

Name the function of each of the buttons on the Formatting toolbar.

_____

_____

_____

_____

_____

_____

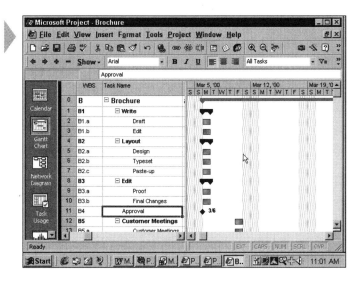

CHAPTER 6

Entering Scheduling Information

Project scheduling may be the primary reason users purchase Microsoft Project 2000. Since scheduling involves numerous calculations and iterations, it is far easier to use software for calculations than to do the manual scheduling yourself.

Many people are reluctant to schedule project work because they think it is likely to change anyway. I have actually seen project managers spend much time laying out a schedule only to throw it away a week or two later because they were attempting to plan reality rather than plan for reality. It's important, however, to keep this simple thought in mind: the point of planning a schedule is to have a roadmap or strategy to follow with enough flexibility to handle the twists and turns encountered along the way. For this reason, most project managers publish and report only on the progress of milestone deadlines and not on every task in the project. This milestone or key deliverable approach seems to give the project manager flexibility to handle everyday occurrences and adjustments between milestones.

As you schedule tasks in your project, keep in mind that you are devising a strategy for completion, and all good strategies allow for the unexpected and can be altered as needed to reach the end goals.

A number of factors affect scheduling in Project 2000. Entered information like task type, task relationships (dependencies), task calendars, constraints, and duration estimates determine the initial schedule. Optionally, you can have the schedule affected by resource availability.

Since your schedule needs adjustments prior to setting a baseline (the historical, not hysterical capture of deadlines and dates), consider working forward from the project start, then enter a deadline date, and then work backward, making necessary adjustments until you are satisfied with your strategy for completing project deliverables.

In this chapter you learn how to enter task types, enter dependencies, and assign task calendars as well as enter duration estimates. You also learn how to adjust the timescale on a graphical task chart and how to customize the Network Diagram.

Understanding the Task Type

A s your project scheduler, Project 2000 needs various pieces of scheduling information like Task type. *Task type* sets the calculation rules for Project 2000 in relation to work (amount of a resource's time such as 60 billable hours), duration, and units (a percentage of a resource's time, such as 50%). A Task type of Fixed Duration is important in the scheduling of tasks in which you establish a maximum amount of time for the resources to complete the assignment. This type is used most frequently when the project manager does not have direct control of the resource's time. Fixed Work and Fixed Units task types become important when resource availability drives the schedule. Let's look at the three choices for task type here briefly and in more detail in "Creating Filters" in Chapter 10.

The formula Project 2000 uses for calculating duration is Duration = Work/Units, in which Duration is calendar time, Work is the amount of effort or billable time the resource will work, and Units is the percentage of the assigned resource time, such as full-time (100%) or half-time (50%).

When you choose a task type, you inform Project 2000 which value to consider invariant. In other words, you tell Project 2000 which value to fix during calculations. The fixed value is the one that you type into the designated field, and Project then calculates the other two values to keep the equation valid.

If you do not intend to assign resources, the Task type entry is irrelevant. Without the introduction of resources, Project 2000 will allow direct entry of duration as if the task is Fixed Duration. However, if you intend to assign resources, the default Fixed Units is probably a good choice. As you enter units and work in a Fixed Unit task, Project recalculates duration. Conversely, as you enter units and duration, Project recalculates work.

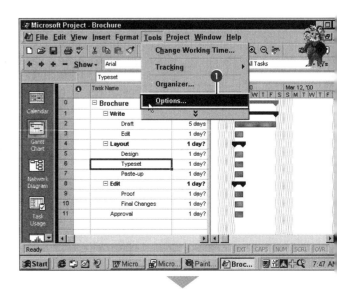

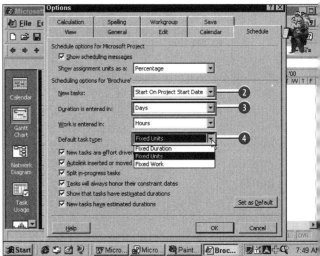

❶ To set Task type defaults, choose Tools ➪ Options, and then select the Schedule tab.

❷ Choose a default "Start On" option for new tasks.

❸ Choose a default unit for duration.

❹ Choose a default task type.

CROSS-REFERENCE

See Chapter 10, "Grouping, Filtering, and Sorting," for more on task types and resource scheduling.

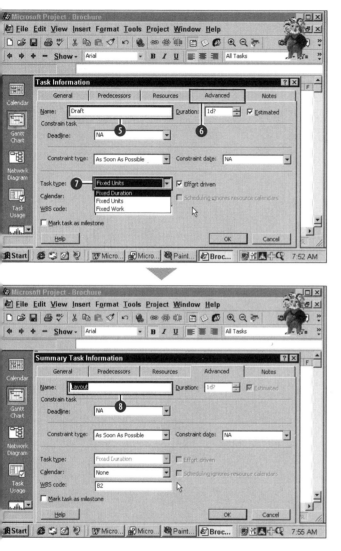

As you begin to enter task names on the initial outline, consider establishing a Task type default on the Schedule tab of the Options dialog box (Tools ⇨ Options). Later, enter a task type for a specific task using the Type column on a Gantt Chart table or select the type using the Task Information dialog box, Advanced tab. Remember, you cannot set the type for a summary task because its information is a summarization of the subtasks.

TAKE NOTE

SCHEDULING DEFAULTS

The Schedule tab of the Options dialog box (Tools ⇨ Options) contains numerous useful fields for establishing task defaults. In the project-specific schedule portion of the box, establish defaults for starting new tasks on the project start date or current date and enter a default unit for duration. Acceptable increments for duration include minutes, hours, days, weeks, and the newly added months. Use this tab to also choose a default task type.

---

⑤ To change task type for individual tasks, first select the task and click the Task Information button.

⑥ Select the Advanced tab.

⑦ Select the Task type from the list.

⑧ To better understand a task type, select a summary (roll-up) task and click the Task Information button.

▶ Notice that you cannot enter a Task type because the scheduling for a summary task is performed at the subtask level.

FIND IT ONLINE

For free Web-based project scheduling and communications systems, see **http://www.scheduleshare.com**.

Estimating Duration

An estimate is your best calculation (or guess) of what you anticipate will happen in the task. Most projects with a great number of unknowns use techniques that allow for a range of values for effort, time, and cost. Another rule of thumb is that the tighter the constraints (time, budget, resources, quality), the more accurate the estimates need to be. More accurate estimates are typically created by developing "bottom-up" calculations at each subtask level. Keep in mind that bottom-up estimates can be used as a comparison against top-down "imposed" constraints. The Gantt Chart is still merely a plan, based on your estimates of what you think is likely.

Task level estimating techniques rely on having a clear definition of the task, along with task deliverables and quality standards. It is very beneficial to also know the resources, their skill sets, and their availability when estimating task effort and duration. Below are descriptions of several common estimating techniques.

▶ *Forecasting* is similar to weather forecasting in that you look at past historical information and then compare the historical actuals to the current task, considering the variables that are different. You then forecast what is likely.

▶ *Delphi*, developed in 1948, involves asking subject matter experts to independently develop estimates and list assumptions for a given task. The premise behind this technique is that estimates, even from experts, can vary dramatically due to differences in assumptions. In this technique, as the experts clarify and agree to a standard set of assumptions, their estimates come closer and closer together.

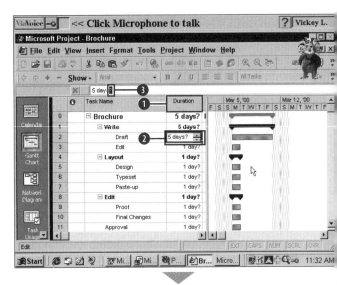

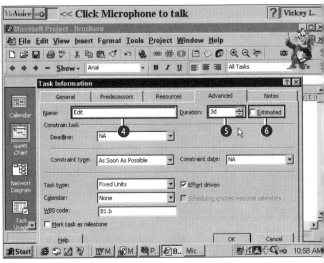

❶ Display a Duration column on the spreadsheet of a Gantt Chart or use the Entry table.

❷ Type the duration in the Duration cell or use the Entry Bar.

❸ Remove the question mark to remove the estimate designation.

❹ Alternatively, select a task and click the Task Information button.

❺ Type or select a duration from the spin control.

❻ Uncheck the box to remove the Estimated designation.

CROSS-REFERENCE

See Chapter 10 for help on applying and creating filters to display a subset of tasks.

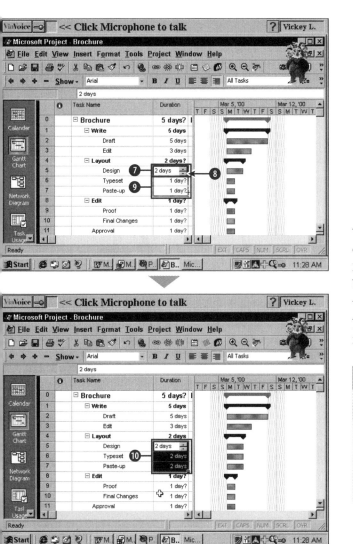

▶ *PERT analysis* looks at risk factors and their relationships to duration estimates. This technique asks for an optimistic estimate (how long will the task take if everything goes according to plan), a likely estimate (how long if the typical number of unplanned events occur), and a pessimistic estimate (how long if most everything that could go wrong does). You can use these three estimates to create three different Gantt Charts or use a weighted average to predict duration.

Project 2000 has no recommended technique for developing estimates. The software accepts whatever you enter into the duration field. A new feature in Project 2000 allows you to enter an estimated duration followed by a question mark. The question mark signifies uncertainty about the estimate. Later, using a predefined filter, you can easily locate these question-mark estimates for revision.

TAKE NOTE

▶ CALCULATING PERT ANALYSIS WEIGHTED AVERAGE

The formula for calculating the weighted average is (most optimistic) + (4) (most likely) + (most pessimistic)/ 6.

7 To populate cells (fill) with a repeated number, select the duration cell to copy.

8 Click the small square located in the bottom right of the highlighted cell.

9 Drag the square to highlight the other cells in the same column to populate.

10 Release the mouse button to populate the cells.

FIND IT ONLINE

For project estimating tips see **http://www.pmi.org/semcat/estimating.htm**.

Adjusting the Timescale

The timescale is the time grid portion of a graphical chart. On a Gantt Chart, for example, the task bars display under the timescale. Previously, you practiced using the Zoom In and Zoom Out buttons on the Standard toolbar to adjust the timescale units. In this task, you'll practice using the Timescale dialog box to make specific formatting choices.

To access the Timescale dialog box, choose Format ⇨ Timescale, or double-click anywhere in the timescale header, or right-click in the timescale header and choose Timescale from the shortcut menu.

The Timescale dialog box uses two tabs, one for working time (Timescale) and one for nonworking time. Let's review the Timescale tab first.

The Timescale tab shows four sections: a Major scale, a Minor scale, a General section, and a Preview, which allows you to see how your adjustments will look when accepted. The Timescale on a graphical chart uses a major scale (the macro time increments) and a minor scale (the micro time increments). For instance, displaying months as the major scale with weeks as the minor scale is common. As you might expect, the minor scale must be a smaller unit than the major scale.

The Major scale section allows you to choose the units for the scale, from minutes to years. Also, you can choose a label for the scale from the drop-down list that includes formats for both words, numbers, and combinations. You can also select the number of units to display per Major scale section. For example, if the Major scale is "months" and the Count is "2," then the scale displays two months per section (such as Jan–Feb, March–April). Additional formatting options include

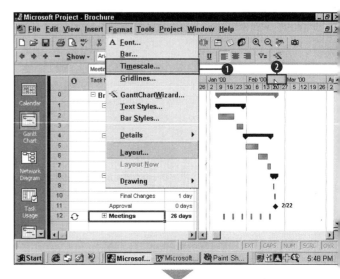

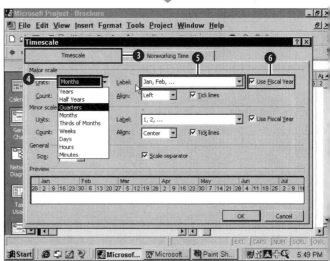

❶ To access the Timescale dialog box, choose Format ⇨ Timescale.

❷ Or, double-click anywhere in the timescale header area.

❸ Choose the Timescale tab.

❹ Choose a Unit for the Major scale.

❺ Choose a Label format.

❻ Uncheck this box to remove the fiscal year format for the timescale.

CROSS-REFERENCE

See "Formatting Bar Styles" in Chapter 12 for more information on changing the appearance of task bars.

the alignment of the scale characters and whether to display *tick lines*, those lines that separate timescale sections. A new feature with Project 2000 is the capability to display a fiscal year scale. To actually use this feature, you must also choose a fiscal year start, other than January, on the Calendar tab of Tools ⇨ Options.

The choices for the Minor scale are very similar, although there are more detailed choices for some of the selections. For example, you can choose monthly ordinal dates (Month 1, Month 2, ...) for the Major timescale and daily ordinal dates for the Minor scale (Day 1, Day 2, ...).

Use the General section to size the scale (same as using Zoom In and Zoom Out buttons) and to decide whether to use a separator line between the major and minor scale.

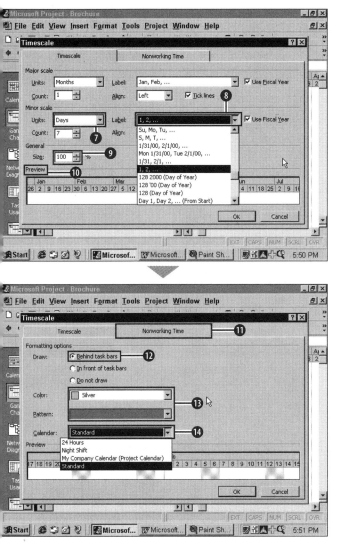

7 Choose a Minor scale unit.

8 Choose a Label for the Minor scale.

9 Choose the Size percentage.

10 Check the Preview as you adjust the timescale preferences.

11 Click the Nonworking Time tab.

12 Click a radio button for Draw options.

13 Choose a color and pattern for nonworking time display.

14 Choose a calendar for display purposes.

FIND IT ONLINE

For a free trial version of Project 2000, go to **http://www.microsoft.com/office/2000/project/trial/info.htm**.

Setting Dependency Links

After entering task names and developing estimates for each, it is now time to schedule the tasks. In its simplest form, scheduling means sequencing the tasks and calculating start and finish dates for each.

When you are sequencing tasks it's helpful to think of the flow of the deliverables through the project. For example, you must create invitations before you can send them out to guests. In this example, the predecessor task is *create invitations* and the task that is dependent on the scheduling of the predecessor is called the successor, *send invitations*.

Establishing dependency relationships allows Project 2000 to schedule your tasks and frees you from remembering all the requirements that go into developing a schedule such as task calendars, predecessors, successors, and constraints. By setting relationships, when the timing of one task changes, it affects its successor tasks, which affects its successor tasks, and so on throughout the project.

Four dependency types are available in Project 2000: Finish-to-Start, Start-to-Start, Finish-to-Finish, and Start-to-Finish. They describe whether the start or finish of the predecessor drives the scheduling of the start or finish of the successor. For example, in a Finish-to-Start link, the finish of the predecessor task determines the scheduling of the start of the successor task.

To make your task relationships more realistic, use *lead* and *lags* where necessary. For example, two tasks may be linked together with a Start-to-Start dependency, but you want the start of the successor task to lag behind the start of the predecessor task by one week. In terms Project 2000 understands, you describe this link as "Start-to-Start plus one-week lag." You can also

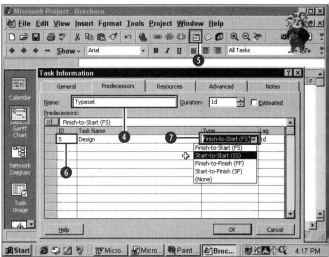

① To set Finish-to-Start dependencies, first highlight the predecessor task, and then highlight the successor task.

② Choose Edit ➪ Link Tasks.

③ Or, click the Link Tasks button.

④ To set a dependency using the Task Information dialog box, select a successor task.

⑤ Click Task Information on the Standard toolbar.

⑥ On Predecessor tab, enter the ID (row) number of the predecessor task or select the task name from the list.

⑦ Select the type of dependency and enter a lag if desired.

CROSS-REFERENCE

See "Formatting the Network Diagram" in this chapter for displaying dependency links graphically.

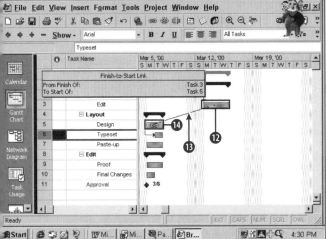

require the start of the successor task to lead the completion of the predecessor task by two weeks. This link shows as "Finish-to-Start minus two weeks lag." In Project 2000, *negative lag* is the same as *lead time*. In addition, you can enter lag time as a percentage of the predecessor's duration: for example, the successor starts when 50 percent of the predecessor's duration has elapsed.

Finish-to-Start links can be set using the menu, the Link Tasks button, or the mouse. Additional techniques include using the Task Information dialog box, the Task Form, or the Entry Table.

TAKE NOTE

▶ **USING THE AUTOLINK FEATURE**

Use caution if accepting the default selection (Tools ⇨ Options and selecting the Schedule tab) for Autolink inserted or moved tasks. The purpose of the feature is to save time by automatically breaking and re-establishing links when you insert a task into an existing chain of tasks or if you move tasks. However, my experience shows that most users forget about this feature, and meanwhile Project 2000 is setting links that may alter the schedule. Unless you are absolutely certain that you want Project 2000 to second-guess your intentions about linking tasks, uncheck the box and reestablish links manually.

---

⑧ To use the Task Form, choose Window ⇨ Split.

⑨ Enter information in Predecessor Name field.

⑩ To use the Entry table, activate the top pane and choose View ⇨ Table and select Entry.

⑪ Type the predecessor task ID number and the relationship type for all types and a lag if desired.

⑫ To use the mouse to set a dependency, click the task bar of the predecessor task.

⑬ Click and drag down until the link tool shows.

⑭ Drag to the successor task bar and release to set a Finish-to-Start link.

FIND IT ONLINE

For estimating models, visit **http://www.angelgroup.com/svc-estm.htm**.

Reviewing and Modifying Dependency Links

Probably the most popular way to view dependency links for the project is to view a Network Diagram. Network Diagrams are commonly known as logic diagrams, precedence diagrams, flowcharts, and PERT charts. The Network Diagram graphically shows the logical sequencing of all tasks in the project using the descriptions of the dependency relationships. The diagram is made up of task nodes, which represent tasks, and arrows, which represent the relationships between tasks.

The Network Diagram in Project 2000, formerly known as a PERT Chart, is completely new. Using its features, you are now able to apply filters in this view to focus on dependency relationships of one WBS family or one phase at a time. You may now use outlining symbols to hide or display subtasks of summary tasks in a network diagram. Additionally, you now have multiple options available to format task nodes (task boxes) for better control over the look of the Network Diagram. You'll try these options in the next task of this chapter.

Consider using the Network Diagram in a split window to not only see the timing of tasks but the logic behind the timing. This information becomes increasingly important if you need to reduce the overall duration of the project. A typical split window might display a Gantt Chart in the top pane and a Network Diagram in the bottom pane. Another useful combination is to display a Gantt Chart in the top pane and a Relationship Diagram view in the bottom pane. Using this combination, as you select a task in the upper pane, the bottom pane displays that task with its links in a Network Diagram-like display.

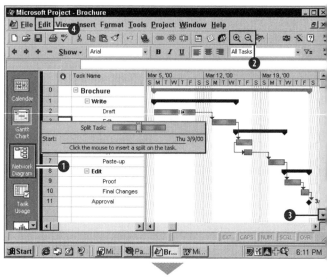

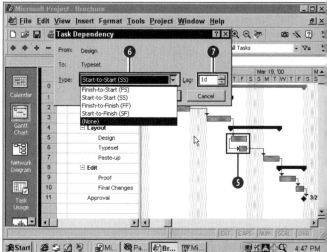

❶ To view the Network Diagram, click Network Diagram on the View Bar or choose View ➪ More Views ➪ Network Diagram.

❷ Click Zoom In and Zoom Out to change the scale.

❸ Scroll to view different tasks.

❹ Choose Edit ➪ Go To to locate a task by ID number.

❺ To modify a link using the Task Dependency box, double-click a dependency line.

❻ In the Type drop-down list, choose a different relationship or choose (None) to remove the link.

❼ Enter lead (–) or lag (+) time if desired. The default is no overlap or lag in the dependency timing relationship.

CROSS-REFERENCE

See "Exploring Formatting Options" in Chapter 12 for information on formatting network diagram nodes.

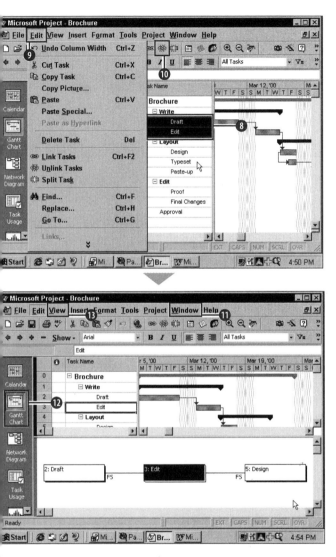

To modify established dependency links, use the Task Information dialog box. Use the Task Form to delete relationship information by deleting the ID number of the predecessor task; to create a different relationship, change the ID number of the Predecessor or successor task. You can also delete the contents of a cell in the Predecessor column on the Entry table to delete a dependency or modify the contents of the cell. Likewise, to delete an unwanted link, first select the linked tasks and then choose Edit ⇨ Unlink Tasks.

TAKE NOTE

▶ TIPS FOR REMOVING DEPENDENCY LINKS

Keep these suggestions in mind when removing dependency links:

▶ Clicking the Unlink Task button or choosing Edit ⇨ Unlink Tasks while a single task is selected removes all dependency links for that task.

▶ Likewise, selecting multiple tasks and selecting Edit ⇨ Unlink Tasks or clicking the Unlink Tasks button removes all dependencies for all selected tasks.

▶ To delete all dependency links, select all tasks by clicking the Task Name column header or clicking the Select All button at the upper left-hand corner of the Gantt Chart window, and choose Edit ⇨ Unlink Tasks or click the Unlink Tasks button.

⑧ To unlink tasks, select the tasks to be unlinked.

⑨ Choose Edit ⇨ Unlink Tasks.

⑩ Or, click the Unlink Tasks button.

⑪ To utilize a Relationship Diagram in a split window choose Window ⇨ Split.

⑫ Activate the top pane. Click Gantt Chart on the View Bar.

⑬ Activate the bottom pane and choose View ⇨ More Views ⇨ Relationship Diagram.

⑭ In the More Views dialog box, click Apply and you will see the combination view.

FIND IT ONLINE

For tips on estimating project time, see **http://www. social.chass.ncsu.edu/~covington/timerequ.htm**.

Formatting the Network Diagram

As mentioned in the previous task, the look and functionality of the Network Diagram is much changed in Project 2000. In this task, you'll explore the many new formatting options.

As in other task views, you can now expand and collapse summary tasks to hide or show the subtasks. Clicking the outline symbol next to each task node alternately changes the summary task from expand to collapse.

Formatting of Network Diagram nodes is achieved in layers, starting from general formatting down to formatting of cells within the task nodes. Format individual nodes by choosing Format ➪ Box, or format all task categories by choosing Format ➪ Box Styles.

Using the Box Styles dialog box, you select the task categories for formatting options. Examples of task categories include Milestones, Critical Tasks, and Noncritical Tasks. As you choose various options, check the node Preview before accepting the choices. Also in the Box Styles dialog box, you choose node border shape, color, and pattern. General formatting extends to gridlines and background color and patterns. The second layer of formatting uses data templates. Data templates offer general formatting selections for the contents of the nodes. In the Box Styles dialog box is a drop-down list to choose a Data Template and two templates show as defaults: Standard and Summary Task Data.

Clicking the More Templates button in the Box Styles dialog box takes you deeper into formatting using the Data Templates dialog box. This box lists all templates available in this project. An Import button allows you to add box templates from other currently open projects by using a convenient dialog box to name the source project, the view containing the template (Network Diagram),

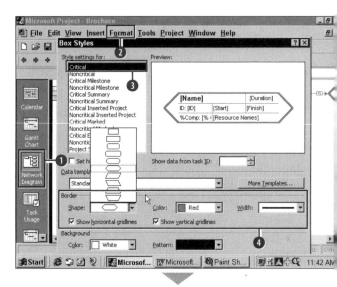

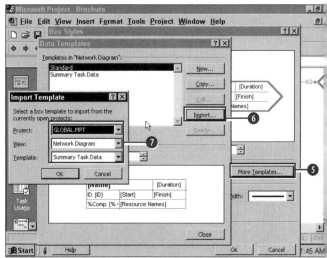

1. To format the Network Diagram, click the Network Diagram button or choose View ➪ Network Diagram.

2. Select Format ➪ Box Styles or right-click a blank area of the diagram; choose Box Styles from the shortcut menu.

3. Choose a category to format in the "Style settings for" list.

4. Choose Border properties.

5. Click the More Templates button in the Box Styles dialog box to open the Data Templates dialog box.

6. Click Import to import a box template.

7. Using the Import Template dialog box, select the source project, view, and template.

CROSS-REFERENCE

See "Using Standard Filters" in Chapter 10 for applying filters to the Network Diagram.

and the name of the template to add. Clicking the Edit button allows you to edit the selected data definition, while clicking the Copy or New buttons generates another formatting layer.

Clicking either the Copy or New buttons opens the Data Template Definition dialog box. Use this box to format the cells within the nodes. You may select the content (fields) and content alignment of the cells as well as make font selections. Clicking the Cell Layout button here takes you to the most detailed level of formatting.

The Cell Layout dialog box establishes the number of rows and columns within a node, the cell width, and the rules governing blank cells.

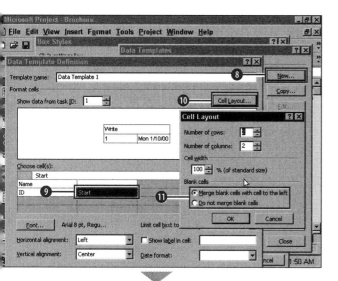

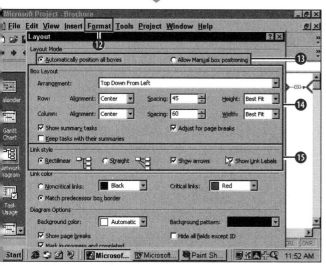

TAKE NOTE

FORMATTING USING THE LAYOUT DIALOG BOX

Options that affect the high-level formatting of the Network Diagram view itself are found in the Layout dialog box. Use the Layout dialog box to choose manual or automatic positioning of nodes as well as select a formatting style for the link lines. This dialog box also shows selections for the arrangement of information within each node, link colors, and page breaks.

- Click the New button in the Data Template dialog box to open the Data Template Definition dialog box.
- Choose fields to show in the nodes using the drop-down lists.
- Click the Cell Layout button for other formatting options.
- Click either radio button for rules on handling blank cells.

- ⑫ For other formatting options, choose Format ➪ Layout.
- ⑬ Select a Layout Mode.
- ⑭ Select Box Layout options.
- ⑮ Select a Link style.

FIND IT ONLINE

For a companion product to develop PERT Charts, see
http://www.criticaltools.com/PERTMAIN.htm.

Scheduling Potpourri

Additional scheduling options available to you include task splitting, using task calendars, setting links in an outlined task list, and formatting the dependency links shown on a Gantt Chart.

Task Splitting

If you look at the task bars showing so far, they are continuous bars representing total duration estimates for the tasks. However, not all task work is done continuously in a project. Some tasks have planned interruptions that you will want to put in the project plan, and some tasks are interrupted after starting, which you can account for during tracking of progress. Placing interruptions in a task is called *task splitting* in Project 2000, and there is no preset limit to the number of splits a task can have. See this page and the opposite page for step-by-step instructions for splitting a task. You might use task splitting if a resource will be unavailable for a period of time during a task for vacation or to attend a conference, or if a scope change causes an interruption of all in-progress tasks. For linking purposes, remember that when you link to a split task you are linking to the entire task, not to a particular split portion.

Using Task Calendars

Chapter 3 covered how to create calendars so, in this task, I'll limit the discussion to applying calendars to specific tasks. Sometimes, not all tasks fit into the scheduling of the master project calendar. Sometimes tasks have specific scheduling needs and for these tasks, you can create a calendar specifically for them and apply the calendar to the task. For example, suppose you are planning an office move in which most of the tasks occur during the project calendar but the actual move tasks

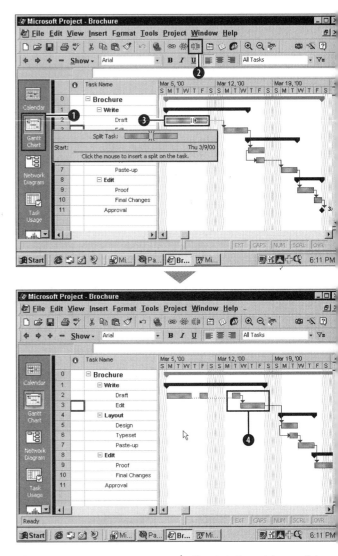

① To split a task, display a Gantt Chart.

② Click the Split Task button, right-click the task bar, and choose Split Task from the shortcut menu or choose Edit ⇨ Split Task.

③ Position the mouse pointer over the task bar to split.

④ Click the task bar and the split occurs. Repeat as needed.

CROSS-REFERENCE

See "Viewing, Printing, and Modifying Standard Reports" in Chapter 12 for more display options.

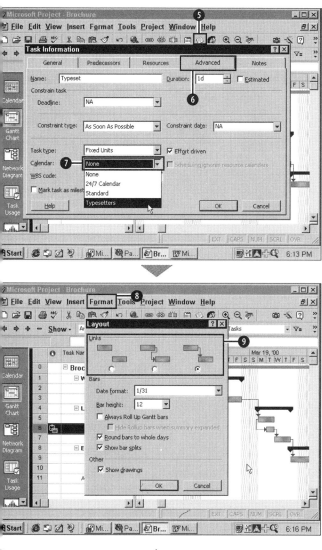

place on a weekend. Create a calendar for the "Move" task that shows the weekend dates and hours scheduled for work, and apply this calendar to the Move task.

Setting Links in an Outlined Task

Decisions around linking tasks become more complex with an outlined task list as you choose whether to link at the summary or subtask level. The following partial task is an example:

Write
    Draft
    Edit
Layout
    Design
    Typeset

The predecessor task for Design could be Edit, the last subtask, or Write, a summary task. In this case the advantage for setting a link at the summary level is that if you add tasks after Edit, you do not need to change the dependency link. However, if you set the dependency at the subtask level (Edit) simply because it is the last task in the family, you would now need to modify the links.

TAKE NOTE

▶ **FORMATTING DEPENDENCY LINKS**

For the dependency links shown on a timescale portion of a Gantt Chart you have two choices for the types of lines to be drawn: straight or 90-degree angle (or display no lines at all). This and the facing page describe the steps.

---

⑤ To apply a task calendar, select the task and click the Task Information button.

⑥ Select the Advanced tab.

⑦ In the Calendar drop-down list, select the desired calendar from the list.

⑧ To format dependency link lines, choose Format ➪ Layout.

⑨ Choose a Links format type.

FIND IT ONLINE

For tools to capture enterprise project schedules see
http://www.projectoffice.com.

Personal Workbook

Q&A

1 What three task types are available in Project 2000?

_____

_____

_____

2 What is the formula that Project 2000 uses to calculate duration?

_____

_____

_____

3 What are acceptable increments for duration estimates?

_____

_____

_____

4 What is the definition of an *estimate*?

_____

_____

_____

5 Which estimating technique mentioned utilizes subject matter experts who independently estimate durations and record their assumptions?

_____

_____

_____

6 What is a *predecessor task*?

_____

_____

_____

7 What is the difference between *lead* and *lag*?

_____

_____

_____

8 When would you use a Network Diagram?

_____

_____

_____

ANSWERS: PAGE 320

① Try using the Delphi technique to estimate task duration.

② Set a Start-to-Start link with lag time.

③ Choose to display no link lines on a Gantt Chart and display rectilinear link lines on a Network Diagram.

④ Remove a link between two tasks.

⑤ Split a task.

⑥ Display a Network Diagram in the top pane and a Gantt Chart in the bottom pane of a split window.

✔ To have Project 2000 calculate the duration of your project you set dependency links for all tasks.

✔ To schedule the overlapping nature of some task relationships, you use Start-to-Start links with lag time.

✔ You print a Network Diagram for your project "War Room" so team members can see the logic flow of work.

✔ You leave your duration entries as estimated until the team leads can defend their estimates.

Visual Quiz

How do you display this dialog box? Which selection places a "?" after an estimated duration? Which selection sets a default duration unit for new tasks?

_____

_____

_____

_____

_____

CHAPTER 7

MASTER
THESE
SKILLS

▶ **Scheduling with Constraints**
▶ **Understanding the Critical Path**
▶ **Optimizing the Schedule**
▶ **Using Rollup Tasks**

Analyzing the Schedule

A long with quality and cost, a project schedule lies at the core of most project plans. Microsoft Project 2000 rolls together the project calendar information, information about whether you are scheduling from the project start or finish date, task duration estimates, task calendars, task link information, and constraints to calculate a project schedule. Project 2000 can even add resource availability and resource calendar information to the mix for added impact to the schedule.

One of the primary benefits of using scheduling software such as Project 2000 is its ability to perform many calculations quickly. Years ago, before scheduling software was available, schedulers made all calculations manually — even for projects with hundreds of tasks. Today, at your fingertips is more computing power than many aerospace schedulers saw in their entire careers!

Even if your project appears rather simple or only contains a few tasks, apply the appropriate techniques so that the resulting schedule is meaningful. Temptation tells you to just grab task bars and manually drag them into a position that pleases your customer or boss, but you're cautioned against such a technique. The resulting

Gantt chart isn't really a schedule; it is merely a graphic chart. With this "picture" Gantt you probably won't be able to see potential problems early enough to do anything about them and you may unknowingly base decisions on inaccurate corresponding dates. You also won't be able to see where the flexibility lies in your schedule.

Experienced project managers manage the schedule by monitoring tasks on the critical path as well as being aware of the flexibility that some tasks have in scheduling. In project management terms, the *critical path* is the longest sequence of tasks in the project. In other words, the length of the critical path is the same as the project duration. The critical path shows us the shortest amount of time scheduled to complete all tasks. Critical tasks make up the critical path chain. Noncritical tasks, those that are not part of the critical path chain, have some flexibility in the way they are scheduled.

In this chapter you'll continue working on the schedule by entering task constraints and deadline dates, by viewing critical path data, and by compressing the critical path to fit a predetermined deadline date.

Scheduling with Constraints

The schedule takes shape as you enter tasks, duration estimates and task linking relationships. Refining the schedule further sometimes requires constraining tasks to dates that differ from the date calculated by merely establishing task relationships. For example, suppose that after setting task links, the start date for the task Design House is May 1. However, the architect for the job is not available until May 10. You apply a Start No Earlier Than date of May 10 for the Design House task to account for this specific date constraint. Or, for another example, you plan a family reunion with a Must Start On constraint of October 12.

The Start No Earlier Than constraint is only one of the numerous constraint types available in Project 2000. The Advanced tab of the Task Information dialog box displays a Constrain task section. (Double-clicking the task name displays the Task Information dialog box as does clicking the Task Information button on the Standard toolbar.)

The Constrain task drop-down list shows eight constraint types. Use these judiciously as you place the finishing touches of realism to your schedule.

The As Soon As Possible choice is the default. This constraint allows tasks to start as soon as the task link relationship requirements with predecessor tasks are satisfied. For example, the task Test Program can start as soon as possible after the task Code Program is finished. Because this type, as well as the As Late As Possible constraint, still allows Project 2000 to calculate dates without regard to a specific date, no date entry is required.

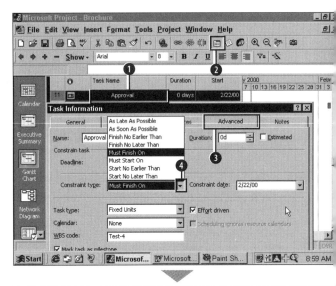

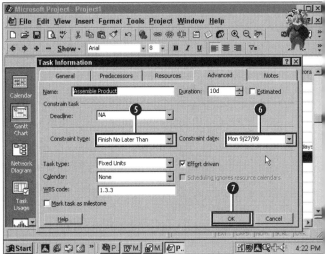

① Select the task to be constrained.

② Click the Task Information button to display the Task Information dialog box.

③ Click the Advanced tab.

④ Click the drop-down arrow for a list of constraint types.

⑤ Choose Finish No Later Than as the constraint type.

⑥ Type in the constraint date or choose a date from the drop down calendar.

⑦ Click OK.

▶ On scheduling messages that might appear, instruct Planning Wizard to Continue and set a Finish No Later Than constraint. Also, allow the scheduling conflict.

CROSS-REFERENCE

See "Exploring Formatting Options" in Chapter 12 for information about displaying slack lines.

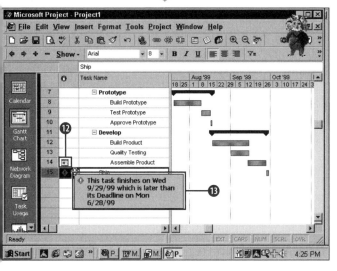

As Late As Possible, on the other hand, instructs Project 2000 to schedule the task so that it finishes just in time for the successor task(s) to start. For example, if you owe money to the government at tax time, you probably pay the bill as late as possible before the due date. Documentation, training, and equipment rental often fall into this category of constraint as well.

The four choices — Finish No Earlier Than, Finish No Later Than, Start No Earlier Than, and Start No Later Than — require date entries but serve as constraint boundaries for positioning of the tasks in the schedule rather than tying the task to a specific date.

The remaining constraint types, Must Finish On and Must Start On, also require date entries and restrict tasks to a specific date.

⑧ To use the deadline date instead of the constraint date, select another task.

⑨ Click the Task Information button and select the Advanced tab.

⑩ Enter a deadline date that is several days earlier than the currently scheduled finish date of the project.

⑪ Click OK.

⑫ Notice the different symbols for constraint and deadline shown in the Indicators column.

⑬ Moving your pointer over the icon will display a pop-up description box.

Understanding the Critical Path

Monitoring the critical path of your project provides valuable information for schedule management. Critical path analysis shows you not only the duration of the project and task start and finish dates but also the latest dates tasks can finish without delaying the project end and the amount of flexibility you have in scheduling a particular task. As you change scheduling input data, Project 2000 recalculates the critical path.

To effectively manage the entire project schedule, you must watch the critical as well as the noncritical tasks with an understanding of how a change in one task affects the others. Critical path analysis helps you gain that understanding.

The start and finish dates show the earliest date the task is scheduled to start and the earliest date the task is scheduled to finish. These are sometimes called Early Start and Early Finish.

At the opposite end of the scheduling spectrum, Late Start indicates the latest date you can start the task without delaying the project end date. Likewise, Late Finish shows the latest date you can complete the task without delaying the project end date.

The difference between when you can finish (Finish date) and when you must finish (Late Finish) is the amount of flexibility available in executing that task. This amount of flexibility is called *slack*. For example, a task finish date is February 22 and the late finish is February 27. The amount of slack time is five days (assuming all days between the 22nd and 27th are work days).

❶ To apply the Schedule table for critical path analysis, choose View ➪ Table: Schedule.

❷ Notice the columns for critical path information: Start, Finish, Late Start, and Late Finish.

❸ Notice that in the example, the Finish of Task 2 is 1/19/00 but the Late Finish is 1/28/00

▶ The difference between the dates is the amount of total slack time in the schedule.

CROSS-REFERENCE

See "Using the GanttChartWizard" in Chapter 12 for more on using the Wizard to format critical path tasks.

If there is no difference between the task finish date and the task late finish date, the slack is zero. Zero slack defines a critical task. Hence all tasks that make up the critical path show zero slack. Slack time is not "extra" time in the schedule. Nor is it padding. Slack time is calculated merely because that particular part of the project chain of events is not part of the critical path.

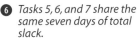

TAKE NOTE

▶ REMOVING CONSTRAINTS

Instead of removing a constraint once set, simply change the constraint type back to the default: As Soon As Possible.

▶ TOO MANY CONSTRAINTS

Use caution when entering schedule constraints because they apply specific limits to the way in which a task can be scheduled. For example, if you calculate every start and finish date and enter those as constraints, you are not benefiting from the scheduling capabilities of Project 2000.

▶ DIFFERENT TYPES OF SLACK

Free slack amounts indicate the amount of time a task can slip without affecting its next successor task. *Total slack,* probably the more useful of the two calculations, shows the amount of time a task can slip without affecting the project end date.

④ *Locate the amounts in the Free Slack column. This is the amount of time each task can slip without delaying its next successor task.*

⑤ *Notice the amounts in the Total Slack column.*

⑥ *Tasks 5, 6, and 7 share the same seven days of total slack.*

FIND IT ONLINE

For a list of project management books, including books on critical path analysis, see **www.pmibooks.org**.

Optimizing the Schedule

Optimizing the schedule includes viewing and analyzing the critical path, troubleshooting constraints, and compressing the critical path if necessary.

The Schedule table supplies critical path data in columns for convenient analysis. It is also helpful to display critical tasks in red so that they "jump off the page" to catch your notice.

The GanttChartWizard is an easy way to change the display options for critical tasks. You can, of course, manually change the formatting for critical tasks.

Many novice Project 2000 users apply constraints inadvertently. For example, if you are "playing" by dragging a task bar across the screen, a constraint is set as you release the mouse! It can be frustrating to have a less than optimum schedule simply because of misplaced constraints. Fortunately, an easy method exists to check for intended versus accidental constraints. The Indicators column (available by default on the Entry table), appearing to the left of the Task Name column, displays a constraint icon for each task with a constraint other than As Soon As Possible or As Late As Possible. By moving your pointer over the icon, a pop-up tip displays showing the type of constraint as well as the constraint date.

Many options exist for compressing the critical path. Situations for which the critical path indicates a twenty-week project and the customer wants it in fifteen require that you compress the critical path. Keep in mind that entering a project deadline and asking Project 2000 to calculate from the project finish can result in negative slack. *Negative slack* indicates the amount of compression required to meet the deadline date.

Let's review some common defendable techniques to compress the critical path, sometimes called "schedule

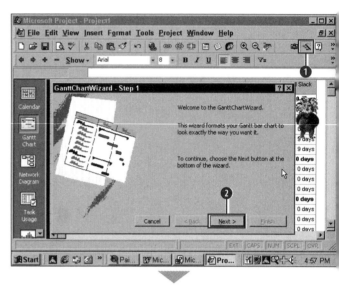

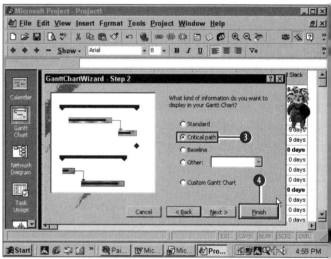

❶ To use the GanttChart Wizard to highlight critical path tasks, click the GanttChart Wizard button on the Standard toolbar.

❷ Click Next after reading Step 1 in the Wizard.

❸ Choose to display Critical path information by clicking the radio button in Step 2.

❹ Skip the remainder of the customization options by clicking the Finish button.

CROSS-REFERENCE

See "Reviewing the Schedule" in Chapter 11 for more suggested ways of reviewing the project plan.

crashing." To compress the time, consider reducing the project scope, completing just the required deliverables now and creating a follow-on project for the remainder, or reducing project quality. Options like adding resources, adding more highly skilled resources, assigning overtime, and buying technology instead of developing it in-house can also reduce the project duration. Reducing the percentage of time allocated to noncritical tasks (it might be acceptable for them to take a little longer) so you can switch the resources to critical tasks is another technique for compressing the schedule.

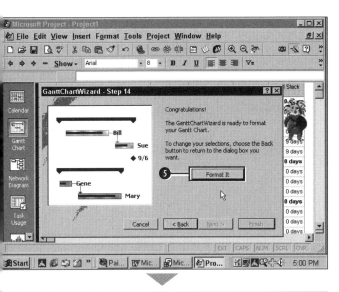

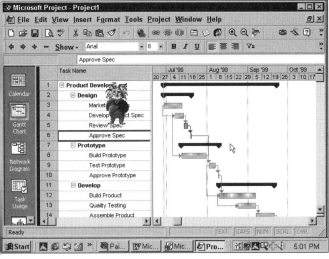

⑤ Click the Format It button to instruct the Wizard to develop the Gantt Chart.

⑥ Locate, on your screen, the critical path tasks shown with red task bars.

TAKE NOTE

▶ **CRITICAL PATH CALCULATION OPTIONS**

The standard definition of a critical task is slack of zero or less, but the Calculation tab of the Options dialog box offers alternatives. On this form you set the definition of critical task to catch the tasks that calculate as "almost critical."

▶ **MULTIPLE CRITICAL PATHS**

Another checkbox on the Calculation tab sets Project 2000 to calculate multiple critical paths in projects that contain independent sections or components.

FIND IT ONLINE

For Microsoft Project 2000 survival tips see **http:// www.alumni.caltech.edu/~dank/project.html**.

Using Rollup Tasks

If you use outlining as your task structure, the details of the subtasks automatically roll up to their summary tasks. To clarify, summary task information is merely the sum of data entered for individual subtasks. For example, summary tasks sum the duration estimates, work, and costs for the subtasks.

In this task, however, you'll look at rolling up task bar or milestone symbols on the chart side of the Gantt Chart. This type of formatting is very useful when printing summary-level reports if you don't wish to display all the subtasks but need more information than a solid summary bar shows. Using rollup formatting techniques, you can display subtask bars or milestone symbols on the summary bar itself, even when the summary is collapsed (subtasks are hidden). In this way, you can show the start and finish dates for the subtasks all on one line.

There are three steps to rolling up task bars. First, select a view that is already formatted for displaying rollup bars. The three default views to choose from include the Bar Rollup view, the Milestone Date Rollup view, and the Milestone Rollup view. In the Bar Rollup view, rollup task bars are shown below or slightly overlapping the summary bar. Use the Milestone Date Rollup view to display milestone symbols as well as their dates on the summary bar. The Milestone Rollup view is similar to the Milestone Date Rollup except that it rolls up only the symbols without the milestone dates.

The second step in using rollup bars is to open the Layout dialog box and check the box to "Always roll up Gantt bars." Checking this box rolls up bars for the entire project. A companion checkbox in the same dialog box enables you to hide the rollup bars on the summary task when the summary task is expanded.

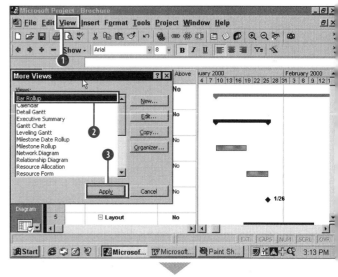

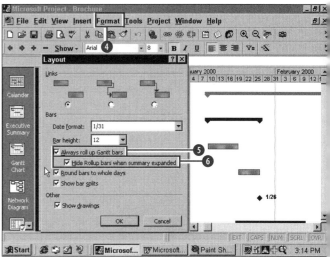

① To display rollup bars and milestones, choose Views ⇨ More Views.

② In the More Views dialog box, select the Bar Rollup view.

③ Click the Apply button to display the view.

④ To allow Gantt bars to roll up from a project level, choose Format ⇨ Layout.

⑤ In the Layout dialog box, check the box to "Always roll up Gantt bars."

⑥ Also, check the box to "Hide Rollup bars when summary expanded" to avoid the duplication of bars.

CROSS-REFERENCE

See "Adjusting the Timescale" in Chapter 6 for more information about using Zoom In and Zoom Out.

The third step is to select and mark the tasks that display as rollups. You can select both task bars and milestone symbols, although it is more common to only use milestone symbols. On the General tab of the Task Information dialog box is a checkbox to "Roll up Gantt bar to summary." This box must be checked for the rollup display to take effect. However, remember that you can select multiple tasks and then activate the Multiple Task Information dialog box, or filter for milestones first and then use the Multiple Task Information dialog box.

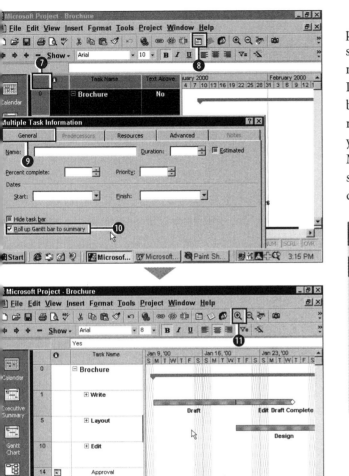

⑦ To roll up all individual tasks when the summary is collapsed, click the Select All button.

⑧ Click the Task Information button.

⑨ In the Multiple Task Information dialog box that opens, select the General tab.

⑩ Check the box to "Roll up Gantt bar to summary."

▶ Notice the multiple task names appearing on one rollup line.

⑪ If task names overlap, click the Zoom In button.

Personal Workbook

Q&A

1 What information does Project 2000 use to calculate a schedule?

_____

_____

_____

2 When would you apply the Must Start On constraint type?

_____

_____

_____

3 What are the two constraint types that don't require a corresponding date entry?

_____

_____

_____

4 What is the definition of *critical path*?

_____

_____

_____

5 How is total slack calculated?

_____

_____

_____

6 What are four ways to compress the critical path?

_____

_____

_____

7 What is the difference between setting a deadline date and establishing a constraint?

_____

_____

_____

8 When would you roll up task bars?

_____

_____

_____

ANSWERS: PAGE 321

EXTRA PRACTICE

① Apply several different constraints to a task and check for schedule changes.

② Use the GanttChartWizard to display critical tasks in red.

③ Locate the constraint icon in the Indicators column.

④ Use one of the techniques mentioned in this chapter to compress a practice schedule by twenty-five percent.

⑤ Remove a schedule constraint (change the type back to As Soon As Possible).

⑥ Roll up milestone tasks and dates to the summary level.

REAL-WORLD APPLICATIONS

✔ You create a file containing three current projects to view common resource commitments. You check the "Calculate multiple critical paths" box to calculate the critical paths of the three projects as if they are contained in three independent files.

✔ Your project has a specific deadline and you use critical path compression techniques to adjust the schedule to match.

✔ As an event planner, you use the Must Start On constraint to assign a specific date to the event task.

✔ You use the GanttChartWizard to display the critical tasks in red prior to an optimization discussion with your planning team.

Visual Quiz

How do you display the two icons in the Indicators column?

_____

_____

_____

_____

_____

_____

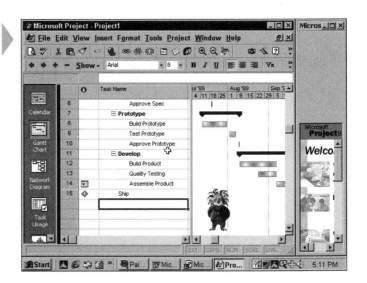

CHAPTER 8

Defining Resources and Costs

You may recall that you do not have to assign resources to tasks in Project 2000. Without resources, Project 2000 schedules tasks according to the scheduling information, as discussed in Chapter 7. However, if you don't assign resources you run the risk of scheduling a task when the resource is unavailable to work on it or the resource is already overallocated on other task assignments. If you do assign resources, Project considers resource availability and resource calendars in addition to task information before scheduling the task.

Features now available in Project 2000 allow for precise definition and allocation of resources. These features allow for more realistic planning and tracking of resources than in previous versions of Microsoft Project. Since defining resources using most of the definition features in this section takes time, make sure you need a high level of precision before creating elaborate resource definitions.

For example, suppose you are a project manager with ten team members who report directly to you on this project. You will probably define the resources quite precisely, using customized calendars and availability changes over time. If your project is of rather long duration, you may need to use cost rate tables to define the rate of pay

changes after performance reviews of your team. If, on the other hand, you "borrow" resources to work on your project from functional managers and you do not have direct control over their work, you probably only need to use basic resource definitions. Basic definitions include fields like Name, Type, Standard Rate, Overtime Rate, and Base Calendar. Some projects only assign a resource name to a task to show responsibility, not work assignments. In these projects, the only definition field needed is the Resource Name field.

As you teach yourself to use Project 2000, explore the different definitions discussed in this chapter. In this way, you will be better prepared to pick and choose the appropriate definitions for your project.

This chapter focuses on defining resources as needed for your project. In Chapter 17, you will learn how to share this list of resources with other projects (see "Creating and Using a Resource Pool" and "Viewing Shared Resources Across Projects"). Topics to look forward to include contouring resource availability, establishing cost rate tables, defining both people and consumable resources, using task notes, customizing resource calendars, entering e-mail and workgroup communication information, and creating standard and overtime pay rates.

Defining Resources

The easiest (and safest) place to define resources is on the Resource Sheet, available on the View Bar. However, you can assign resources to tasks without defining them first, and allow Project 2000 to add the resource name to the Resource Sheet for you and complete the definition at a later time. You can select this option by going to Tools ⇨ Options, choosing the General tab, and placing a checkmark by "Automatically add new resources." Be cautious when using the automatic add feature. For example, if you assign Bob as a resource to Task 1 and assign Robert, the same resource, to Task 2, Project 2000 will add two resource names. For this reason, I recommend defining the resources first and then assigning them to tasks.

Let's review some of the definition fields found on the Resource Sheet. The Resource Name field can include the names of individuals such as Vickey, or a job category like engineers, typesetters, or carpenters. Resource groups like engineers or carpenters will be scheduled according to one resource calendar but you can plan for different numbers of resources in the group by using an *availability table*. New to Project 2000 is the ability to define a material resource. A *material* resource is a consumable resource like gasoline, lumber, paper, silk, or irrigation line.

The Type field contains designations for Work or Material. Use Work for resources that count their project contribution in work like 200 billable hours or 40 hours of machine production time. The other choice, Material, is the designation for the consumable resources.

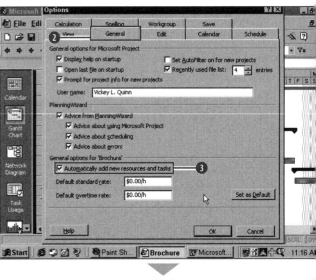

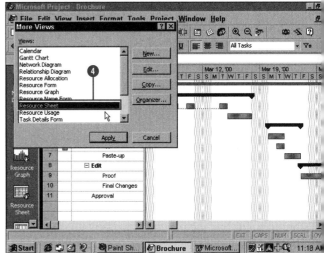

❶ To assign resources first and have Project 2000 automatically add them to the list of resources, click Tools ⇨ Options.

❷ Select the General tab.

❸ Check the box for "Automatically add new resources and tasks."

❹ To use the Resource Sheet t‹ define resources, click the Resource Sheet button on t‹ View Bar or choose View ⇨ More Views ⇨ Resource She and click Apply.

CROSS-REFERENCE

See "Using the View Bar" in Chapter 2 for information about switching views.

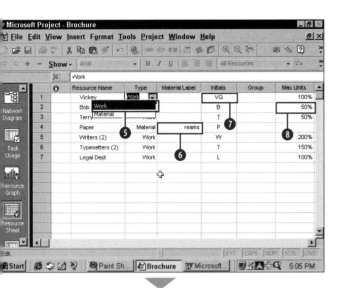

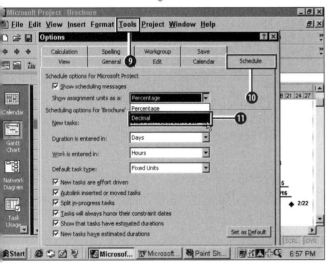

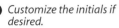

The Material Label field is just for the Material type resource. For example if the resource name is "cement," the label could be yards.

Maximum Units defines the maximum amount a resource is available at any time in the project. Exceeding this maximum level results in overallocation flags. Units can be defined as a percentage (default) or a decimal. To switch to decimal designations, choose Tools ➡ Options on the Schedule tab and then select the "Show assignment units as a" list box.

For a single resource, entering 100% (1 if using decimals) in the Max Units field indicates the resource is available full-time for this project. Similarly, entering 50% (.5) for a single resource indicates half-time availability for this project. For a resource group, like writers, enter full-time equivalent (FTE) values. For example, if you have two writers full-time and one part-time writer, enter 250% (2.5). Material resources don't have maximum units as it is assumed that, in theory, they are unlimited.

TAKE NOTE

USING RESOURCE INITIALS

To save time when typing resource names or to save space when printing a Gantt Chart displaying resource names, consider using initials instead of the full name.

5 Enter resource names and select the resource type from the drop-down list.

6 Enter material labels for materials resources.

7 Customize the initials if desired.

8 Enter the maximum units available per resource.

9 To change the maximum units from a percentage to decimals, choose Tools ➡ Options.

10 Select the Schedule tab.

11 From the drop-down list for "Show assignment unit as a," select Decimal.

FIND IT ONLINE

For a free Web-based project-management tool, see
http://www.iteamwork.com/figure.

Defining Resource Costs

The *Standard Rate* is the cost per unit of time to charge for the use of the resource. For example, you can enter $50/hr, $1000/mo, or $65,000/yr for an annual salary. If you enter a rate without a corresponding unit, Project assumes the default designation of hours. When you assign a resource to tasks, the annual Standard Rate converts to hours to calculate project costs.

The *Overtime Rate* is the rate that will be incurred if a resource works overtime. If the resource is paid the same rate for overtime as standard hours, enter the standard rate in the overtime rate field (notice the rate defaults to $0.00). Some of you salaried folks are smiling right now thinking about actually getting paid for all those hours per week above 40 that you work. But to truly measure the costs of a project — not accounting costs but spent costs plus opportunity costs — consider entering a rate for all employees, salaried and hourly. Using this technique you can track the cost of this project compared to time the salaried resources could have spent on other projects.

Cost per Use is used only for resources that incur a cost each time they are used. For example, your Legal department may charge one hundred dollars each time you consult with them about a vendor contract.

The *Accrue At* field is for project cost accounting and plays a large part in how spent costs are reported during the project. Accrue At Start front-loads the entire cost of the task as if it is already spent as soon as the task starts.

① To continue defining resources on the Resource Sheet, enter both standard and overtime rates.

② Enter cost per use if required.

③ Select an accrual method and a base calendar.

④ Enter a code if desired.

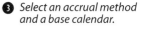

CROSS-REFERENCE

See "Creating Groups" in Chapter 10 for an example of using cost account codes to band or group tasks.

Defining Resources and Costs

Accrue At End back-loads the spent costs to the date the task finishes regardless of the way the money was actually paid out. The Prorated choice spreads out the costs evenly throughout the task duration. For example, if 40 percent of the task is complete, 40 percent of the costs will be incurred.

Base Calendar assigns a calendar to use as the starting point for the resource calendar. If, for example, you assign the Standard calendar as the Base Calendar, then the work hours and workdays of the Standard calendar will be passed along to the resource calendar for that person. You may then customize the resource calendar that is automatically created for each resource to include resource-calendar specifics.

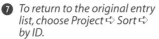

5 To sort your list alphabetically, choose Project ➪ Sort.

6 Click "by Name" to complete the sort.

7 To return to the original entry list, choose Project ➪ Sort ➪ by ID.

Defining Availability and Calendars

The Resource Information dialog box contains numerous fields for making advanced resource definitions. If your scheduling and resource definitions aren't yet ready for these features, at least give this section a quick glance. It is beneficial to know what features are available for future reference.

The Resource Information dialog box serves as a convenient location to define availability of resources as well as customize resource calendars. From the Resource Sheet, right-click and choose Resource Information from the shortcut menu to access the dialog box. Alternatively, choose Project ➪ Resource Information. As a shortcut, from any resource-focused view (Resource Sheet, Resource Usage, Resource Allocation) right-click the mouse and choose Resource Information from the shortcut menu.

The Resource Information dialog box contains four tabs: General, Working Time, Costs, and Notes. In this task, you'll look at the General and Working Time tabs.

The General tab contains several fields as part of the Resource Sheet such as Resource Name, Resource Type, Initials, Code, and Material Label. Using the Email field, enter the address for each project participant to use for communication purposes such as communication regarding task assignments. Similarly, if you have an Office address book available, you can establish workgroups in Project 2000 for sharing information among all project participants using e-mail and the World Wide Web.

The Resource Availability feature is very useful, especially when using resource groups. Establishing resource availability allows you to contour the definition of available units over time for a resource group. This contouring affects both scheduling and leveling, thus giving you

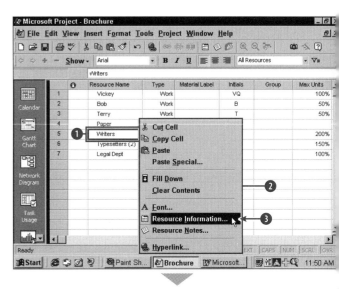

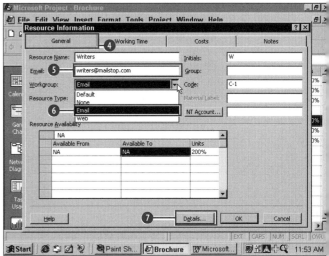

① To access the Resource Information dialog box from the Resource Sheet, select any resource.

② Right-click the mouse for the shortcut menu.

③ Select Resource Information.

④ Choose the General tab in the Resource Information dialog box.

⑤ Enter the e-mail address for intranet communications.

⑥ Select a workgroup mode of communication.

⑦ Click the Details button to select e-mail specifics.

CROSS-REFERENCE

See Chapter 13 for more information about using the Web for communicating project information.

a greater degree of accuracy than in previous versions. For example, suppose that in your project from March 1 to March 30 you have two writers (2 units), from April 1 to June 30 you have four writers (4 units), and from July 1 to the end of the project you have one writer (1 unit). Entering that information here helps you plan for the ramping up and down of resource numbers. You can also use Resource Availability for a single resource whose available project time fluctuates.

The Working Time tab presents individual resource calendars. Enter calendar changes using the same techniques as when changing project calendars. Use these individual calendars to account for resource time away from the project that is not already accounted for using the project calendar. Common uses for resource calendars include planning for vacations, conferences, meetings, medical appointments and recovery, and travel time between client sites.

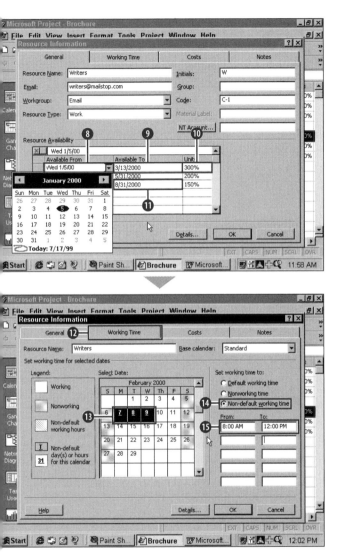

TAKE NOTE

USING THE DETAILS BUTTON

The Details button found on the bottom of the Resource Information dialog box is for identifying any e-mail specifics (like the type of e-mail system) that your e-mail program may need to know in order to correctly send and receive project messages. You may want to seek the advice of your LAN Administrator before changing or adding new e-mail profiles.

---

⑧ Click an Available From cell and select a date.

⑨ Click the Available To cell and select a date.

⑩ Enter the percentage of resource units available for this time period.

⑪ Repeat for subsequent changes in resource availability.

⑫ To access a resource calendar, click the Working Time tab.

⑬ Select date(s) to modify.

⑭ Click the radio buttons to switch between Default working, Nonworking, and Non-default working time.

⑮ If the date(s) are workdays, enter the corresponding work times (From and To).

FIND IT ONLINE

For handouts and project management-related hot links, see **http://michaelgreer.home.mindspring.com/.**

125

Defining Cost Rate Tables and Notes

For those interested in tracking resource costs, using rate tables can provide a high level of accuracy and realism. In the last section, you learned about the value of contouring resource availability compared to using one value for maximum units throughout the project. Similarly, resource cost rate tables provide a greater degree of accuracy than using a single standard rate or single overtime rate. In this section you will learn about cost rate tables and their use, and resource notes. They are easily accessible using the Resource Information dialog box.

There are two main purposes for cost rate tables. First, they allow you to account for changes over time in the standard rate, overtime rate, and cost per use rate for a resource (both material and work resources) or resource group. These changes may be due to inflation or pay rate increases. For example, suppose at the beginning of the project a resource is paid $50 per hour, but you know that starting second quarter the resource will receive a pay increase of 10 percent. To plan a more accurate budget it is important that these increases are included in the plan.

Using the default table (Table A) these cost rate changes appear on subsequent lines (25 changes maximum per resource or resource group) showing an effective date for each change. Project 2000 will then automatically adjust the rate and cost of using that resource on that date.

When entering rates you may enter a new dollar amount, such as a standard rate increase for Vickey from $75 per hour to a new rate of $85 per hour. Or, you may

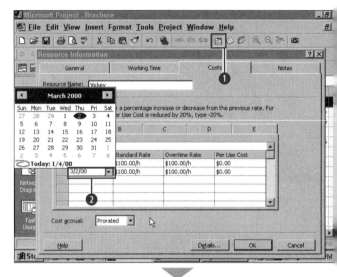

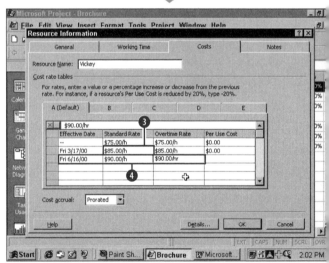

① To access cost rate tables from the Resource Sheet, click the Resource Information button.

② Using the Costs tab, type in an effective date or choose the date from the drop-down calendar.

③ Enter the new rate.

④ Repeat as necessary.

CROSS-REFERENCE

See Chapter 9 for information about assigning resource cost rate tables to specific task assignments.

Defining Resources and Costs

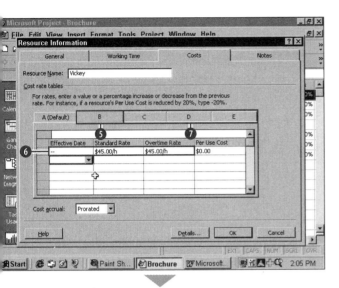

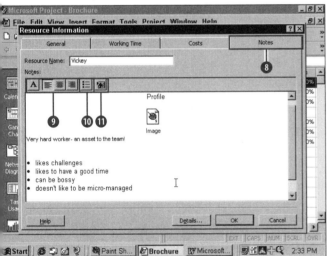

enter the rate as a percentage change; for example, the new rate for paper is a decrease of 20 percent and is entered as −20% for the new standard rate.

Use the remaining tables (B, C, D, and E) to establish rates if the amount charged differs depending on the work being performed. For example, a consultant in your company uses Table A (default) for on-site consultation fees, Table B for phone consultations, Table C for emergency consultation fees, and Table D for consultation prep.

Resource Notes provide documentation space to capture resource information. Common information includes skill set, recent training, birthdays, a picture of the resource, or work style preferences.

TAKE NOTE

COST RATES AND RESOURCE GROUPS

Remember that when defining a resource group (carpenters, writers, engineers, typesetters, clean-up crew) the resource definition fields, such as availability contouring, cost rate tables, resource calendars, and e-mail addresses, apply to the entire resource group as a whole. For example, if you have three writers defined as a group, you will not be able to define three separate calendars for them. All three writers will be scheduled according to the one calendar assigned to the resource group "writers."

---

5 To create additional tables, click B (Table B).

6 Enter an effective date and the new rates.

7 Repeat with tables C, D, and E if desired.

8 To enter task notes, click the Notes tab.

9 Click these buttons to determine font and text alignment.

10 Click this button for a bulleted list.

11 Click this button to insert an object such as a picture.

FIND IT ONLINE

For a project management forum of nonprofit resources, see **http://www.pmforum.org**.

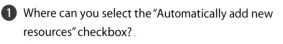

Personal Workbook

Q&A

1 Where can you select the "Automatically add new resources" checkbox?.

_____

_____

_____

2 What is a *material resource?*

_____

_____

_____

3 How many "full-time-equivalent" writers are available if the maximum units is 250 percent?

_____

_____

_____

4 How does a prorated cost accrual operate?

_____

_____

_____

5 What is the purpose of a base calendar?

_____

_____

_____

6 What are the four main definition tabs of the Resource Information dialog box?

_____

_____

_____

7 What are two ways to access the Resource Information dialog box?

_____

_____

_____

8 What are two reasons for using cost rate tables?

_____

_____

_____

ANSWERS: PAGE 322

Defining Resources and Costs

EXTRA PRACTICE

1 Define three different cost rate tables for a resource.

2 Define a material resource using a Material Label and Material Type.

3 Establish three changes to availability for a single resource.

4 Create a resource group of four writers and a group of two typesetters.

5 Customize a resource calendar.

6 Deselect the "Automatically add new resources" option.

REAL-WORLD APPLICATIONS

✔ Your resource manager looks at resource needs based on job category so you plan resource needs by resource group rather than individual names.

✔ The scheduling of your project tasks must be as realistic as possible so you use resource calendars to account for time away from the project.

✔ Your project uses many part-time available resources so you use resource contouring to manage the changes in availability.

✔ Employee hourly pay rates are confidential in your organization so you ask Finance or Human Resources for an average standard pay rate for project accounting purposes.

Visual Quiz

How do you display this dialog box? What do the two re-source availability entries mean? What does *Resource Type* mean?

_____

_____

_____

_____

_____

CHAPTER 9

**MASTER
THESE
SKILLS**

▶ **Understanding Resource Scheduling**

▶ **Understanding Task Type and Resource Scheduling**

▶ **Using the Assign Resources Dialog Box**

▶ **Assigning Resources Using Alternate Methods**

▶ **Understanding Effort-Driven Scheduling**

▶ **Using the Task Usage View**

▶ **Using the Resource Usage View**

▶ **Assigning Fixed Costs and Material Resources**

Project Staffing and Budgeting

In the last chapter, you learned how to define the resources and material resources that are needed for this project. As you saw, many options are available for defining resources, depending on how accurate or how detailed your schedule and cost information needs to be. When assigning resources you have just as many options.

Try not to become overwhelmed by the number of options available in this chapter. Remember that the developers of Microsoft Project 2000 make a product with a broad target audience. The same product serves the needs of a 100 dollar project as well as the needs of a ten million dollar project. Simply choose the options that you want to use, start simple, and ignore the rest. You can grow into the options as you need them, so keep this book in a convenient place for quick reference.

In this chapter you will review how Project calculates resource assignments and task scheduling. You will use task type and effort-driven scheduling choices to dictate how Project calculates. There is

no mystique here — they simply consist of mathematical formulas and a scheduling algorithm. If you understand the techniques being used, then you can control what is happening in your schedule. Too often, clients call me to lament that they were "just making a small change" only to have their project finish date suddenly and unexplainably extend three years into the future.

You will also explore numerous ways to assign resources to tasks so that you can choose a method that feels comfortable. You will practice entering assignments using forms, tables, and dialog boxes.

You will have the opportunity to contour resource assignments for those who need precise resource scheduling such as those in "job shop," professional, skill-driven, or consulting environments. Finally, you will assign fixed costs and material resources to tasks to complete your project budget.

The following chapter will present numerous additional resource views.

Understanding Resource Scheduling

Just as Microsoft Project 2000 uses numerous pieces of entered data to schedule tasks, it also uses resource information, if entered, to further define the scheduling of the task in light of the resource information. Before assigning resources to tasks, let's review six key points to remember when scheduling resources on project work.

By default, Microsoft Project schedules resource work to begin at the same time as the task start date. Also by default, the resource continues to work on the task uninterrupted until the task finishes.

Project will only schedule resource work during the dates and times shown as working time on the individual resource calendar. For example, Project will not schedule resources during their designated nonworking times like weekends and holidays.

If you schedule the resource units less than 100 percent for any task, Project will schedule work on that task for less than the total available time defined on the resource calendar. Let's consider two examples. First, suppose Vickey's calendar is 40 hours per week. If you schedule her to work 50 percent on a task, Project will schedule her 20 hours per week. However, suppose Bob's calendar is a part-time 20-hour-per-week calendar. If you schedule Bob at 100 percent for a task, he will be scheduled for 20 hours per week; 50 percent allocation for Bob represents 10 hours per week. Use your own discretion when deciding to reflect a resource's availability by altering the resource calendar or adjusting the units available per task. Although both methods yield the same results, it may be more difficult to use the calendar method because it requires that you remember how each resource's availability was entered.

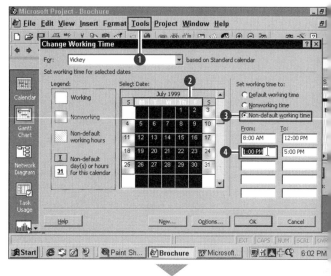

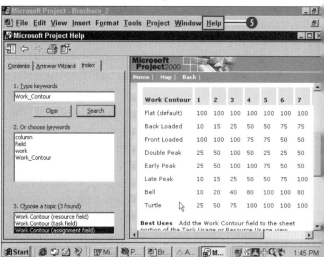

① For a part-time resource calendar, choose Tools ➪ Change Working Time. Select the part-time resource.

② Select Monday–Friday for a 20-hour-per-week calendar.

③ Click the Non-default working time radio button.

④ Erase the work time from 1:00 PM to 5:00 PM for a 4-hour-per-day calendar.

⑤ To preview the predefined resource contours, choose Help ➪ Contents and Index.

CROSS-REFERENCE

See "Assigning Resources Using Alternate Methods" in this chapter for information on using resource delays.

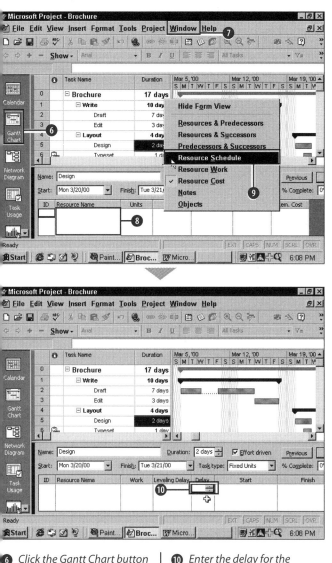

Further refinements to resource scheduling include manually overriding the even loading of resources by entering work hour variations or applying one of the predefined work assignment contours.

If one of the resources will not be available to begin work on the start date of a task, you can introduce a delay. Establishing a delay in your project allows the other resources to begin work as scheduled while enabling the delayed resource to join the task later.

A split in the task results in a split in the resource assignment as well. Task splitting works well when resources are pulled from one task to work on another task such as a critical path task.

⑥ *Click the Gantt Chart button on the View Bar.*

⑦ *To split the screen, choose Window ➪ Split.*

⑧ *Right-click the mouse button anywhere in the bottom pane to activate it.*

⑨ *Choose Resource Schedule from the details shortcut menu.*

⑩ *Enter the delay for the resource.*

FIND IT ONLINE

For employee scheduling software, see **http://www.f-tech.com**.

Understanding Task Type and Resource Scheduling

In Chapter 6, I began a discussion of task type and its role in task scheduling. In this section you will review fixed duration as a task type and look at two additional task types, fixed units and fixed work.

As a reminder, *duration* is the elapsed time from start to finish of a task, *units* is the percentage of time a resource is assigned to a task, and *work* is the amount of effort or billable time a resource is assigned to the task. Your display options for duration and work of minutes, hours, days, weeks, or months and work is either a percentage or decimal.

The three entries of duration, work, and units are mathematically related. The formulas used are *work = duration times units*, *duration = work divided by units*, and *units = work divided by duration*. Since these numbers are related, Project is forced, through programming (not stubbornness), to keep them balanced. As we look at the three task types more closely, keep in mind that a built-in programming bias drives Project to calculate duration before work and work before units.

The task type alerts Project to hold this entry in the formula fixed and calculate the other two numbers. For example, a fixed duration type signals to keep the duration as you have entered it and recalculate work and units to balance.

A fixed duration task might have its duration set as the maximum amount of time you can spend on the task as set by a customer, government agency, deadline, or senior management. If you enter duration and work, Project calculates the units required to complete that work within the timeframe. However, if you enter duration and units available, Project calculates how much work can be completed in the timeframe. Using the calculation bias, if you only enter duration, Project will recalculate work and leave units as is.

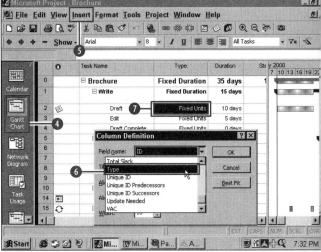

① To change task type for an existing task, select the task and click the Task Information button.

② Click the Advanced tab.

③ Select the task type from the drop-down list.

④ Alternatively, click the Gantt Chart button on the View Ba

⑤ Click any column header an choose Insert ⇨ Column.

⑥ In the Column Definition dialog box select Type as the field name from the drop-down list.

⑦ Type the task type or select the task type from the drop-down list.

CROSS-REFERENCE

See "Understanding the Task Type" in Chapter 6 for a discussion about task type and task scheduling.

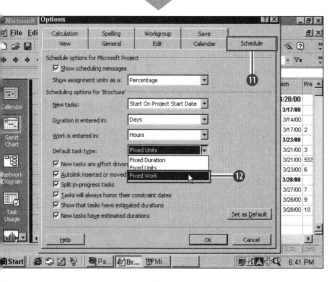

The default, *fixed units,* is typically used when you have a limited amount of a resource and want to carefully spread its time among various simultaneous tasks. If you enter units and work, Project calculates duration. If you enter units and duration, Project calculates work. Due to the bias, if you enter units only, Project calculates duration while leaving work as is.

Fixed work is typically used when resources have estimated the effort that is scheduled to be used in the project or when scheduling contractors' time if there is a maximum time allowed. If you enter work and duration, Project calculates the units required. Again, due to the programming bias, if you enter work only, Project calculates duration, leaving units as is.

TAKE NOTE

▶ ENTERING TASK TYPE

Change the task type using the Task Information dialog box, the Task Details form, or the Type column in a table.

---

⑧ *To change task type from the Task form, click the Gantt Chart button on the View bar.*

⑨ *Choose Window ⇨ Split.*

⑩ *Change the task type from the drop-down list.*

⑪ *To change the default task type for new tasks, click Tools ⇨ Options and select the Schedule tab.*

⑫ *Change the default task type from the drop-down list.*

FIND IT ONLINE

For courses offered by the American Management Association, see www.tregistry.com/s011projmgt.htm.

Using the Assign Resources Dialog Box

One common assignment method displays a Task Entry View showing a Gantt Chart in the top pane and a Task Form in the bottom pane. In addition, add the Assign Resources dialog box for a powerful entry combination.

You can use drag-and-drop features with the Assign Resources dialog box to quickly assign single or multiple resources to single or multiple tasks on the Gantt Chart and then modify the resource assignments using the Task Form.

The Assign Resources dialog box is a versatile dialog box enabling you to not only assign resources but also replace one resource with another on single or multiple tasks or to remove resources from tasks. Checkmarks indicate assignment to the currently selected task. In addition, use the units field in this dialog box to enter unit assignments other than 100 percent for the specific resource assignments. Leaving the units field blank uses the default unit assignment of 100 percent.

Six buttons display along the right side of the Assign Resources dialog box:

▶ *Cancel* or *Close* closes the dialog box.
▶ *Assign* assigns selected resources to selected tasks.
▶ *Remove* deletes the resource assignment or removes the assignment from the resource.
▶ *Replace* offers a pop-up list of all resources available in the project so you can choose a replacement for the currently selected resource.
▶ *Help* accesses a typical dialog box help screen.
▶ *Address* references the intranet workgroup e-mail address.

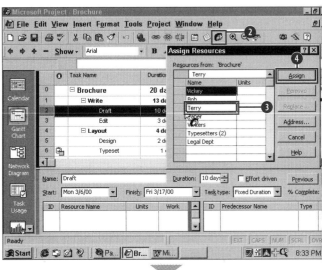

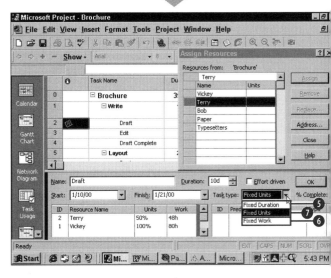

① To assign resources to tasks, select View ➪ More Views; select Task Entry; click Apply.

② Click the Assign Resources button.

③ Select the name(s) of the resources to assign.

④ Drag Assign Resources icon to the task in the Gantt Chart or click Assign if desired target task is highlighted.

⑤ Using the Task Form in the bottom pane, enter a duration, if the task type is fixed duration, and either units or work and click OK.

⑥ If the task type is fixed work, enter the work and either duration or units and click OK.

⑦ If the task type is fixed units, enter the units and either duration or work; click OK.

CROSS-REFERENCE

See "Copying, Deleting, and Moving Tasks" in Chapter 5 for more information about using drag and drop.

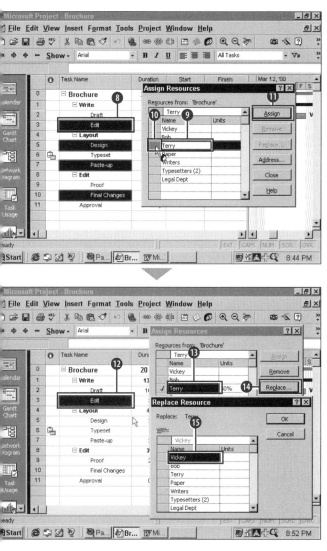

Keep in mind that Project cannot automatically match skills or availability of resources for replacement. It merely presents the entire list from which you can choose.

The Task Form, located at the bottom of the Task Entry view, is a convenient place to enter or change task type and effort-driven status for tasks. It is also a convenient place to enter duration, work, or units on a per-resource basis. You can also assign resources using this form by selecting resources from a pop-up list by clicking in the Resource Name field or typing the name or the resource ID number (from the Resource Sheet).

TAKE NOTE

▶ ### CALCULATING DURATIONS WITH MULTIPLE RESOURCE ASSIGNMENTS

The use of resource calendars and resource delays can make understanding Project calculations difficult. It becomes especially important when assigning multiple resources to the same task to remember that duration is the elapsed time between the start of the task and the finish. For example, suppose Don works for 20 days straight on a task and Clara works for 15 days, goes on holiday for 5 days and returns to work her remaining 5 days after Don has finished. The duration is calculated to be 25 days or the longest time for either Don or Clara. Clara's time includes the 5-day interruption for vacation.

---

⑧ To assign a resource to multiple tasks, select all the desired tasks on the Gantt Chart.

⑨ Select the resource name(s) to assign in the Assign Resources dialog box.

⑩ Drag the name(s) to the Gantt Chart onto any highlighted task and release for the multiple assignment.

⑪ Or, click the Assign button.

⑫ To replace one resource with another, select the tasks for which the resource will be replaced.

⑬ Select the resource to replace in the Assign Resources dialog box.

⑭ Click the Replace button.

⑮ Select a replacement resource and click OK.

FIND IT ONLINE

For the Institute of Project Management of Ireland, see
http://www.iol.ie/~instpmgm/index.html.

Assigning Resources Using Alternate Methods

For those of you who like tables, you can use the Resource Names column to directly enter resource assignments and units. You can use any table that contains the Resource Name column such as the Entry table.

The resource name entry is a text field, and the entry must follow the exact pattern that Project 2000 recognizes. The pattern when assigning resources using this method is

ResourceName1[Units], ResourceName2[Units]

Notice that the name of the resource is followed by the unit entry in square brackets with no space between the name and the left bracket. Multiple entries must be separated by commas. For example a typed entry might be Vickey[50%] or Vickey[50%],Bob[50%]. Unit entries of 100 percent do not need to be entered since that value is the default.

For those who like forms, the Task Information dialog box offers an alternative method for assigning resources. Using this box, you can assign resources to one or several tasks at once. This form is also a convenient place to change and delete resource assignments.

To enter assignments using this box, type or select from the drop-down list the resource name. Then, enter the units if different than the 100 percent default. To use this form to assign a resource to multiple tasks, select all the tasks prior to clicking the Task Information button. The Multiple Task Information dialog box opens for the multiple assignments.

The Resource Schedule details form at the bottom half of a split window is another convenient way to enter resources and resource delays. The resource delay field is used when a resource will not start work the same date

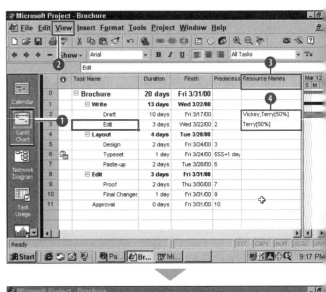

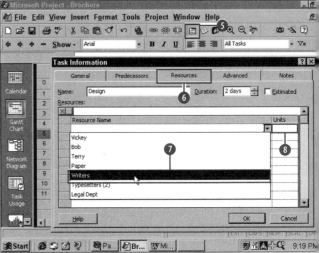

① To assign resources using the resource name column, click the Gantt Chart button.

② Display the Entry table by selecting View ⇨ Table ⇨ Entry.

③ Scroll to locate the Resource Names column.

④ Type your resource assignment into the column.

⑤ To assign resources with the Task Information dialog box, select a task and click the Task Information button.

⑥ Select the Resources tab.

⑦ Select a resource name from the drop-down list.

⑧ Enter the units value.

CROSS-REFERENCE

See "Applying Standard Tables" in Chapter 2 for more information about using spreadsheet tables.

as the task start date. You can either enter the delay amount and Project will calculate the new start and finish dates for the resource work, or you can enter the new resource start date and Project will calculate the delay amount and the new finish date for resource work.

Be careful if you enter a finish date for resource work here. The result will probably surprise you! If you enter a finish date, Project doesn't recalculate the start and delay amounts; rather, it recalculates the work amount so that the task can finish by that date.

To schedule resource delays, choose Views ⇨ More Views, select the Task Entry view, and click Apply.

Right-click the bottom pane and choose Resource Schedule as the detail form.

Enter a delay in the delay field and click OK.

▶ The resource start date is changed to reflect the delay.

Understanding Effort-Driven Scheduling

In project management terms, a task is effort driven if the task duration varies with the number of resources assigned. For example, suppose you have a task that requires 40 hours of work and you assign one person to it full-time. Adding a second full-time resource reduces the duration to half a week. Reality isn't usually so mathematically neat. Adding another person usually adds to the communication or decision-making time and could actually add time to the task!

New tasks are effort driven by default, but you can change the default before entering tasks using Tools ➪ Options and selecting the Schedule tab. Once tasks are entered, you can change the choice of effort-driven tasks using either the Task Form or the Task Information dialog box.

The choice of effort-driven tasks has no effect on the calculations performed during initial resource assignments. The choice only takes effect when adding or removing resources after the initial entries.

If you mark a task as effort driven, then in theory the more people you add to the task, the less time it takes to complete because each person shares the total work. For example, you assign three resources to a 2-day task that requires 48 hours of work total, or 16 hours each. You now decide that you want to shorten the schedule, so you add a fourth person to the task. Project holds the work at 48 hours but now each person has only 12 hours of work each so the task duration is cut to 1.5 days. Similarly, if you remove people from an effort-driven task, the task duration increases as each person takes longer to do more work.

① To see the effects of effort-driven scheduling, choose View ➪ More Views, select the Task Entry view, and click Apply.

② Right-click the bottom pane and choose Resources and Predecessors.

③ Click the Effort driven box if unchecked.

④ Add an additional resource and click OK.

▶ Notice the decrease in work per resource as well as the decrease in duration.

CROSS-REFERENCE

See "Setting Default Options" in Chapter 3 for more on setting initial task entry defaults.

In a task that's not effort driven, adding a fourth person adds 16 more hours of work to the task. This change results in 64 hours of work scheduled to be accomplished in the same two days.

With these examples, it becomes easy to see why you need accurate estimates about both the amount of work required for each task as well as the total elapsed time in which the resources will work.

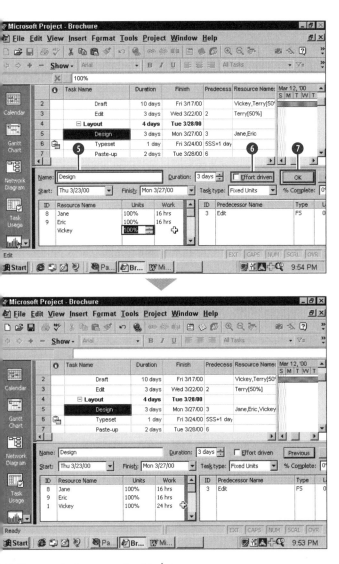

TAKE NOTE

DRIVING RESOURCES

With multiple resource assignments to the same task, Project calculates the duration of the task (fixed units or fixed work task types) to accommodate the longest time needed by any resource to complete his or her work. For example, if Terry has 16 hours of work to do on a task and Mary has 8 hours of work, the duration of the task will be calculated to accommodate Terry's work. In this example, Terry is called the *driving resource* since his work drives the duration.

⑤ To see a similar example with a non-effort-driven task, choose another task.

⑥ Uncheck the Effort driven box.

⑦ Add an additional resource and click OK.

▶ Notice the work is added to the work of the original resources rather than dividing up the workload, and the duration remains unchanged.

FIND IT ONLINE

For project management books, see
http://www.amazon.com.

Using the Task Usage View

The Task Usage view is a good choice for those who want to contour resource assignments or see details of resource work distribution. The Task Usage view displays tasks with assigned resources listed underneath each one as well as a time-phased distribution worksheet showing work assignments in hours. Many of the features mentioned in this chapter are found in the Task Usage view, and because of its popularity, the Task Usage view is available from the View Bar.

It is probably easiest to use the Task Form or the Assign Resources dialog box for initial resource assignments with this view. Use the Task Form to enter work and units as well.

The main additions offered by the Task Usage view include delaying or splitting resource assignments, changing the even work distribution to a contoured distribution, and applying cost rate tables that apply different cost rates to different types of work done by a resource.

To delay or split an assignment, simply insert blank cells for the time period in which no work will be done by that resource, thereby shifting work to another time period. As soon as you modify cells or insert blank ones, Project immediately recalculates the work for the resource and duration, and the total work for the task.

Resource distribution contours refer to the pattern made by the resource allocation over time. By default, Project assigns an even or flat distribution. You can manually adjust the cells to create your own work pattern (named Contoured) or you can choose from one of the eight predefined contours available when using the Assignment Information dialog box. The Assignment Information dialog box is only available through the Task Usage or Resource Usage views.

① To use the Task Usage view, click the Task Usage button on the View Bar.

② To delay a resource assignment, click the cell where the delay is to start and press the Insert key on your keyboard.

③ Manually adjust work hours by typing an entry.

④ Notice an increase in work per day leads to an increase in the total work for the task as well.

⑤ A delay was entered using blank cells.

CROSS-REFERENCE

See "Defining Cost Rate Tables and Notes" in Chapter 8 for more information on this topic.

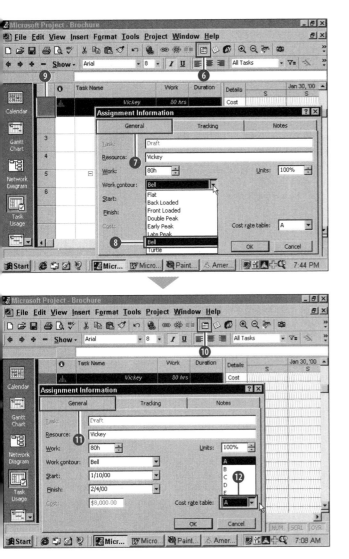

Choosing a different pattern alters the numeric contents of each cell in the Task Usage view. The eight contours are Flat, Back Loaded, Front Loaded, Double Peak, Early Peak, Late Peak, Bell, and Turtle. For example, a front-loaded distribution peaks at the start by scheduling most of the work for the resource up front and tapers off during the task duration. A turtle distribution rises to a plateau and tapers off. For easy reference, an icon in the Indicators column displays the type of distribution you have assigned.

Use the Assignment Information dialog box to assign a cost rate table to a specific resource for a specific task assignment.

TAKE NOTE

CAUTIONS WHEN USING A DISTRIBUTION WORKSHEET

Be careful when using contours with fixed duration tasks. Since the duration cannot change, all the work scheduled using the contour may not fit in the set duration.

To restore a contour edited manually or assigned back to the default assignment pattern, choose the contour pattern called "Flat."

⑥ To assign a resource contour, select a resource on the table and click the Assignment Information button.

⑦ Click the General tab.

⑧ Choose a work contour from the drop-down list.

⑨ Locate the icon in the Indicators column displaying contour type.

⑩ To change the cost rate table applied to a resource, select the resource on the table and click the Assignment Information button.

⑪ Click the General tab.

⑫ Select a cost rate table for this resource assignment.

FIND IT ONLINE

For project costing software, see
http://www.pricekey.com.

Using the Resource Usage View

The Resource Usage view is quite similar to the Task Resource view except that the focus is on resources and their task assignments. After assigning resources, you may find that this view is more useful in reviewing assignment information than the Task Usage view. Because of its popularity, the Resource Usage view is available from the View Bar.

Like the Task Usage view, the Resource Usage view also displays a table on the left and a distribution worksheet on the right. The table lists unassigned tasks under a heading of the same name, followed by each resource listed separately. Under each resource name, Project displays the tasks assigned to that resource.

Numerous tables are available for the view. For example, the cost table supplies not only costs per task per resource, but also displays the costs rolled up to total costs of the resource for the entire project. In addition, the work table displays work information for each task per resource as well as for the project.

The distribution worksheet side of the view is equally valuable. Because you can choose to display different data items, you can actually type in different work information directly on the worksheet. For instance, entering a new work amount alters the duration for a non-fixed duration task.

This worksheet can also be used as a time-tracking system. For example, right-clicking the mouse on the distribution side displays a shortcut menu with row choices. Since you can choose to display numerous items from this menu at once, display Actual Cost, Actual Overtime, and Actual Work to create a time-tracking worksheet. After the project gets under way, you can enter costs, overtime, and work expended for each resource for each task.

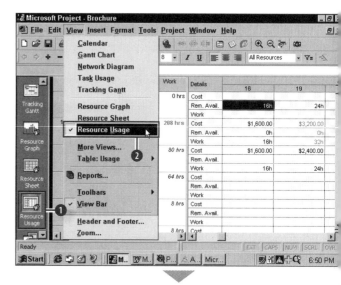

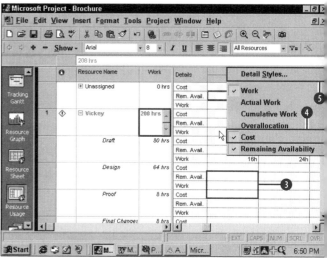

❶ To access the Resource Usage view, click the Resource Usage button on the View Bar.

❷ Or, choose View ➪ Resource Usage.

❸ To display different rows on the distribution worksheet, right-click the distribution side of the screen.

❹ Choose an element to display from the context menu.

❺ For more choices, click Detail Styles.

CROSS-REFERENCE

See Chapter 14, "Tracking Progress," for more information about earned value and time tracking.

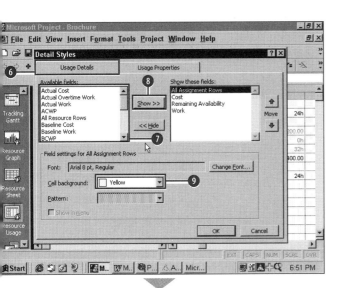

By choosing Detail Styles on the context menu, you can add to the list of menu options simply by choosing them from a list. For example, earned value fields can show on the distribution worksheet. Earned value formulas attempt to present project progress in terms of dollars earned. Two typical earned value fields that appear here include ACWP (Actual Cost of Work Performed) and BCWP (Budgeted Cost of Work Performed).

Using the Detail Styles dialog box, you can also set cell background color and font as well as the alignment of data within the cell.

Right-clicking the mouse on the left side of the Resource Usage view displays a context menu. Both the Assignment Information and Assignment Notes dialog boxes appear here.

TAKE NOTE

FILTERING THE RESOURCE USAGE VIEW

For added assistance in focusing on specific resource issues or for printing purposes, consider filtering the Resource Usage view. Some of the more popular filters to use here include material resource, work resource, resources with overtime, overallocated resources, work incomplete, and work overbudget.

---

6 Choose the Usage Details tab.

7 To show additional fields not on the shortcut menu, select a field in the left-hand list.

8 Click the Show button.

9 Select a different cell background color using the drop-down list.

10 To access the Assignment Information dialog box, right-click anywhere on the table side of the screen.

11 Choose Assignment Information from the context menu.

FIND IT ONLINE

For distance learning opportunities in project management, see **http://www.sbpm.gwu.edu/mspm**.

Assigning Fixed Costs and Material Resources

The fixed cost field, available on the Cost table, allows you to directly enter a cost amount applied to the task. This cost is then added to the resource costs to calculate the total cost for the task.

For example, suppose you hire a vendor to complete a deliverable in four weeks for $10,000. You first enter the task as a fixed duration task of four weeks and enter $10,000 into the fixed cost field for that task. If you want to enter the vendor's name as a reminder that the deliverable is being produced outside, enter it on the Resource Sheet as a new resource. Then assign the vendor to the task but use units of 0% since you don't care how much work the vendor expends on the tasks due to the fixed cost nature (contract) of the work.

For those users who do not wish to assign resources as we have done in this chapter but do want to track higher-level costs (labor and material) associated with each task, using fixed costs offers a simple solution. Let's say that you use an Excel spreadsheet to calculate labor, materials, travel, overhead, and other expense categories for budget preparation. Enter these totals per task in the fixed cost field and track them using totals per task as well. This technique offers a simple project accounting system without the complexity of entering all project costs as separate items.

Use any of the techniques mentioned in this chapter for assigning work resources to assign material resources to tasks. In the Units field, for material resources, enter the number of units that match the material label. For example, assign paper to the Publication task and in the Units field enter 100 reams. Based on the cost per ream entered on the Resource Sheet, the cost for the 100 reams is added to any work resource costs of this task plus any fixed costs to calculate a total cost.

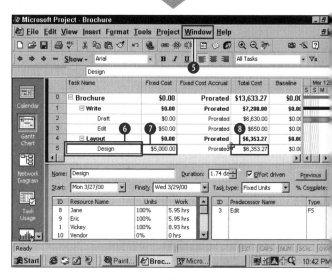

❶ To assign fixed costs, click the Gantt Chart button on the View Bar.

❷ Apply the cost table by choosing View ➪ Table ➪ Cost.

❸ Type an entry into the fixed cost field or use the spin control button.

❹ Notice the change in the Total Cost field.

❺ To enter a vendor as a fixed cost yet retain the name, choose Window ➪ Split.

❻ Assign the vendor to the task with 0 units and click OK.

❼ The work is also calculated to 0 so enter the contract price.

❽ Notice the Total Cost for the project.

CROSS-REFERENCE

See "Defining Resources" in Chapter 8 for more information about material resources.

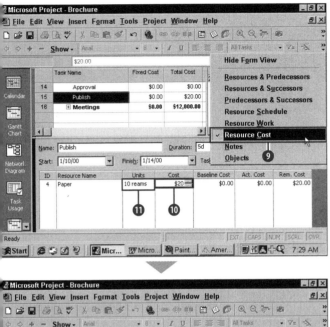

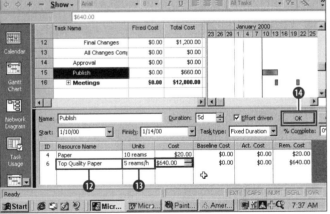

⑨ To assign a fixed consumption material resource using the same split window, right-click the bottom pane and select Resource Cost from the shortcut menu.

⑩ Assign a material cost.

⑪ In the Units field, enter the amount followed by the units: for example, "10 reams" (of paper).

⑫ To assign a variable consumption material resource using the same split window, assign the material resource.

⑬ For Units, enter the amount followed by the time period: for example, "5 reams/h" as in 5 reams per hour.

⑭ Click OK for the cost recalculation.

FIND IT ONLINE

For project budget estimating software, see **http://www.rms.net/product_fast_planner.htm.**

Personal Workbook

Q&A

1 What are the three task types?

_____

_____

_____

2 What is a *fixed duration* task?

_____

_____

_____

3 What is an advantage to using the Assign Resources dialog box?

_____

_____

_____

4 What are three ways to assign resources to tasks?

_____

_____

_____

5 What is the primary difference between the Resource Usage and Task Usage views?

_____

_____

_____

6 What are four kinds of resource contour patterns?

_____

_____

_____

7 What are *fixed costs*?

_____

_____

_____

8 What are the two kinds of consumption of material resources?

_____

_____

_____

ANSWERS: PAGE 322

EXTRA PRACTICE

1 Make resource assignments and enter numbers for duration, work, and units with the three kinds of task types.

2 Make multiple resource assignments to multiple tasks using the Assign Resources dialog box.

3 Assign resources using the Task Information dialog box.

4 Assign resources using the Resource Names column.

5 Add a resource to an effort-driven task.

6 Enter a fixed cost amount.

REAL-WORLD APPLICATIONS

✔ In an effort to assign resources quickly, you use the Assign Resources dialog box for multiple resource assignments to multiple tasks.

✔ For some of your tasks, resources do most of their work at the beginning of a task and then taper off so you assign a front-load contour.

✔ You use an Excel spreadsheet to budget all task expense items and then you enter this total in the fixed cost column.

✔ Most of your task durations are determined by the number of resources assigned, so you use effort-driven scheduling.

Visual Quiz

How do you access the Assignment Information dialog box?

_____

_____

_____

_____

_____

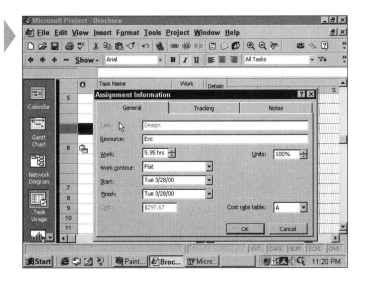

CHAPTER 10

MASTER THESE SKILLS

- ▶ Grouping Tasks
- ▶ Creating Groups
- ▶ Developing Custom Grouping Codes
- ▶ Using Standard Filters
- ▶ Creating Filters
- ▶ Sorting Lists

Grouping, Filtering, and Sorting

By this point in developing your project plan, you have developed a task list or outline, entered scheduling information, analyzed the schedule, defined available resources and cost amounts, staffed your project, and developed a budget. In preparation for reviewing and finalizing the plan, you now need skill in manipulating and sifting through your project data. Microsoft Project 2000 increases in value as a scheduling, tracking, and reporting tool in direct proportion to your ability to not only enter accurate data but also communicate project information in an effective manner.

Since your project data resides in a database, it is important that you are comfortable manipulating the data and rearranging it during analysis and prior to reporting. Several techniques discussed in this chapter assist you in handling not only the numerous pieces of data but multiple reporting needs as well.

A new feature of Project 2000 is grouping. *Grouping* allows you to band tasks together temporarily for analysis or reporting. Previous versions of Microsoft Project offered task grouping only by outline summary and subtask groups.

Grouping greatly enhances your ability to support multiple reporting requirements. In this chapter you will practice using predefined groups, creating new groups, and using custom fields in conjunction with groups. Grouping techniques work with task lists as well as resource lists.

Filters enable you to work with a subset of project database information rather than all data. For example, you may only want to print next month's critical tasks for a team meeting. Filters allow you to display and print this required data as opposed to printing all tasks. Filters are available for both task and resource information. In this chapter you practice using predefined filters as well as creating custom task and resource filters.

The third main feature discussed in this chapter, *sorting,* enables you to rearrange the order in which tasks or resources display in lists or on forms. For example, you may want to sort your Resource Sheet in alphabetical order or sort a task list so that the critical tasks are listed first.

Some of the features mentioned here rely on practicing features in previous chapters. Return to those chapters mentioned in the Cross-Reference sections to practice, if needed.

Grouping Tasks

I n previous versions of Microsoft Project the outline structure was the basic foundation for any project. If you wanted tasks to appear in a different place in the task list, you had to manually move them or apply a sort that rearranged tasks within each outline group. Limiting users to only one format, the WBS format, which corresponds to the outline structure, is at best frustrating as people involved with projects often need to see data in different configurations. The good news is that Project 2000 gives you the capability to design and display tasks and resources in any grouping that you can imagine, all without manually moving any tasks! Of course, you can still use WBS numbers and the outline structure in addition to grouping.

The Grouping feature enables you to organize tasks or resources in meaningful groups and see rolled-up totals for these groups. Each group is shown with a band or title for the group followed by resources or tasks that match the group criteria. By changing the way tasks are grouped together, you can focus on numerous important aspects of the project. Consider grouping tasks based on user-entered task data, on WBS codes, or on user-defined outline codes. These choices provide virtually unlimited ways to rearrange project tasks and resources.

Suppose you are preparing reports for several different project meetings. The focus of one meeting is the WBS family groups, the goal of another meeting is to focus on high-risk tasks, and the focus of yet another meeting is costs associated with vendor tasks. Meanwhile, the

❶ To use grouping, select Project ➪ Group By ➪ More Groups.

❷ Choose the Task radio button.

❸ Select Duration and click Apply.

▶ The tasks are grouped or banded according to milestones first.

❹ To group by critical versus noncritical tasks, choose Project ➪ Group By ➪ More Groups.

❺ Choose Critical.

❻ Click Apply.

▶ The tasks are separated into critical and noncritical.

CROSS-REFERENCE

See "Creating Custom Fields" in Chapter 17 for information about developing custom outline codes.

team leads want to focus on their responsibilities while yet another group wants to focus on critical path tasks assigned to the engineers. Using the same task list, you can meet all of these reporting needs through grouping.

Sometimes it is not useful to group for each unique value. For example, suppose you are grouping by Cost. It is probably better to define grouping intervals that span cost ranges than to have each separate cost with associated tasks listed.

To group tasks, first create a group definition or use one of the default group definitions and then apply the definition. The task list is then rearranged according to the group definition. In this way you can change grouping criteria as often as you wish or choose No Group to revert back to your original task list. Project 2000 gives you eight task group definitions and five resource group definitions, plus the No Group choice for both.

TAKE NOTE

SHARING GROUPING INFORMATION

Custom group criteria that you establish can be shared using the Organizer as previously discussed in Chapters 3 and 4. To reach the Organizer to copy custom group information from one project to another, go to Tools ⇨ Organizer, Group tab.

⑦ To group a Resource Sheet, click the Resource Sheet button on the View Bar.

⑧ Choose Project ⇨ Group By ⇨ Resource Group.

▶ The resources are now banded based on group identity.

⑨ To group by Work vs. Material Resources, choose Project ⇨ Group By ⇨ Work vs. Material Resources.

▶ The resource list is divided into two types.

FIND IT ONLINE

For examples of Project 2000 in the workplace go to
www.microsoft.com/ office/project/casestudies.htm.

153

Creating Groups

Grouping opens vast opportunities to rearrange your data for analysis as well as reporting needs. Consider using a color printer for full effect in banding that uses multiple criteria.

In the last task you practiced applying predefined task and resource group bands. In this task, you'll look at creating new group definitions, modifying existing definitions, copying definitions, and sharing definitions among projects.

The first step in successful use of groups is to enter the relevant data. For example, if you want to band by resource group, then you need to enter resource group names on the Resource Sheet. Or, if you want to group by responsible team member, then you should create a custom column for "Responsible" using one of the available text fields (Text 1–10) and enter appropriate names. As you can see grouping is not necessarily for data entry purposes but rather for analysis and reporting.

Click the New button in the More Groups dialog box to open a Group Definition dialog box. Use this box to name the new group and decide whether to show it on the More Groups menu. "Group By" enables you to select one or more fields to use when banding your tasks together. To use multiple banding criteria, choose subsequent field names to create a list of criteria. For example, choosing Critical first and then Responsible will band your tasks first by Critical and Noncritical and within those groups band by the Responsible team names. Typical multiple combinations include Cost and Responsible, Responsible and On Time, Responsible and Late, and Responsible and Over Budget. As you can see, the choices become almost limitless.

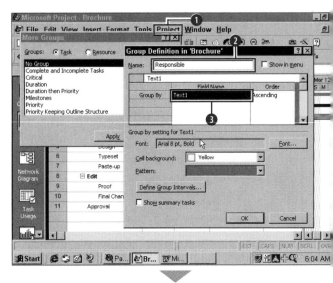

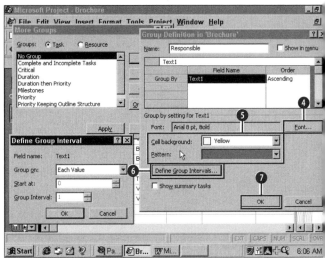

1 To create a user-defined group definition, choose Project ⇨ Group By ⇨ More Groups, and click the New button.

2 To group by Text 1 (Responsible custom column) enter Name of definition as Responsible

3 In the Group By field, choose Text 1 from the drop-down list; choose Ascending order.

4 Select a font style and size.

5 Choose a cell background color and pattern.

6 Click Define Group Intervals to establish a banding interval.

7 Click OK.

CROSS-REFERENCE

See "Creating Custom Fields" in Chapter 17 for more information about creating a Responsible column.

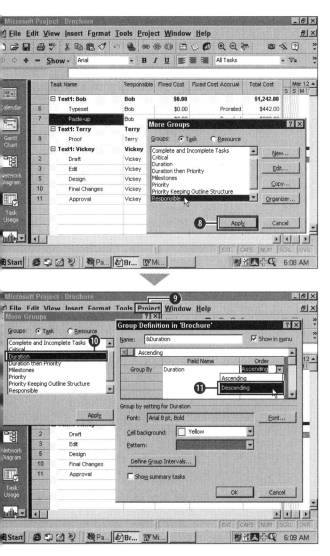

The Group Definition dialog box also contains fields for ordering the groups in ascending or descending order, and choosing a font and cell background color and pattern for each band. Use this form to establish a group interval; an *interval* is a band that represents more than one value. For example, if you band by cost you probably don't want a new group for every dollar range in the project. Instead establish an interval that bands costs in $10,000 or $100,000 intervals.

Clicking the Copy button in the More Groups dialog box opens the Group Definition dialog box as well. The Copy command allows you to copy an existing definition for modifications and a new name.

Clicking the Edit button also opens the Group Definition dialog box. Edit allows you to modify an existing custom or predefined definition. As usual, the recommendation is to copy an existing predefined group definition for modifications rather than editing it.

TAKE NOTE

SHARING GROUP DEFINITIONS

Clicking the Organizer button opens the Organizer dialog box in which you can copy your custom group definitions to another project or to the Global.mpt file so that they are available to all projects. Use the Groups tab to share group definitions.

● Click Apply to display the banded grouping.

❾ To modify an existing group definition based on duration, choose Project ⇨ Group by ⇨ More Groups.

❿ To modify duration group definition, select Duration; click Edit.

▶ &Duration is a default Project definition; you can use D as a shortcut in the menu name.

⓫ Change the order to Descending and click OK.

FIND IT ONLINE

Visit **www.microsoft.com/office/project/default.asp** for ideas on grouping.

Developing Custom Grouping Codes

Microsoft Project 2000 now contains the functionality that allows you to create custom user-defined fields. In previous versions of Project you could customize fields in limited ways like renaming fields or renaming and using blank fields like the Text 1–30 fields. However, in Project 2000 you can create fields containing values that are selected from pick-lists, or create fields that contain formulas, such as formulas for calculating overhead costs or capital expenses. You can now truly add to the "out-of-the-box" functionality of Project in ways that you could not before.

Although the topic of creating custom fields is covered in detail in Chapter 17, let's look at a sample in this task to illustrate the powerful combination of custom fields with grouping in data entry, management, display, and reporting.

This process of using custom fields with grouping involves five steps:

1. First, you must create a custom field with name and type entries. For this example, suppose you want to group tasks by the responsible team member's name. Project 2000 does not currently contain a Responsible field. Using the Customize Fields dialog box shown in the top figure on this page, you can define the custom field — Responsible, for example.
2. Next, you must define values for that field. In this example, create a list of names of the project team leads as text entries. Later, you can choose the names from an automatically generated pick-list.

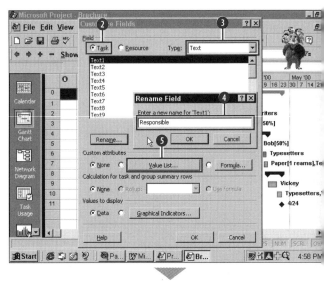

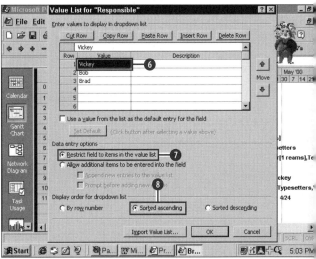

❶ To create a custom field, choose Tools ⇨ Customize ⇨ Fields.

❷ Choose the Task radio button.

❸ Choose Text.

❹ Highlight Text1, click the Rename button, and rename the field Responsible.

❺ Click the Value List button to create a list of choices.

❻ Click the Value field for Row and enter a team member name. Repeat for Rows 2 and 3.

❼ Click the radio button to restrict the field to these three choices.

❽ Click the Sorted Ascending radio button so that the pic list names are alphabetized

CROSS-REFERENCE

See "Creating Custom Fields" in Chapter 17 for more examples of the power of customizing Project 2000.

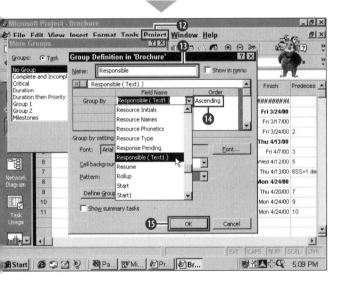

3. Then, choose a task view and include this new field as a column on the table shown; you can also do this for resource fields and resource tables. (See "Applying Standard Tables" in Chapter 2 for information about inserting a column into an existing table or see "Creating New Tables" in Chapter 17 for information about adding this field column to a new table.)

4. Enter or select from a pick-list the appropriate entry for each task. In this example, choose the responsible team member name for each summary or subtask.

5. Finally, create the group definition to group by Responsible field. In this example, grouping results in tasks being banded beneath each responsible team member's name. See "Creating Groups" earlier in this chapter for more information.

TAKE NOTE

COMMON TEXT CUSTOM FIELDS

In addition to Responsible as a custom text field valuable in grouping, other useful fields include phase name, responsible department name, resource manager name, cost account, and subproject name.

---

9 Display the newly created Responsible field (column) on a task table.

10 Click the arrow for a drop-down list and make a selection.

11 Complete the entries for all remaining tasks.

12 To create a new group that uses this field, choose Project ⇨ Group By ⇨ More Groups; click New.

13 Name the group Responsible and group by the field name Responsible.

14 Choose Ascending order to alphabetically sort groups.

15 Choose OK and apply the group definition.

FIND IT ONLINE

For a Microsoft Project 2000 users group go to
http://www.mpug.org/.

Using Standard Filters

For Project 2000 to be truly useful, you need the ability to manipulate and extract data specific to your current needs. Before printing views or reports or during onscreen data analysis, consider filtering to display or highlight only pertinent information.

When applying a filter, select whether the tasks or resources that match the criteria for the filter are displayed or highlighted. The Display Only option displays the tasks that match the filter and hides those that do not. For example, when you filter for critical tasks, only those tasks that are calculated as critical will be shown on the screen, the noncritical tasks will not show.

When the filter is set to Highlight instead of Display Only, the tasks or resources that match the criteria appear in a different color or in a different font while leaving non-matching items as they are.

Project 2000 ships with a number of predefined task and resources filters. Task filters may be applied to task views while resource filters only apply to resource views. New to Project 2000 is the ability to filter tasks in a Network Diagram view.

In addition to using predefined filters you may wish to create new filters or edit or copy existing filters. You can also use the Organizer to copy new or modified filters to other projects or to the Global.mpt file for use by all projects.

In addition to the basic filters, there are special interactive filters. An interactive filter asks the user to enter values that are then used as search criteria. The Date

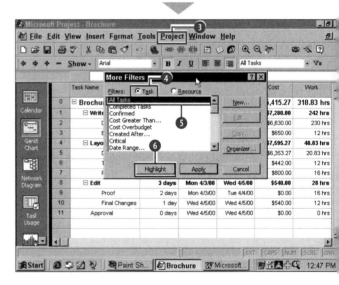

① To apply a Display Only filter, click the filter selection arrow.

② Choose a filter from the list.

③ To use a Highlight filter or choose a filter not on the short list, choose Project ⇨ Filtered for: ⇨ More Filters.

④ Select Task (or Resource) to select the filter type.

⑤ Choose a filter by name and click Apply for a Display Only filter.

⑥ Or, choose a filter by name and click Highlight.

CROSS-REFERENCE

See "Exploring Formatting Options" in Chapter 12 for more on using filters prior to printing views and reports.

Range filter and the Cost Greater Than filter are both examples of interactive filters. For example, if you supply the value of $25,000 in the Cost Greater Than interactive dialog box, Project will display or highlight tasks whose cost value is more than $25,000.

Another special type of filter compares two different field values found in the project database. The Cost Overbudget filter is an example of a database comparison filter. The Cost Overbudget filter compares the baseline cost to the current cost.

Examples of predefined filters include the All Tasks filter that displays all tasks in the list with no criteria applied: a nonfiltered condition. The Completed Tasks filter displays tasks that are 100 percent complete. The Critical filter displays all critical tasks. The Incomplete Tasks filter displays tasks that are not yet 100 percent complete. The Milestone filter displays all milestone tasks. The Material Resources filter looks for and displays material resources assigned to tasks.

TAKE NOTE

USING AUTO FILTERS

The AutoFilter command displays a drop-down menu with filter values at the top of each column in a resource or task table. You may choose a value from the menu to filter that column.

⑦ To use AutoFilters, click the AutoFilter button on the Formatting toolbar.

⑧ Click any of the arrows on the column headers for a drop-down list of values.

⑨ Select the desired option.

⑩ Repeat for other columns if desired.

⑪ To return to an unfiltered condition, choose All Tasks from the toolbar filter drop-down list.

FIND IT ONLINE

For a Microsoft online location in South Africa, see
http://www.microsoft.com/southafrica/downloads.

Creating Filters

If a standard filter doesn't provide the capability that you need, consider creating a new filter. As with many other features in Microsoft Project 2000 such as calendars, tables, groups, and reports, you can modify an existing filter, copy an existing filter to use as a base for the new filter, or create an entirely new filter. You can also use the Organizer to make custom filters available to all projects.

It is again recommended that you not modify a standard filter. You may decide later that you need that filter and may have forgotten how to create it. Instead, copy an existing filter to use for the new filter. Whether you are creating a new filter from scratch or copying and modifying an existing filter, you use the Filter Definition dialog box, described in the remainder of this task.

When naming a new filter, use descriptive words that describe the purpose of the filter. For example, it is easier to remember the purpose of "Next month's critical tasks" than "Filter 23." Also decide at this time whether the filter should be shown on the filter menu. If the filter is one that you use often, show it on the menu for ease of selection.

Next, turn your attention to creating search criteria statements consisting of a field name, a test, and a value. For example, a search criteria statement might read, "task type (field name) equals (test) fixed duration (value)" to locate all fixed duration tasks. Another example might read, "budgeted cost (field name) is greater than (test) $10,000 (value)" to locate all tasks whose baseline cost is more than $10,000.

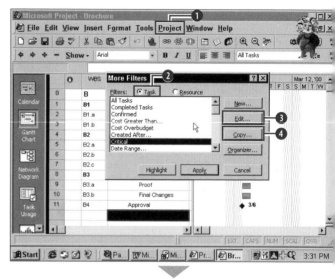

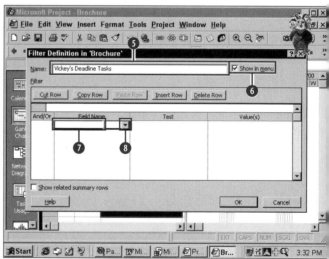

❶ To create or modify filters, choose Project ➪ Filtered for ➪ More Filters.

❷ Choose Task (or Resource) radio button for a filter type.

❸ To modify, select a filter and click Edit.

❹ To copy and modify a filter, select a filter and click Copy or click New to create a new filter.

❺ Name the filter "Vickey's Deadline Tasks" for this example.

❻ Click the checkbox to show this filter in the menu.

❼ Click the first row under Field Name.

❽ Click the drop-down arrow.

CROSS-REFERENCE

See "Creating Custom Fields" in Chapter 17 for more about maximizing the power of filters.

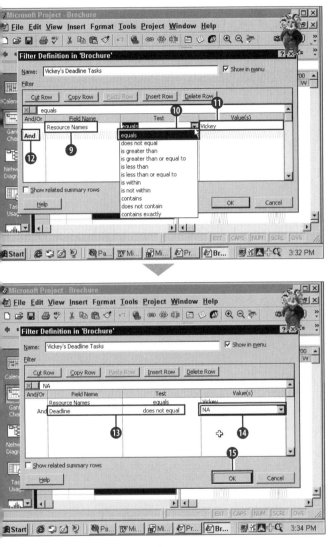

Field names appear on a drop-down list of all field names found in a project database. Test choices also appear on a drop-down list. Test conditions include equals, does not include, is greater than, is greater than or equal to, is less than, is less than or equal to, is within, is not within, contains, does not contain, and contains exactly. Values are database field values like fixed duration ([task type]) or a specific entry like $5,000.

To create more complex filters using multiple criteria, use "and/or" between condition statements. The *and* choice means that the task or resource must meet all selection criteria statements in order to display or highlight. The *or* choice, on the other hand, means the task or resource must meet at least one of the selection criteria statements to display or highlight.

Lastly, decide whether to display or highlight only the subtasks that meet the criteria or to include their roll-up summary tasks as well.

TAKE NOTE

▶ **CREATIVITY AND FILTER CREATION**

You can create almost an unlimited number of filters using predefined and custom fields. Reporting just the right information for the intended audience can be very powerful.

⑨ Make a selection from the list (Resource Names, in this example).

⑩ Click the first row under Test and choose "equals."

⑪ Click the first row under Value(s) and type the entry, "Vickey" in this example.

⑫ Click the second row and choose And for a multiple condition statement.

⑬ In the second row, choose Deadline as the field name, and "does not equal" as the test.

⑭ For the Value, type NA which means not blank.

⑮ Click OK to complete the Filter Definition dialog box and click the Apply button to activate the filter.

FIND IT ONLINE

Find a preparation coach for the Project Management Professional certification exam at **http://www.iil.com**.

Sorting Lists

Sorting provides another useful technique for manipulating data. Sorting allows you to rearrange the order in which tasks or resources appear on a list or in forms. For example, tasks and resources appear in ID order by default. You may decide to sort alphabetically by name or to sort by start date, cost, resource group, or finish date.

You can sort any view that presents data in a list or on a form. This includes all views except the Calendar, Network Diagram, Resource Graph, and Relationship Diagram.

There are three main types of sorts: sorting a task list displaying outline order, sorting a task or resource list using grouping, and sorting forms.

Sorting a Task List in Outline Order

Let's look first at sorting a task list in outline order. The outline order already establishes family groups: summary tasks with related subtasks. When sorting these tasks, first the summary tasks sort based on your selection of sorting criteria and sort order (ascending or descending). Then, the subtasks within each summary task sort following the same criteria. For example, suppose you sort by cost in descending order. First, all summary tasks sort with the most costly summary task at the top of the list. Then the subtasks within each summary task also display according to cost in descending order.

Sorting a Task or Resource List with Grouping

When grouping task or resource lists (that is, Resource Sheet, Task Sheet, Gantt Chart) the grouping definition

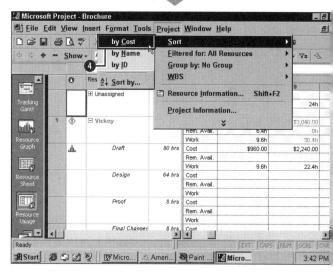

1. To use predefined task sort criteria, select the task view or form to sort and group if desired.

2. Choose Project ➪ Sort, and choose to sort by Start Date, Finish Date, Priority, Cost, or ID.

3. To use predefined resource sort criteria, select the resource view or form to sort and group if desired.

4. Choose Project ➪ Sort, and choose to sort by Cost, Name, or ID.

CROSS-REFERENCE

See "Grouping Tasks" earlier in this chapter for more information about grouping prior to sorting.

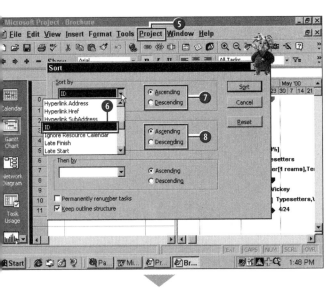

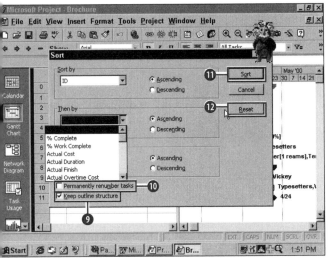

determines ascending or descending order for sub-groups. Sorting under grouping conditions is a secondary function as it next sorts the tasks or resources within each group using the sort criteria and order you choose. For example, grouping a task list by resource group assigned and then sorting by finish or deadline date is a popular combination.

Sorting Forms

Forms present one resource or task at a time for modification or review. Applying sort criteria and order to forms determines the order in which each form displays. For example, if you sort Resource Forms alphabetically, the resource forms cycle through in alphabetical order as you click the Previous and Next buttons found on each form.

TAKE NOTE

▶ **CAUTIONS WHEN SORTING**

When defining a sort, you can choose to have the tasks or resources permanently renumbered (ID number). Although you can undo a sort if you change your mind quickly enough, it is recommended that you save a copy of the project file if choosing to permanently renumber. If you do not permanently renumber, you can always go back to the original list by sorting by ID number.

For task lists, the Keep Outline Structure checkbox keeps all tasks under their respective summary tasks during the sort. If you clear this box in the sort definition, tasks sort without regard to their outline position.

---

5 For a user-defined task sort definition, choose a task view or form and choose Project ⇨ Sort ⇨ Sort by.

6 In the primary sort definition box, choose the sort criteria.

7 Choose Ascending or Descending order.

8 Repeat for second- and third-level sorts ("tie-breakers" if two items from a primary sort have the same data).

9 Check or uncheck the Keep outline structure checkbox

10 Check or uncheck the box to Permanently renumber tasks.

11 Click the Sort button to sort now.

12 Click the Reset button to return to the default sort by ID number.

FIND IT ONLINE

For access to the latest developments and experts in project management, see **http://www.pmblvd.com/**.

Personal Workbook

Q&A

1 What is the purpose of grouping?

_____

_____

_____

2 How do you make custom group definitions available to other projects?

_____

_____

_____

3 What are the five steps needed to group tasks using a custom field?

_____

_____

_____

4 What is a *Display only* filter?

_____

_____

_____

5 What is a *Highlight* filter?

_____

_____

_____

_____

6 What is an *Interactive* filter?

_____

_____

_____

7 What are four views that cannot be sorted?

_____

_____

_____

8 How do you return to an "unfiltered" view?

_____

_____

_____

ANSWERS: PAGE 323

EXTRA PRACTICE

1. Practice grouping tasks by finish date.

2. Create a custom group to group by finish date and then critical.

3. Use a display only filter for critical tasks.

4. Use a material resource Highlight filter to locate those resources on a Resource Sheet.

5. Sort your resource list alphabetically.

6. Return your resource list back to the default sort order, using ID numbers.

REAL-WORLD APPLICATIONS

✔ You report project data to different stakeholders so you group data to make the reports more meaningful.

✔ To produce individual team member reports with assignments you use an interactive filter.

✔ To create an alphabetized list of resources for ease in selecting from a pick-list, you sort by name.

✔ You use the Organizer to share custom group definitions with other project managers in your group.

Visual Quiz

How do you complete this dialog box to group by resource group (primary) and then by standard pay rate?

_____

_____

_____

_____

_____

_____

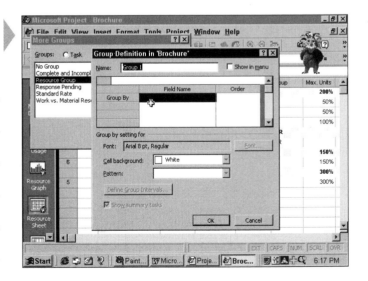

CHAPTER 11

MASTER THESE SKILLS

Reviewing the Project Plan

As the last chapter in Part III, "Creating a Project Plan," it is appropriate that we spend some time reviewing the data entered and finalizing the plan. In this chapter you are asked to analyze the plan you have created using the "realism yardstick." Remember, this may be your final opportunity to fine-tune the plan before it is submitted for approval.

Many of the ideas in this chapter are covered in previous data entry chapters but it's important to review them once again. In addition, it is often difficult to switch from data entry mode to analysis mode without some guidance about where to look for flags and warnings. It is also difficult to remember which pieces of data are strung together and how changing one piece affects numerous other pieces. It is the goal of this chapter to show you some schedule and resource/cost analysis tools available in Project 2000.

It is possible that you use a project coordinator to gather and enter data in Project 2000. At this point in planning, however, the project manager can greatly benefit from knowing enough about how Project 2000 works to perform the analysis firsthand. There is a wealth of information stored in your project database, and it is difficult to analyze project information using only static reports and charts.

In this chapter, you review the schedule, resource allocations, and costs to make sure they don't exceed project constraints. You also practice using the Calendar view as a means of communicating task assignments. After viewing the calendar you will practice customizing various calendar components.

On the resource management side, you will practice identifying overallocated resources as well as resolving the conflicts both manually and automatically, using automatic resource leveling. You will also explore the Resource Management toolbar as a convenient means of accessing often used resource features.

Reviewing the Schedule

At this point in creating a plan, it is probably a good idea to step back and review the information you have supplied Project 2000. In this task, you'll find some suggestions or tips for reviewing your schedule.

Gantt Chart

Consider alternating between the outline structure, a WBS structure, and grouping as a means of viewing your schedule from different perspectives. For example, the WBS structure could show project deliverable phases while the grouping shows critical and noncritical tasks.

Indicators Column

Remember to check the Indicators column for warnings or task constraint dates. Add the Indicators column to any table for the Gantt Chart.

Schedule Table

Apply the Schedule table to the Gantt Chart for effective review of task dates. This table shows important critical path information such as start and finish dates for each task and "late start" and "late finish" of each task. This table also includes columns for Free Slack and Total Slack. Review "Understanding the Critical Path" in Chapter 7 for definitions of these scheduling terms.

GanttChartWizard

Using the GanttChartWizard to custom format the Gantt Chart is useful during schedule review. Using the wizard, you can display critical tasks in a different color, display total slack, and display finish dates next to each task bar easily.

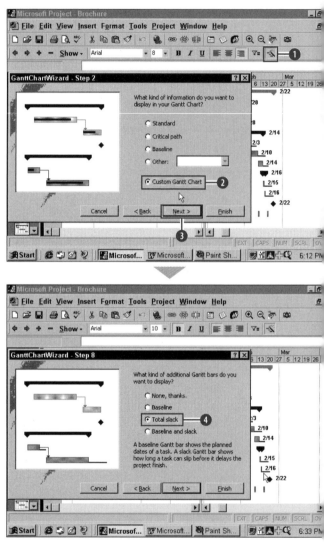

❶ To display Total Slack lines on a Gantt Chart, click the GanttChartWizard button.

❷ On Step 2 of the Wizard, click the radio button for Custom Gantt Chart.

❸ Click the Next button until you reach Step 8, making decisions along the way if you like.

❹ On Step 8, click the radio button to display Total slack.

❺ Notice the slack lines on this Gantt Chart.

CROSS-REFERENCE

See "Setting Dependency Links" in Chapter 6 for descriptions of the types of links available.

Network Diagram

Use the Network Diagram to double-check the logical flow of work through the project. Reviewing the schedule using this diagram provides the opportunity to challenge the types of dependency relationships set in this project. Pay careful attention to those points in the diagram where several "paths" converge. These convergence points represent areas of increased risk as a delay in any converging path often delays important milestones or approvals affecting the other paths.

Filters

Use filters to either highlight or display valuable schedule information. Consider using these filters during schedule review to show milestones, critical tasks, tasks with estimated durations (these also represent more risk in scheduling), tasks with deadlines, tasks with a task calendar assigned, and tasks with fixed dates.

TAKE NOTE

▶ **SPLIT WINDOWS**

Since many pieces of information contribute to the final scheduling of tasks, it is often helpful to display as much of that information on the screen as possible. One way to do this is to split the screen and show, for example, a Gantt Chart on the top pane and the Task Form on the bottom pane. To change the information displayed on the Task Form either right-click anywhere in the form and choose Predecessors and Successors from the shortcut menu or activate the Task Form view and choose Format ⇨ Details and choose Predecessors and Successors from the cascading menu.

⑥ To display the Schedule table, choose View ⇨ Table ⇨ Schedule.

⑦ Compare the Finish dates to the Late Finish dates.

⑧ Locate the amount of Total Slack per task.

⑨ Notice the Constraint Indicator.

⑩ To view many pieces of scheduling data at once, choose Window ⇨ Split.

⑪ Display a Gantt Chart in the top pane and a Task Form in the bottom pane.

⑫ Right-click anywhere in the bottom pane to show a shortcut menu.

⑬ Choose Predecessors & Successors from the shortcut menu.

FIND IT ONLINE

For information about the art of influencing, see
http://www.trg_mcber@haygroup.com.

Reviewing Resource Allocations and Costs

As in the last task, when finalizing your project plan, also review the planned resource assignments and costs. A number of standard views are very useful for this task.

Task Usage View

As you saw in Chapter 9, the Task Usage view is tremendously helpful for seeing each task listed with assigned resources indented beneath. Right-clicking anywhere on the distribution side of this view (the right-hand side) displays a shortcut menu. You can select which data to display per resource per task. More than one piece of data may be shown per resource. For example, while reviewing resource and cost assignments, consider choosing Cost and Work.

Resource Usage View

The Resource Usage view is arranged opposite the way the Task Usage view is arranged but just as useful. You can right-click anywhere on the distribution side in this view to access a shortcut menu. Useful items to show include Work, Cost, and Remaining Availability. Remaining Availability shows you how efficiently you have scheduled your resources.

Resource Allocation View

The Resource Allocation view is a combination of a Resource Usage view on the top pane and a Leveling Gantt View on the bottom pane. This view is helpful because you not only see hours, costs, and available hours for each task a resource is assigned to but you also see the timing of the task.

CROSS-REFERENCE

For information about applying standard views, see "Changing Standard Views" in Chapter 2.

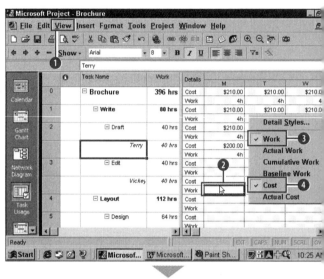

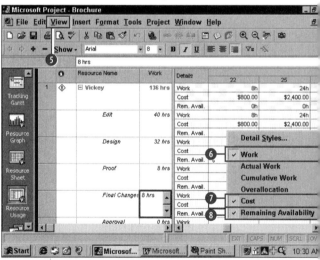

1 To apply the Task Usage view, click the Task Usage button or select View ⇨ Task Usage.

2 Right-click anywhere on the distribution side.

3 Select Work from the shortcut menu.

4 Right-click again and choose Cost as an added display item from the shortcut menu.

5 To select the Resource Usag view, click the Resource Usage button or select View ⇨ Resource Usage.

6 Right-click on the distributic side and choose Work from the shortcut menu.

7 Right-click again and choos Cost from the shortcut men

8 Right-click again and choos Remaining Availability.

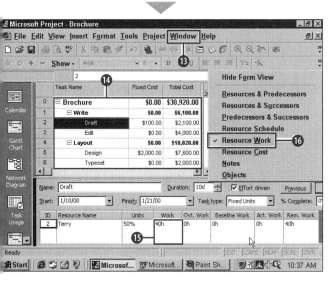

Filters

Filters help you focus on items in the project plan that need attention. For example, use the interactive task filter, Cost Greater Than..., to highlight or display your "big ticket" or high-cost tasks. If you use the Workgroup features covered in Chapter 15, use resource filters to check for either confirmed or unconfirmed assignments. One common problem in working on cross-functional teams is lack of clarity about who is doing what when. Checking for unconfirmed assignments is a good way to find those assignments that are still unclear or not yet agreed to.

Resource Form

Using the Previous and Next buttons on the Resource Form, you can cycle through your resources one by one to gather a large amount of information. This form contains information about individual resource cost rates, maximum units, base calendar, group, and code. At the bottom of this form is a listing of all the task assignments this resource has in all currently open projects by project name, task name, task ID, and start and finish of the assignment.

> ### TAKE NOTE
>
> #### USING A SPLIT WINDOW TO REVIEW ALLOCATIONS AND COSTS
>
> Once again, split windows offer an excellent view into the costs and resource needs of your project. A combination that offers many possibilities is a Gantt Chart in the top pane showing either the Cost or Work table with a Task Form in the bottom pane showing either Resource Schedule, Resource Work, or Resource Cost details.

---

⑨ To access the Resource Form, select View ➪ More Views, choose Resource Form, click Apply.

⑩ For different display information, right-click anywhere on the form and choose a different table.

⑪ Edit resource assignment information from this form.

⑫ Click Previous or Next to move to another resource.

⑬ To see many pieces of resource information at once, choose Window ➪ Split.

⑭ Apply a Gantt Chart displaying a Cost table in the top pane.

⑮ Apply a Task Form in the bottom pane.

⑯ Right-click in the bottom pane and select either Resource Cost, Resource Schedule, or Resource Work.

> ### FIND IT ONLINE
>
> If you are looking for project management employees, see **http://jetechdata.o8.net/project_costing.html**.

171

Using the Calendar View

The Calendar view is a popular means of printing or displaying task assignments for use by members of the project team. Because of its similarity to non-software printed calendars, its format is readily understood. In this task, you'll become familiar with the Calendar view by learning formatting techniques and how to navigate around the calendar.

The default Calendar view shows a month and year title at the top and displays four weeks of time. Task bars "float" on top of the calendar from the start to the finish of each task. Summary tasks may also display. The Calendar view may display in a split window but only in the top pane.

Although you can insert, delete, and edit tasks as well as set dependency links in the Calendar view, I don't recommend that you do so except, perhaps, with small, rather simple projects. Even as a veteran user of Project, I still accidentally make changes in the Calendar view that I don't intend. For example, if you insert a task at a specific date or drag the task into position on this view, a constraint is set for that task. This may go unnoticed and cause scheduling errors later.

However, using the Task Information dialog box while in the Calendar view seems to be a safe way to change task information. Double-clicking the name of a task in the Calendar view displays the Task Information dialog box for that task. Because you use this form to make changes and not the Calendar view itself, the results are the same as if you entered the information on a Gantt Chart.

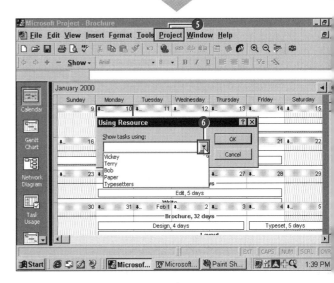

CROSS-REFERENCE

See "Formatting the Calendar View" later in this chapter for customizing the Calendar appearance.

172

① *For Calendar view, click the Calendar button or choose View ➪ Calendar.*

② *Double-click overflow indicator arrow for all tasks occurring on that date.*

③ *Use the title arrows to move forward and back one month at a time.*

④ *Use the scroll bar and buttons to "advance" the calendar.*

⑤ *To personalize a calendar fo each resource's tasks, choose Project ➪ Filtered for ➪ Usin Resource.*

⑥ *Using the drop-down list, select the desired resource.*

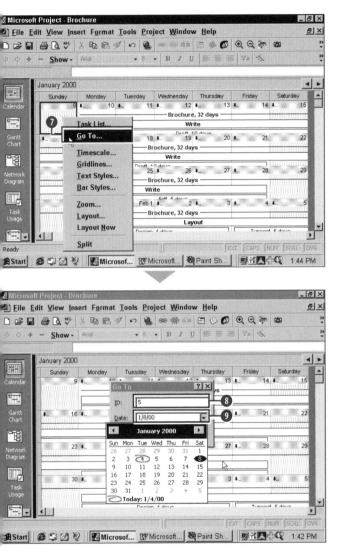

Since many of my project team members are unfamiliar with Gantt Charts, this view is a perfect alternative, especially when filters are applied to create personal calendars for each member of the team. Use the interactive Resource Group filter to show tasks belonging to a specific department. Or, use another interactive filter, Using Resources, to filter for each specific resource by name.

Many options are available for navigating around the calendar. Right and left pointing arrows at the top of the Calendar move the calendar forward or backward one month. Scroll buttons and bars allow you to move horizontally through days of the week or vertically through weeks of the month. Use Alt+Home and Alt+End to jump from the beginning to the end of the project. Page Up and Page Down move you quickly through the calendar in two-week intervals.

TAKE NOTE

USING THE GO TO COMMAND

The Go To command is also available in the Calendar view so that you can quickly locate a task by ID or name. Select Edit ⇨ Go To from the menu or right-click in the Calendar view and choose Go To from the shortcut menu.

⑦ To quickly locate a task or time period, right-click any blank section of the Calendar and choose Go To from the shortcut menu or select Edit ⇨ Go To.

⑧ In the Go To dialog box, enter the ID number of the task you are looking for.

⑨ Or, select a date to locate a specific time period.

FIND IT ONLINE

For free Web-based team collaboration product information, see **http://www.eproject.com/**.

Formatting the Calendar View

Formatting options abound in the Calendar view. The most basic change is to click the Zoom In and Zoom Out buttons on the formatting toolbar to change the number of weeks that show. You can also grab the lines that define boxes and drag the mouse pointer to change the size.

Right-clicking anywhere on the calendar displays a shortcut menu containing many formatting options, or you can locate these options from the Format menu.

To format the timescale, use the Timescale dialog box, which contains three tabs: Week Headings, Date Boxes, and Date Shading. The Week Headings tab presents choices for various calendar component titles: whether to use a 5- or 7-day week and whether or not to show small versions of last month's and next month's calendars in the upper left-hand corner of the calendar.

Use the Date Boxes dialog box to design the content of the date boxes. For example, by default the Overflow Indicator shows in the upper left-hand corner of the box with the date in the upper right. The overflow indicator shows if there are more tasks scheduled for that date than can fit on the calendar. Double-clicking on the Indicator displays a list of all tasks occurring on that date.

The third tab, Date Shading, establishes the calendar to use for determining working time and how to display calendar exceptions like Resource Calendar Nonworking Days.

Formatting gridlines sets the look of all title and box lines in the Calendar, whereas formatting text styles sets the font, font style, size, and color selections.

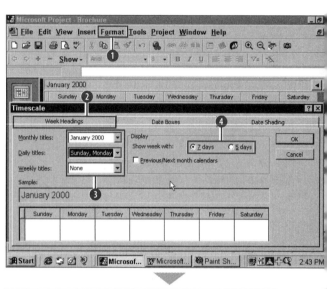

1. To format the Calendar timescale, right-click in a blank area of the Calendar and choose Timescale from the shortcut menu, or choose Format ⮕ Timescale.

2. Choose the Week Headings tab.

3. Select title formats.

4. Click either radio button to display a 5- or 7-day week.

5. Select the Date Boxes tab.

6. Choose up to four items to display in the task box corners.

▶ Notice the Overflow indicator.

▶ Notice the Date display.

CROSS-REFERENCE

See "Scheduling Potpourri" in Chapter 6 for information about splitting tasks.

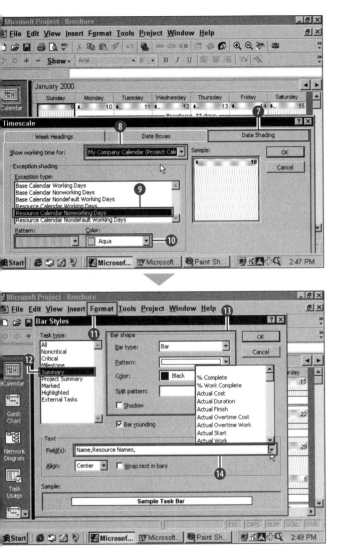

Formatting bar styles enables you to customize the bar appearance on the Calendar by task type. Examples of task types include Critical, Noncritical, Milestone, and Summary. For each type, you select the look of the bar from a drop-down list. Bar Style choices also include the pattern and color of each bar or line and what text appears in the task box. Select the text by choosing which fields to show. Separate multiple field choices with commas. For example, to show the task name, duration, and resources assigned, enter **Name,Duration,Resource Names**.

When you choose Format ⇨ Layout, the Layout dialog box appears. Use this box to determine whether tasks display according to the current sort order, ID number by default, or whether Project 2000 should try to fit as many tasks as possible into the allotted space without regard to sort order. A checkbox in this dialog box provides options for how to handle the look of split tasks. By default, the period of time between task parts in a split task displays with dotted lines.

TAKE NOTE

SETTING THE CALENDAR VIEW START DAY

Use the Calendar tab of the Options dialog box to determine the first day of the week for the Calendar view. Make this selection in the Week Starts On field.

---

⑦ Click the Date Shading tab.

⑧ Choose a calendar on which to base working and nonworking time displays.

⑨ Choose an Exception type.

⑩ Choose a pattern and color for the exception.

⑪ To format bar styles, choose Format ⇨ Bar Styles, or right-click in a blank area of the Calendar view and select Bar Styles from the shortcut menu.

⑫ Choose a task type to format.

⑬ Select Bar shape information.

⑭ Choose fields to display in the boxes.

FIND IT ONLINE

For Project 2000 product support, see **http:// officeupdate.microsoft.com/welcome/project.htm.**

Identifying Resource Overallocation Conflicts

During project plan review it is a good idea to make sure your resource assignments are realistic. It is better to know up front that resources will not be available as planned rather than be surprised later when deadlines are missed. In this task, you'll explore the reasons behind resource overallocation conflicts and several techniques for identifying which resources are in conflict.

A resource overallocation conflict arises when the sum of the units or hours assigned to a resource or resource group is greater than the maximum number of hours or units available during that time period. For example, let's say that you enter 100% in the Maximum Units field for Vickey on the Resource Sheet. After assigning Vickey to numerous simultaneous tasks, her workload totals 150% for the third week of the project. This represents a resource conflict situation. The same is true for resource groups. If you have three part-time typesetters (total maximum availability of 150%) and you schedule them for full-time work (300%) for two weeks, this also represents a resource conflict situation.

You can specify at what level of conflict Project 2000 raises the conflict "flag." For example, suppose you have assigned a resource to work on three tasks on the same day, each of two-hour duration. But, suppose all three tasks are scheduled from 8:00 a.m. until 10:00 a.m. If you ask Project to monitor the schedule hour by hour, it raises the conflict flag. If, however, you want to monitor daily allocations and allow individual team members to manage their time during the day, then choose daily

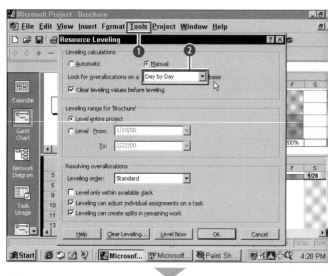

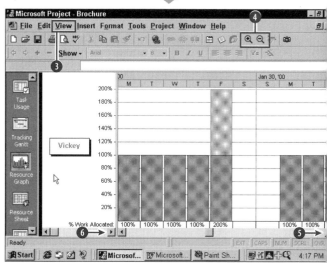

① To set the resource allocation monitoring and red flag level, choose Tools ⇨ Resource Leveling.

② In the Resource Leveling dialog box, select a monitoring basis from the drop-down list.

③ To view a Resource Graph, click the Resource Graph button or choose View ⇨ Resource Graph.

④ Use Zoom In and Zoom Out to adjust the timescale to match your monitoring precision level.

⑤ Use this scroll bar to view different time periods.

⑥ Use this scroll bar to view a different resource.

CROSS-REFERENCE

See "Using the Resource Usage View" in Chapter 9 for more information about applying this view.

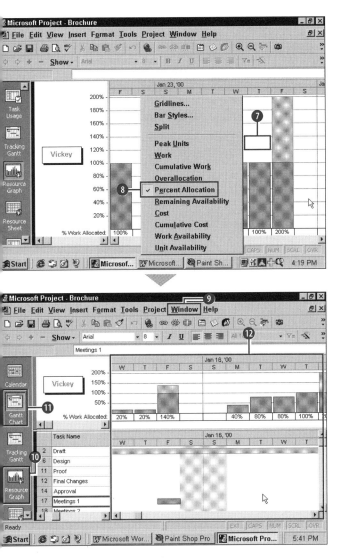

monitoring. It is also common for the project manager to monitor on a weekly basis with individual resources monitoring their own schedules daily. The monitoring precision is set in the Resource Leveling dialog box.

The four best views to spot overallocation conflicts are the Resource Sheet, Resource Usage, Resource Allocation, and Resource Graph. The names of overallocated resources appear in red on all these views.

In addition, using these views in combination with filters not only helps you identify which resources are overallocated but when and why.

TAKE NOTE

▶ USING THE RESOURCE GRAPH

The Resource Graph is a histogram (bar chart) view that is a graphical display of resource allocation information. You can Zoom In and Zoom Out in this view to match your monitoring precision. Use the scrollable time periods to locate the "when" of overallocations. Scroll buttons and arrows allow you to look at graphs for different resources. Using this view in combination with a Gantt Chart helps you locate the "why" of the overallocations. Right-clicking on the left-hand side of the graph displays a shortcut menu listing different bar chart data display choices. The most useful ones for identifying resource scheduling problems include Work, Percent Allocation, and Overallocation.

⑦ To change display data on the Resource Graph, right-click anywhere on the right-hand side of the graph.

⑧ Select data to display in histogram (graph) format.

⑨ For reviewing resource allocations, choose Window ⇨ Split.

⑩ Activate the top pane and click Resource Graph.

⑪ Activate the bottom pane and click Gantt Chart.

⑫ Use the Resource Graph to locate the details of the overallocation; use the Gantt Chart to locate the conflicting task assignments.

FIND IT ONLINE

For enterprise-wide project management software solutions see **http://www.microframe.com**.

Exploring the Resource Management Toolbar

In your efforts to review and finalize the project plan, you have accessed numerous views, forms, and dialog boxes. It might prove more efficient (and easier) to use the Resource Management toolbar as a means of accessing some of the more commonly used means of managing resources.

To display the Resource Management toolbar, choose View ⇨ Toolbars ⇨ Resource Management. This toolbar displays in addition to the default standard and formatting toolbars. Notice that the Resource Management toolbar is divided into seven sections, with each section being defined by a toolbar divider line:

▶ Section 1 shows buttons for two popular resource views, the Resource Allocation View and the Task Entry view, both familiar to us already. The Resource Allocation view is a combination view of the Resource Usage view and the Leveling Gantt view. The Task Entry view is also a combination view showing a Gantt Chart and a Task Form.

▶ Section 2 consists of one button, the Go To Next Overallocation button. Clicking this button locates overallocations for you automatically. To find all overallocations, scroll to the beginning of the project timescale or task list before clicking the button. If you display a Resource Graph, and click the Go To Next Overallocation, the timescale automatically scrolls to the beginning of the next time period that has an overallocation. Clicking the button again moves the timescale to the subsequent period of overallocation. However, using this button with a Gantt Chart simply scrolls to the first task that is involved in an overallocation.

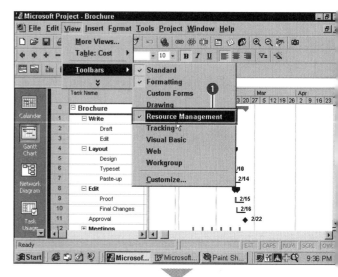

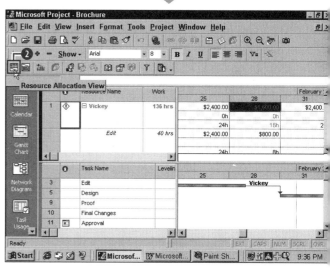

1 To display the resource Management toolbar, choose View ⇨ Toolbars ⇨ Resource Management.

2 Click this button to display the Resource Allocation view

CROSS-REFERENCE

See Chapter 17 for more on displaying additional buttons on the Resource Management toolbar.

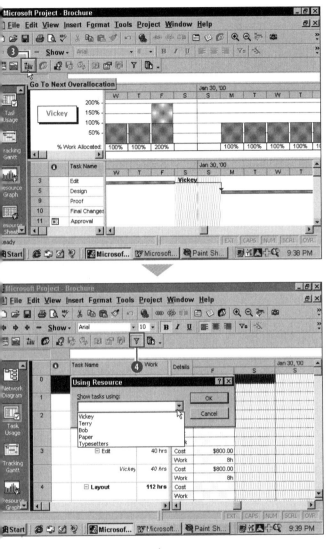

▶ Section 3 also contains only one button, the Assign Resources button. This is the same button as shown on the Standard toolbar and clicking it displays the Assign Resources dialog box.

▶ Section 4 contains three buttons for sharing resources across projects using a resource pool. You'll learn more about these techniques in Chapter 16, "Working with Multiple Projects."

▶ Section 5 contains buttons for quickly locating your Web Address Book and other information-sharing features. You'll learn more about these features in Chapter 15, "Using Microsoft Project 2000 in Workgroups."

▶ Section 6 contains one button, the Using Resource Filter button. This interactive filter lets you highlight or display tasks assigned to a specific resource.

▶ Section 7 contains a Leveling Help button that answers some question about resource leveling or attempting to flatten out the resource allocation peaks and valleys.

❸ *Click here to locate the next resource overallocation conflict.*

❹ *Click here to use the interactive Using Resource filter.*

TAKE NOTE

▶ **RESOLVING RESOURCE CONFLICTS**

It is not mandatory to resolve resource allocations before finalizing project plans. Many project managers prefer to wait until the actual conflict time approaches to see if the schedule or resource availability changes before making any decisions. Other project managers prefer to resolve major resource conflicts before the project plan is submitted for approval.

FIND IT ONLINE

For a companion resource planner for MS Project, see **www.projectmanagement.com/prp1.htm.**

179

Resolving Resource Conflicts

Project managers use numerous strategies to resolve resource overallocation conflicts. You'll review several in this task.

One strategy is to increase the availability of the resource to cover the time period of the overallocation. Perhaps the resource can be available 100 percent instead of 50 percent, or perhaps the resource is willing to work extra hours and not bill overtime rates. Remember to change the maximum units and resource availability entries as well as add extra work time to the resource's calendar for this option.

Another option is to assign overtime hours for the overallocated resource so that the work that exceeds the availability can be done during overtime hours. Again, remember to adjust the resource calendar to make more hours (that is, evenings or weekends) available. The Task Entry view with the Resource Work details table applied offers a convenient way to make these changes.

In some cases it is acceptable to hire additional resources to handle some of the overallocated workload. If this is the case, don't forget to define them on the Resource Sheet.

Sometimes the choice is made to contract out part of the work that your team can't handle. The easiest approach with contractors is to assign them to tasks at 0 percent and enter the contract cost for their services as a fixed cost amount. It is usually helpful to document this in the task notes.

The Assign Resources dialog box offers a convenient way to substitute one resource for another. Choose the task(s) for the substitution, and click the Replace button in the Assign Resources dialog box. A subsequent box appears asking you to select a substitute resource.

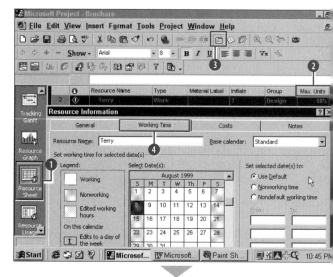

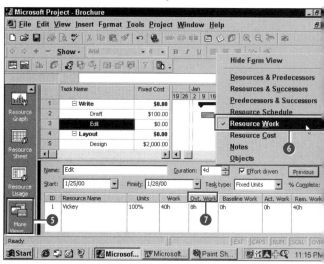

① To change resource availability information, click the Resource Sheet button.

② Select a resource; increase the maximum units available.

③ Click the Resource Information button; change the resource Availability on the General tab.

④ Click the Working Time tab and add hours to the resource calendar.

⑤ To schedule overtime, click More Views and select the Task Entry view.

⑥ Right-click in the bottom pane and select Resource Work.

⑦ Enter the assigned amount of overtime per resource.

CROSS-REFERENCE

See Chapter 9 for more information about assigning, removing, and replacing resources.

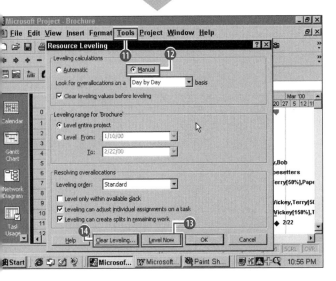

You can delay the start of a resource assignment on a task until the resource has available time. Complete this change in the Task Entry view with the Resource Schedule detail table applied.

You can also contour a resource assignment to a workload other than flat if that helps eliminate the problem (Assignment Information dialog box) or delay the start of a task using the Resource Allocation view. You might also consider reducing the scope or quality of the project by changing the requirements or specifications or eliminating tasks.

TAKE NOTE

USING AUTOMATIC RESOURCE LEVELING

As the name implies, Project 2000 can attempt to resolve resource conflicts for you. Unfortunately, it doesn't use an optimization algorithm to create the best schedule with the resources you have. Instead it uses a simple delay algorithm to delay tasks until resources are available. What this means in reality is that you can almost always generate better alternatives and decisions about resource scheduling than Project. As a warning, keep Resource Leveling set to manual. Otherwise, Project attempts to flatten out resource overallocation problems as they occur, often shifting task scheduling without your knowledge or consent.

---

8 To delay the start of a task, select View ⟶ More Views, select Leveling Gantt and click Apply.

9 In the Leveling Delay column, enter the amount of the delay in elapsed days (edays) for the selected task.

10 Locate the delay line on the task bar.

11 To use automatic resource leveling, choose Tools ⟶ Resource Leveling.

12 Set calculations to Manual.

13 Accept the other defaults and click Level Now.

14 To return to an unleveled state, choose Tools ⟶ Resource Leveling and click Clear Leveling.

FIND IT ONLINE

For multiproject resource management software, see http://www.pmsolutionsinc.com/index.htm.

Personal Workbook

Q&A

1 How do you jump from the beginning to the end of the project in the Calendar view?

_____

_____

_____

2 How do you access the Go To command in a Calendar view?

_____

_____

_____

3 What is an *overflow indicator* on a Calendar view?

_____

_____

_____

4 What are three techniques for identifying resource overallocation conflicts?

_____

_____

_____

5 Name three buttons found on the Resource Management toolbar.

_____

_____

_____

6 What are two manual techniques for resolving resource conflicts?

_____

_____

_____

7 What is the drawback to using automatic resource leveling?

_____

_____

_____

8 Where do you establish the first day of the week as shown on the Calendar view?

_____

_____

_____

ANSWERS: PAGE 324

EXTRA PRACTICE

1. Use a filter to identify resource overallocations in your schedule.

2. Modify the Bar Styles for your Calendar view.

3. Modify a resource calendar to add Saturdays as a workday.

4. Display the Resource Management toolbar and use it to access the Using Resource filter.

5. Substitute one resource for another on a task assignment.

6. Try resource leveling on a practice project and then clear the leveling calculations.

REAL-WORLD APPLICATIONS

✔ You need to notify your resources about task assignments so you create individual calendars for each.

✔ You have a number of part-time resources assigned to your project so you filter for overallocated resources.

✔ As a method of resolving a resource conflict you replace one resource with another.

✔ You print resource graphs as a visual way to demonstrate the workloads of your team members.

Visual Quiz

How do you display slack lines on your task bars?

_____

_____

_____

_____

_____

_____

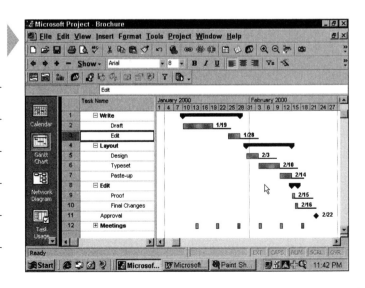

Contents of 'Desktop'

Name

My Computer

Network Neigh

Internet Explore

Microsoft Outlook

Recycle Bin

My Briefcase

3252-9

3259-6

3261-8

3262-6

3281-2

3286-3

DE Phone List

Device Manager

In

Iomega Tools

PART

IV

Printing and Publishing the Plan

Now that you have created a project plan, it is time to concentrate on project communications. Team members, sponsors, customers, and other stakeholders are just a few of the people who require regular "feedings" of project information. Project communications include initial schedule and assignment information as well as ongoing updates of project status, accomplishments, and issues.

Part IV covers techniques for communicating through printed reports and charts as well as through intranet and Internet channels.

Specifically, you'll learn how to use the spell checker for document accuracy, and you'll discover various formatting options for reports and views. Additionally, you can exercise your creative talents by including drawings and objects in your reports. You will also practice printing standard views and reports and creating your own custom reports.

Finally, you'll be able to create a Web page for use on your company's intranet or over the World Wide Web. On this Web page, you can make project data available to a wide range of people, thereby simplifying the distribution of project information.

CHAPTER 12

MASTER THESE SKILLS

- ▶ Using the Spell Checker
- ▶ Exploring Formatting Options
- ▶ Using the GanttChartWizard
- ▶ Formatting Bar Styles
- ▶ Inserting Drawings and Objects
- ▶ Preparing to Print Views
- ▶ Using Setup Commands
- ▶ Designing Margins, Borders, Headers, Footers, and Legends
- ▶ Using Print Preview and Print
- ▶ Viewing, Printing, and Modifying Standard Reports
- ▶ Creating Custom Reports

Printing Views and Reports

Communication is a large part of any project manager's job. It is estimated that an effective project manager spends 90 percent or more of his/her time communicating project information. Status reporting, issue resolution, planning, problem solving, listening, negotiating, defining the scope, gaining commitment, assigning tasks are all examples of project communication.

To use your project database to its full potential, extracting and printing meaningful charts and reports must be part of your repertoire of techniques.

Fortunately, you have already practiced a number of techniques that help create professional, memorable reports. Options like adjusting the timescale, changing views and tables, filtering, sorting, outlining, and grouping all assist in effective communication.

Reporting options seem the easiest to understand if you consider the communication from the holistic or "big picture" down to the details. For example, when creating a report, consider the audience and their reporting needs first. Are you creating a management report with summary information or a team member level report with task details? Would a graphic chart serve the purpose or is a table of numbers and dates more

appropriate? An understanding of your audience's preferences will help you produce the right report for the occasion. If you don't know the communication preferences of your audience, there's a simple solution. Just ask them!

Next, choose the view or report type that you want as the basis for the communication. Then, choose whether to use outlining, WBS, or Grouping if appropriate with the chosen view, or choose to use a specific table or form details. Techniques like collapsing and expanding the outline, filtering, sorting, and adjusting the timescale all add to the look and functionality of the communication.

In this chapter you will practice preparing and printing both views and reports. You will preview numerous standard reports available in Project 2000 as well as practice modifying these reports and creating new ones. You will also use the spell checker function and several formatting options not previously introduced. I also discuss inserting drawings and objects to liven up your communications, using the GanttChartWizard as an aid in choosing custom format options, and using Page Setup, Print, and Print Preview.

Using the Spell Checker

Although good spelling is not usually a required skill for the job of project manager, sending out a report with typos can be a source of embarrassment as well as inaccurate data. For these reasons, run Project 2000's spelling checker before printing reports.

Before using the spell checker the first time, set up the options for the spell checker through the Spelling tab in the Options dialog box (Tools ⇨ Options). Twenty-two fields are listed on the tab with "Yes" preselected to ask the spell checker to check the entries in these fields against words in both the standard and custom dictionaries. If you do not want the field data checked, simply change the entry to "No" using the drop-down choices. Typical fields for checking include Task Name, Task Notes, Resource Names, Resource Notes, and Resource Groups.

Checkboxes on the right side of the Spelling tab enable you to turn on or turn off options to Ignore words in UPPERCASE, Ignore words with numbers, Always suggest (spelling alternatives), and Suggest (other words) from the user dictionary. Changing these options affects the way the spell checker operates.

To run the spelling checker after setup, click the Spelling button on the Standard toolbar, choose Tools ⇨ Spelling, or press the F7 function key. If an error is detected, a Spelling dialog box automatically opens. The misspelled or questionable word shows as being not in the dictionary. If you checked the box to "Always suggest" alternatives, then an alternative displays. Choose this word, select another from the suggestions list below,

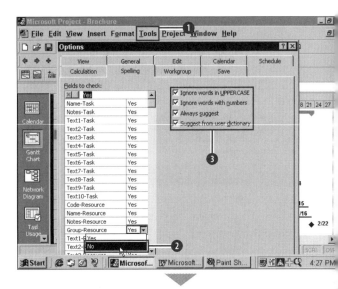

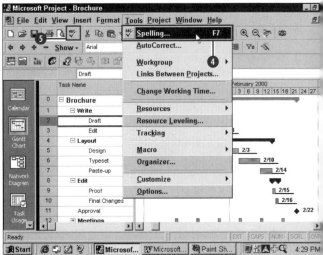

❶ To set up the spell checker, choose Tools ⇨ Options and select the Spelling tab.

❷ If you do not want listed field entries checked, choose No.

❸ Deselect any checkboxes to change the operation of the spell checker.

❹ To run the spell checker, choose Tools ⇨ Spelling.

❺ Or, click the Spelling button.

❻ Or, press the F7 function key.

CROSS-REFERENCE

See "Defining Cost Rate Tables and Notes" in Chapter 8 for more on using the Resource Note field.

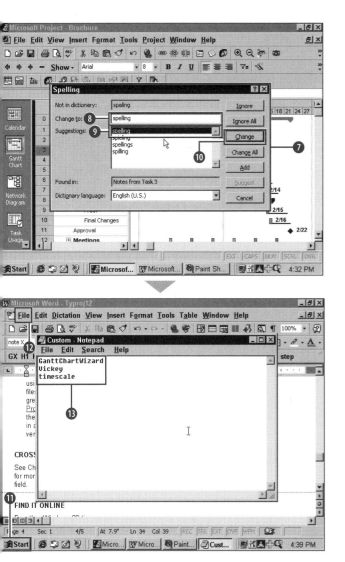

or type in your own entry. The box also lists in what field the questionable word is found and the dictionary language that determines the acceptable word spellings.

You now instruct the spell checker to either ignore the word, change it, or add it to your custom dictionary. More specifically, the choices are to ignore this word, ignore all occurrences of this word in the list or text, change this word, change all occurrences of this word, or add this word to your custom dictionary so that it is not questioned in the future. The Suggest button is only available if you deselected the Always suggest option; otherwise it is not needed.

TAKE NOTE

USING A CUSTOM DICTIONARY

The custom dictionary available during spell check (Custom.dic) is found in the folder Program Files\Microsoft Office\Office. This file can be edited using various text editors such as Notepad for text-only files less than 64K in size, or WordPad for files greater than 64K. Both are found through Programs ⇨ Accessories or Quick View available on the Windows File menu. Make sure your new entries are in alphabetical order before you save the edited version of the dictionary.

---

7 When a spelling error is detected, the Spelling dialog box opens.

8 Type a correction in the "Change to" field.

9 Or, select from the Suggestions list.

10 Click the Change button to correct the spelling.

11 To edit your custom dictionary, choose Start ⇨ Programs ⇨ Accessories ⇨ Notepad.

12 Choose File ⇨ Open and open the custom dictionary (Custom.dic) (Program Files/MS Office/Office/).

13 Add each word on a separate line before saving.

FIND IT ONLINE

For other Windows 98 tips, see **http://www.chami. com/tips/.**

Exploring Formatting Options

In addition to the formatting techniques already covered in this book, this task covers changing table row height, formatting gridlines, and formatting fonts and text styles.

Project 2000 now supports variable row heights for table rows, which means that long task names now word-wrap automatically if you reduce the width of the row and instead increase the row height. To change row height, simply drag the row line between tasks to the height you want. To change multiple rows, select the rows and then drag any one of the row lines in the selection and a uniform height is set for all selected. Any data that is too long to fit in a column width automatically "wraps."

Gridlines are vertical and horizontal lines that appear in the chart portion of any view containing a timescale. Some gridlines serve as task bar reference points like Gantt rows, bar rows, and sheet rows and columns. Other gridlines serve as timescale reference points such as major and minor timescale column lines. The project start and project finish date gridlines serve as project reference points while the current date and status date gridlines show important time reference points. The vertical and horizontal title and page break gridlines help in page preview or before printing.

As you might guess, you would create a very confusing and busy chart if you used all of these gridline choices at once. The idea is to use the gridlines that you find useful. Typically, users display the current (computer) date in

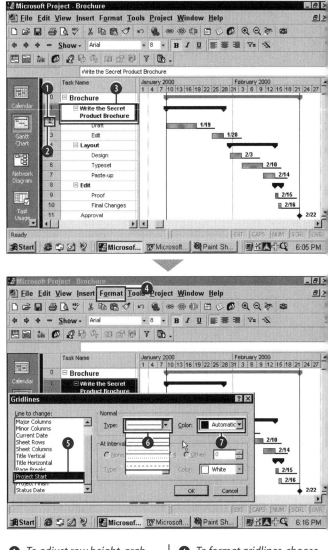

❶ To adjust row height, grab the row divider line.

❷ Drag the double-sided arrow to the desired row height and release.

❸ Notice the automatic word wrap.

❹ To format gridlines, choose Format ➪ Gridlines.

❺ Select the line to change (or show).

❻ Select a line type from the list.

❼ Select a line color.

CROSS-REFERENCE

See Chapter 14 for more information about using a status gridline during progress tracking.

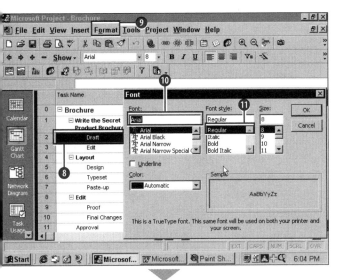

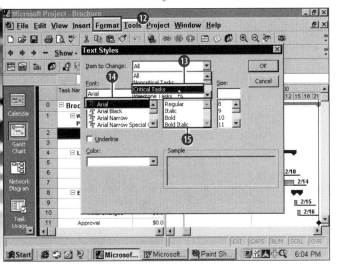

one color and line shape, the project start date in another color and shape, and the status date (tracking progress through date) in a third color and shape. These three lines together give good visual reference points on reports and views. The figures on this page and the next provide steps for formatting gridlines.

Formatting text gives you the opportunity to add style or visual appeal to your reports. To format a single text selection, choose the text and then choose Format ➪ Font. Using the dialog box that opens, select the font (Arial, Courier, or Freestyle, for example), font style (regular, italic, bold), and the size, color, and underline options.

To create text palettes for task types, choose Format ➪ Text Styles. The same selections show here as show for the font formatting above but using this dialog box, you can create a palette based on task category. Categories exist for noncritical tasks, critical tasks, milestone tasks, or all tasks.

TAKE NOTE

USING THE FORMATTING TOOLBAR

Several "easy-change" options display on the default formatting toolbar. Use the drop-down lists to change font and point size for selected text. Three font style buttons are available: bold, italic, and underline. You can also choose the alignment — center, left, or right — of selected text.

---

⑧ Select the text to be formatted.

⑨ Choose Format ➪ Font.

⑩ Select a Font.

⑪ Select a Font style.

⑫ To format text styles by task category, choose Format ➪ Text Styles.

⑬ Choose an item to change from the drop-down list.

⑭ Choose a Font.

⑮ Select a Font style.

FIND IT ONLINE

Find additional fonts at
http://www.fontsnthings.com/.

Using the GanttChartWizard

In previous chapters, you glimpsed the power of the GanttChartWizard for formatting the chart side of a Gantt Chart. In this task, you'll practice using all the powers of the Wizard to customize the chart.

Start the Wizard either by clicking the GanttChartWizard button on the Formatting toolbar or choosing Format ➪ GanttChartWizard. The Format options screens present as numbered steps or pages. The pages are "smart" pages in that each early choice determines which subsequent pages appear.

Your first formatting choice involves basic formatting of bars. Sixteen predefined bar styles are available here plus the option to create a custom chart. Clicking the Standard radio button gives you all bars of the same color with progress lines. Clicking the Critical path radio button displays the critical path in a different color than noncritical tasks and progress lines. If you prefer baseline bars and actual bars with progress lines to appear as two separate bars per task, choose the Baseline radio button. The fourth predefined option is the Other button. Notice the drop-down list available after you click the Other radio button.

The Other list displays thirteen bar style choices for bar color, pattern, and symbol. Watch the preview box in the left of the dialog box to help you make a selection. The choices include four baseline styles, three critical path styles, four standard styles, and two status styles.

After selecting one of the predefined styles, other steps move you through questions about adding information to the left, right, or inside the task bars. You

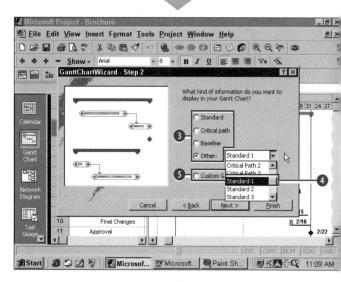

❶ To access the GanttChartWizard, choose Format ➪ GanttChartWizard.

❷ Or, click the GanttChartWizard button on the formatting toolbar.

❸ To use one of the predefined bar style options, click one of these radio buttons.

❹ Or, click the Other button and select a style from the drop-down list.

❺ Choose the Custom Gantt Chart button to design a custom look for task bar styles.

CROSS-REFERENCE

For more information about critical path and slack, see Chapter 7.

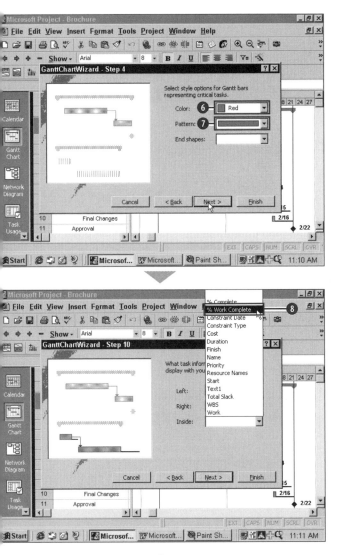

select from resources and dates, resources, dates, none, or custom task information which displays a drop-down list of task fields. Lastly, decide whether or not to show link lines (dependency lines) between tasks on the chart.

If, however, you decide not to use one of the predefined bar styles but instead choose to create a custom Gantt Chart, the path of Project's questions is a bit different. Using the custom choice, you first decide if you want critical and noncritical tasks to display differently. A "Yes, please" response elicits questions asking you to select colors, patterns, and end shapes for critical tasks, noncritical tasks, summary tasks, and milestone tasks. Summary tasks include one extra choice for bar style.

Next, if you're following the path of the custom choice, you're asked about adding any additional bars like a baseline bar, total slack bar, or baseline and slack. Project then asks you to define the look of the bar.

The custom choice concludes with the same questions presented with the predefined choices: "What information do you want to display with bars?" and "Do you want to display link lines?"

TAKE NOTE

▶ **ACCESSING THE GANTTCHARTWIZARD**
You can also access the GanttChartWizard by right-clicking on any blank area of the chart and choosing GanttChartWizard from the shortcut menu.

---

⑥ For the custom choice, select a critical-task bar color.

⑦ Also, select a critical-task bar pattern.

⑧ Also part of custom choices, select field data (using the drop-down list) to place to the right of task bars.

FIND IT ONLINE

For an enterprise solution that accepts Project 2000 information, see **http://www.artemispm.com**.

Formatting Bar Styles

If the GanttChartWizard doesn't offer the right formatting options for your needs, try formatting task bars using the Bar Styles dialog box or format a single task selection.

To format a single task, open the Format Bar dialog box. This box contains two tabs, one for altering the shape of bars and the other for adding bar text. Remember, if you adjust a single bar and you want to revert to the original format, select the task, return to this dialog box, and click the Reset button.

On the Bar Shape tab select the appearance of the (middle) bar and what shapes, if any, appear as start and finish points at either end of the bar. A drop-down list offers a blank space for a "no end point" option.

The Bar Text tab enables you to select, using drop-down lists, field data to place around task bars. Fields can be placed to the left or right of task bars, on top or bottom of bars, or even inside task bars.

To globally alter task bars on the Gantt Chart, open the Bar Styles dialog box. Using this dialog box you can truly customize the appearance of all bars and symbols on the chart. When using this dialog box, remember that the text and bar appearance in the bottom portion of the box display for the name selected in the top portion.

The Name column appears first in the table. Select a name that already displays to edit, or click Insert Row and type your own custom name. Names appearing by default include critical task, slack, milestone, summary, project summary, and split task.

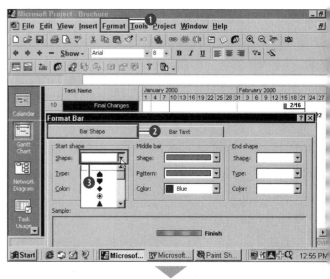

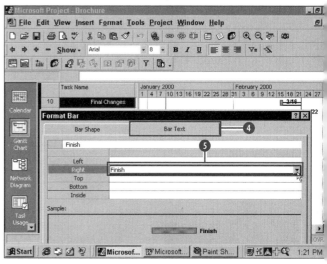

① To format a task, select the task and choose Format ⇨ Bar.

② Click the Bar Shape tab in the Format Bar dialog box.

③ Using the drop-down choices, alter the appearance of the middle bar or start and end shapes.

④ Click the Bar Text tab.

⑤ Select Finish to display the finish date to the right of the task bar.

CROSS-REFERENCE

See "Using Rollup Tasks" in Chapter 7 for more information about this task category.

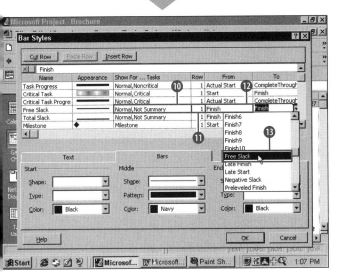

Next, select the appearance of the item listed in the Name column using the selections on the Bars tab, and use the Text tab to enter text around bars. Both tabs function in the same way as described earlier.

Use the "Show For ... Tasks" column to designate the task category to represent with this item. Multiple entries use commas to separate the categories. For example, the Task item definition lists Normal, Noncritical as the category definition.

Next, select a row in which to display the item. There are four rows available for each task and it is typical, for example, to display a baseline (planned schedule) on Row 2 below the Actual (current) bar.

Use the From and To columns to indicate the start and finish points of each item.

TAKE NOTE

CREATING A FREE SLACK LINE

The default slack definition on the Bar Styles table is for Total Slack. Use the steps on this page and the facing page to create a Free Slack line as well.

6 To globally alter task bars, choose Format ⇨ Bar Styles.

7 Click Total Slack under the name field, and click the Insert Row button.

8 Type **Free Slack** as the name in this new row.

9 Click the Appearance field, and select the middle line, solid pattern, navy color.

10 In the "Show For ... Tasks" field, type **Normal, Not Summary**.

11 Keep the row as number 1.

12 Choose Finish in the From field.

13 Choose Free Slack in the To field.

FIND IT ONLINE

For a reporting system that uses Excel workbooks, see
http://www.projectreportingsystem.com/.

Inserting Drawings and Objects

Drawings and objects add variety, interest, explanation, or data into your charts. It is common practice to add objects to schedules submitted as part of a proposal package or use objects on status reports. In this task, you'll see a variety of additional uses for both objects and drawings.

When inserting drawings, a floating Drawing toolbar opens. You can drag the toolbar to the top of the screen and "dock" it with your other toolbars or allow it to "float." Use the buttons that display to create arrows, rectangles, ovals, arcs, polygons, and text boxes. Using the Cycle Fill button, cycle through a color palette to choose a color for your object. The Attach to Task button enables you to anchor the object to a specific task on the Gantt Chart instead of having it attached to a date on the timescale with a relative vertical offset. Attaching to a date allows the object to move with the task during scrolling. The drop-down choices for the Draw button enable you to arrange the object either in front of or behind other screen objects, like task bars.

You can use drawing objects to include explanatory text in a text box for a late task or to circle tasks of note for a report. Arrows also draw attention to a particular task bar or milestone. In addition, drawing a line through a task and recommending that it be deleted from the project makes a strong visual statement.

The capability to insert files as objects provides extensive opportunities to use multimedia to create professional-looking output. Consider, for example, adding a company logo to report headers, or adding a photo of each team member in the resource note field, or placing

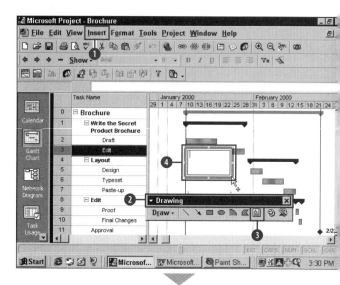

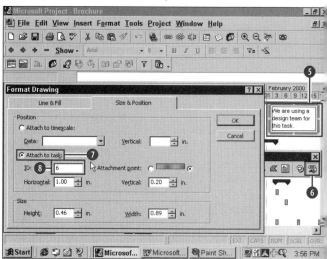

① To insert a drawing object in a Gantt Chart, choose Insert ⇨ Drawing.

② Drag the title of the Drawing toolbar to move it to a new location.

③ To create a text box, click the Text Box button and the pointer becomes a crosshair.

④ Click at one corner of the box and drag to the left or right and down to create the box.

⑤ Click inside the box and type the desired text.

⑥ To anchor this box to a task, click the Attach to Task button.

⑦ Click the Attach to task radio button.

⑧ Enter the ID number of the task to attach the object to.

CROSS-REFERENCE

See "Creating Milestone and Recurring Tasks" in Chapter 5 for more about using milestone tasks.

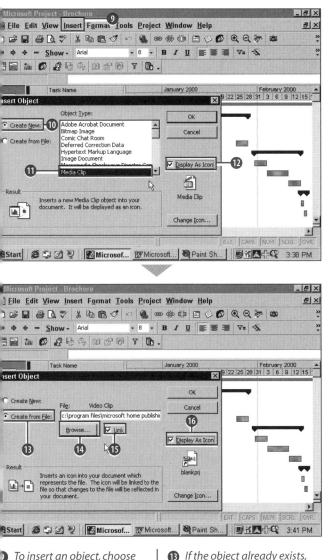

a diagram in a task note, or adding a wave file for an auditory explanation for a cost variance, or including a "flag" graphic to indicate a problem or issue. These are just a few of many such uses.

A variety of file formats work as objects. For example, scanned images, photo files, illustrations, Excel charts and spreadsheets, video clips and wave (audio) files provide many sources. Clipart is another object source and the Microsoft Clip Gallery comes with Project 2000.

Project 2000 accepts graphics in four places: in the task bar section of a Gantt Chart; in resource, task, and assignment notes; in headers, footers, and chart legends; and in resource and task forms.

TAKE NOTE

CREATING SYMMETRICAL OBJECTS

To make perfectly symmetrical objects, such as circles or squares, click the drawing tool and then hold down the Shift key as you drag the mouse to create the object.

GRAPHICS CAUTION

Although it is exciting to fill your notes and charts with objects, be judicious in their use. In addition to appearing "too cute," the object files can be rather large and can slow down calculations in Project 2000.

---

⑨ To insert an object, choose Insert ⇨ Object.

⑩ Click Create New radio button to create a new object.

⑪ Select the Object Type that you will create.

⑫ Click the checkbox to display the object as an icon that is available by double-clicking it.

⑬ If the object already exists, click the Create from File radio button.

⑭ Use the Browse button to locate the file.

⑮ Click the Link box to keep the object refreshed from the source file.

⑯ Click the Display As Icon box to show the object in the chart.

FIND IT ONLINE

For a selection of clipart, see **http://www. desktoppublishing.com/cliplist.html**.

Preparing to Print Views

Although reports are valuable, the most common printing assignment is printing views. As you might expect, the Gantt Chart is probably the most often printed view. The Calendar and Network Diagram are also extremely popular views to print. This task concentrates on preparing to print views while a later task in this chapter covers printing Project 2000 reports.

When preparing to print a view, the first step is to display the desired view onscreen since how views display onscreen is how they look when printed. Choose whatever formatting and table options you prefer as well as sorting and filtering options. Include drawings and objects and, for views that contain a timescale, make sure it shows the major and minor timescales that you want. Unless otherwise indicated, for views that contain tables, only the columns visible onscreen will print. For multipage views, all the left-hand pages print before the right-hand pages. For a Gantt Chart, for example, all the table pages print before the timescale pages print, if the printout is more than one page across.

Adding page breaks may help you adjust the amount of information that displays on a page. To insert a page break on a Gantt Chart, for example, select a task that will be the task immediately below the page break or, in other words, the task that will start the new page. From the menu, select Insert ➪ Page Break. A dashed line appears in the view indicating the manually inserted page break.

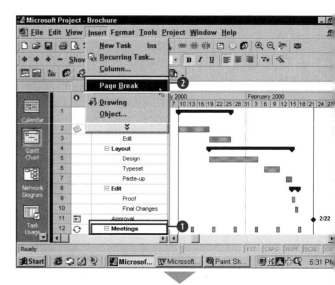

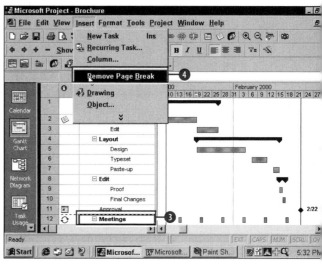

① To set a manual page break, select the task that will start a new page.

② Choose Insert ➪ Page Break.

③ To remove a manually set page break, choose the task that starts a new page.

④ Choose Insert ➪ Remove Page Break.

CROSS-REFERENCE

See "Changing Standard Views" in Chapter 2 for more information about the default views available.

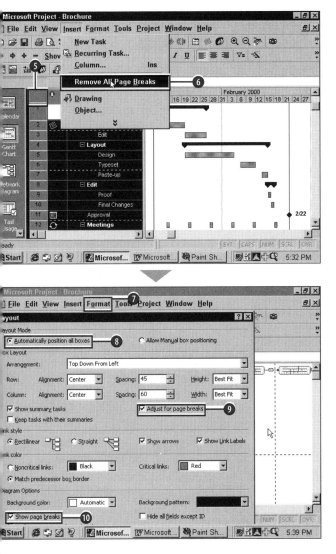

To remove a page break, click the task just below the break and choose Insert ⇨ Remove Page Break. The dashed line disappears. To remove all manually set page breaks at once, click the button in the upper left-hand corner of the pane, which selects all rows and columns. Then, choose Insert ⇨ Remove All Page Breaks.

You cannot set page breaks on the Network Diagram but you can direct Project 2000 to adjust for page breaks so that task nodes are not placed across pages (on a page break). When setting up a Network Diagram, choose Format ⇨ Layout and check for three things. Ensure that the "Automatically position all boxes" radio button is selected so Project 2000 will redraw boxes for you if necessary. Second, check the box to adjust for page breaks so nodes don't appear across pages, and third, check the box under Diagram Options to show page breaks so that you can see them prior to printing.

TAKE NOTE

PRINTING COMBINATION VIEWS

When displaying combination views, only the active view prints. If you print the top pane, the entire view prints. However, remember that the bottom view displays information that relates to the selected resource or task from the top pane. If you print the bottom pane, you will only print selected information.

---

⑤ To remove all manually set page breaks at once, click the Select All Rows and Columns button.

⑥ Choose Insert ⇨ Remove All Page Breaks.

⑦ To adjust for page breaks in a Network Diagram, choose Format ⇨ Layout.

⑧ Click the radio button to Automatically position all boxes.

⑨ Check the box to Adjust for page breaks.

⑩ Check the box to Show page breaks.

FIND IT ONLINE
For more clipart see, **http://www.bizart.com/**.

Using Setup Commands

A typical sequence for printing is to first set up the page to include headers, footers, and page numbers, then preview it to make sure it looks the way you expect, and then print.

The Page Setup dialog box lists options that change the look of printed views and conveniently displays six tabs for easy definition of page elements. The settings in the Page Setup dialog box for any view are saved with the project file. This means that once you choose settings for each view, you only need to make minor adjustments with each print if you choose, rather than undertaking a complete setup with each view change. For example, changing the header for Gantt Charts does not affect the designed header for Resource Usage views.

You can go directly to Print or Print Preview from the Page Setup dialog box. In addition, clicking the Options button located at the bottom of this dialog box enables you to select a paper source and set printer resolution (dots per inch).

The Page tab provides two choices for paper orientation: portrait (vertical) or landscape (horizontal). Keep in mind that the orientation you choose here overrides the orientation set in the Print dialog box (Properties button) at the printer level. However, the orientation set through the Page tab automatically updates the same choice in the Options dialog box and vice versa. Most of the views look best when printed in landscape mode. However, the format of many of the predefined reports is best suited for portrait orientation.

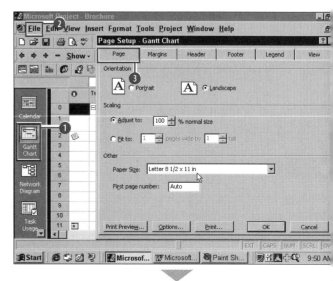

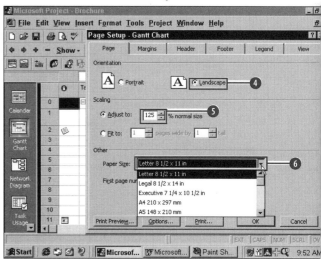

❶ To set up prior to printing a view, select the view to be printed (click the Gantt Chart button on the View Bar, for example).

❷ Choose File ➪ Page Setup.

❸ Select the Page tab.

❹ For the Gantt Chart, click the Landscape orientation button.

❺ Adjust the scale to 125% of normal size.

❻ Use the drop-down list to select a paper size.

CROSS-REFERENCE

See "Creating New Views" in Chapter 17 for information about designing your own views.

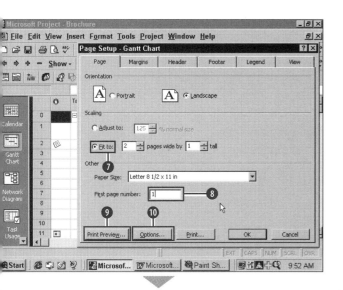

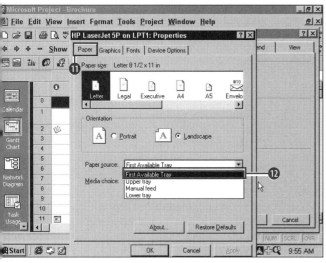

The scaling command, on the Page tab, changes printout size anywhere from 10 to 500 percent of the original size, or you may choose to fit the output into a user-defined number of pages wide and tall. For example, it is often difficult to guess whether to scale from 110 percent to 120 percent but easy to describe four pages tall and two pages wide and let Project 2000 determine the scale necessary. These scaling options are available for all printers, not just PostScript printers with built-in scaling ability.

Another choice on the Page tab, the "First page number" option, is new in Project 2000. Suppose you have previewed a six-page report but only want to print pages five and six. If you leave the First page number option set to Auto numbers, the printed pages are numbered 5 and 6. However, if you want these two pages to number as 1 and 2, as if they were stand-alone pages in a report, simply type 1 as the first page number of this print run.

TAKE NOTE

CHOOSING PAPER SIZE

In Project 2000, you can now select paper size from the Page Setup dialog box rather than at the printer level. Examples of available paper sizes include letter, legal, executive, envelope, A4, A5, and user-defined.

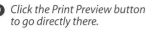

7 For practice, scale the printout to fit two pages wide by one page tall.

8 Type **1** as the first page number.

9 Click the Print Preview button to go directly there.

10 Click the Options button to select printer properties.

11 In the printer properties dialog box, look at the choices you have for your selected printer.

12 If necessary make changes here for printer-specific items such as paper source, paper size, or page orientation.

FIND IT ONLINE

For tips on writing a project proposal, see **www.wpi. edu/Academics/Projects/Proposal/fig3.html**.

Designing Margins, Borders, Headers, Footers, and Legends

Another tab in the Page Setup dialog box is the Margins tab. Use this tab to set both margin and border commands. Margin widths can be set independently for top, bottom, left, and right page margins. You'll find it helpful to look at the margin Preview box while adjusting these settings.

If you choose to have page borders print, they print around every page. For Network Diagrams you can also choose to print borders around the outer pages. For example, suppose you create a three-page by five-page Network Diagram, (fifteen pages total), and you plan to tack these pages on the wall of the "war room" as one report. If you print borders on every page, you will have fifteen separate pages with "picture frame" borders. Printing borders on just the outer pages makes the border look like it is one "picture frame" surrounding all fifteen pages.

The Header, Footer, and Legend tabs are all similar. When designing a header, footer, or legend, imagine that the area for each divides into three sections: left, center, and right. Decide what information, if any, displays in each of the three sections. The top portion of each tab contains a preview area, and the bottom portion is the work area.

While designing headers, footers, and legends, try to avoid typing "hard" data. For example, don't type in the current data or the project filename. Instead, use the field buttons or lists provided to create header, footer, and legend templates. During preview and printing, these field name place holders are replaced with project data from the view being printed.

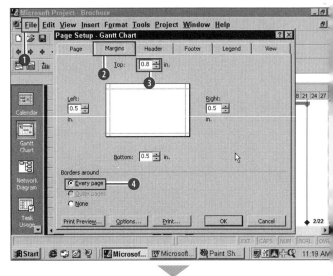

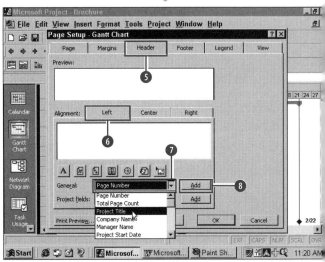

❶ To set margins, choose File ⇨ Page Setup.

❷ Click the Margins tab.

❸ Adjust any margin setting using its spin button.

❹ Click a radio button to choose a border option.

❺ Click the Header tab.

❻ To include a project title in the left portion of the header click the Left tab.

❼ Using the General drop-down list, select Project Title.

❽ Click the Add button to insert the field placeholder on the Left tab.

CROSS-REFERENCE

See "Inserting Drawings and Objects" earlier in this chapter for adding objects to project printouts.

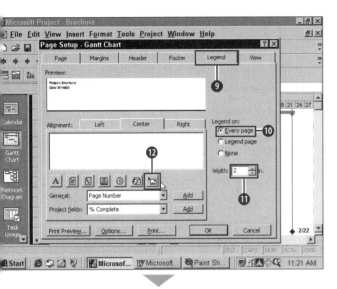

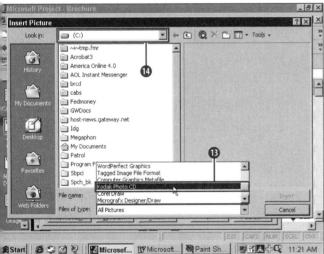

Click any of the predefined buttons found on the bottom portion of each tab to quickly add page numbers, total page count, or current date, for example. Or, optionally, choose a display field from the drop-down General list such as project title, company name, or project start date. Clicking the Add button after making a choice from this list adds it to the working area. A third option is to select a project field from the list and click Add to display the field which, like the others, is replaced with data during preview and print.

The Legend tab supplies one additional choice — whether to show a legend on every page or on a separate page, appropriately named a legend page.

TAKE NOTE

ADDING PICTURES TO HEADERS AND FOOTERS

Click the Insert Picture button, found on the header and footer tabs, to insert a picture into either a header or footer. For example, you may want to include a company logo in the header. Clicking the button opens an Insert Picture dialog box in which you select the file to be inserted. Typical file formats include photos, graphics, drawings, and clipart.

---

⑨ Click the Legend tab for more options.

⑩ Click a radio button to determine where the legend prints.

⑪ Using the spin control, select a legend width.

⑫ To insert a picture into the legend, click the Insert Picture button.

⑬ Use the drop-down list to select a file type.

⑭ Locate and select the file using Look in.

FIND IT ONLINE

For the Bitmap of the Month Club, see
http://baderb.jerseycape.net/bitmapc.htm.

Using Print Preview and Print

Use Print Preview to see a preview of printouts before sending them to the printer. Much time and paper can be saved by viewing a file first in preview mode. Because many users adjust options on the View tab of the Page Setup dialog box and then go directly into Print Preview, this tab is included in this task's discussion along with Print Preview and Print.

The choices on the View tab adjust according to the view selected prior to choosing Page Setup. For example, if the view does not contain a table, then the choice concerning whether to show all sheet columns is unavailable on the View tab. A checkbox enables you to print all sheet columns; otherwise, only columns completely visible onscreen print. Similarly, check the box to print task, assignment, or resource notes.

When finished making all page setup choices, review your work in Print Preview mode. Although you can see the output, you can't make direct changes in preview mode. For example, to adjust the view itself, you must close the preview box and return to the view. However, if the changes are setup changes, then return to the Page Setup dialog box.

When moving your mouse pointer over the preview pages, a magnifying glass appears. Clicking the mouse acts as a zoom in and out.

Other buttons on the preview screen enable you to view the printout page by page or several pages at once. Also, use the arrow buttons to page left, right, up, and down.

When selecting File ➪ Print, or clicking the Print button from Print Preview, the Print dialog box opens. If

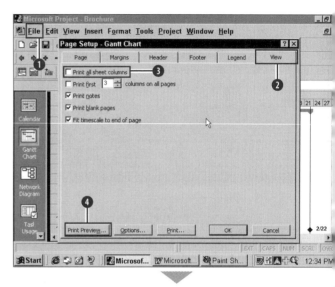

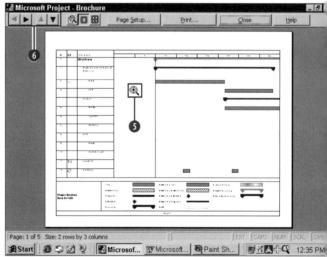

❶ To change view printing options, choose File ➪ Page Setup.

❷ Select the View tab.

❸ Check Print all sheet columns.

❹ To preview these options, click the Print Preview button or choose File ➪ Print Preview.

❺ Click the magnifying glass to zoom in and out.

❻ Click the arrows to scroll through pages.

CROSS-REFERENCE

See Chapter 15 for information about sending output to mail recipients.

you click the Print button on the Standard toolbar, however, the output goes directly to the printer, bypassing the Print dialog box.

Use the Print dialog box to select a specific printer and the number of copies to print. Likewise, use the Print range option to print selected pages from a multi-page report.

If you inserted manual page breaks into the view, check the box to accept them. Another checkbox limits the printing to only the table columns and rows and not the chart.

For many reporting purposes, you might be interested in a specific time period — next month, for example — rather than the entire project duration. Set the From and To dates in the Timescale option to print just a section of the timescale.

TAKE NOTE

▶ TIMESCALE PRINTING TIPS

If you do not want the timescale to print flush with the end of the last column or if printed text runs off the page for the last few tasks, adjust the From and To timescale dates in the Print dialog box. Start printing a few days earlier than the first date in the project and continue printing until a few days after the project to capture all information at either end.

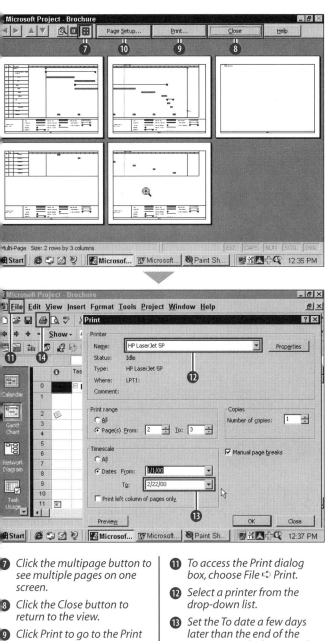

7 Click the multipage button to see multiple pages on one screen.

8 Click the Close button to return to the view.

9 Click Print to go to the Print dialog box.

10 Click Page Setup to return to that dialog box.

11 To access the Print dialog box, choose File ➪ Print.

12 Select a printer from the drop-down list.

13 Set the To date a few days later than the end of the project to include text to the right of task bars.

14 To bypass the Print dialog box, click the Print button.

FIND IT ONLINE

For printer comparisons, see **http://www.4printers.com/main.shtml**.

Viewing, Printing, and Modifying Standard Reports

Project 2000 ships with twenty-two standard text reports divided into five categories. In this task, you'll review the standard reports available and practice printing reports. The Reports choice box displays the five main categories of reports plus a Custom reports section.

Overview Reports

The *Project Summary* report shows project-level information about dates, duration, costs, task status, and resource status.

The *Top-Level Tasks* report shows schedule start and finish dates, percent complete, cost, and remaining work for summary tasks as of the present (status) date.

The *Critical Tasks* report shows planned duration, start and finish dates, resources, predecessors, and successors of tasks on the critical path.

The *Milestones* report displays the planned duration, start and finish dates, predecessors, and resources for each zero-duration milestone task. This report also includes each non-zero-duration task marked as a milestone (Task Information dialog box).

The *Working Days* report shows information from the project calendar.

Current Activities Reports

The *Unstarted Tasks* report lists the duration, predecessor, and resource information for each task that has not yet started, sorted by start date. The earliest date prints first.

The *Tasks Starting Soon* report begins with two interactive filters. You supply the start and end dates for the date range for use in determining which tasks are starting soon.

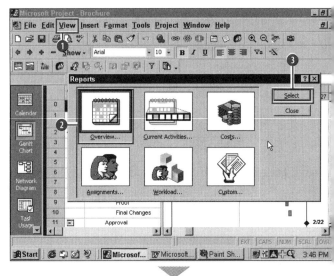

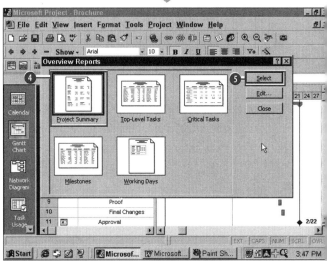

① *To preview the list of standard reports, choose View ➪ Reports.*

② *Double-click the Overview Reports to see the list of summary reports.*

③ *Or, click the report category and click the Select button.*

④ *To preview an Overview report, double-click the report.*

⑤ *Or, click the report and click the Select button.*

CROSS-REFERENCE

See Chapter 14 for information about baselines, actuals, and variances.

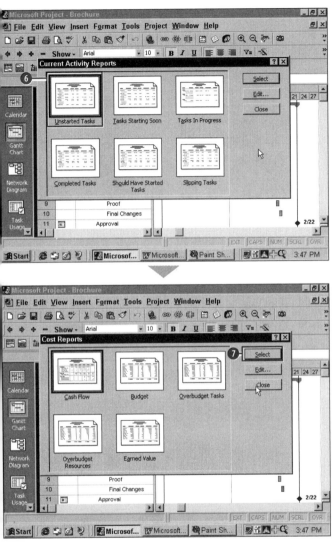

The *Tasks In Progress* report lists the typical duration, start and planned finish dates, and resource information for tasks that have started but are not yet complete.

The *Completed Tasks* report displays actual information for tasks marked as 100 percent complete.

The *Should Have Started Tasks* report also relies on a user-entered date to determine the late tasks. This report shows tasks that should have started by that date but haven't and variance information.

The *Slipping Tasks* report focuses on tasks that are rescheduled from their originally planned baseline dates.

Cost Reports

The *Cash Flow* report uses a table format to report weekly costs by task.

The *Budget* report is a columnar report listing tasks with cost and cost variance information.

The *Overbudget Tasks* report shows information for tasks that currently exceed their planned (baseline) budget amounts. Similarly, the *Overbudget Resources* report highlights resources whose cost is predicted to exceed the planned (baseline) cost based on usage to date.

The *Earned Value* report lists task progress in terms of dollars earned. Earned value reporting is the standard reporting format in government contracting.

Continued

⑥ To select a Current Activity Report, double-click the report.

⑦ To select a Cost Report, choose a report and click the Select button or double-click the report.

TAKE NOTE

EARNED VALUE CALCULATIONS

Use Project 2000 Help to find definitions and formulas used in calculating the eight earned value computations on the Earned Value report.

FIND IT ONLINE

For free software for calculating earned value, see
http://www.nnh.com/.

Viewing, Printing, and Modifying Standard Reports *Continued*

Assignment Reports

The *Who Does What* report lists each resource along with their task assignments and task information.

The *Who Does What When* report also lists each resource with task assignments but does so on a daily basis.

The *To-do List* report shows, on a weekly basis, the assignments of a particular resource. After selecting this report, an interactive filter box opens asking you to select the resource by name.

The *Overallocated Resources* report lists the overallocated resources and their assigned task information.

Workload Reports

The *Task Usage* report is similar to the Task Usage view. The report lists each task with the corresponding resources assigned and assignment information.

The *Resource Usage* report focuses on each resource with corresponding task assignments.

After your previous work in printing views, printing these reports is easy. Many of the same dialog boxes apply and only brief reminders will be repeated here.

Printing any of the standard reports is a short three-step process. Simply choose the report category, choose the report, and click the Select button. The report automatically displays in Print Preview mode. The Print Preview for reports is exactly the same as for views. However, since the report formats are predefined, only the Page and Margin tabs are available in the Page Setup dialog box.

Even the standard reports can be moderately modified. After clicking a specific report, instead of clicking

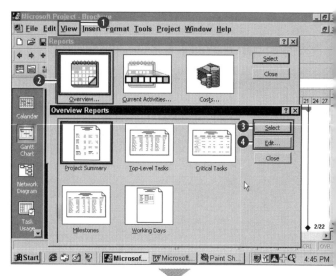

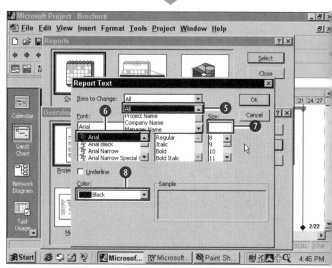

❶ To preview the Project Summary report, choose View ➪ Reports.

❷ Double-click the Overview reports.

❸ Click the Project Summary report and click the Select button.

❹ To edit the Project Summary report, click the Edit button.

❺ In the Report Text dialog box that opens, choose an item to change.

❻ Choose a font.

❼ Choose a font size.

❽ Choose a font color for use with a color printer.

CROSS-REFERENCE

See "Creating Filters" in Chapter 10 for more on using filters to focus attention on specific tasks or resources.

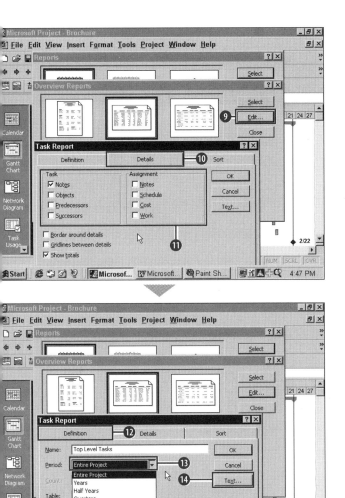

the Select button to display it in Print Preview mode, click the Edit button right below. Depending on the report selected, one of two dialog boxes appears. For some reports, like the Project Summary report, the only modifications you can make are to the text font and font style, size, and color in the Text dialog box.

However, some reports, like the Top-Level Task report, display three modification tabs in the Report dialog box. Typical options on the Definition tab include choosing the time period for the report, the report table, which filter to use, and whether the filter is "display only" or "highlight."

To decide what task and assignment details to print per task or resource as well as whether to print totals on tables, use the Details tab.

To define a sort order other than the default for the report, click the Sort tab. Set up the sort definition here in the same way you would when sorting a view.

Look for the Text button in the Report dialog box. Click this button to open the Text Styles dialog box and choose font, font style, color, and size.

TAKE NOTE

CUSTOM FONT SIZES

If the font size you want isn't listed in the Text or Text Styles dialog boxes, simply highlight the entry box and type in the size you want. This becomes a custom font size.

---

⑨ To modify the Top-Level Tasks report, select the report and click the Edit button.

⑩ Choose the Details tab.

⑪ Check information that you want to display in the report body.

⑫ For further modifications, choose the Definition tab.

⑬ Choose the report time period.

⑭ To modify fonts, click the Text button.

FIND IT ONLINE

See **http://www.drivershq.com/** for printer driver updates.

209

Creating Custom Reports

As with other aspects of Project 2000, if the standard reports fail to satisfy your reporting needs, you can create custom text reports. In this task, you will explore not only creating a custom report but editing and copying custom reports as well.

From the Reports dialog box, choose Custom to open the Custom Reports dialog box. Several familiar buttons grace this dialog box. For example, the Print, Setup, and Preview buttons are the same as seen before.

The twenty-two standard reports from the previous task appear in this list, and you can edit them or copy them to use as the basis of a new custom report. Let's discuss the seven that are new. From the list, locate the Crosstab, Resource, Resource (Material), Resource (Work), Resource Usage (Material), Resource Usage (Work), and Task reports. If you select one of these and click the Edit button, the Report dialog box opens. You are already familiar with this dialog box and its three tabs: Definition, Details, and Sort. You can also copy these seven to use as the basis for a custom report.

More exciting perhaps is the chance to create a custom report from the beginning. Clicking the New button opens a Define New Report dialog box. Four report types appear in a list from which you create new reports. Choosing either the Task or Resource report opens the familiar Report dialog box in which you can select your own definitions, details, and sorting order.

The Monthly Calendar choice opens a Monthly Calendar Report Definition dialog box. Here you can design a calendar format by choosing filters, the specific calendar to print, formatting for task bars and labels, as well as formatting for nonworking days. This custom report format is a text version of the Calendar view.

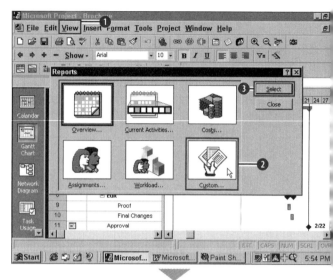

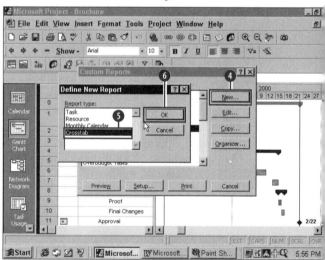

❶ To create a custom Resource by Remaining Availability crosstab report, choose View ⇨ Reports.

❷ Click the Custom report category.

❸ Click the Select button.

❹ Click the New button in the Custom Reports dialog box.

❺ Select Crosstab as the report type in the Define New Report dialog box.

❻ Click the OK button.

CROSS-REFERENCE

For more information on sorting, see "Sorting Lists" in Chapter 10.

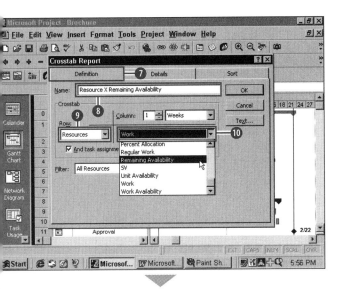

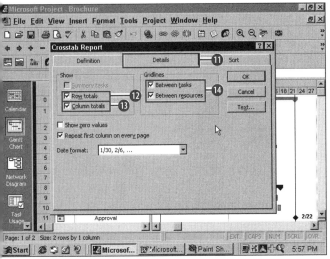

Crosstab Reports

The Crosstab is probably the most useful and unique of the custom report formats. Crosstab reports "cross" rows by columns with data displaying at the intersections. Of the standard reports, the Task Usage, Resource Usage, and Cash Flow reports are examples of crosstab reports.

Typical crosstab reports you may consider developing are Resource by Percent Allocation, Resource by Work, Resource by Remaining Allocation, Task by Overtime Work, or Task by Work. Having this type of information readily available is of great benefit to a project manager.

Using the Definition tab in the Crosstab Definition dialog box, you decide the rows, columns, and time increments. Using the Details and Sort tabs, choose which task and resource details to print in addition to the crosstab information and a sort order.

⑦ Using the Crosstab Report dialog box, click the Definition tab.

⑧ Type the name **Resource X Remaining Availability**.

⑨ From the drop-down list for Row, select Resources.

⑩ Select Remaining Availability for Column.

⑪ Click the Details tab.

⑫ Check the box for Row totals.

⑬ Check the box for Column totals.

⑭ Check both boxes for Gridlines.

FIND IT ONLINE

For information about USB (Universal Serial Bus) peripherals, see **http://www.intel.com/design/usb/**.

Personal Workbook

Q&A

1 How do you add words to your custom dictionary for use with the spell checker?

_____

_____

_____

2 How do you set a variable row height?

_____

_____

_____

3 What is the difference between Format ⇨ Bar and Format ⇨ Bar Styles?

_____

_____

_____

4 What are three buttons found on the Drawing toolbar?

_____

_____

_____

5 What is the primary difference between printing a view and printing reports?

_____

_____

_____

6 What are the two scaling options available when resizing output?

_____

_____

_____

7 How do you add a company logo to a view's footer printout?

_____

_____

_____

8 What are the five categories of standard report groups?

_____

_____

_____

ANSWERS: PAGE 325

EXTRA PRACTICE

1 Add four new words to your custom dictionary for use with the spell checker.

2 Preview all twenty-two standard reports.

3 Format an individual task bar on a Gantt Chart.

4 Use the Drawing toolbar to draw and fill in a text box on the chart side of a Gantt Chart.

5 Add a company logo or other graphic to a view's footer or header.

6 Create a custom Task by Work crosstab report.

REAL-WORLD APPLICATIONS

✔ You want to draw attention to the project start date and the current date on a Gantt Chart so you add gridlines.

✔ You want to do some quick formatting of task bars prior to printing a Gantt Chart view, so you use the GanttChartWizard to help.

✔ For a presentation to your Executive Committee, you add a company logo to all footers.

✔ In preparation for a weekly status meeting with your project sponsor, you print a combination of reports and views.

Visual Quiz

How do you display this dialog box? What purpose does it serve?

_____

_____

_____

_____

_____

_____

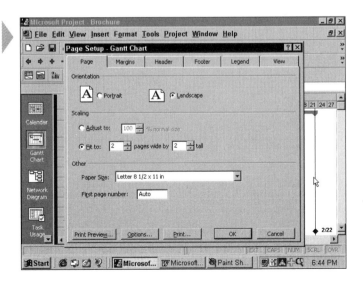

CHAPTER 13

MASTER THESE SKILLS

▶ Saving Project Information as a Web Page

▶ Defining an Import/Export Map

▶ Viewing Your Web Page

▶ Modifying Your Web Page

▶ Adding Hyperlinks

Publishing the Plan on the Web

Until recently, professional Webmasters designed and created Web pages, home pages, and hyperlinks to make information-sharing across the Internet or your company intranet possible. With the templates and maps accompanying Project 2000, you can start to feel like a Webmaster with a little practice. You may not want to publish your first attempts to the World Wide Web, but using your company intranet as a way to share project information is a good starting point.

For example, imagine sending task assignments, personal Gantt Charts, or status updates to a project Web page for access by all team members. You can even include an e-mail link so questions and comments can be sent directly back to you.

Web pages can also serve as the reporting medium rather than printing hard copies of project reports. This format greatly reduces printing and distribution time and works extremely well with distributed teams. Distributed teams are teams whose members are not all in the same physical location. By publishing your project information to an Internet-accessible Web page, your team members have access to project data from anywhere in the world.

Another common use of an intranet Web page is to create an Executive Information System. This system usually contains dynamic links to a storage database that contains summary level information about all the current company-wide projects. Executive Management uses this information for project tracking, project prioritization and selection, budgeting, and capacity planning issues. These systems are increasingly easier to create using Web-based features of Project 2000.

In this chapter, you will explore some of the many Web-based features available in Project 2000. You will start by creating and publishing project information as a static Web page for viewing before attempting to create a dynamic Web-based communication system in Chapter 15. You will also use standard Import/Export maps as well as create your own maps in order to choose which data to export as part of your document.

Additionally, you will use and modify the standard document formatting templates included with Project 2000. For example, you may want to add a custom title for your Web page or change the font style or page background color.

Lastly, you will establish hyperlinks from your "home page" and create task or resource hyperlinks.

Saving Project Information as a Web Page

Before discussing Web pages, here's an examination of some common terms to set the stage for your work throughout this chapter:

▶ *Web browser* is an application, like Microsoft Internet Explorer or Netscape Communicator, that allows you to access Web pages.

▶ *Web address* is the location, or Uniform Resource Locator (URL), of the Web page. For example, the address of IDG Books Worldwide is **http://www.idgbooks.com**.

▶ *Hyperlink* is a link between Web addresses that allows you to jump from location to location, usually by clicking a graphic or icon or by clicking underlined words.

▶ *Hypertext Markup Language (HTML)* is the format used for Web pages or documents.

▶ A *server* is the hardware and software controlling the accessibility of information in a networked environment.

▶ *Clients* access the server to view Web pages.

To create a static Web page (HTML document) from your current project, you simply save it as such. The html extension, for HTML document, is automatically added. The HTML document is the format to house your Web browser-accessible data. This data is exported once, and because it does not contain a link to a database to keep it current, it is called a static Web page. Creating static pages is a good starting place for Web page design beginners.

Let's start with the simplest method for creating a Web page, which is to use standard templates and maps supplied with Project 2000 to create the HTML file. Later in this chapter, you will practice modifying and adding elements to the standard templates.

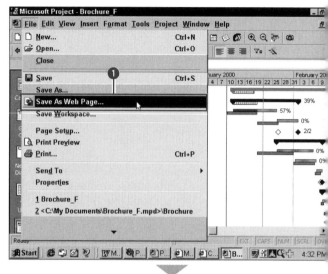

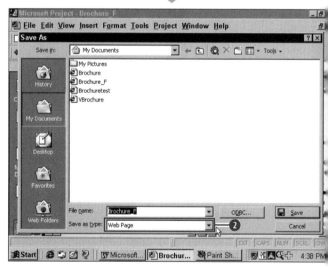

❶ To save a project as a Web page, choose File ➪ Save As Web Page.

❷ In the Save As dialog box that opens, choose Web Page as the file type.

CROSS-REFERENCE

See "Understanding File Types" in Chapter 4 for a discussion of saving project files as different file types.

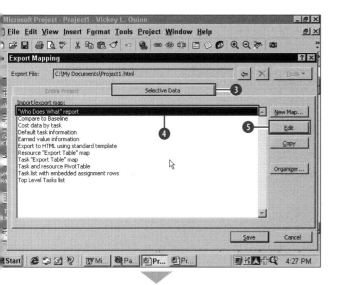

When you click the Save button to save a file as a Web page, the Export Mapping dialog box automatically opens. There are two tab choices for what information to include: either the entire project or selective data.

The information that is part of your Web page or HTML document is exported using an Import/Export map. A map simply identifies which information to include. HTML documents contain information about project tasks, resources, assignments, or combinations of these. For example, if you click the Selective Data tab, you can choose from among the predefined maps showing in the list.

Some of the predefined maps include the "Who Does What" report, Earned value information, Export to HTML using standard template, Cost data by task, Resource "Export Table" map, Top Level Tasks List, and the Task "Export Table" map. To view the included fields, select a map and click the Edit button.

TAKE NOTE

▶ **STANDARD TEMPLATE FIELDS**

Task, resource, and assignment fields are included on the "Export to HTML using standard template" map. Task fields include ID, Name, Duration, Start, Finish, Resource Names, and % Complete. Similarly, the map contains the resource fields of ID, Name, Group, Max Units, and Peak. The assignment fields are Task ID, Task Name, Resource Name, Work, Start, Finish, and % Complete.

---

① In the Export Mapping dialog box, click the radio button to export selective data.

② Choose a default export map, such as the "Who Does What" report map.

③ To preview the fields that are included as part of the export map, click the Edit button.

⑥ In the Define Import/Export Map dialog box for the "Export to HTML using standard template" map, click the Task Mapping tab.

⑦ Using the scroll arrows, preview the fields that will be exported using the From: Microsoft Project Field column.

FIND IT ONLINE

See **http://www.matisse.net/files/glossary.html** for a glossary of Internet terms.

Defining an Import/Export Map

Before viewing your Web page, let's explore creating Import/Export maps to select data to include in your Web page. In the last task, you selected a predefined map from the list in the Export Mapping dialog box. Rather than use a predefined map, click the New Map button to open the Define Import/Export Map dialog box.

The Define Import/Export Map dialog box contains four tabs. The first tab, Options, includes checkboxes for task, resource, and assignment categories of data to include in the "Data to import/export" section. As you check a box, the corresponding tab becomes available to select specific fields. The Task Mapping, Resource Mapping, and Assignment Mapping tabs all function in the same way. In the material that follows, I'll use the Task Mapping tab as an example.

The export HTML information for each of the task, resource, and assignment maps is sent as a table. The title for the destination HTML table shows as the title for the table on your Web page.

To apply a filter so that only information about particular tasks and resources is exported, choose a filter from the drop-down list. This follows the same functionality as general filtering does in Project 2000.

Two choices exist for choosing export fields. If you already have a table that contains all the fields you want to export, click the Base on Table button. (For example, predefined task tables include the Entry, Schedule, and Tracking tables.) This opens the Select Base Table for Field Mapping dialog box from which you can select the table.

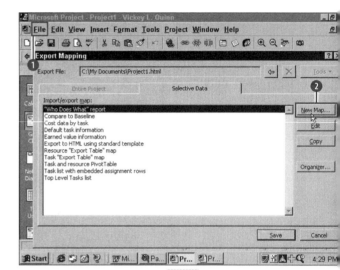

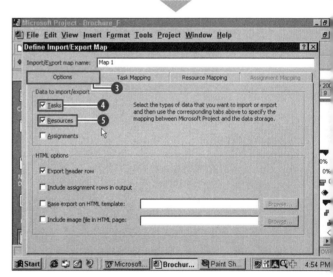

❶ To create a custom Import/Export map, return to the Export Format dialog box by choosing File ⇨ Save As Web Page.

❷ Click the New Map button found in the Export Mapping dialog box.

❸ In the Define Import/Export Map dialog box that automatically opens, select the Options tab.

❹ Click the Tasks box to activate the Task Mapping tab.

❺ Click the Resources box to activate the Resource Mapping tab.

CROSS-REFERENCE

For more about creating filters that can be used when creating Web pages, see Chapter 10.

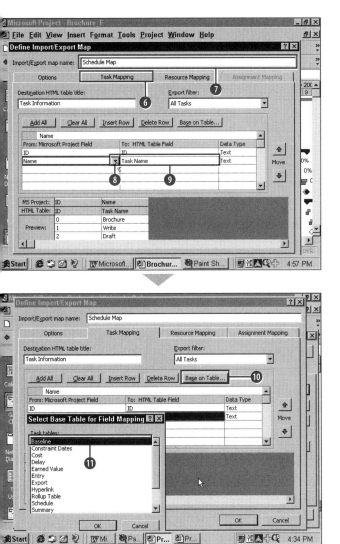

Otherwise, choose which project fields to include as part of the export. The available project fields change depending on the particular mapping tab you select. Use the HTML Table Field to give your data field a custom name on the Web page. For example, you might use "Task Name" on the Web page in place of the field name, "Name."

As you create your table, review the look of it by using the preview section at the bottom of the tab. The preview shows how the table will look on the Web page.

A number of available buttons on this dialog box make manipulating fields easier. Use the Move buttons to move fields vertically in the list. Remember that the first field listed here is the first column on the Web page table, the second field listed here appears as the second column, and so on. Use the Insert Rows and Delete Rows buttons to add and remove fields. Lastly, use the Add All button to add every field available for that data type. This actually creates a very large HTML file and is probably not too practical.

TAKE NOTE

SAVING CUSTOM MAPS

When you save a custom export map, it saves directly into the Global.mpt file. Locate it using the Maps tab.

⑥ Click the Task Mapping tab.

⑦ Enter a map name and a table name.

⑧ Select the fields to export using the drop-down arrow.

⑨ Enter a custom header name as the field will appear on the Web page.

⑩ As an alternative to selecting fields, click the Base on Table button.

⑪ Select a table, the Baseline table for example, as a supplier of fields.

FIND IT ONLINE

For a list of Web browsers, see **http://browserwatch. internet.com/browsers.htm/**.

Viewing Your Web Page

Before viewing your Web page, I'll discuss the four options available at the bottom of the Options tab on the Define Import/Export Map dialog box. These options determine the format of the page.

The first option is a checkbox to export the header row. The header row is the field name or the custom field name that you assigned on the export map. Without the header row, actual data appears in the first row.

The second checkbox enables you to print the assignment rows below each task on the Web page table. You can use this option even if you are only displaying task information (task map). The format of this table looks like the Task Usage view in that resources are listed below the tasks to which they are assigned.

Project 2000 ships with a number of predefined templates for Web page design. The HTML templates determine such formatting options for the page as background color or graphics, font and font size, hyperlinks and e-mail links, and page headers or titles. The default template is Centered Mist Dark.html and will be applied unless you select a different one from the list available in this dialog box. If you create your own style templates, their names will appear in the list as well. The predefined templates are typically stored in Program Files/Microsoft Office/Templates/Microsoft Project Web/.

The final option enables you to include an image file, such as a company logo or graphic, on the Web page. A browse button allows you to locate the image files. There are numerous image capture programs available. You

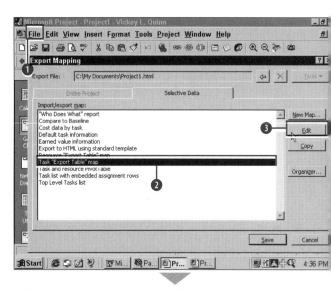

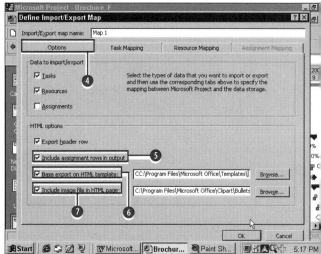

① To select display options for your Web page, return to the Export Format dialog box via File ▷ Save As Web Page.

② Select the map you created in the last step.

③ Click the Edit button to define options.

④ Click the Options tab to set display options.

⑤ Click the "Include assignment rows in output" box to add this to the Web page.

⑥ Check the box to base this export on a default table and click the Browse button.

⑦ Check the box to include an image on your Web page and click the Browse button.

CROSS-REFERENCE

See Chapter 12 for more information about using drawings, objects, and pictures.

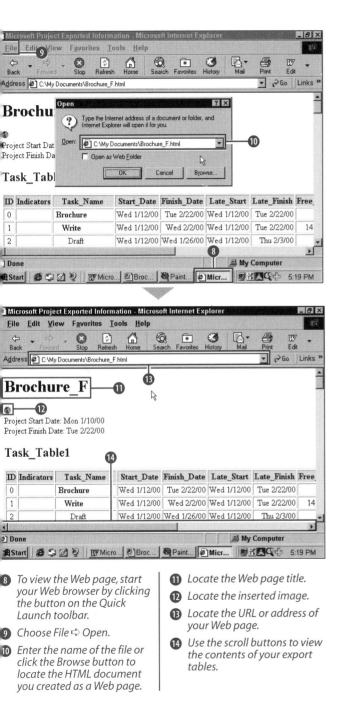

might already be familiar with CompuServe graphics interchange (.gif), Windows meta file (.wmf), Windows/OS2 bitmap (.bmp), Paintbrush (.pcx), Kodak Photo CD (.pcd), PC Paint (.pic), Tagged Image File Format (.tif), or PhotoShop (.psd) file formats. However, for Web page development purposes, these files need to be converted to jpg, gif, or png formats.

Finally, let's view your first Web page. To do this, start your Web browser. In this example, I will use Microsoft Internet Explorer, but Netscape Navigator (Communicator) is similar. From the Web browser, choose File ➪ Open and locate your HTML Web page. As you view it on the screen, remember that it is currently static, which means that it is for viewing purposes only and needs to be saved as an HTML file and updated again following any changes to the project data.

The Web page on the screen is currently formatted according to the predefined Standard Export template and several items you entered. Your items include the table or fields that display, the destination table title, the order of the fields, the custom field headers if you display row headers, any assignment rows, graphic images, and the project title.

⑧ To view the Web page, start your Web browser by clicking the button on the Quick Launch toolbar.

⑨ Choose File ➪ Open.

⑩ Enter the name of the file or click the Browse button to locate the HTML document you created as a Web page.

⑪ Locate the Web page title.

⑫ Locate the inserted image.

⑬ Locate the URL or address of your Web page.

⑭ Use the scroll buttons to view the contents of your export tables.

FIND IT ONLINE

For free software to cut "snippets" from Web pages to place on your desktop, see **http://www.snippet.net/**.

Modifying Your Web Page

In this section you will practice modifying the format of the default HTML template to add some pizzazz to your Web page. For example, you can change the Web page background color, add "wallpaper" as background for the page, and change the title bar text.

Default HTML templates are documents that contain lines of formatting code. Project 2000 and Web authoring tools supply you with templates containing HTML formatting code so that you do not need to be an expert to create Web pages. Since this is formatting code, it is probably a good idea to copy all templates before modification in case you want to return to them later. Additionally, code modifications must also be typed exactly as expected or the browser will not know how to display the document properly.

Use a text editor such as Notepad to edit the HTML template, or you can also access the document from the Internet Explorer notepad, which is probably the easiest because you can make changes and immediately see the results.

To change the background color of your Web page, locate the line (about line 6) of the code that says `<Body>`. Without a specific color listed, the background is typically a shade of gray. To specify a color, add the color information within the brackets for `<Body>`. For example, to specify light green as the background color, type `<Body BGCOLOR="#CCFFCC">` where CCFFCC is the hexadecimal representation of the color light green.

Some hexadecimal colors display in the following table.

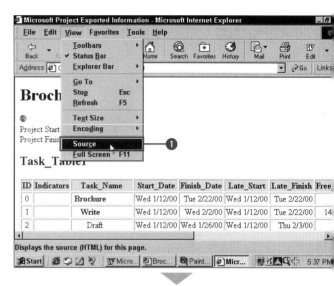

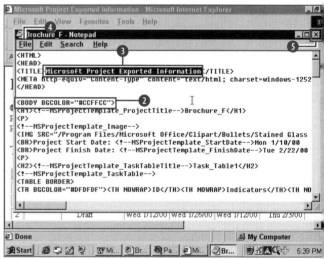

1 To customize the format of the Web page using a notepad included with Microsoft Internet Explorer, choose View ➪ Source.

▶ The notepad opens, displaying the source code.

2 To change the background color to light green, type the following in the Body tag: `<BODY BGCOLOR="#CCFFCC">`

3 To add your own custom Web page title, highlight the default title and type your own text.

4 To see your changes, choose File ➪ Save.

5 Click the Close button.

CROSS-REFERENCE

See "Viewing, Printing, and Modifying Standard Reports" in Chapter 12 for more on standard export maps.

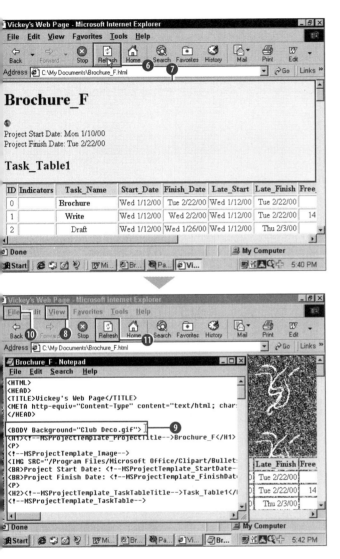

HEXADECIMAL COLOR REPRESENTATIONS

Color	Hexadecimal Code
Black	000000
Yellow	FFFF00
Blue	0000FF
Sky Blue	00CCFF
Gray	808080
Orange	FF6600
Gold	FFCC00
Aqua	33CCCC
White	FFFFFF
Light Blue	CCFFFF

To add a background graphic such as Windows "wallpaper" graphics, copy the graphic (.gif file format) into the same directory as the HTML document. Microsoft Office contains a number of these wallpaper styles. The default location is Program Files/Microsoft Office/Office/Web Page Templates/Styles. Some graphics available include Brick Wall, Club Deco, Fancy Green Patterns, Granite Edifice, and Wheat. Use the following code change to add a background graphic instead of color:

```
<Body Background="filename.gif">
```

The title bar is the title at the top of the Web page window. About three lines down in the code, locate `<Title>Microsoft Project Exported Information</Title>`. Being careful not to disturb the title markers at either end, simply delete the current title and type in your own.

⑥ *To see the changes, click the Refresh button.*

⑦ *Notice the change in background color to light green.*

⑧ *To change the background pattern, choose View ⇨ Source.*

⑨ *In the Body tag, type <BODY BACKGROUND="Club Deco.gif"> where Club Deco is the background pattern.*

⑩ *To save this change, choose File ⇨ Save.*

⑪ *Click the Refresh button to see the pattern.*

FIND IT ONLINE

To download a Windows shareware HTML editor, see http://www.mcWebsoftware.com/Webweav.htm/.

Adding Hyperlinks

yperlinks can be added to Web pages or to individual project tasks or resources. Adding hyperlinks to Web pages allows users of your page to jump to another page or another site, or to download a project file. A similar link (mail link) allows users to automatically open their mail program with a new message preaddressed to you.

For example, to add a hyperlink to the bottom of the Web page, you will again modify the source code. The format or syntax for adding a hyperlink to a URL is `<A HREF="URL or address of site"><B>Text the user will click to go to that address </B></A></TD>`. For example, typing `<A HREF= http://www.microsoft.com><B> Microsoft Home Page</B></A></TD>` creates a hyperlink to the Microsoft Home Page, and the user will see Microsoft Home Page as the underlined text that displays at the bottom of the Web page. Clicking that underlined text will take the user to the Microsoft Home Page address.

Creating an e-mail link is similar. Instead of using the Web address, use the e-mail address. Also, include the text to be underlined for the user as the link. The following is an example of an e-mail link:

```
<A HREF=
"mailto:vickey@mycompany.com"><B>Click
here to send an e-mail to
Vickey</B></A></TD>
```

Consider expanding the functionality of Project 2000 by adding hyperlinks to tasks and resources in your project plan in addition to those added to Web pages. For example, you may want to give quick access, via hyperlinks, to an Excel spreadsheet or a PowerPoint presentation or slide, or link to a Word document to check product specifications.

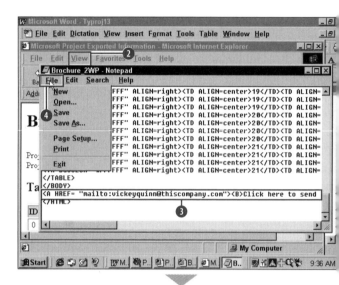

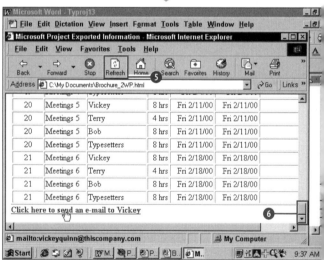

❶ To add an e-mail hyperlink, access the Web page from your browser.

❷ To change the source code, Choose View ⇨ Source.

❸ Add this line above the `</HTML>` tag: `<A HREF= mailto:e-mail address of recipient><B>e-mail link underlined text that users will see on the Web page </B></A></TD>`

❹ To view your e-mail link, clic_ the Refresh button.

❺ Scroll to the bottom of the Web page and locate the underlined text that points t_ the e-mail address.

CROSS-REFERENCE

See "Creating New Tables" in Chapter 17 for information about creating a table that contains the Hyperlink field.

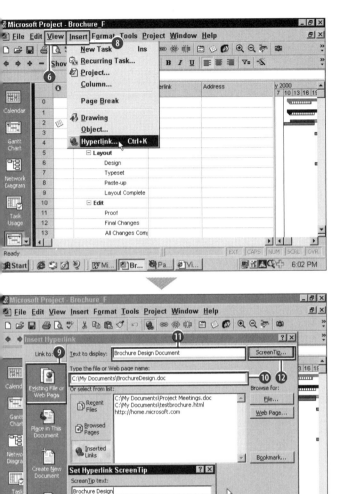

When creating a hyperlink to a task or resource, you have numerous choices. For example, you can link to an existing file or Web page. You can even link to another task or resource in the open project file by supplying the Task or Resource ID number for the link. A third choice is to link to a new document. In addition to supplying a path to save the document, you can choose to immediately go to the document for editing or to edit the new document later.

The final choice is to create a hyperlink to an e-mail address. This choice opens a dialog box in which to type the e-mail address or select it from a list of recently used e-mail addresses.

TAKE NOTE

DELETING HYPERLINKS

To edit or remove a hyperlink, choose Insert ➪ Hyperlink or click the Insert Hyperlink button on the Standard toolbar. To delete a hyperlink, click the Remove Link button at the bottom of the dialog box.

⑥ Before adding hyperlinks to project tasks or resources, select the Hyperlink table by choosing View➪Table and selecting Hyperlink.

⑦ To add a hyperlink to a task, select the task.

⑧ Choose Insert ➪ Hyperlink.

⑨ In the Insert Hyperlink dialog box, click Link to: Existing File or Web Page.

⑩ Type in the name of the file to link to or click the Browse for File button to locate it.

⑪ Type in text to display in the Hyperlink table.

⑫ Click the ScreenTip button and type in your custom screen tip.

FIND IT ONLINE

For information about uploading your Web page to an Internet-accessible server at no cost, see **www. homepage.com/**.

Personal Workbook

Q&A

1 What is a *URL?*

_____

_____

_____

2 What is an *HTML document?*

_____

_____

_____

3 What is the purpose of an Import/Export map?

_____

_____

_____

4 What is a *hyperlink?*

_____

_____

_____

5 How do you save a Project 2000 project as a Web page?

_____

_____

_____

6 What is the name of the default HTML document template that comes with Project 2000?

_____

_____

_____

7 What are the four tabs in the Define Import/Export Map dialog box?

_____

_____

_____

8 What is a *Web browser?*

_____

_____

_____

ANSWERS: PAGE 325

EXTRA PRACTICE

1 Save a project file as a Web page.

2 Using a Web browser, open the Web page.

3 Using a text editor, change the background color of your Web page.

4 Add a hyperlink to a task.

5 Define an Import/Export map to send specific data to your Web page.

REAL-WORLD APPLICATIONS

✔ Your project sponsor likes to see project summary information every Friday so you save the project as a Web page for easy viewing on the company intranet.

✔ For ease in accessing detailed task specifications, you add hyperlinks within each task to the specification documents.

✔ To manage communications among a distributed team, you customize the Web page with the team logo, title, and background color.

Visual Quiz

How do you access this dialog box?

_____

_____

_____

_____

_____

_____

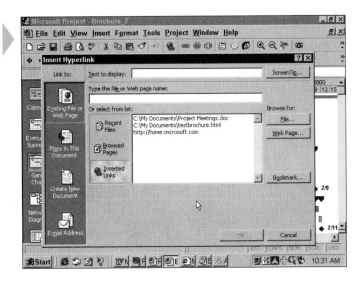

PART V

CHAPTER 14 Tracking Progress

15 Using Project 2000 in Workgroups

Controlling and Closing the Project

Developing a project plan is only one aspect of successful project management. To be successful, you now need to manage the work, using the plan as the roadmap. By tracking progress and making comparisons against the plan, you can check for variances. The severity of the variance will tell you whether you need to take corrective action (whether you're in a ditch, to use our roadmap analogy), or whether your strategy is working (you're still between the ditches).

Part V guides you through the process of tracking progress, controlling project work, and analyzing variances. You'll learn how to set a baseline or "snapshot" of the plan and then how to enter actual schedule, resource, and cost progress information. This part also covers checking for variances and taking corrective action.

Additionally, you'll discover various techniques for managing and closing the project efficiently using workgroups. You'll see how communication across a workgroup occurs through the use of e-mail, a corporate intranet, or the Internet.

CHAPTER 14

MASTER
THESE
SKILLS

▶ Setting a Baseline

▶ Viewing Baseline Information

▶ Selecting Automatic Update Options

▶ Using the Tracking and Forms Toolbars

▶ Entering Actual Schedule Data

▶ Entering Actual Resource and Cost Data

▶ Analyzing Variances

▶ Understanding Earned Value

▶ Revising the Current Plan

▶ Preparing Status Reports

Tracking Progress

If a project plan serves as a roadmap for how you intend to reach the project goals, then tracking progress serves as the reality check along the way. Tracking progress of the schedule, budget, and resource usage tells you if your strategies for achieving the goals are working or if you are currently on a side road or maybe even in a ditch and need to change your strategies.

Without tracking where you are and comparing that to where you thought you would be, it is difficult to tell if significant variances exist. Not only is tracking progress mandatory for good project control but how frequently you track progress is important as well. Tracking helps spot variances early enough to allow you to take appropriate corrective action or change your strategies. For example, if you're changing out a piece of equipment in a manufacturing plant and the entire execution of the change-out occurs within a 24-hour timeframe, tracking would probably occur every one-half to one hour depending on the complexity of the work. On the other hand, if your project tasks are estimated in days and weeks, weekly tracking and analysis may be sufficient.

Your project level of detail established during initial planning should be consistent with the frequency that you plan to analyze variances. For example, planning a project to the hourly level while planning to track weekly probably won't work very well. Too many successor tasks will start and finish between updates for you to take any meaningful corrective action. This type of tracking leaves you feeling like you are chasing after your project rather than managing or controlling it.

In this chapter you will learn how to save and view a project baseline, and you will practice a number of tracking or updating techniques using various views, forms, and toolbars. In particular, you will become familiar with the Tracking Gantt view, the Tracking toolbar, and the Custom Forms toolbar. These updating techniques are for tracking the progress of resource utilization, schedule, and budget.

You will also explore options available within Project 2000 to analyze variances and earned value. You will explore suggestions for revising the current plan and taking corrective action. This chapter concludes with tips on preparing status reports.

Setting a Baseline

A baseline is a snapshot or record of the planned start and finish dates, duration estimates, work, and cost information for each task and resource. This data is stored in fields known as *baseline fields*. Unless you manually reset the baseline, this record does not change during the project, thus allowing you to compare current and actual information against this baseline plan.

You can set a baseline in Project 2000 in two ways. When you save a project file, the Planning Wizard asks if you would like to save the file with or without a baseline. You can elect to save the file with a baseline. Another option is to use the Save Baseline dialog box to save a baseline for the entire project.

If you set the baseline prematurely, use the Clear Baseline dialog box to clear the baseline from the entire project or just the task(s) currently selected. The functionality to clear the baseline was not previously available in Microsoft Project.

Sometimes, after the project is under way, tasks are added to the plan or a portion of the plan is changed. Again, using the Save Baseline dialog box from any task view, you can choose to save a baseline for just the selected task(s). This baseline information replaces any original baseline information.

If the project scope or other negotiated constraints change so drastically during the project that the original plan and baseline no longer serve as an adequate roadmap, there are three possible baseline responses. Your first option is to do nothing, simply allow the actual information to be very different from the original plan to highlight the magnitude of the changes.

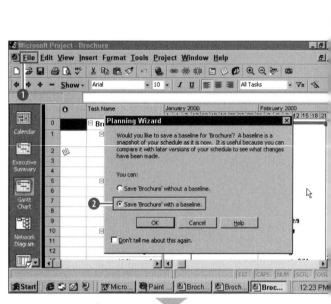

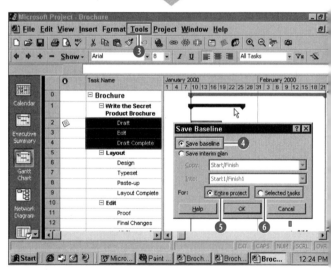

❶ To set a baseline using the Planning Wizard, choose File ➪ Save.

❷ In the Planning Wizard dialog box, click the button to save the project with a baseline.

❸ To save a baseline with the Save Baseline dialog box, choose Tools ➪ Tracking ➪ Save Baseline.

❹ Click the button to save a baseline.

❺ Choose to set a baseline for the entire project.

❻ To set a baseline for selected tasks, you must select the tasks before opening the dialog box.

CROSS-REFERENCE

See Chapter 11 for tips on finalizing your project plan prior to setting a baseline.

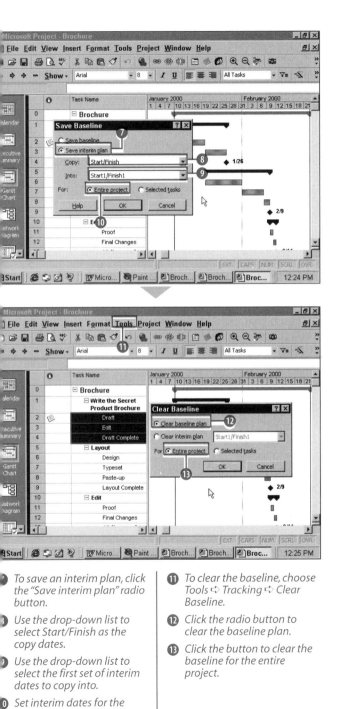

The second option is to save the baseline again, replacing the original. This option provides the needed current roadmap but doesn't provide an audit trail of the changes.

The third option is to make a copy of the project file to use as an audit trail. Store this copy with the original information in a secure place along with the date and explanation. Then, using the original file, clear the baseline from all tasks that are not yet complete. Make all necessary changes to the plan and, as a final step, save the baseline again.

▶ **USING INTERIM PLANS**

Project 2000 has the capacity to store and clear ten sets of dates as interim plans. This is useful if your project is temporarily placed on hold or to track schedule progress from one development phase to another. Using interim dates, for example, you can save the current start and finish dates into Start1 and Finish1 to capture projected dates as of today. Renaming this column as "Phase 2 Start" lets you compare another set of dates to the baseline as well as to actual information.

● To save an interim plan, click the "Save interim plan" radio button.

● Use the drop-down list to select Start/Finish as the copy dates.

● Use the drop-down list to select the first set of interim dates to copy into.

● Set interim dates for the entire project.

⓫ To clear the baseline, choose Tools ⇨ Tracking ⇨ Clear Baseline.

⓬ Click the radio button to clear the baseline plan.

⓭ Click the button to clear the baseline for the entire project.

Viewing Baseline Information

To view baseline task bars and actual task bars on the same screen, you need to use a Gantt Chart. In Chapter 12, you practiced creating your own task bar definitions for slack but not for baseline bars. Until you have time to practice creating custom baseline bars, there are two standard ways to view baseline and actual bars together.

The Tracking Gantt view displays baseline task bars on the bottom (Row 2) with bars representing actual progress on top (Row 1). Without entering any progress data, the actual progress bars parallel the baseline bars. With the addition of tracking data, tasks starting earlier than the baseline start will show shifted to the left of the baseline bar start position while tasks starting later than baseline start will show bars starting to the right of the baseline bar start.

In addition to the Tracking Gantt view, the Gantt Chart Wizard allows for easy selection and display of baseline bars. However, the Wizard places the baseline bars on top with the actual progress bars on the bottom. Using the custom Gantt Chart option the Wizard offers, you can also show baseline bars with a different default style but still in the top position.

In addition to baseline task bars, baseline data is readily available as well. Numerous standard task tables show baseline information by default. The Baseline table shows the recorded values for Baseline Start, Baseline Finish, Baseline Duration, Baseline Work, and Baseline Cost. The Cost table shows baseline costs, and the Work table displays baseline work data.

CROSS-REFERENCE

See "Exploring Formatting Options" in Chapter 12 for information about displaying gridlines.

234

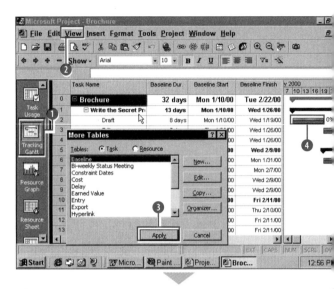

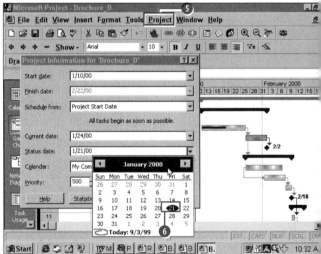

① To display baselines, click the Tracking Gantt button.

② To display baseline data, choose View ➪ Table ➪ More Tables, and select the Baseline table.

③ Click Apply to view the table data.

④ Locate the baseline (bottom) bars on your Gantt Chart.

⑤ To change the status date prior to updating, choose Project ➪ Project Information.

⑥ Using the pop-up calendar, change the status date to reflect the date through which you are reporting progress.

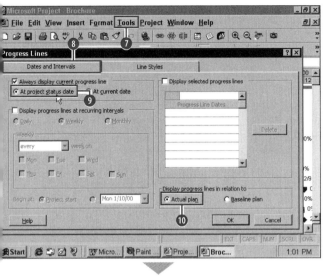

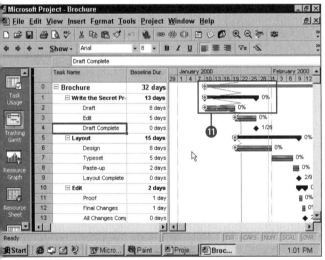

Most of the other views have detail tables or rows containing baseline information. Both the Task Usage and Resource Usage views have options to display baseline cost (Cost details) and baseline work (Work details) data on the distribution side of the view. Standard tables for the Resource Sheet show both baseline cost and work information. Even the Task and Resource Forms can display baseline cost and work information using the standard detail tables. All of these detail tables are available through the shortcut menus accessible by right-clicking on the form or view.

TAKE NOTE

▶ SHOWING PROGRESS LINES

In addition to showing the current date gridline on the chart, consider displaying progress lines as well. *Progress lines* are a helpful visual means of determining progress as compared to the baseline or actual plan. Progress lines connect the progress indicators on each task for a visual reference. Using the Progress Lines dialog box, options are available to display progress lines for the current date or the project status date (report-through date as set in the Project Information dialog box). As an alternative, progress lines can display at regular daily, weekly, or monthly intervals. You can also select user-defined dates for progress line display.

---

7 To add progress lines to your chart, choose Tools ⇨ Tracking ⇨ Progress Lines.

8 Select the Dates and Intervals tab.

9 Click the checkbox to always display current progress line at the project status date (radio button).

10 Click the radio button to display progress lines in relation to the actual plan.

11 Locate the progress lines drawn from progress point to progress point in each task. In the example, the progress is 0% to date.

FIND IT ONLINE

For Project 2000 companion reporting tools, see
http://www.mspug.com/Reporting%20Tools.htm.

Selecting Automatic Update Options

Before updating schedule, resource, or cost information, decide whether to enter these values manually or have Project calculate spent information based on the percent complete of the task to which they are assigned. For example, Project can automatically calculate spent work and cost based on the percent complete of the task. The drawback to this feature is that the calculations may not be very accurate if the task is not progressing according to plan. However, you can still update an individual resource's spent work if it is significantly different than the calculated amount.

The two important checkboxes that determine these automatic update calculations are both found on the Calculation tab of the Options dialog box. By default, both boxes are checked to provide the automatic work and cost updates. Let's review the choices prior to entering progress information.

The "Updating task status updates resource status" checkbox offers the opportunity to have Project 2000 automatically calculate work spent by your resource (and cost) based upon the percent complete entered for the task. For example, suppose the baseline data shows Vickey scheduled for 20 hours of work at a cost of $2,000.00. Later, as you enter 50% complete for the task, Project 2000 will calculate 10 hours of spent work for Vickey at a spent cost of $1,000.00. This option often saves time but the results are not as accurate as if you entered them resource by resource. Unchecking this box unhooks these two calculations so that they are treated separately.

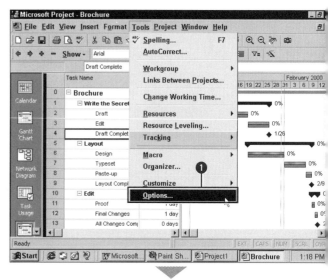

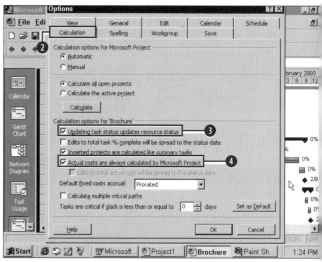

❶ To set automatic updating of resource and cost data, choose Tools ⇨ Options.

❷ Click the Calculation tab.

❸ Check the box to have Proje automatically update resource and cost status. Uncheck the box to "unhook the formulas.

❹ Check the box to have Proje always calculate costs. Uncheck for manual entry o spent costs.

CROSS-REFERENCE

See "Selecting Default Options" in Chapter 3 for information about selecting other defaults.

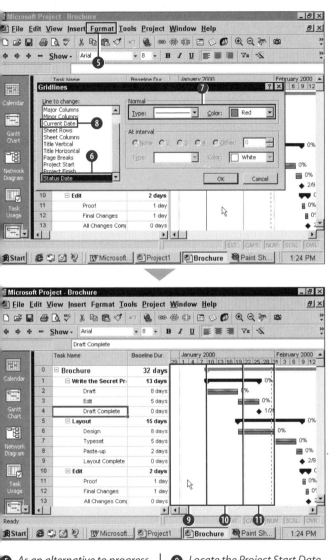

The other important updating checkbox on the Calculation tab is the "Actual costs are always calculated by Microsoft Project" checkbox. This choice is similar to automatic calculations for resource status as it allows Project to calculate costs based on percent complete. Unchecking this box leaves the actual cost field at $0.00 unless you enter a spent amount.

TAKE NOTE

PREPARING TO UPDATE

Before beginning your first update cycle, check the Status date in the Project Information dialog box (Project ⇨ Project Information). Three dates display in this dialog box; the *start date*, the *current date*, and the *status date*. When scheduling from the project start date, the start date is a user-entered date or, when scheduling from the project finish date, a calculated date. The current date is today's date and is regulated by your computer. The status date is another user-entered date and represents the reporting date or the "update through" date in Project 2000. A number of tracking calculations use the status date. Remember to return to the Project Information dialog box and enter a different status date prior to entering actual progress data for the next reporting cycle. For example, using a weekly reporting cycle, leave the status date "frozen" from Friday to Friday so that all calculations are viewed from the same instant in time.

5 As an alternative to progress lines, display various gridlines by choosing Format ⇨ Gridlines.

6 Select Status Date from the Line to change list box.

7 Select a line type and color.

8 Choose Current Date as the line to change and select a line type and color.

9 Locate the Project Start Date gridline.

10 Locate the Status Date gridline.

11 Locate the Current Date gridline.

FIND IT ONLINE

For product information to integrate your Project 2000 data and financial data, see **www.mantix.com/youcan**.

Using the Tracking and Forms Toolbars

Now that you have saved a baseline, it is time to begin tracking and entering actual project progress. Decide what information is important to gather on a regular basis and enter into Project 2000 for tracking purposes. Typical data to collect includes start and finish dates of each task, percent complete, remaining duration, spent hours, spent costs, and unplanned work or tasks.

Before you enter information, let's explore two specialty toolbars that make tracking easier. See Tables 14-1 and 14-2.

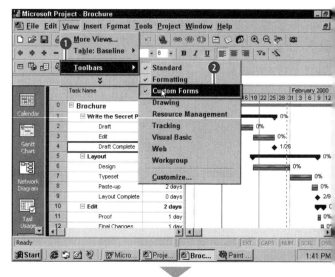

Table 14-1: CUSTOM FORMS TOOLBAR

Button Name	Description
Entry	Useful during initial task entry
Cost Tracking	Provides data fields useful for tracking costs per task
Work Tracking	Provides data fields useful for tracking resource work
Task Earned Value	Supplies earned value calculations per task
Schedule Tracking	Useful during tracking of schedule information
Task Relationships	Allows you to enter ID numbers of Predecessor and Successor tasks
Tracking	Provides easy entry of actual progress data
Forms	Displays the Customize Forms dialog box

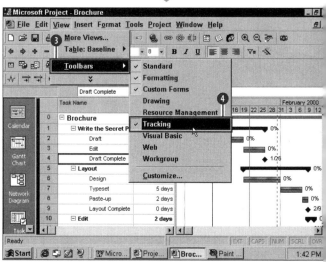

❶ To display the Custom Forms toolbar, select View ➪ Toolbars.

❷ Select Custom Forms to display that toolbar.

❸ To display the Tracking toolbar, select View ➪ Toolbars.

❹ Select Tracking to display that toolbar.

CROSS-REFERENCE

See "Customizing Toolbars" in Chapter 17 for information about creating your own Tracking toolbar.

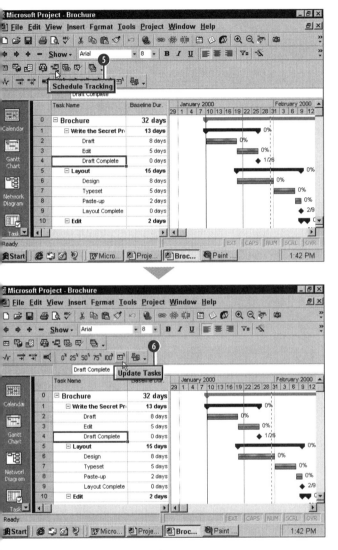

5 *Read the tool tips for each button on the Custom Forms toolbar.*

6 *Read the tool tips for each button on the Tracking toolbar.*

Table 14-2: TRACKING TOOLBAR

Button Name	Description
Project Statistics	Supplies current, baseline, actual, and variance information
Update as Scheduled	Transfers baseline start dates into actual start date fields and enters percent complete in the Project Information dialog box
Reschedule Work	Displays the Update Project dialog box to select a date to reschedule work from
Add Progress Line	Displays a progress line tool to click and place a progress line on the timescale portion of a Gantt Chart
0%	Marks the selected task(s) as 0 percent complete
25%	Marks the selected task(s) as 25 percent complete
50%	Marks the selected task(s) as 50 percent complete
75%	Marks the selected task(s) as 75 percent complete
100%	Marks the selected task(s) as 100 percent complete
Update Tasks	Displays the Update Tasks dialog box
Workgroup Toolbar	Displays an additional toolbar for easy access to Workgroup features

FIND IT ONLINE

For a companion product to track issues and progress, see **www.projectassistants.com/ts/usingpc.html.**

Entering Actual Schedule Data

As you explore a variety of ways to enter schedule progress data, double-check field names prior to entry. For example, users are often confused between Baseline Start, Start, and Actual Start dates. For each task, the *baseline start* is the recorded planned start date. The *start* is the calculated start date of the task based on scheduling criteria, and the *actual start* is the date work physically began for this task.

The Tracking Gantt view with the Tracking table shows task bars for comparison and "actual" columns for data entry. For example, type the actual start date of the task into the Actual Start cell or choose the date from a pop-up calendar. Other fields on this table include Actual Finish, Percent Complete, Actual Duration, and Remaining Duration.

Both the Task Information and Multiple Task Information dialog boxes contain a percent complete field. You can also click the Schedule Tracking button on the Custom Forms toolbar to enter percent complete. Clicking any of the percent complete buttons on the Tracking toolbar enters percent complete, too.

Use the Update Task (Tools ➪ Tracking ➪ Update Task) dialog box to record actual progress information such as that found on the Tracking table. This dialog box conveniently lists the current task information as read-only for easy data comparison.

The Update Project (Tools ➪ Tracking ➪ Update Project) dialog box establishes update preferences for the project as a whole. This feature is useful if your project is progressing as planned. Using this dialog box, you can choose to update the project through a user-selected date. Project 2000 will then enter the baseline data into

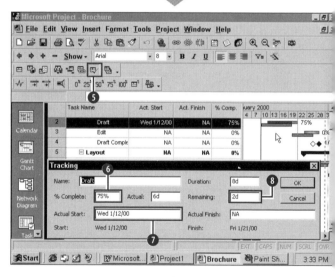

❶ To enter actuals using the Tracking table, click the Gantt Chart button on the View Bar.

❷ Choose View ➪ Table, and select the Tracking table.

❸ Enter the actual start date or select it from the pop-up calendar.

❹ Enter the % complete or click the % complete button on the Tracking toolbar.

❺ As an alternate means of data entry, click the Tracking button.

❻ Enter percent complete.

❼ Enter an actual start date.

❽ Update remaining duration if necessary.

CROSS-REFERENCE

See Chapter 2 for more information about changing views and tables.

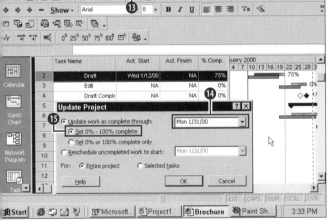

the actual fields to show the project is exactly on schedule, and it will enter percent complete as well. Radio buttons offer choices for percent-complete entries that range from 0 to 100 percent based on the percent of the task that should be complete by the entered status date.

Clicking the Tracking button on the Custom Forms toolbar displays a form containing the same "actual" fields as those found on the Tracking table. Clicking the Update Tasks button on the tracking toolbar displays the same Update Tasks dialog box described earlier. Both of these buttons offer excellent, safe means of entering actual schedule data. Consider using these, especially if an inexperienced Project user is entering the update information or you like having the fields presented in form format.

TAKE NOTE

▶ CHANGING PERCENT COMPLETE USING THE MOUSE

To use this technique, position the mouse pointer over the start of the task bar until the pointer changes to a percent symbol (%). Click and drag the mouse until the percent complete in the pop-up box matches your desired entry, and then release the mouse.

⑨ For a third data entry option, click the Update Tasks button.

⑩ Alternatively, open the Update Tasks dialog box by selecting Tools ⇨ Tracking ⇨ Update Tasks.

⑪ Enter the actual start date.

⑫ Update % Complete.

⑬ To access the Update Project dialog box, choose Tools ⇨ Tracking ⇨ Update Project.

⑭ To update several tasks at once, click this radio button and select a date.

⑮ Click the button to allow percent complete values between 0 and 100 percent.

FIND IT ONLINE

For project time accounting software solutions, see
http://www.timewzrd.com.

Entering Actual Resource and Cost Data

Project 2000 contains a variety of views, forms, and dialog boxes suitable for updating resource and cost information. If Project 2000 already calculates resource and cost information for you, use these updating methods to alter only those resource expenditures that are significantly different from the Project 2000 calculated values. Otherwise, if you "unhook" automatic update calculations, actual work and costs fields are currently blank and you will have to enter the data manually.

Clicking the Work Tracking button on the Custom Forms toolbar displays a convenient dialog box containing typical work update fields like Actual (spent) Work, % Work Complete, and Remaining Work. Baseline fields also display for easy comparison. Consider asking your data entry team members to use this dialog box rather than a free-form use of table fields in which baseline or current work information could be inadvertently changed.

Similarly, clicking the Cost Tracking button on the Custom Forms toolbar offers fields for updating Actual Cost, Remaining Cost, Fixed Costs, and % Work Complete while viewing baseline data for comparison.

Both the Task Usage and the Resource Usage views offer excellent opportunities to enter resource work and cost progress data. In the Task Usage view, useful tables for the spreadsheet include Tracking, Cost, and Work. Likewise, both Cost and Work tables are available for the Resource Usage spreadsheet. The right side of both views, the distribution worksheet, provides significant detail for updating work and cost information. Remember to change the scale for the distribution worksheet by zooming in and out to track hourly, daily,

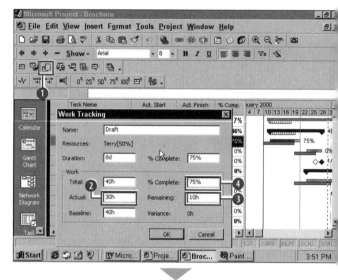

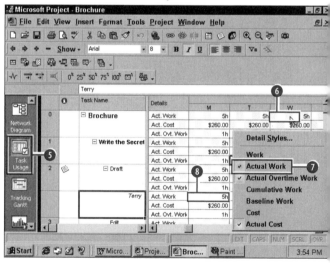

❶ To update resource and cost information with the Work Tracking dialog box, click the Work Tracking button.

❷ Enter actual work, or change the value calculated by Project 2000.

❸ Enter remaining work, if necessary.

❹ Enter work percent complete.

❺ To enter data using the Task Usage view, click the Task Usage button.

❻ Right-click in the distribution side to show shortcut menu.

❼ Display the menu three times, selecting Actual Work, Actual Overtime Work, and Actual Cost to display.

❽ Enter actual work amounts in the Actual Work field per resource assignment.

CROSS-REFERENCE

See Chapter 9 for more information about using the Task and Resource Usage views.

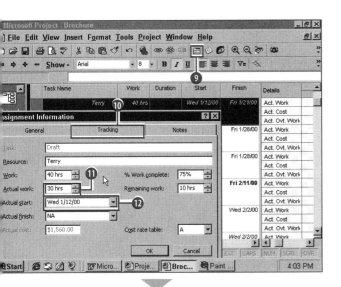

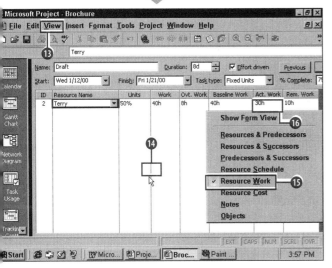

weekly, or monthly. The shortcut menus for both views contains details of Actual Cost, Actual Work, and Actual Overtime, that display on the distribution worksheet and allow direct manual entry.

The bottom pane of the Task Entry view (Task Form) or the Task Form as a single view also offer convenient places to enter actual work and cost information. Three tracking tables are available for the column portion of the form and are accessible from the details shortcut menu by right-clicking anywhere in the form. The Resource Work table contains fields for entering Actual Overtime Work, Actual Work, and Remaining Work. The Resource Cost table supplies fields for Actual Cost and Remaining Cost. The Resource Schedule table displays fields for the start and finish dates of the resource work efforts.

TAKE NOTE

USING THE ASSIGNMENT INFORMATION DIALOG BOX TO TRACK PROGRESS

The Tracking tab of the Assignment Information dialog box contains update fields for resource and cost data like Actual Work, Actual Start, Actual Finish, % Work Complete, and Remaining Work. Use the Notes tab on the same dialog box to document reasons for variances between baseline estimates and actual data.

⑨ *From the Task Usage view, click the Assignment Information button for an alternate data entry option.*

⑩ *Click the Tracking tab.*

⑪ *Enter actual work.*

⑫ *Enter actual start date of the work.*

⑬ *To use the Task Form as a means of data entry, select View ⇨ More Views, and select Task Form.*

⑭ *Right-click in the bottom of the form to display a shortcut menu.*

⑮ *Select Resource Work as the detail table.*

⑯ *Enter actual work on this table.*

FIND IT ONLINE

For resource management software that integrates with Project 2000, see **http://www.amsusa.com**.

Analyzing Variances

Generally, it is not adequate to merely record actual progress routinely during the execution of the project. Rather, to manage the project work effectively, consider analyzing the variances routinely as well. When analyzing the differences between the baseline estimates and the actual results, determine the reasons for the variances and decide whether you need to take corrective action or whether your plan is working well.

Variance analysis usually involves establishing a variance threshold for the level of corrective action needed. For example, during the first few weeks of the project, you may be able to accept a 15 percent variance in duration or cost without taking immediate corrective action due to your ability to correct slowly over time. However, during the last few weeks of the project, any variance may necessitate that corrective action be taken. In this task, you'll explore numerous ways within Project 2000 to check for variances.

Variance fields reside on at least three predefined tables for use with any view that accepts tables. The Variance table lists the amount of variance between baseline and actual start and finish dates. Likewise, the Cost table shows variances between baseline and actual costs. In addition, the Work table provides variance information between baseline and actual work.

The distribution worksheet of both the Task Usage and Resource Usage views contains fields for baseline and actual fields. For example, display choices include Baseline Work and Actual Work, and Baseline Cost and Actual Cost. There aren't any specific variance fields here, but you can manually check for differences or use a filter to help you locate variances.

① To view start and finish date variances, click the Gantt Chart button.

② Choose View ➪ Table, and select the Variance table.

③ Locate the Start Variance column.

④ To view cost variance, select View ➪ Table, and select the Cost table.

⑤ Locate the Variance column.

CROSS-REFERENCE

See "Using Standard Filters" in Chapter 10 for more information about applying filters.

If you prefer forms to views, consider using the Resource Form and applying either the Cost or Work detail table. Similarly, the Task Form showing either the Resource Work or Resource Cost detail table supplies variance information.

For a quick look at variances related to a specific task or resource, click the Cost Tracking, Schedule Tracking, or Work Tracking buttons on the Custom Forms toolbar. Clicking the Statistics button on the Tracking toolbar displays variance information for the entire project rather than for a specific task.

TAKE NOTE

▶ USING FILTERS TO LOCATE VARIANCES

Filters offer a quick and easy way to locate specific variances in both tasks and resources. When looking for task variances, the Cost Overbudget, Late/Overbudget Tasks Assigned To, Slipped/Late Progress, Slipping Tasks, and Work Overbudget filters provide useful assistance. When working with resource views, try the Slipping Assignments, Cost Overbudget, Slipped/Late Progress, or Work Overbudget filters.

▶ OTHER USEFUL TRACKING FILTERS

To help focus on important aspects of the project during execution, use the Update Needed filter to locate tasks due for a status update. The Tasks with Deadlines filter helps locate important milestones, and the Incomplete Tasks filter finds tasks that can possibly be altered as part of a corrective action plan.

---

⑥ To see work variance, click the Work Tracking button on the Custom Forms toolbar.

⑦ Locate the read-only Variance field.

⑧ To view a read-only cost Variance field, click the Cost Tracking button on the Custom Forms toolbar.

⑨ Locate the Variance field.

FIND IT ONLINE

For a Web-based time collection system that integrates with Project 2000, see **http://www.journyx.com/**.

Understanding Earned Value

Earned value is an objective way of stating the value (in monetary terms) earned by the work performed to date in a project. Because of its objective nature, earned value reporting is used as the basis for contract payments in government contracting and often in construction contracts, and is becoming increasingly more popular in other industries.

Project 2000 calculates typical industry standard earned value results for you. One goal of this task is to help you become familiar with earned value terms and definitions so that you understand and can participate in earned value discussions. The second goal is to help you display earned value progress using Project 2000.

The following is a list of standard earned value terms and their definitions:

▶ *Budgeted Cost of Work Scheduled* (BCWS) is the baseline cost multiplied by the planned completion percentage (by the reporting date) or the percentage of the budget that should have been spent by this date. If the baseline cost is $10,000 and the planned completion percentage is 50 percent, the BCWS is $5,000.

▶ *Budgeted Cost of Work Performed* (BCWP) is the achieved cost of the task, calculated as Baseline Cost multiplied by Percent Complete. If the Baseline cost is $10,000 and the task is 60 percent complete, the BCWP is $6,000.

▶ *Schedule Variance* (SV) is calculated as BCWP minus BCWS. A negative amount indicates the task is ahead of schedule.

▶ *Actual Cost of Work Performed* (ACWP) is the total amount spent on a task to date.

▶ *Budgeted at Completion* (BAC) is a task's total baseline cost.

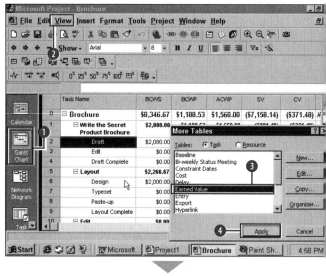

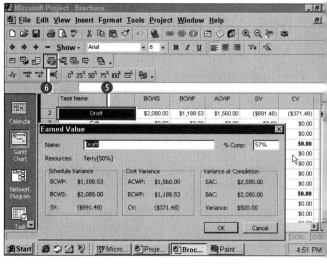

① To view earned value calculations, click the Gantt Chart button.

② Choose View ➪ Table ➪ More Tables.

③ Select the Earned Value task table.

④ Click the Apply button to view the table.

⑤ To see earned value calculations for a specific task, first select the task.

⑥ Click the Task Earned Value button on the Custom Forms toolbar to display earned value calculations for the task.

CROSS-REFERENCE

See Chapter 9 for more information about creating project budgets.

▶ *Cost Variance* (CV) is BCWP minus ACWP. A negative number represents an amount overbudget.

▶ *Estimated at Completion* (EAC) is a task's total cost.

▶ *Variance at Completion* (VAC) is BAC minus EAC. A negative number indicates amount overbudget.

Project 2000 offers three primary ways to display calculations. To see earned value calculations for all tasks, display the Earned Value table with any view that accepts tables (for example, Gantt Chart or Task Sheet). Notice that you cannot directly edit most of these fields as Project calculates them for you. However, you can edit both the Estimated at Completion and Budgeted at Completion entries directly.

To see earned value calculations on a task by task basis, click the Task Earned Value button on the Custom Forms toolbar. The fields divide into three categories: schedule variance, cost variance, and variance at completion.

The distribution worksheets for both the Task Usage and Resource Usage views contain display options for ACWP, BCWP, BCWS, CV, and SV.

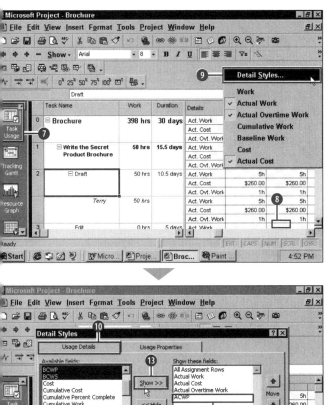

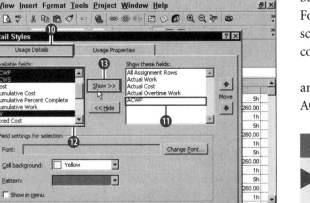

TAKE NOTE

▶ **BURN RATES**

In discussing earned value it is common to hear project managers discuss burn rate. *Estimated burn rate* refers to the amount of your budget you should have spent to date compared to your *Actual burn rate,* which is how much you have actually spent. A negative number indicates you are spending at a faster rate than planned or progressing more slowly than planned.

---

⑦ To display earned value calculations in the Task Usage view, click the Task Usage button on the View Bar.

⑧ Right-click anywhere on the distribution side of the view to display a shortcut menu.

⑨ Select Detail Styles to select the earned values to show in the shortcut menu.

⑩ In the Detail Styles dialog box, click the Usage Details tab.

⑪ Click ACWP in the Show these fields box and click the Show button.

⑫ Select BCWP, BCWS, and CV in the Available fields box.

⑬ Click the Show button to move all three into the Show these fields box.

FIND IT ONLINE

For software to integrate project data into an enterprise system, see **http://www.dtrakker.com**.

Revising the Current Plan

After capturing and entering actual progress data and analyzing variances and earned value, at times you will need to correct or change your current plan in order to meet the project goals. For example, if variance analysis shows that you are three weeks behind schedule, your choices are to try to alter some aspect of the plan to reduce the remaining time by three weeks or negotiate with your customer for a three-week deadline extension. In this section, you'll review various techniques for revising the current plan.

The techniques for revising a plan are basically the same as the techniques used to plan the project initially. After all, revising is just planning some parts of the project again. For example, in development projects with many unknowns, planning time remains rather constant throughout the project, even until close-out.

Before revising your plan, make a number of backup copies of your project file. Consider revisions as "what if" scenarios and experiment with different revisions before accepting one. You may also need to obtain approval on a "what if" before it becomes the agreed upon method of correction.

There are three main areas open to correction in your project; the scope and quality, the schedule, and the budget and resources. As you choose a corrective action or series of actions, consider the impact on the other areas.

Options for reducing the schedule or duration of a project involve reducing the length of the critical path. Breaking finish-to-start dependency links for critical tasks and allowing them to overlap (lag) shortens the project schedule. However, this technique may add to the project risk or increase the amount of rework needed for each task.

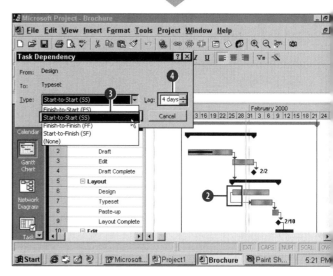

❶ To make backup copies of your file prior to "what if" revisions, choose File ⇨ Save As.

❷ To reduce the length of the critical path by overlapping task link, double-click the link line between the two linked tasks.

❸ In the Task Dependency dialog box, change the type to Start-to-Start.

❹ Enter a lag (overlap) amount

CROSS-REFERENCE

See "Reviewing the Schedule" in Chapter 11 for more about revising the plan.

248

Sometimes resources are added to the project in an effort to reduce the time necessary to complete all tasks. However, adding new people could negatively impact the synergy already established in the project team or slow down the work due to the communication time needed to bring these new people "up to speed" on task work. An alternative is to ask current team members to work overtime or devote a higher percentage of their time than originally planned.

Other alternatives to compress the schedule include reducing the scope or quality of the project deliverables, or using more experienced resources.

If your resources spend more time on tasks than planned, consider the skill level of the team. Are your expectations realistic in light of the skill level? Can you provide training to increase skill level? Can you provide better tools to make the resources more productive?

TAKE NOTE

CORRECTING POOR QUALITY

If the quality of your project is low, again consider the skill level of your team members. Do they have the expertise to do top quality work? Also, did you clearly document the deliverables and specifications (quality standards) for each task?

⑤ To add Saturdays as available overtime hours for a resource, click the Resource Sheet button.

⑥ Right-click any resource name to display a shortcut menu.

⑦ Select Resource Information as an easy place to change the resource calendar.

⑧ Select the Working Time tab.

⑨ Click the second S column header for Saturday, to select all Saturdays.

⑩ Click the Nondefault working time radio button to change Saturdays to available working time.

⑪ Enter the working time for Saturdays (From and To).

FIND IT ONLINE

For job-costing software, see **http://www.costcomp.com**.

Preparing Status Reports

For tracking purposes, you can print any of the views and tables discussed in this chapter with many customizing options applied. Since you've already practiced printing and customizing views in Chapter 12, in this task you'll look at various standard reports that serve as status reports. You will also practice including view and table information in a report document.

Several of the standard reports serve as progress update reports. In the Current Activities report category, the Unstarted Tasks report displays potential tasks available for modification during "what if" scenarios. The Tasks Starting Soon report is a good way to give advanced notice to team members. The Tasks in Progress report identifies which tasks need to be updated and included in reports. The Completed Tasks report can be used in team meetings as a list of accomplishments and successes. At the other end of the scale, the Should Have Started Tasks report highlights potential problems, as does the Slipping Tasks report.

The Costs report category contains a report to display cash flow for the project as a prediction of burn rate. The Overbudget Tasks and Overbudget Resources reports filter for specific project problem areas. The Earned Value report displays an objective look at the value earned in your project to date.

In addition to printing Project 2000 reports, you may want to use a view or table containing information in a report document. Copying a Project 2000 graphical display is possible using the Copy Picture button on the Standard toolbar. Views available for copy include Gantt Chart, Network Diagram, Calendar, Task Usage, Resource Usage, and Resource Sheet.

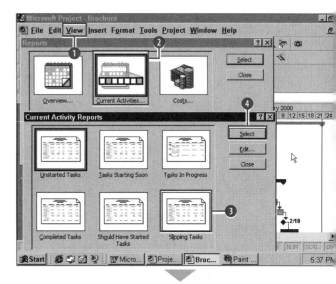

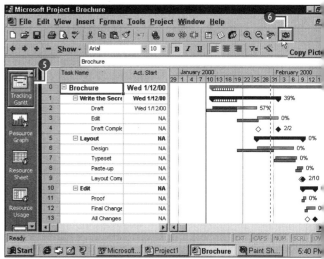

❶ To print standard status reports, select View ➪ Reports.

❷ Double-click the Current Activities report category.

❸ In the Current Activity Reports dialog box, click any report.

❹ Click the Select button to display the selected report.

❺ To copy a view for placeme in a Word document, select the view. In this example, click the Tracking Gantt button on the View Bar.

❻ Click the Copy Picture butto on the Standard toolbar.

CROSS-REFERENCE

See Chapter 12 for more information about printing reports and views.

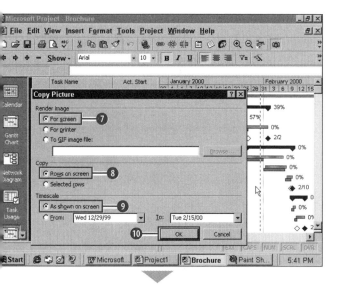

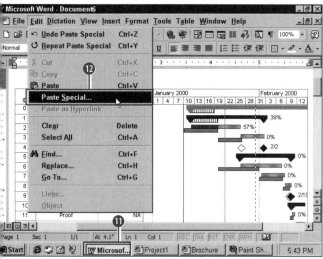

Use the Copy Picture dialog box to prepare the view for capture. Determine whether you are capturing the image to be pasted into another application (like Microsoft Word) for onscreen viewing or for printing purposes. A third option allows the image to be captured as a GIF (Graphics Image Format) image file for use on a Web site.

If the image you capture contains a table, you can decide to capture just the rows visible onscreen, or selected rows. As the image is captured, unselected rows between selected rows are removed, and the final image displays without blank or empty rows.

If the image contains a timescale, you can choose to capture the image as shown onscreen or specify a specific timeframe (From and To) for capture.

TAKE NOTE

▶ USING EDIT ⇨ COPY

Using the Edit ⇨ Copy command also captures an image to the Clipboard, typically as tab-delimited text, but it does not provide you with capture preferences as the Copy Picture command does. The Copy Picture command is better suited for capturing graphical images.

⑦ Click the radio button to send the image to screen for practice.

⑧ Click the radio button to capture all rows onscreen.

⑨ Click the radio button to capture the timescale as shown onscreen.

⑩ Click the OK button to make the screen capture.

⑪ Switch to Microsoft Word or open Word.

⑫ Choose Edit ⇨ Paste Special.

▶ View the pasted timescale.

FIND IT ONLINE

For image management software, see
http://www.jasc.com.

Personal Workbook

Q&A

1 How do you save a baseline?

_____

_____

_____

2 What is a _progress line?_

_____

_____

_____

3 What is the difference between Start date and Actual Start date?

_____

_____

_____

4 What are three useful tracking buttons on the Tracking toolbar?

_____

_____

_____

5 What are two places to enter actual schedule data into Project 2000?

_____

_____

_____

6 What does BCWP mean?

_____

_____

_____

7 How do you save an interim plan?

_____

_____

_____

8 What does the Copy Picture button do?

_____

_____

_____

ANSWERS: PAGE 326

EXTRA PRACTICE

1. Set a baseline for your project and view it using the Tracking Gantt view.

2. Clear the baseline from your project.

3. Display both the Tracking and Custom Forms toolbars.

4. Enter actual schedule data for a task using the Schedule Tracking button on the Custom Forms toolbar.

5. Display the Earned Value table for a Gantt Chart view.

REAL-WORLD APPLICATIONS

✔ Your project coordinator is new to Project 2000 so you advise him to use the Tracking and Custom Forms toolbars to make data entry easier.

✔ Before tracking progress, you set a baseline to record the original plan.

✔ You enter actual work spent by your resources on the distribution worksheet on your Task Usage view.

✔ You use the Statistics button on the Tracking toolbar for a global look at project status.

Visual Quiz

How do you access this dialog box? What purpose(s) does it serve?

_____

_____

_____

_____

_____

_____

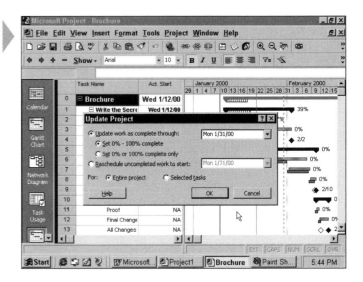

CHAPTER **15**

Using Project 2000 in Workgroups

Most projects require a group of people to make them successful. Whether you call them resources, a team, or stakeholders, good communication and task coordination between all project players is essential to the successful execution of a project.

Project 2000 includes two sets of workgroup features, *team messaging* and the new Web-based *ProjectCentral*, that encourage and help facilitate good team communication and coordination. Workgroup features, in general, work best when one person takes the role of facilitator or administrator of project data, security, and accessibility by new team members. This person is usually the project manager but on large or complex projects, a project coordinator frequently takes on this role. In addition, the project administrator usually has a level of authority and accessibility higher than that established for team members or "resources." Organizing data flow and solving data flow issues prior to setting up a workgroup can prevent communication disasters.

The team messaging features are familiar to users of Project 98, Microsoft's previous Project release. With messaging, a team can communicate using e-mail, the company intranet, or the World Wide Web. Messaging enables a project manager to send out team task assignments, send out and collect task update information during tracking, send out and collect status information, and send out schedule notes and reminders — all from his or her computer. It is easy to see how valuable these features become, especially with a distributed team. (A *distributed team* is one in which the team members are not all in the same physical location.) A Workgroup Toolbar also adds to the functionality of this feature set.

The new Web-based ProjectCentral data repository is a remarkable set of features. ProjectCentral is actually an interface between a server that supplies access to data for many users and the database that stores the data. Users save project data to the database either automatically or with simple menu choices, and ProjectCentral accesses the database where the project data resides and extracts requested information. ProjectCentral is easily accessible to anyone with access to the World Wide Web or your company's intranet, and it lets you establish security levels around accessibility to project, task, and assignment data.

In this chapter you will explore both the team messaging features and ProjectCentral. The chapter closes with techniques for closing out the project.

Creating a Workgroup

A *workgroup* is a collection of people that you designate as having the capability to communicate with one another through e-mail, a company intranet, or the World Wide Web. Workgroups are the core of both team messaging and ProjectCentral accessibility. Tapping into workgroup functionality is particularly useful when workgroup members don't all have access to Microsoft Project 2000. Both team messaging and ProjectCentral require that the project manager alone (or designated workgroup manager) must have Microsoft Project 2000 on his or her computer; it is optional for other workgroup members.

Everyone who wishes to use workgroup features of Project 2000 with a company intranet or the Web (Internet) must have a browser, such as Microsoft Internet Explorer 4.*x* or higher. (Caution: Test other non-Microsoft browsers for compatibility.) Workgroup members must also have access to the company server that controls the communication exchange for this workgroup, while those wishing to use the Web must have access to an Internet Service Provider. Lastly, each workgroup member must be identifiable with a unique e-mail address to use those features and a unique username and password for access to the workgroup Web site.

For e-mail access, each workgroup member must have a unique e-mail address on a MAPI-compliant, 32-bit e-mail system, as described in Chapter 13.

For help setting up a company intranet, Internet, or e-mail system, typical choices include your company network administrator, your IT/IS department (Information Technology/Information Services), or your company Webmaster.

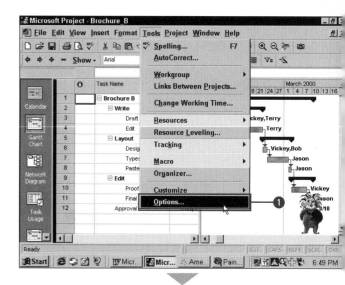

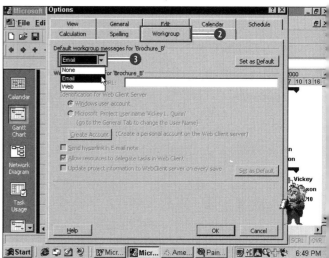

❶ To select default workgroup message type, (Web or Email) choose Tools ➩ Options.

❷ Click the Workgroup tab.

❸ For this example, using the drop-down arrow, select Email for workgroup messages.

CROSS-REFERENCE

See Chapter 13 for definitions related to intranet, Internet, and e-mail systems.

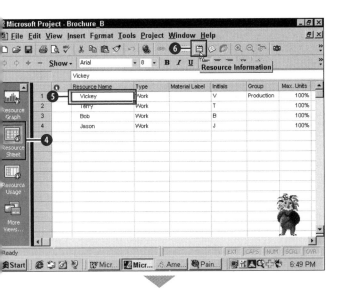

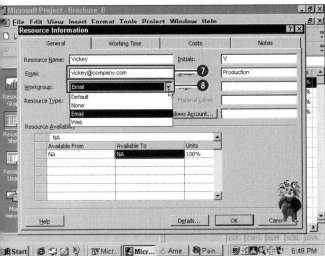

Setting up the workgroup in Project 2000 involves several simple steps. In this task, you set up team messaging to work with an e-mail system. Later in this chapter, you will set up ProjectCentral to work with Web messaging.

To further clarify, setting up for e-mail access requires both a general workgroup message choice on the Workgroup tab of the Options dialog box and three pieces of resource (workgroup member) information. The Resource Information dialog box is a convenient place to set up the e-mail address of the member, access by e-mail or Web, and the resource group. See this page and the facing page for instructions on setting up your workgroup.

④ To set up resources as part of a workgroup, click the Resource Sheet view on the View Bar.

⑤ Select a resource.

⑥ Click the Resource Information button on the Standard toolbar.

⑦ Enter the e-mail address for the selected resource.

⑧ Using the drop-down arrow for resource, select Email for Workgroup.

TAKE NOTE

▶ PERSONAL WEB SERVER

Windows 2000 contains Microsoft Personal Web Server so that you can set up your computer to act as a workgroup server for access by others.

▶ E-MAIL ACCESSIBILITY

If some members of your workgroup do not have Project 2000, they will need to run an executable file called wgsetup.exe (found on the Project 2000 CD-ROM). This file establishes the location of the member's inbox to send and receive messages. Setting up the inbox is easy. Simply copy the wgssetup folder (from the CD) to the drive on the network accessible by the e-mail system. Each workgroup member without Project 2000 should run the wgsetup.exe file, which opens the Workgroup Message Handler Setup dialog box.

FIND IT ONLINE

For a beginners guide to effective e-mail, see **http://www.Webfoot.com/advice/e-mail.top.html**.

Using Team Messaging

Team messaging, in Project 2000, includes a set of predesigned message forms that allow the project manager (workgroup manager) to send task assignments to workgroup members as well as request updates on task progress. In Chapter 14, you set up a system to track progress on project tasks, but that system was manual. Using these team messaging components, you can automate an updating system by communicating electronically with all workgroup members.

For example, in this task, you look at TeamAssign, TeamUpdate, TeamStatus, and TeamInbox. Let's explore these workgroup messaging components in the context of using an automated tracking system.

After the project plan is complete and a baseline is set, the workgroup manager (project manager) uses TeamAssign to send out task assignment messages for all tasks or just selected tasks. Using a message box, much like a memo pad, the project team members (memo recipients) receive notification of work assignments. The notification lists, in a table format, fields such as task name, work, start date, finish date, and comments. A default message asks recipients to respond if the assignment is not acceptable.

TeamAssign recipients, using TeamInbox, can view the table of task assignments. Each team member can respond "Yes" if accepting the assignment or "No" to show nonacceptance of the assignment before returning the message to the project manager.

TeamUpdate notifies team members of changes to task start or finish dates. TeamUpdate is only available after the original task assignment is accepted. Otherwise, there is no need to notify recipients of a change if the change doesn't affect them.

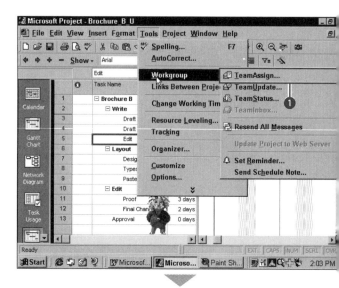

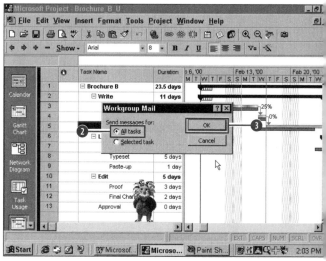

❶ To send a TeamAssign message, choose Tools ➪ Workgroup ➪ TeamAssign.

❷ In the Workgroup Mail dialog box, click the radio button for All tasks since this is our first assignment notice.

❸ Click OK.

CROSS-REFERENCE

See Chapter 14 for more information about tracking project progress.

TeamStatus is a powerful feature allowing the project manager to send out an automated request for update information about task progress. Team members then enter completed work and remaining work for each assigned task and send the information back to the project manager. The project manager can then click the Project Update button, and the TeamStatus information automatically updates the project plan. This results in no manual entry of tracking information except at the team member level.

Lastly, TeamInbox serves as the location to retrieve and read workgroup messages. TeamInbox displays all messages so that you can open them individually for response. Using TeamInbox is very similar to using any e-mail inbox.

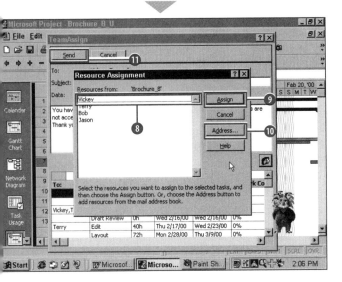

ESTABLISHING GOOD WORKGROUP HABITS

Project "kick-off" is a good time to plan your team workgroup communication procedures. For example, you may want all team members to check their inboxes regularly for messages and reply promptly to information requests. As the project manager, you will probably want to send out task update reminders immediately after the change takes place. You may also want to send out requests for status updates regularly, maybe even on the same day each week. As the project manager, you will also want to make sure that all members using this system understand how to receive and send messages.

④ In the TeamAssign dialog box, change the subject, if desired.

⑤ Enter a message in addition to or to replace the default message.

⑥ Review the assignments in the table.

⑦ If you wish to make a task assignment or add an e-mail address, click the Assign Resources button.

⑧ Select a resource(s) to assign to tasks selected in the TeamAssign dialog box.

⑨ Click the Assign button.

⑩ Click the Address button to add resources from the e-mail address book.

⑪ Click Send to send the TeamAssign notices.

FIND IT ONLINE

For information about public e-mail etiquette, see
http://www.iwillfollow.com/e-mail.htm.

Sending Schedule Notes and Reminders

The Send Schedule Note menu choice opens a dialog box that allows you to address the note to various project participants. You can choose to send the note to the project manager, resources (team members), or to contacts, which might include vendors or support personnel. To send the note to everyone in the workgroup, choose Entire project. Otherwise, to send the note to just the resources assigned to a specific task or tasks, choose Selected tasks. You can attach either a file or a picture of selected tasks with the note.

After clicking OK in the Send Schedule Note dialog box, an e-mail message form opens with the selected icon representing either the file or picture of selected tasks already attached. The project manager can simply complete the e-mail form and send it.

The Set Reminder menu choice opens a Set Reminder dialog box. Using this box you can request that a reminder notice automatically appear in the TeamInbox of the recipient prior to the start or finish of assigned tasks. You can set the notice to appear a user-entered number of minutes, hours, days, weeks, or months prior to the beginning or end of the task.

Another useful workgroup feature lets you route a file to various workgroup recipients. This feature might prove useful if you need to send the project file from team lead to team lead with each person adding to or building onto the current project plan. This might include adding a phase, deliverable, or component part to the plan. This technique is also useful while working with large projects that contain several smaller project plans.

CROSS-REFERENCE

See Chapter 1 for a reminder about a project life cycle and its applicability to an electronic messaging system.

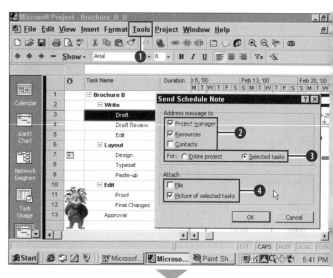

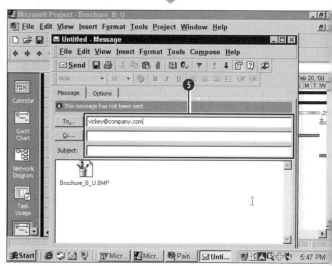

❶ To send a schedule note, choose Tools ➪ Workgroup ➪ Send Schedule Note.

❷ Check the appropriate Address message to boxes.

❸ Click either Entire project or Selected tasks.

❹ Check the boxes to attach a file and/or picture of selected tasks, or leave boxes unchecked if not applicable.

❺ Complete the top portion of the automatic e-mail message that opens.

▶ Notice the automatic attachment.

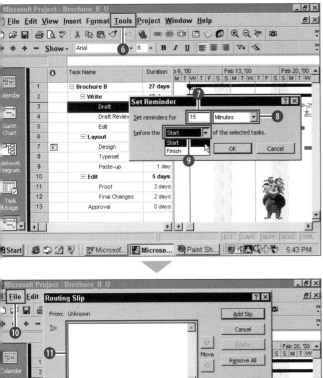

When setting up a routing plan, you can send the file to one recipient after another or to all recipients at once. You might consider using the "All at once" choice if the parts of the plan are independent of one another.

You can also choose to have the file automatically returned to you after all routing recipients are finished. Additionally, you can ask that automatic messages alert you when the file moves from one recipient to another. In this way you will know where the file is at all times and the progress it is making during the routing procedure. This technique is called "Track status."

⑥ To set a reminder notice, choose Tools ➪ Workgroup ➪ Set Reminder.

⑦ Enter an amount of time.

⑧ Select a time increment from the drop-down list.

⑨ Select to set the reminder before the start or finish of the task(s).

⑩ To route a project file, choose File ➪ Send To ➪ Routing Recipient.

⑪ Complete the To portion for the routing recipient.

⑫ Choose the appropriate radio button for routing sequence.

⑬ Check the boxes to Return when done and Track status.

FIND IT ONLINE

For information on the implications of universal e-mail, see www.rand.org/publications/MR/MR650/.

Customizing Workgroup Messages

Before sending out workgroup messages, you may want to spend a little time customizing the message to include only the information that seems appropriate. Project 2000 includes an easy, convenient method to customize messages. In this task you will explore four customization options.

The TeamAssign, TeamUpdate, and TeamStatus messages all contain a table that displays task and assignment information. The default fields include Task Name, Work, Start, Finish, Completed Work, Remaining Work, % Work Complete, and Comments. Using the customization options available, you can change the table to include just the fields that you find useful as well as arrange the table columns in the order that you prefer. For example, you might include an Assignment delay field for notification that a resource cannot start the task with other assigned resources, or include a Constraint Date field to show a date tied to a calendar date rather than driven by its predecessors. Other useful fields include Contact, Critical (Yes or No), Deadline, Duration, Hyperlink, Predecessors, and Successors.

As you add fields, message text in the middle of the dialog box tells you which team message will include this table column (TeamAssign, TeamUpdate, TeamStatus) and who can change data contained in the fields: the project manager or resources, or both.

The second customization option enables you to define how you will ask for completed work requests using TeamStatus messages. The project manager can request that team members respond by entering a total for the entire time period or by entering completed work by time phases. The time phases include daily or weekly accounting for completed work. The person responsible for tracking progress on this project should indicate to

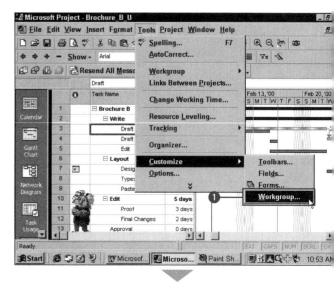

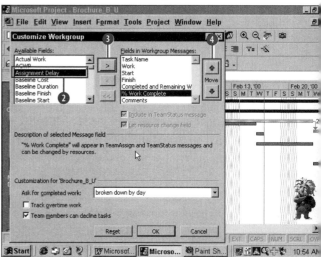

① To customize workgroup messages using the Customize Workgroup dialog box, choose Tools ⇨ Customize ⇨ Workgroup.

② To add a field to the workgroup message table, select the field from the left-hand list.

③ Click the right-pointing arrow.

④ Click the Move arrows to rearrange the order of the fields in the right-hand list .

▶ Notice the message text that corresponds to the two grayed-out checkboxes.

CROSS-REFERENCE

See Chapter 2 for more information about applying and changing standard tables.

all team members the desired tracking interval for completed work to ensure consistency of data collection.

The third customization option is a simple checkbox to indicate whether you wish to track overtime work. Even if overtime work is not charged to the project, it is still a good idea to track the amounts as a way to check and improve the accuracy of your estimates.

The fourth option is also a checkbox that gives team members the ability to decline tasks. In a matrix organization in which the project manager often does not have "line authority" over team members, it seems important to allow team members the right to decline tasks. From a project management perspective, it is probably better to know early on in the project that a resource is not committed to the task and deal with it as opposed to finding out the day the task is supposed to start that no one is working on it.

TAKE NOTE

▶ **USING THE WORKGROUP TOOLBAR**

For those using workgroup features, the Workgroup toolbar offers a convenient way to access all workgroup features.

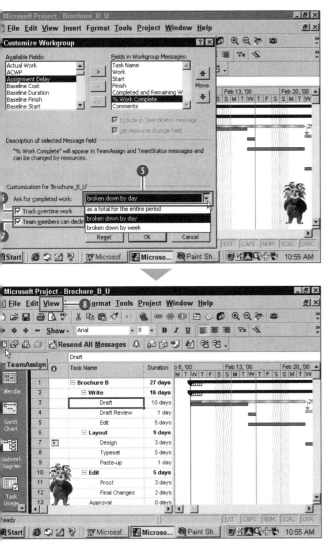

5 Using the drop-down list, select a completed work breakdown method.

6 Check the box to track overtime work.

7 Check the box to allow team members to decline task assignments.

8 To include the Workgroup toolbar, choose View ➪ Toolbars ➪ Workgroup.

FIND IT ONLINE

For a resource to help you reduce spam (unwanted e-mail), see **http://do-not-spam.com/**.

Understanding Microsoft ProjectCentral

Web-based messaging in Project 2000 represents the next generation of exciting and powerful project communication tools. Using the new Web-based features, you have access to dynamic database tools that allow all team members to access current project information anytime, anywhere. The Web-based features truly give you a repository for project information, not merely static Web pages of information.

The Web-based messaging in Project 2000 consists of a server (Microsoft ProjectCentral Server) and a client (Microsoft ProjectCentral) which serve as the interface between you and the database of project information. The server provides an Internet Information Server (IIS) and the database. Project 2000 Central Server supports Oracle, SQL Server, and Microsoft Database Engine (MSDE), a version of SQL Server. The only additional component you need is a browser to access the World Wide Web. (Again, check compatibility if using a non-Microsoft browser.)The Project 2000 installation CD-ROM contains the files for both Microsoft ProjectCentral Server and Microsoft ProjectCentral. (If you are not familiar with setting up a client/server application, consider seeking advice or support from an expert.) For Web client and server installation tips and requirements, see the Websetup.doc document in the Docs folder on your Project 2000 installation CD-ROM.

After your client/server application is up and running, all you need to do as the project manager is to enter server and access information on the Workgroup tab of the Options dialog box. On the Workgroup tab, you will select Web as the default workgroup message preference. Next, enter the URL (Uniform Resource Locator),

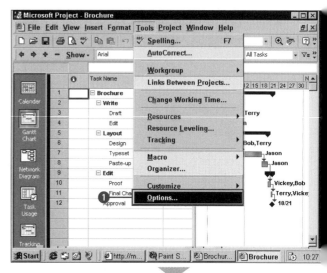

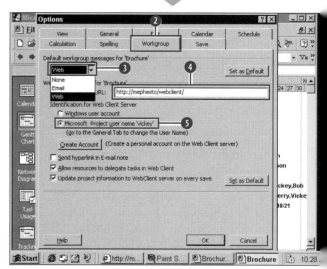

❶ To set up the Web-based workgroup, choose Tools ➪ Options.

❷ Click the Workgroup tab.

❸ Select Web as the default workgroup message type.

❹ Enter the Web Client Server URL.

❺ Click the radio button for identification to be authenticated by the Microsoft Project user name

CROSS-REFERENCE

See Chapter 13 for a contrast between static and dynamic Web pages.

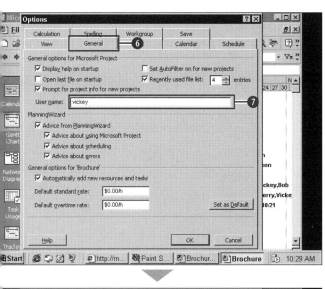

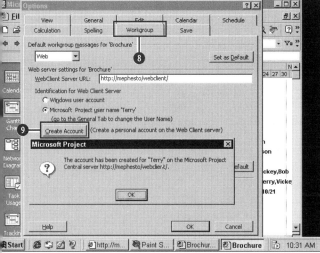

or address, of the Web Client server where you installed Microsoft ProjectCentral Server. This is known as your "Web site."

Also on the Workgroup tab, specify how you want users to log on to the Web site. Choices include logging on using a Windows user account, logging on using a Microsoft Project username (the "User name" that appears on the General tab of the Options dialog box for each user), or creating a personal account on the Web Client server for those without access through the other two methods.

Lastly, decide whether you will allow resources to further delegate their assigned tasks to other resources in ProjectCentral (the Web Client). This feature might be helpful, for example, where team leads need to delegate portions of their responsibilities to other, more remote, team members.

TAKE NOTE

UPDATING THE SERVER DATABASE

As a convenience, Project 2000 can automatically update the Web Client server database with current project information on every file save. The benefit to updating with each save is that you have the most current information accessible through the database. However, you need access to the server with each save, and updating the database requires more time than the regular save procedure. Without the automatic update, you can still update the database whenever you like, using menu choices.

⑥ To double-check the user name for Web access identification, click the General tab.

⑦ Enter the correct username if incorrect.

⑧ Click the Workgroup tab to complete the selections.

⑨ If the name you entered on the General tab does not already have a user account, click the Create Account button.

▶ Project automatically creates a new account based on the username entered on the General tab.

FIND IT ONLINE

See **www.tznet.com/busn/advocate/designer.html** for information on Web site management and design.

Accessing ProjectCentral

ProjectCentral not only gives you access to current data but gives you the capability to restrict data access rights based on each user's logon account name. These features help you create a secure data repository. Remember, even with password protection, once a user opens the file, all information is available as at least read-only.

For security and operational reasons, it is important to choose a ProjectCentral (or database) administrator. This person is typically responsible for assigning access rights, creating accounts for new users, teaching new users how to use ProjectCentral, creating project views and task access rights, and working with your company's network administrator to ensure that all team members can access the server. Two other roles are part of ProjectCentral: project manager and resource. Of course, the project manager can also serve as the administrator.

The administrator should log on to ProjectCentral first to set up the interface for other users. You will look at some of the administrator's responsibilities in the next task.

After accessing your project database Web site, you see a ProjectCentral logon screen similar to the home page in Project 98. Users are asked to select their username from a drop-down list and enter their password. If the user's name does not appear on the list, users can click "Setting up a Web Client Account" on the left side of the logon screen to ask Project 2000 to automatically create an account. Users accessing the Web site with Microsoft Windows network account authentication will bypass the login page.

After logging on, the ProjectCentral home page displays. Actions, or options that you can choose, show in two places. They show along the left-hand side of the page as collapsible and expandable list categories. As

CROSS-REFERENCE

See Chapter 4 for information about sharing information between software applications.

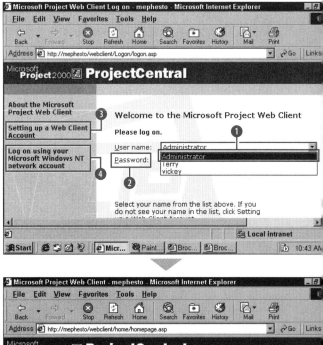

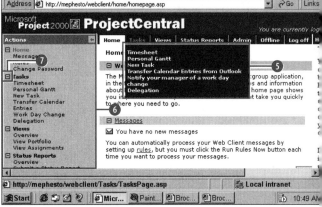

① To log on to ProjectCentral, choose your name from the drop-down list.

② Enter your password.

③ Click "Setting up a Web Client Account" if your name does not appear on the list.

④ Click "Log on using your Microsoft Windows NT network account" if that is your preferred logon method.

⑤ Choose actions from the menu choices.

⑥ Or, choose action items from the Actions list.

⑦ Click the minus sign to collapse the list to just the category name.

with a task list, click the minus sign to collapse the list to just the category title. Options also show along the top of the home page as menu items. The categories of menu choices with option actions are listed in Table 15-1.

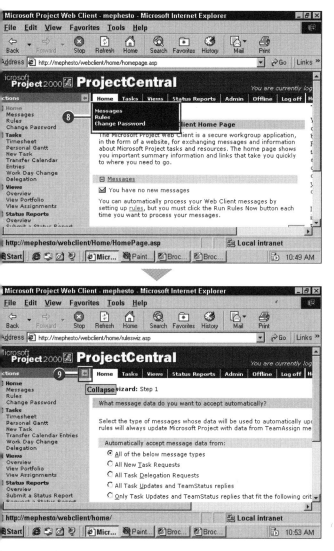

Table 15-1: PROJECTCENTRAL HOME PAGE MENU CHOICES

Menu Choice	Action Options
Home	Messages
	Rules
	Change Password
Tasks	Timesheet
	Personal Gantt
	New Task
	Transfer Calendar Entries
	Work Day Change
	Delegation
Views	Overview
	View Portfolio
	View Assignments
Status Reports	Overview
	Submit a Report
	Group Status Reports
	Request a Status Report
Admin	Overview
	Add, Remove, or Modify User Accounts
	Delete Items From Database
	Customize
	Manage Views
	Server Mode

⑧ To feel more comfortable with ProjectCentral, use the menu to move around to different Web pages.

⑨ To collapse the entire left-hand list of Actions and use the menu choices only, click the Collapse arrow.

Help is available by clicking the word "Help" at the top right of the home page.

FIND IT ONLINE

For information on Internet and intranet project management communications, see **www.vcsonline.com/**.

Performing Administrator Tasks

As mentioned in the last task, it is important for the ProjectCentral administrator to log on to the Web site and set up access and view rights for other users. You will preview some of these activities in this task.

The *Overview* choice gives you a brief summary of all Admin menu choices.

Add, Remove, or Modify User Accounts lets the administrator add project team members to the list of authorized users, delete no longer authorized users, change user e-mail addresses or logon names and account numbers, and change user roles (Resource, Manager, Administrator).

Server Mode indicates whether the server is accessible to all users or to the Administrator only. To perform many of the Admin tasks, the administrator needs to have sole access to the database.

Delete Items From Database is one of the choices that requires single server mode before its action is performed. This step actually allows the administrator to remove items from the server database and should only be completed by an experienced database user because certain database relationships between data may not be readily apparent.

The *Customize* choice contains numerous sub-actions. For example, the administrator can set up categories of nonworking or nonproject time to show in users' timesheets. The administrator may also choose which Gantt Chart to show and which formatting options of the timescale to display in the Views section. Task delegation is another customization option available to the administrator. The administrator also decides whether managers and resources can create user accounts for themselves and for other resources as well as how users gain access to the server.

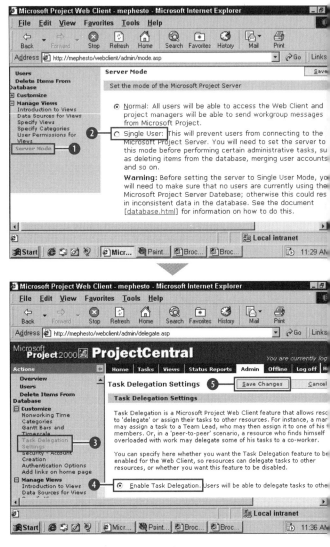

① To change the server mode to single user for administrative tasks, click Server Mode under the list of Actions.

② Click the radio button for Single User.

③ To enable or disable task delegation authority, choose Task Delegation Settings (in the Customize category) from the Action list.

④ Click the radio button to enable task delegation.

⑤ Click the Save Changes button when complete.

CROSS-REFERENCE

See Chapter 2 for information about project views.

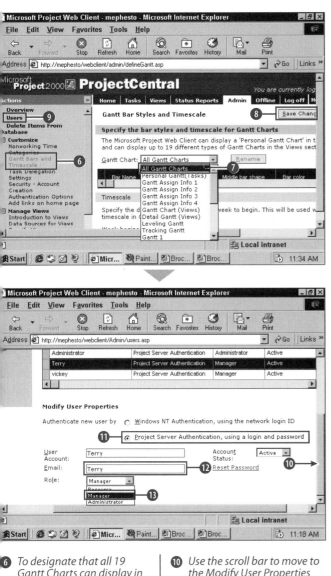

Administrators also control *Manage Views.* Administrators can decide, per user, which views and what data is accessible. Views allow users to access data without having direct access to the database. Like project views, these views are a set of fields and filters that allow you to see parts or all of a project. The administrator can create views that enable users to see a list of projects, then drill down to individual projects, and then continue to drill down to specific tasks and assignments. Part of managing views is also deciding not only what information is relevant to the individual user but also deciding if the user has permission to see information for another user or group of users.

TAKE NOTE

▶ DATABASE ACCESS RIGHTS

It is typical that the database administrator has access to both network and project information in order to effectively manage the data — not necessarily the data content. It is also typical that the project manager have access to all project data. It is usually the project manager's choice as to what data is relevant to team members. The administrator then sets up the system according to the preferences of the project manager.

⑥ To designate that all 19 Gantt Charts can display in the View section, choose Gantt Bars and Timescale.

⑦ Using the drop-down list for Gantt Chart, choose All Gantt Charts.

⑧ Click the Save Changes button when complete.

⑨ To modify user properties, choose Users from the Action list.

⑩ Use the scroll bar to move to the Modify User Properties section.

⑪ Click the radio button to authenticate the new user using Project Server authentication.

⑫ Enter the e-mail address of the user.

⑬ Using the drop-down list, choose a Role for this user.

FIND IT ONLINE

See **http://www.mcafee.com/** for information about network security and antivirus products.

Using ProjectCentral

After the administrator sets up ProjectCentral, users may log on and access data according to their current authorization levels. In this task, you will preview some of the many features available in ProjectCentral to help users manage their project commitments.

When you first log on, the Web Client Home Page displays. You can use this page to check change highlights. For example, check the Home Page Messages section to see if you have new messages. Or, check the Tasks section to see if you have new tasks added since the last time you viewed the home page. Also, check to see if you have overdue tasks for which you are receiving a gentle reminder!

The *Rules* choice runs the Rules Wizard, which helps you set up procedures for automatically processing your messages. For example, you can set up rules for accepting and declining messages or new tasks.

The *Change Password* command allows the currently logged on user to change his or her password.

There are three types of *Views* available: portfolio views, project views, and assignment views. In portfolio views, each table row represents a project. You can click one of two project links to either open the project in Project 2000 or see the project as shown in a project view in ProjectCentral. In other words, a project view shows one specific project from the portfolio list of all assigned projects. The assignment view drills down further still to display work assignments related to the chosen project.

Status reports allow users to request status reports, submit requested and unrequested reports, and create group status reports. The status reports form allows users to create user-defined sections. You might use these sections to list highlights, issues, unplanned work,

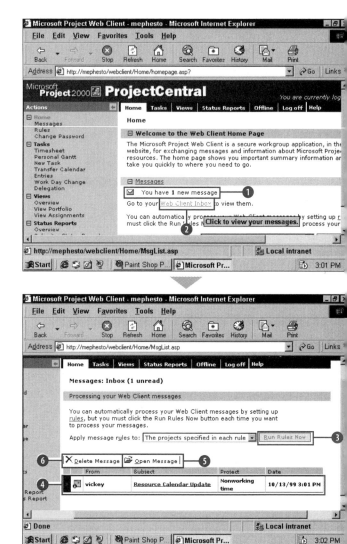

❶ When logging on to ProjectCentral, check for new messages.

❷ If you have new messages, click the Web Client Inbox hyperlink to read new messages.

❸ To automatically process rules according to the rules established, click the Run Rules Now button.

❹ Select the message you want to read.

❺ Click the Open Message button.

❻ To remove the message, click the Delete Message button.

CROSS-REFERENCE

See Chapter 12 for more information about generating status reports.

accomplishments, risks, or upcoming activities. To augment or substantiate your text, you can cut, copy, paste or insert tasks from the timesheet into the report.

Working *Offline* enables users to track task status even if they are not connected to the Web server. Once reconnected, users can resynchronize their information because it is being "pulled" from a single source: the database behind ProjectCentral. This is especially useful if server access time is limited in your organization.

Users should use the *Log off* procedure to exit ProjectCentral.

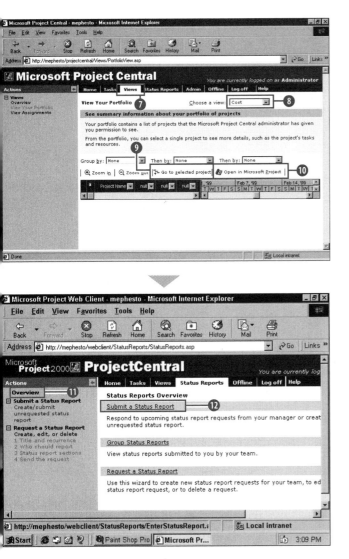

TAKE NOTE

COMMUNICATION PLANS

Project communication plans are usually created during the planning cycle of a project. Communication plans list the names of the project stakeholders, what type of communication they will receive or send, how frequently the communication should take place, and what medium (voice mail, phone, e-mail, videoconference, conference call, face-to-face, letter, memo) should be used. Many communication plans even list separate procedures to handle project emergency situations. Communication plans seek to limit the amount of miscommunication or "dropped" communication that can occur in a project.

⑦ To view your portfolio of projects, choose Views ⇨ View Portfolio.

⑧ Select a view from the drop-down list.

⑨ To drill-down to the project level within ProjectCentral, click "Go to selected project."

⑩ To open the project in Project 2000, click the Open in Microsoft Project button.

⑪ To access summary descriptions of status report functions, click Overview in the Actions list.

⑫ To create and send an unrequested status report, click the Submit a Status Report hyperlink.

FIND IT ONLINE

For books on database administration, see
http://www.barnesandnoble.com.

Accessing Task Information

The Task category offers numerous options for accessing task information. Here are brief summaries of some available options.

The Timesheet option displays a timesheet-like form to enter expended work data when tracking task progress. Based on your administrator's setup, the timesheet displays a table that usually contains project and task assignments as well as nonworking time such as vacations or sick time. The timescale looks like the work distribution side of both the Resource and Task Usage views. The timescale adjusts to track work by days, weeks, or months. This tracking information is usually entered by the resource or team member and sent to the project manager. Scroll buttons and bars provide access to portions of the Timesheet currently off-screen.

Other choices include a tab at the top of the Timesheet to filter and group tasks for more meaningful display. Users can also create a new unassigned task from the Timesheet to alert the project manager that unplanned-for work needs to be added to the project plan. A button to send an update back to the project manager displays on the Timesheet as well. Users can even jump to the Personal Gantt Chart by clicking the Gantt View button found on the Timesheet.

The Personal Gantt displays a Gantt view customized to contain your projects and tasks. This view looks like a Gantt Chart in Project 2000 with task bars and columns of data. Users can delete tasks, or zoom in and out to change the time increments for the timescale. Similar to a Gantt view in Project 2000, filtering, grouping, and the Go to selected task options are all available.

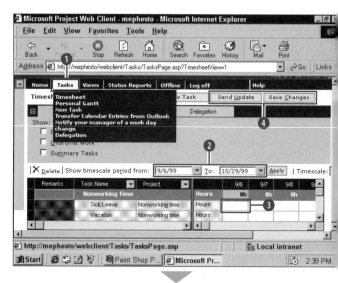

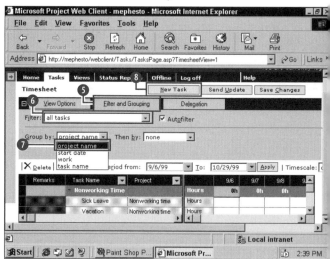

① To view or enter values on your timesheet, choose Tasks ➪ Timesheet.

② Select the timescale tracking interval (time period).

③ Enter hours (in the example) spent during this time period.

④ Click Save Changes; then click the Send Update button to send the information to your project manager.

⑤ To use filtering or grouping techniques, click the Filter and Grouping tab of the Timesheet.

⑥ Choose a filter from the drop down list.

⑦ Select grouping criteria using the drop-down list: "project name" in this example.

⑧ To create a new, as yet unplanned, task click the New Task button.

CROSS-REFERENCE

See Chapter 17 for creating a toolbar to combine features from the Web and Workgroup toolbars.

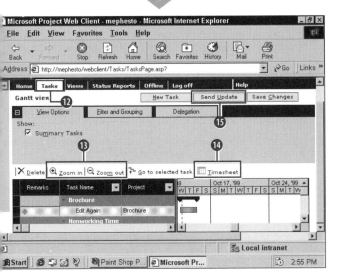

Also, users can jump back to the Timesheet from the Personal Gantt or create a new task, send updates to the project manager, or even delegate assignments to other resources. With proper authorization, you can delegate assignments for those tasks that you track, those you are the lead for, or those you track but are not the lead for. These choices, and others, are also available from the Tasks menu.

As you can see, the ProjectCentral interface is a convenient and powerful way to access database information without setting up queries and formatting displays yourself. In fact, team members don't even need to own or know how to use Project 2000 to be able to communicate effectively by using ProjectCentral.

TAKE NOTE

USING THE WEB TOOLBAR

Project 2000 contains a Web toolbar as one of the standard default toolbars. This toolbar contains some of the same functionality as your Web browser's toolbar buttons. Buttons that display on this toolbar include Back, Forward, Stop Current Jump, Refresh Current Page, Start Page, Search the Web, Favorites, Go, and Show Only Web Toolbar.

⑨ On the New Task screen, select the project associated with the new task.

⑩ Using the scroll buttons or bar, or pressing the Tab key, continue down the screen, answering questions about the new task.

⑪ When complete, click the Create Task button to add this task to your timesheet.

⑫ To view your Gantt chart, select Tasks ⇨ Personal Gantt.

⑬ Click the Zoom in and Zoom out buttons to change the timescale portion of the Gantt chart.

⑭ To return to the Timesheet, click the Timesheet button.

⑮ After saving any changes, click the Send Update button.

FIND IT ONLINE

For links to network and security information, see
http://www.telstra.com.au/info/security.html/.

Closing out a Project

Y ou can glean much information from conducting a post-project close-out. The close-out focuses on the project management process used, the final deliverables, how successful the team was in meeting goals, and issues and accomplishments.

Creating a project plan without tracking actual results has little value as a learning tool. Closing out a project provides the time and opportunity to capture all the important lessons learned from this project for use in subsequent, similar projects.

During close-out, it is typical to focus on the actions in the project that obtained desired results and also to concentrate on those activities that should be improved for the next project. Typically, the project manager collects the team members for this type of feedback and self-critique session. Let's look at several techniques for passing on the valuable data you have collected in your project file.

Consider using your project database created with ProjectCentral as a knowledge warehouse to store typical tasks with their original estimates and actuals so you can continuously improve your estimating ability based on specific company history. Remember than you can also save the project file in a format readable by other database applications.

For historical purposes, you can also save your file in a format readable in Excel (Microsoft spreadsheet program) as a record of planned versus actual work.

Consider saving a copy of your project file as an archival record of both the baseline plan and documentation of changes and final results. If you have a project office in your organization, it serves as an ideal project library for future reference. A project office is a virtual or physical office set up to assist in the implementation

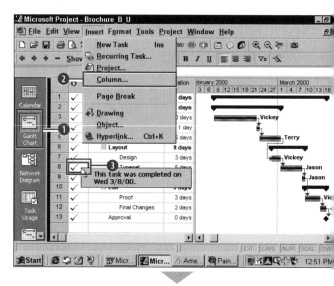

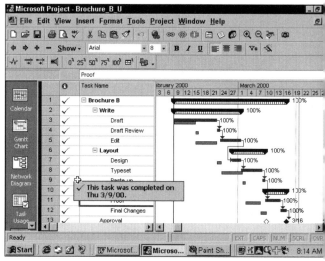

1 To view checkmarks for completed tasks in the Indicators column, click the Gantt Chart button on the View Bar.

2 Choose Insert ⇨ Column and insert the Indicators column, if needed.

3 Point your cursor to a checkmark to see the pop-up description of the completion date.

▶ A checkmark for every task indicates a completed project.

CROSS-REFERENCE

See Chapter 6 for information about estimating project task duration.

of projects and project management within an organization. The file can be saved on disk, or to a shared drive on the intranet, or saved for accessibility from a Web page. Also consider saving a hard copy as an archival record or save the project file on microfiche.

If you used a project template to begin your planning efforts, give feedback to the "owner" of the template as to the validity of estimates and tasks supplied with the template.

As you turn over deliverables to the project client, it can be valuable to ask questions about your success in meeting expectations.

Project 2000 provides two close-out features that you will explore in this task. A checkmark shows in the Indicators column for all complete tasks. The pop-up box indicates that the task is complete and gives the completion data.

The second close-out feature is a summary of final project statistics. The Statistics box gives read-only Current, Baseline, Actual, and Variance information for project Start date, Finish date, Duration, Work, and Cost.

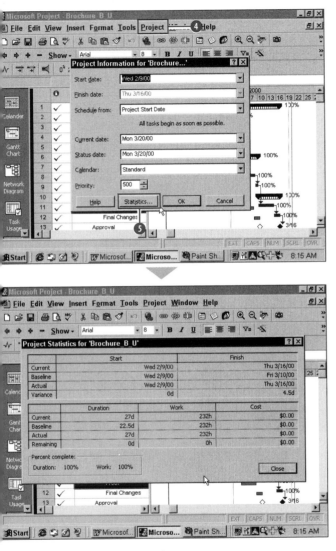

TAKE NOTE

▶ FOSTERING GOOD TEAM COMMUNICATION

One useful technique to foster good communication is to ask the team, during "kick-off" to create a Team Operating Agreement that lists team communication "standards."

❹ To view project statistics, choose Project ⇨ Project Information.

❺ Click the Statistics button at the bottom of the Project Information dialog box.

▶ The Project Statistics box shows a summary of project tracking information.

FIND IT ONLINE

For information about data warehousing, see
http://pwp.starnetinc.com/larryg/eis.html.

Personal Workbook

Q&A

1 What are two workgroup communication options?

_____

_____

_____

2 Web-based messaging in Project 2000 consists of what two major components?

_____

_____

_____

3 What three database types are supported with Web-based messaging in Project 2000?

_____

_____

_____

4 What is the name of the Microsoft Project Web Client?

_____

_____

_____

5 What should you do if your name does not appear in the list of users eligible to log on to ProjectCentral?

_____

_____

_____

6 What does the acronym MAPI mean, as in MAPI-compliant, 32-bit e-mail system?

_____

_____

_____

7 What is the name of the Web server included on the Project 2000 CD-ROM?

_____

_____

_____

8 Which tab in the Options dialog box is used to establish the Web Client Server URL for use by the Web Client?

_____

_____

_____

ANSWERS: PAGE 327

EXTRA PRACTICE

1. Install the client and server applications included on the Project 2000 CD-ROM.

2. Display both the Web and Workgroup toolbars.

3. Use TeamAssign with your e-mail system to notify team members of task assignments.

4. Access your ProjectCentral Web site remotely.

5. Update task tracking information in ProjectCentral, and use the information to automatically update the project plan.

6. Assist the administrator or serve as the administrator to set up view rights in ProjectCentral.

REAL-WORLD APPLICATIONS

✔ Before tackling ProjectCentral, you use the Team features with your company e-mail system.

✔ You work with a large, geographically separated team. You use ProjectCentral as the warehouse for all project task and assignment information.

✔ Using the administrator features in ProjectCentral, you restrict the access by a contractor to just her tasks.

✔ You use the Status Reports options with ProjectCentral as your report distribution method.

Visual Quiz

Where do you enter the default workgroup messaging options and establish the Web Client Server URL? How do you access this dialog box?

_____ _____

_____

_____

_____

_____

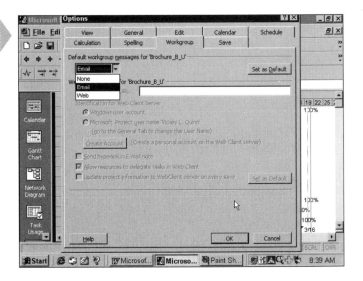

PART

VI

Working Beyond the Basics

This book has shown you how to develop a project plan, produce reports and other project communications, and manage a single project to completion. However, most projects and project managers don't exist alone in an organization. The multiproject environment is probably far more common than the single-project one.

For this reason, Part VI is focused, in part, on managing multiple projects. You'll learn to consolidate projects into one file, set dependency links between tasks in different projects, and create a common resource pool and share those resources across projects. You'll also learn about techniques for viewing resource allocations across projects.

The final chapter in this book presents numerous powerful techniques for customizing Project 2000 to fit your specific project management needs. For example, you'll learn how to create new tables and views for data management and presentation. To structurally change Project 2000 so it is more "user-friendly" for your users, you'll explore creating new menus and toolbars. Finally, to add functionality to Project 2000 you will develop custom fields and formulas and custom forms for data entry.

CHAPTER **16**

**MASTER
THESE
SKILLS**

▶ **Viewing Multiple Open Files**

▶ **Creating a New Window**

▶ **Inserting Projects**

▶ **Working with Inserted Projects**

▶ **Setting Cross-Project Dependency Links**

▶ **Creating a Resource Pool**

▶ **Working with Shared Resources**

Working with Multiple Projects

So far, you have worked with single projects contained in a single file. Although single projects are the foundation for an organization's overall management strategy, it is often necessary to bring projects together to obtain "across projects" data. For example, multiple project managers may in fact be managing pieces of a much larger project; the manager overseeing the entire project can benefit from pulling all the pieces together to view the project as a whole for scheduling, critical path, or reporting purposes.

Also consider the possibility that several projects may be part of a larger department, division, or corporate umbrella objective. These projects are said to be a related group of projects usually called a *program*.

Resource management relies heavily on the ability to pull projects together. A resource manager or department head needs to see the total individual workloads and schedules of workers for all current project assignments. Likewise, a look at proposed resource needs across future projects is needed for long-term resource planning.

Windows provides the capability to open numerous files at once, and Microsoft Project 2000 provides numerous tools for managing multiple open files containing projects and resources. In this chapter, you will practice techniques for managing multiple projects.

Each of the techniques presented in this chapter have specific uses, and you will be able to choose the best technique for your particular project management needs by the chapter's end. For example, you will practice opening several projects at once for reporting purposes. You will also practice combining several projects into one window for a *consolidated* or combined look.

As a second consolidation technique, you will practice inserting projects into other projects. This chapter also covers establishing dependency links between tasks of different projects where the timing or scheduling of a task in one project (or subproject) determines the scheduling of a task in another project (or subproject).

In the last two tasks in this chapter, I discuss creating and working with a resource pool of shared resources. You will practice creating the resource pool, sharing resources across projects, viewing shared resource assignments, looking for overallocations among shared resources, and discontinuing sharing.

Viewing Multiple Open Files

The most basic strategy to work with multiple projects is to view multiple open files, each in a distinct window. This technique is most useful for quick and easy report printing from numerous open projects. Having several projects in side-by-side windows on the same screen also allows you to compare information from one project with information in another. In addition, you can try different "what if" scenarios with different versions of the same project file by using separate windows for each project.

In Microsoft Project 2000, you can — depending on your computer system and memory constraints — open up to 50 files (projects) in separate windows at any one time. Use the Window commands from the main menu to move between open project files.

When you access the Window menu, a list of open windows (projects) displays at the bottom of the menu with a checkmark next to the active project. Up to nine open windows show on the menu, with any other open windows accessible from the More Windows choice.

If you choose to display only one window, it is the active window that displays. The other windows aren't closed; they're still open but in the background. This Windows functionality allows you to switch between project windows as easily as you switch between open applications.

To display multiple project windows on the same screen simultaneously, open all project files first. By choosing Window ➪ Arrange All, the windows will be sized and arranged, also known as *tiled* because of the cosmetic similarity to floor tiles. When windows are

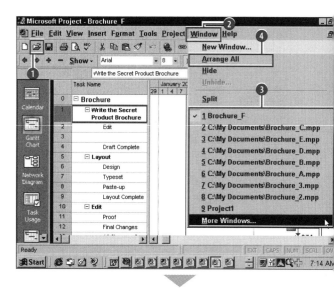

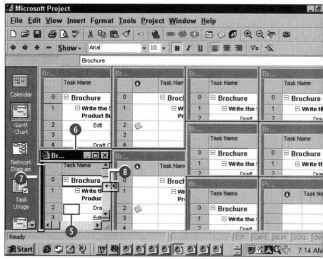

❶ Click the Open button to open multiple project files.

❷ To see a list of open files, click Window.

❸ Locate the list of open windows, the active window (checkmark), and More Windows (when more than nine windows are open).

❹ Click Arrange All to tile all open file windows.

❺ Click any window to make it active.

❻ Locate the active title bar (darker).

❼ Locate the active window indicator (left-hand margin).

❽ To resize a window, click the window divider for a two-headed arrow and drag to the desired size.

CROSS-REFERENCE

See "Creating a New Project" in Chapter 3 for more on using the Project Information dialog box.

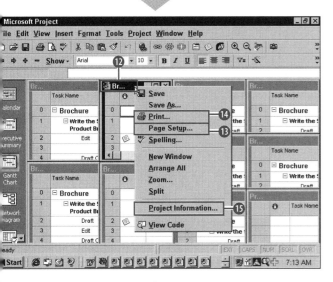

tiled, each project resides in a separate window with the project name in a Title bar. The project that is active when you select the Arrange All command now appears in the top left-hand corner of the screen and is still active.

To activate another project window, click anywhere in the window. The Title bar will change colors or become a brighter shade to indicate its active status. The active indicator bar also displays along the left-hand margin of the active window.

If you don't want an open project to display in this currently tiled group of projects, choose the project and select Window ➪ Hide. The project file is not closed; it's just hidden. To display this window again, choose Window ➪ Unhide and choose the projects to unhide or show from the Unhide dialog box that opens.

TAKE NOTE

▶ USING THE SHORTCUT MENU

When displaying windows in a tile format, right-clicking anywhere in a window opens one of two shortcut menus. Right-click on the Title bar to quickly save or print reports from the active window. This shortcut menu also contains a spelling command to run the spell checker for the active project window. You can also access the Project Information dialog box for each project through this shortcut menu.

⑨ To hide a window, click to activate the window.

⑩ Choose Window ➪ Hide.

⑪ To unhide a hidden window, choose Window ➪ Unhide and select the window to unhide from the Unhide dialog box.

⑫ To display the shortcut menu for printing, right-click the title bar of a window.

⑬ Click Page Setup.

⑭ Click Print to open the Print dialog box.

⑮ Click Project Information to open the Project Information dialog box.

FIND IT ONLINE

For companion program management software, see
www.projectlearning.com/project-software/ppm.htm.

Creating a New Window

A *consolidated project file* combines several files (up to 1,000 files maximum) into one file as if they were entered that way. Using consolidated files, you can bring project pieces together to create the overall project plan or combine subproject pieces together to make a master project plan. Initially, the projects maintain their separate identities as they are consolidated and look much like a summary task with subtasks. After consolidation, you may group, filter, and sort as if the file contains only one project.

Project 2000 offers two primary techniques to consolidate projects. In this task, you will practice the first technique, creating a new window to house the consolidated version. In the following task, you will insert projects to achieve the same result.

Whereas the Window ⇨ Arrange All command displays each project in a separate window, the Window ⇨ New command lets you create a single window that displays all combined projects. This command supplies a list of open project files from which you can choose files to consolidate together into a new window. After selection, the name of the new window is Project # with the number representing the last new project you created in Project 2000. If you save this new consolidated version, simply give it a new name when saving.

When viewing tasks from the various projects in this new window, the Indicators column shows an icon for inserted projects. In this case, the projects are inserted into a new blank window in the order in which they are selected from the list for merging. A project summary task is automatically added for easy distinction between projects.

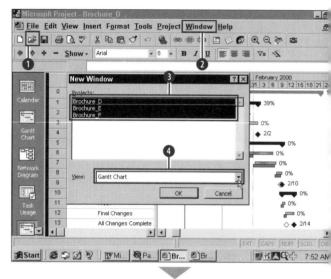

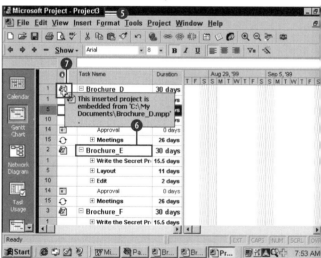

① To create a new window for inserted projects, open the files.

② Choose Window ⇨ New Window.

③ Select projects to be inserted into the new window, using the New Window dialog box.

④ Select a view from the drop-down list for the default view of the new window.

⑤ Locate the default new window name (Project #).

⑥ Locate the individual projec[t] appearing one below the other.

⑦ Locate the indicators icon fo[r] inserted projects in the Indicators column.

CROSS-REFERENCE

See "Changing Standard Views" in Chapter 2 for more information about displaying combination views.

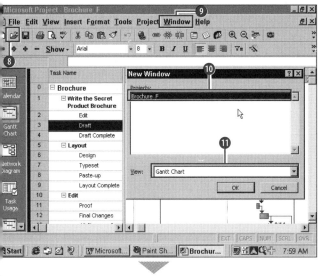

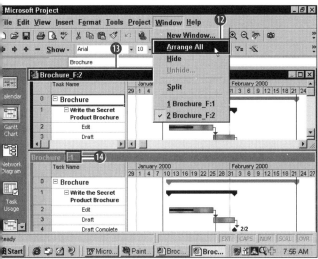

You can also use the Window ⇨ New command in conjunction with the Window ⇨ Arrange All command to see multiple versions of the same project side by side for easy multiple-data analysis. For this technique, choose only one project file from the list for projects to merge. Then arrange (tile) the project files to have the two versions of the same project display next to one another. In other words, you have one open file showing in two windows.

Any changes you make in one project window affects the other. This technique is similar to displaying a combination view except that now you can display a combination view in each window, or two full-screen views, or one of each.

TAKE NOTE

▶ **VALUABLE VIEW DISPLAY COMBINATIONS**

When displaying multiple windows of the same project, consider displaying a full-screen Gantt Chart in one window to view conflicting resource time periods and show a Resource Graph in the other full-screen view to look for underallocated resources as substitutes.

Another useful combination is to display a Tracking Gantt in one window to track the schedule and a resource Usage view in the other window to track actual work and cost information.

---

⑧ To display two instances of the same project in separate windows, open the desired project.

⑨ Choose Window ⇨ New Window.

⑩ Select the one project for the second instance.

⑪ Choose a view for the default.

⑫ To see both instances in separate windows, choose Window ⇨ Arrange All.

⑬ Locate the active Title bar.

⑭ Locate the numbers 1 and 2 for the multiple instances of the same project.

FIND IT ONLINE

For information about project portfolio management and prioritization, see http://www.pmsolution.com.

Inserting Projects

Using the Window ➪ New command from the previous section, a list of open file names appears for selection into a newly created consolidated project. However, if the project files you want to consolidate are not currently open you may choose to insert the projects rather than open them first by using the new window command. The end result of both techniques is exactly the same, and icons in the Indicators columns of both the new window command and insert project commands show the consolidated projects as inserted projects.

The files that you consolidate will perform in the same way as any other project file you create in Project 2000. The only difference is in the way the files are created.

You can choose to insert a project into an existing project that already contains tasks or insert projects into a file that does not yet contain any other project tasks. If your file already contains tasks, select the task below where you want to insert the project file. Then choose Insert ➪ Project to access the Insert Project dialog box.

Using the Insert Project dialog box, you select the project file (source file) to insert. To copy the tasks and task information from the source file into the host file, click the Insert button. It is important to remember that by clicking the Insert button, you have the same tasks and information in two places: a destination file and a source file.

You can create a dynamic link between the source project and the destination project by clicking the Link to Project box. A data change in either project file will update the other automatically. This is extremely useful if multiple project managers will track, update, and change their own project pieces, but you want to reflect

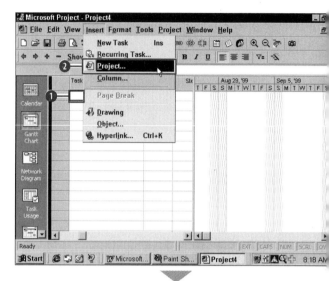

1 To insert a project into a file, select the task you want the inserted project to follow in the list.

2 Choose Insert ➪ Project.

3 Select a project as the sourc(e) file.

4 Check the Link to Project bo(x) to create a dynamic link.

5 Click the arrow on the Inser(t) button to insert the project (or) insert as read only.

CROSS-REFERENCE

See Chapter 4 for information on exchanging project information with databases.

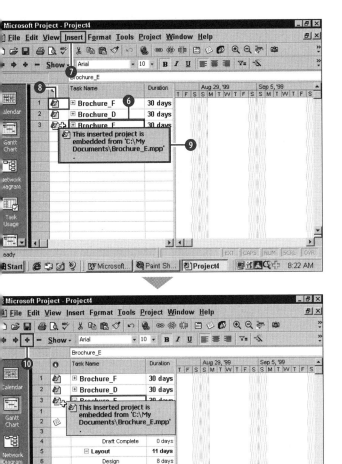

the most current information in the consolidated (master) project. Remember, the data updates, not the formatting options. Users of both the source and destination files retain their current formatting selections.

To restrict the ability to change the inserted project from the destination version, perform the insert as "read only." Clicking the small arrow on the Insert button gives two choices: insert or read only. Read only leaves the project control with the individual project owners but allows reporting from a consolidated level.

After insertion, the project summary task for the inserted group of tasks is collapsed, which means the subtasks do not show. Of course, you can expand the complete list of tasks after insertion by clicking the Show All Subtasks button on the Formatting toolbar.

TAKE NOTE

▶ **INSERTING A DATABASE FILE**

Clicking the ODBC (Open Database Connectivity) button in the Insert Project dialog box enables you to insert a database project file into a Microsoft Project 2000 project file. ODBC-compliant applications (like Access) store information in a format easily read by Project 2000.

---

⑥ To insert additional projects, select a blank row for the inserted project.

⑦ Choose Insert ⇨ Project and repeat Steps 1–5.

⑧ Locate the outline symbol identifying hidden subtasks.

⑨ Read the inserted project icon in the Indicators column.

⑩ To expand the outline or show the subtasks for an inserted project, click the Show Subtasks button on the Formatting toolbar.

FIND IT ONLINE

For information about a companion product that fosters team collaboration, see **http://www.cpts.com**.

Working with Inserted Projects

While working with consolidated project files, remember the following tips to make your efforts more productive and less frustrating! Information about the inserted file is available on the Advanced tab of the Task Information dialog box. A Link to Project checkbox indicates the source file location and name. Unchecking this box breaks the link, and the files will no longer update each other. Unlike previous versions of Microsoft Project, Project 2000 stores the relative path name to linked projects. This means that you can now move the inserted projects without re-saving them to a new location from within Project 2000.

A "read only" checkbox also indicates that restriction. Remember, an inserted project icon appears in the Indicators column for all inserted projects. If the inserted project is available as read only, an exclamation mark appears after the icon.

If using grouping techniques with a consolidated project, it is often difficult to determine the origin of individual tasks. Inserting a Project column next to the ID column on a table shows the project name for the task. Notice that duplicate task ID numbers display because of the multiple inserted projects. Having a method to determine the source project for a specific task is absolutely necessary.

Another useful technique for locating inserted projects is to display a Subprojects File column on the active table. The path and name of the inserted project appear there.

The sort command sorts tasks within each project independently. Grouping techniques, on the other hand, treat all tasks as if from one project.

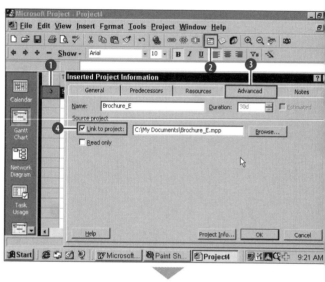

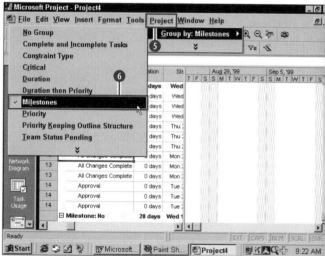

❶ To view information about an inserted project, select a project summary task.

❷ Click the Task Information button.

❸ Click the Advanced tab.

❹ Uncheck the Link to project box to terminate the dynamic link.

❺ To see the value of the Projec column when grouping tasks, first group by choosing Project ➪ Group by.

❻ Choose Milestones from the list to group by milestone tasks.

CROSS-REFERENCE

See "Grouping Tasks" in Chapter 10 for information about using grouping features.

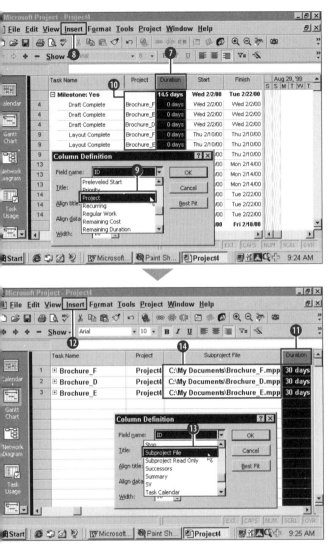

By default, Project 2000 calculates the critical path for each inserted project independently of the other projects. To calculate critical tasks for the project as a whole, regardless of the inserted projects, or to calculate multiple critical paths, use the Calculation tab of the Options dialog box. Check the box to instruct Project to calculate multiple critical paths.

TAKE NOTE

BREAKING APART LARGE PROJECTS

The concept used for inserted projects can be used in reverse to break a large project apart into subprojects while still maintaining the links between the individual components.

First, select the task ID for each task that will be part of the first subproject. Selecting the ID number selects the entire row, not just the contents of the name cell, for example.

Next, use either the Cut or Copy commands to save the tasks to the Clipboard. If you cut the tasks to paste them into a new file, the dependency links between cut tasks and those not cut will be lost. However, copying the tasks copies the link information, too.

Then, open the new project file for the subproject, and select the first blank task name cell. Choose Edit ⇨ Paste to copy the tasks from the Clipboard.

To maintain the dynamic link information between source and destination files, establish this subproject as the inserted file.

---

7 To add the Project column to easily see the source project for the tasks, click the column header after the Task Name or Name column.

8 Choose Insert ⇨ Column.

9 From the drop-down list for Field name, select Project.

10 Locate the project name next to each task using the Project column.

11 To add another valuable locator column, select the column header to the right of the Project column.

12 Choose Insert ⇨ Column.

13 From the drop-down list, select Subproject File.

14 Locate the file path to the source file using the Subproject File column.

FIND IT ONLINE

See **http://www.imscorp.com** for information about executive information systems using consolidated data.

Setting Cross-Project Dependency Links

Due to the quantity of tasks involved, or the independent nature of some subprojects, or even limits imposed by memory constraints of your computer system, consolidating projects is not always the answer to working with multiple projects. In this task, you'll practice establishing dependency links between projects that are not already consolidated.

Using cross-project links is common when a milestone or deliverable from one project is the predecessor or successor to a task in another project. The scheduling date of the predecessor impacts the successor so you want to create a dynamic link that automatically adjusts the schedule of the successor.

To establish a dependency link between tasks of non-consolidated projects, simply type the full path to the predecessor or successor task in the corresponding column in a table. The path includes the drive, directory, project filename, and task ID of the predecessor or successor task. For example, if you type C:\my documents\brochure.mpp\6 in the predecessor column for a task, you have established Task 6 in the Brochure project as the predecessor to this task. Any of the standard dependency types along with lead and lag times are available.

After the link is set, an automatic task is created by Project 2000 in the destination file representing the predecessor task. The task name appears in gray as do the start and finish dates, the duration, and the task bar. These tasks look like ghost or shadow tasks as they are not really in this project plan but should be seen because of their influence on the scheduling of tasks in this plan.

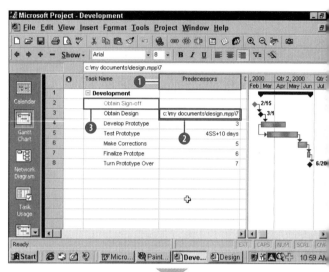

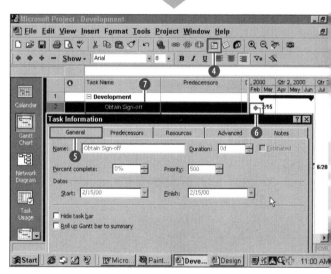

1. To create an external dependency link, display a Predecessors column on the current table.

2. In the predecessor cell for the successor task, type the complete path to the predecessor task, including the task ID number.

3. Locate the "shadow" task that is automatically placed as an external link reminder.

4. To view information about the "shadow" task, select it and click Task Information.

5. Select the General tab.

6. Double-click the link line between the external link and the successor task to change the dependency typ[e]

7. Double-click the name of th[e] external task to switch to th[e] source file.

CROSS-REFERENCE

See "Setting Dependency Links" in Chapter 6 for more information about dependency types.

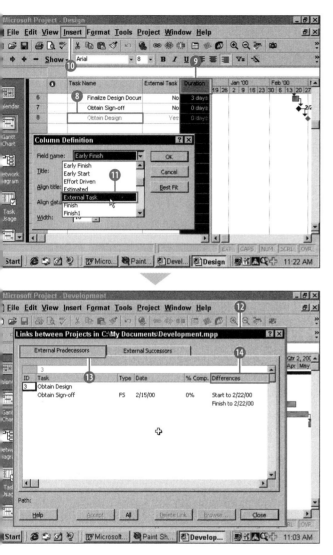

Double-clicking the dependency link opens the Task Dependency dialog box so you can change dependency type. However, double-clicking the "shadow" task name opens the file that contains the predecessor task.

Conversely, in the project that contains the predecessor task, an automatic task is also created to represent the linked successor task. This "shadow" task is also gray, and double-clicking the task name moves you back and forth between predecessor and successor tasks.

When opening a file that contains cross-project links, the Links Between Projects dialog box automatically opens to advise you of changes to either external task. An *external* task is one that has a dependency link outside of the project. The Difference column in the Links Between Projects dialog box describes the changes.

This dialog box also enables you to refresh changes to external files, reestablish file locations for the predecessor or successor paths, or delete an external link.

TAKE NOTE

▶ LOCATING EXTERNAL LINKS

An easy way to locate tasks with external links is to filter for them. If you display the External Task column on a table, a "Yes" appears in the column for all tasks with an external link. Filtering for those tasks locates those displaying a "Yes" in the field.

● Locate the successor task "shadow" in the source file.

● To add an External Task column for ease in locating external tasks, select the column header to the right of where you want the column inserted.

● Choose Insert ➪ Column.

● Select External Task.

⑫ When opening a file that contains external links, the Links between Projects dialog box may open.

⑬ Choose the External Predecessors tab.

⑭ Check the Differences column to note the delay from 2/15 to 2/22 for the Obtain Sign-off task.

FIND IT ONLINE

For an Internet enterprise multiple project solution, see
http://www.systemcorp.com.

Creating a Resource Pool

A *resource pool* is a group of resources shared across multiple projects. With Project 2000, you can maintain one list of resources yet use them across many projects. A resource pool can reside in any project file, but creating a project file that contains just resources has its advantages. For example, if the project contains only resources and no tasks, presumably someone can update the list with current resources and definitions without disturbing the access of anyone else waiting for a project file. More importantly, for security reasons, creating a separate "read only" resource file ensures that a limited number of people can change resource definitions.

To create a resource pool, create a Resource Sheet listing all resources, both work and material, along with resource definitions. Then open all files that will share the resource pool including the one that currently stores the pool. Select any sharing file (not the file that contains the pool) and choose Tools ⇨ Resources ⇨ Share Resources to access the Share Resources dialog box.

The Share Resources dialog box contains a radio button to Use Resources From a user-selectable list of open files. Select the file that houses the resource pool. All the resource information from the pool will automatically copy to the Resource Sheet of the sharing file. If names already exist on the Resource Sheet of the sharing file, the pool names will add to this list. However, if the same name appears in both original files with different definitions, you must choose which list takes precedence; the pool list or the sharer list.

The resource names and definitions stay on the sharer Resource Sheet even if the sharing is terminated. Restoring resource definitions to their original state before sharing took place requires manual changes.

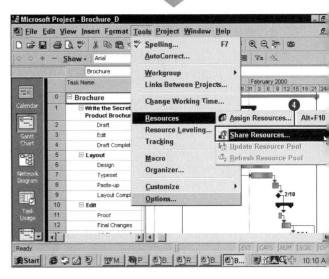

❶ Create a project file that contains no tasks, just resources, on the Resource Sheet.

❷ Open all project files that will use the resource pool, including the file that contains the pool.

❸ From the Window menu, switch to a file that will share resources (not the file that contains the pool).

❹ To establish sharing, choose Tools ⇨ Resources ⇨ Share Resources.

CROSS-REFERENCE

See Chapter 4 for information about creating template files.

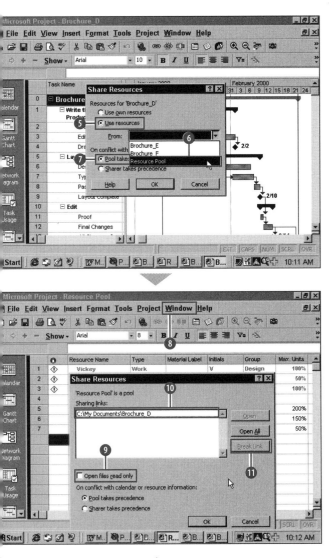

If you open the Share Resources dialog box for the file that contains the resource pool, it looks a bit different. Instead of asking which file to draw resources from, it lists all the files that currently use the resource pool. You can use this version of the dialog box to easily terminate sharing.

When opening a file that shares resources from the pool, an Open Resource Pool Information dialog box opens asking if you want to open all the files sharing the same pool. If you intend to view resource assignments across projects, then open all related project files. If your activities are limited to a single project, you probably don't need to open all files that share the pool.

▶ ORGANIZING MULTIPLE PROJECTS

If you intend to consolidate project plans after they are prepared, consider supplying each subproject manager with a template file that contains calendars and completing the Share Resources dialog box to look for the resource pool. This technique minimizes differences in calendars and resource definitions, thereby preventing problems that can take hours to sort out.

---

⑤ Check the radio button to Use resources.

⑥ Select the From file that contains the pool.

⑦ For conflicts with resource definitions, click the radio button for the pool to take precedence.

⑧ To see the Share Resources dialog box with a different appearance, choose the file that contains the resource pool from the Window menu.

⑨ Check the box to have sharing files open as read only.

⑩ To discontinue sharing, select a file in the list of sharing files.

⑪ Click the Break Link button.

FIND IT ONLINE

For information about a database to warehouse multiple Microsoft Project files, see **http://www.abtcorp.com**.

Working with Shared Resources

A final technique for working with multiple projects is to save the workspace in which they reside. Saving a workspace tells Project 2000 to record which files are currently open and, when you open the workspace file again, to open these same files. Saving a workspace saves time by opening all sharing files together rather than opening them one by one as a "Yes" answer in the Open Resource Pool Information dialog box instructs Project to do.

The default name of the workspace is resume.mpw. The mpw extension is the automatic extension given to workspace files. The default name, "resume," indicates that you will presumably resume work using these same open files at a later time. You can, of course save the file using a different name.

Since you now know how to share resources, it is appropriate that you know how to discontinue sharing resources across projects. There are two techniques to switch from sharing to non-sharing. In the Share Resources dialog box accessible from one of the sharing files, click the radio button to "Use own resources." This file will no longer use the shared resources. However, all resources currently on the Resource Sheet remain.

The second alternative to discontinue sharing is to use the Share Resources dialog box from the file that contains the pool. Since this box displays a list of all files that share the pool, you can simply remove a file from the list to discontinue sharing.

If you consolidate projects first, then viewing resource allocations is the same as described for any single project file. For nonconsolidated projects that share resources, the techniques are slightly different.

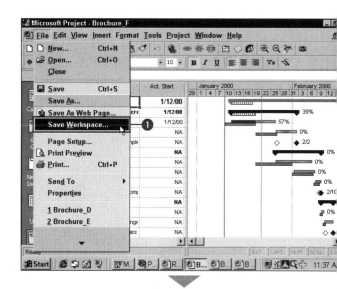

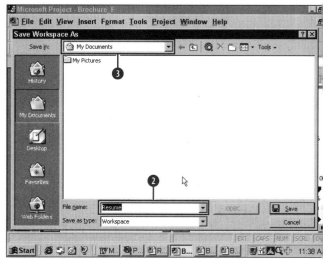

❶ To save multiple files in a workspace, first open all relevant files and choose File ⇨ Save Workspace.

❷ The Save Workspace As dialog box automatically opens so you can change the file name if you like.

❸ Change the "Save in" location, if desired.

CROSS-REFERENCE

See Chapter 11 for more information about checking resource allocations.

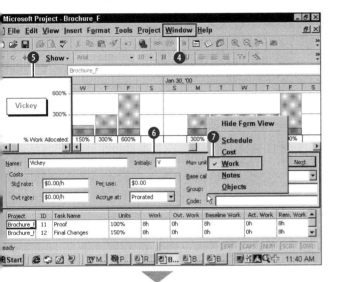

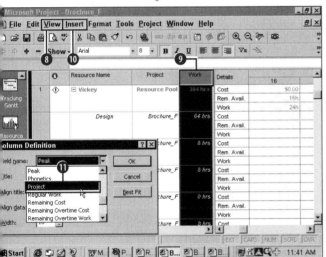

First, either open the workspace or open all project files that share resources. As you open views like Resource Graph, the allocation information represents totals for all tasks in all open projects. For example, if the Resource Graph shows a current allocation of 300% for a specific time period for Vickey, this number is a total of all Vickey's assignments across all the open projects for that same time period. To make working with all the open files easier, add the Project column to tables so that you can identify task assignments with corresponding project names.

TAKE NOTE

USEFUL VIEWS TO SEE SHARED RESOURCE ALLOCATIONS

The following views are particularly useful when viewing resource allocations across projects:

▶ A combination window with the Resource Graph in the top pane and a Gantt Chart with the Project column in the bottom pane

▶ Both Resource Sheet and Resource Usage views displaying the Project column

▶ The Resource Form displaying either the schedule, cost, or work detail table with the Project column

▶ The Resource Allocation view with the Project column added to the table on either the top or bottom pane

---

④ For a combination view, select Window ➪ Split.

⑤ Activate the top pane; select View ➪ Resource Graph.

⑥ Activate the bottom pane and select View ➪ More Views; select Resource Form and click the apply button.

⑦ Right-click in the Resource Form view; select Work from the shortcut menu to see the Project column.

⑧ To use another useful view, select View ➪ Resource Usage.

⑨ To add the Project column, select the column header to the right of the Resource Name column.

⑩ Choose Insert ➪ Column.

⑪ Select Project.

FIND IT ONLINE

For an enterprise solution that accepts Project 2000 project files, see **http://www.microframe.com**.

Personal Workbook

Q&A

1 What are three techniques for working with multiple project files?

_____

_____

_____

2 What is the function of the Window ⇨ Arrange All command?

_____

_____

_____

3 What are two project consolidation techniques that produce the inserted projects icon in the Indicators column?

_____

_____

4 What is the purpose of saving a workspace?

_____

_____

_____

5 How do you set a dependency link between tasks in different project files?

_____

_____

_____

6 What is an _external_ task?

_____

_____

_____

7 How do you discontinue using a shared resource pool?

_____

_____

_____

8 What does the exclamation point next to the inserted projects icon in the Indicators column indicate?

_____

_____

_____

ANSWERS: PAGE 327

Working with Multiple Projects

EXTRA PRACTICE

1 Open four project files and arrange (tile) them to display each in a separate window.

2 Create a new window and consolidate at least three project files.

3 Insert three project files into an empty project file.

4 Set a dependency link between two tasks in different nonconsolidated project files.

5 Create a resource pool and set up three project files to access the resources from the pool.

REAL-WORLD APPLICATIONS

✔ You consolidate the five subprojects planned by your team leads to view the overall project schedule.

✔ To share resources across three projects from the same department, you create a resource pool.

✔ The completion of your Design milestone determines the start of the Development phase so you set a cross-project dependency link.

✔ To consolidate four projects that are already open you use the New Window command.

Visual Quiz

What is the purpose of this dialog box? How do you access it?

_____

_____

_____

_____

_____

_____

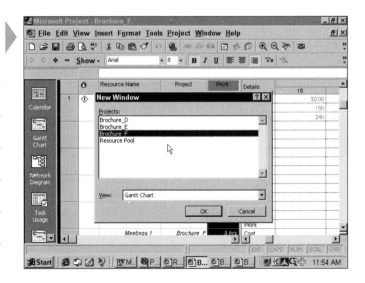

CHAPTER 17

MASTER
THESE
SKILLS

▶ Creating New Tables
▶ Creating New Views
▶ Customizing the Menu
▶ Customizing Toolbars
▶ Creating Custom Fields
▶ Creating Custom Forms
▶ Developing Macros

Customizing Project 2000

Microsoft Project 2000 stands far above other project management software applications for its ease of customization by end users. Furthermore, Microsoft is a leader in supplying users with the tools necessary to customize its applications. These two factors result in a powerful tool that is both functional and tailored to meet different needs.

You might think that you need to be an "expert" in software use or maybe even a programmer to customize Project, but you don't. All necessary tools are included, and customizable items like the menu and toolbars can be reset to their original form.

This chapter supplies you with examples of customizations useful in the workplace and step-by-step instructions for customizing. If you run short on ideas for customizing, ask other Project users in your company what additional tables, views, forms, or toolbar buttons would make using Project easier. The customizations in this chapter are listed in relative order of difficulty so as you complete one you will gain the knowledge and confidence to try the next.

All custom items that I discuss in this chapter are saved in the files in which they are created except the toolbars and the menu changes. Changes to these two items are saved directly into the Global.mpt file. This means that changes to the menu and toolbars affect everyone that launches Project using that same Global.mpt file. Users that share Project 2000 on a network are most typically impacted. However, all other custom items can be saved to the Global.mpt file or another project file using the Organizer.

In this chapter, you will create new tables for use with views and create new single pane or combination pane views. You'll add menus to the menu bar as well as create toolbars and toolbar buttons. This chapter also covers creating fields that return values based on user-defined formulas, a feature new to Project 2000. Finally, you'll create custom forms for updating purposes and record macros to make the performance of routine tasks easier.

Creating New Tables

Tables serve as the building blocks of views and, as such, play a key role in data entry and reporting. In order to develop a new view that uses tables, you must first create the table to be used by the new view. In this task, you'll explore designing and creating custom resource and task tables.

The Table Definition dialog box serves as the means for creating new tables. As you define a new table, notice that the table definition is for the currently open project only. However, you can use the Organizer, Table tab, to copy tables to other projects or to the Global.mpt file for use by all projects.

As you name your new table, give it a name that is both meaningful and concise. For example, the purpose of the "Bi-weekly Status Meeting" table is easier to remember than "Table 1."

Simply check the box to have this table name added to the main menu under Views ⇨ Tables. If you intend to include the name on the menu, consider assigning a shortcut character as an alternative to clicking the name.

The next row in the Table Definition dialog box provides five buttons to assist you in cutting, copying, pasting, inserting, and deleting rows. You can also simply click an empty row to begin.

As you select field names for the table from the drop-down list, you are actually selecting columns that appear on the table. The order that the fields show vertically in the definition is the same order they will appear from left to right in the actual table.

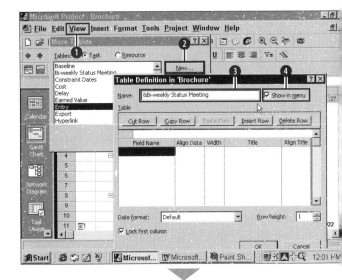

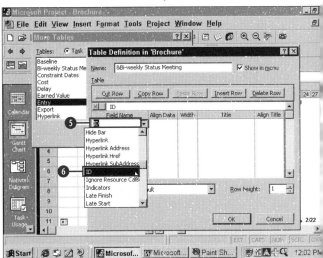

① To create a new table, choose View ⇨ Table ⇨ More Tables.

② Click the New button.

③ Type the name **&Bi-weekly Status Meeting**.

④ Check the box to show this table in the menu.

⑤ Click the first blank cell in th[e] Field Name column.

⑥ Using the drop-down list, choose ID as the first colum[n].

CROSS-REFERENCE

See "Applying Standard Tables" in Chapter 2 for examples of shortcut characters.

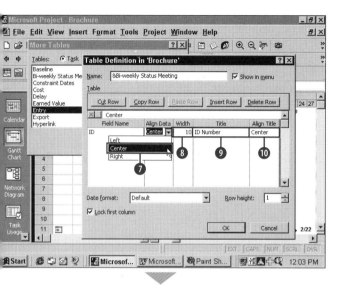

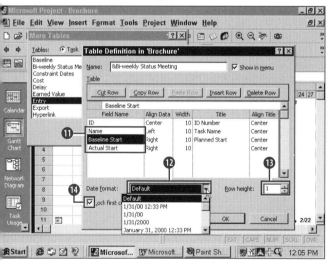

Both data and titles can be aligned either left, right, or center. Data items are the entries that appear in column cells, and titles are column headers. You can choose a column width here, let Project 2000 enter a default width, or adjust the width while entering data on the actual table.

Project 2000 uses field names to store data but you can give the field a new column header title for use on the table. For example, the field "Name" might use "Activity Name" as the title or the field "Baseline Start" might appear with "Planned Start" as the title.

The last definition items include selecting a date format, determining a row height, and choosing whether to lock the first column. Locking the first column prevents it from scrolling off the screen.

TAKE NOTE

CREATING A MENU SHORTCUT

To create a shortcut character, add the ampersand (&) symbol immediately before the shortcut character as you type the name of the new table. For example, you could create "&Bi-weekly" to define and underline the letter *B* as the shortcut character, or type "B&i-weekly" to use the letter *i* as the shortcut character.

⑦ Choose to align the ID data in the center.

⑧ Enter a width of 10.

⑨ Type **ID Number** for the title.

⑩ Choose to align the title in the center.

⑪ Enter the remaining fields.

⑫ Choose a date format from the drop-down list.

⑬ Select a row height.

⑭ Check the box to lock the first column.

FIND IT ONLINE

For Microsoft Project 2000 customizing tips see, **http://www.microsoft.com/project/prk/text/toc.htm**.

Creating New Views

The potentially time-consuming part of creating new views is first developing all of the component pieces used in views. For example, before creating a new Gantt Chart view, you must have available the table, group, and filter you will use. So, keep in mind that in order to build a new screen you must start by building all the small components. I'll assume for this task that you have the component pieces available and now want to design the new view.

Defining the new view is a two-part process. Using the Define New View dialog box, first decide whether to create a single or combination view. The combination view makes selections for both the top and bottom pane together.

To create a single view, use the View Definition dialog box. As with the New Table Definition dialog box, notice that this view is for the current project only. Likewise, use the Organizer, View tab, to copy the view to other project files. After naming the view, decide what screen type serves as the foundation for this view. The drop-down list contains the names of all the standard views in Project 2000 like the Calendar, Gantt Chart, Network Diagram, Resource Form, Resource Graph, and Task Sheet.

Depending on your choice for screen type, the Table and Group choices are either available for selection or grayed out. For example, a Gantt Chart needs to display a table but grouping is optional. Neither the Calendar nor the Network Diagram view, however, displays a table; therefore no grouping is possible.

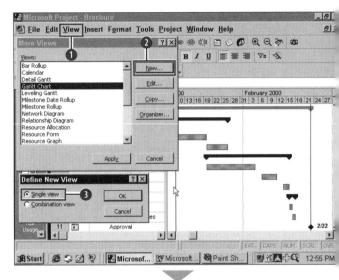

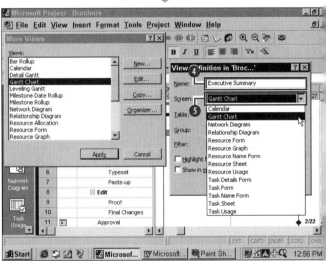

① To create a new view, choose View ➪ More Views.

② Click the New button.

③ Click the radio button to develop a new single view.

④ Name the view.

⑤ Choose a screen type from the drop-down list, Gantt Chart in this example.

CROSS-REFERENCE

See "Exploring the Global.mpt File" in Chapter 4 for more information about using the Organizer.

Next, choose the filter to apply to the view. This field is mandatory so select All Tasks if you do not wish to filter out any tasks or resources. If you select a filter other than All Tasks, you can use it as a highlight filter by checking the box.

As with tables, this view may be shown in the More Views menu. The same rules for assigning shortcut characters in table names also apply to view names.

The View Definition dialog box for a combination view contains only four selections. The Name and Show in menu items are familiar. Using the drop-down lists, choose which view to display in the top pane and which to display in the bottom pane. Before developing combination views, you must first create the tables, groups, filters, and single views that make up the combination views.

TAKE NOTE

▶ **REVERSING CHANGES TO TABLE AND VIEWS**

If you have edited standard views and tables and want to return to the originals, use the Organizer. For example, using the View tab, rename your edited version to keep it intact and copy the original from the Global.mpt file back into your project file.

---

⑥ Choose a table to display in the view.

⑦ Choose a group or no group to display.

⑧ Choose a filter name or All Tasks to display.

⑨ Check the box to show in the menu.

⑩ To create a combination view, choose View ➪ More Views, click the New button, and then click the radio button for Combination view.

⑪ Name the view.

⑫ Select a view to display.

⑬ Select a view to display in the bottom pane.

⑭ Check to show in menu.

FIND IT ONLINE

For examples of customizing wizards, see **www.coe. missouri.edu/~perfsppt/Dbell/gery13.html**.

Customizing the Menu

With the capability to customize menus come great power and responsibility. Unlike many of the other custom items you create, when you customize menu items, the changes are saved directly into the Global.mpt file. This means that any changes you make alter the menus for everyone that launches Project 2000 using the same global file. This deserves special consideration if a number of people start Project 2000 from the same place on the network server.

Now that I've sufficiently scared you about the responsibilities of customizing Project 2000, let's consider the power of customizing menus. By customizing the presentation of commands — either by changing default menus or building new menus — you can develop a very user-friendly, timesaving system. For example, you can add two new menus to the default menu bar. One menu lists the reports that you print weekly so all you do is point and print. The second new menu might be a list of the eight to ten most common commands that you execute. Further customizations might include removing menu items that you don't use or totally removing the default menu bar and creating your own.

A menu bar is very similar in function to a toolbar. For example, using a menu bar you choose an item from a list rather than click the button. In fact, for customization and selection purposes, the menu bar is considered a toolbar and included with the other toolbars in Project 2000. The menu bar is actually comprised of numerous menus and like toolbars, the menu bar appears docked at the top of the screen by default, but you may drag it to the side or bottom of the screen or simply allow it to "float."

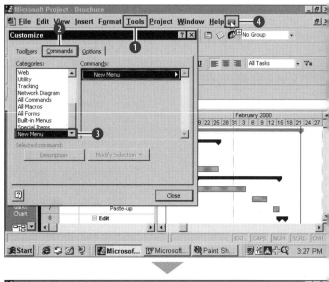

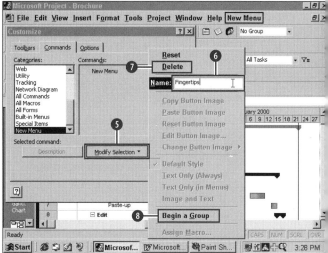

❶ To add a custom menu to the default menu bar, choose Tools ➪ Customize ➪ Toolbars.

❷ Click the Commands tab.

❸ Select New Menu from the list on the left.

❹ Click and drag the New Menu command on the right to the desired place on the menu bar and release.

❺ Click the Modify Selection button.

❻ Type the name.

❼ To delete this custom menu or any item added to it, select the item and click Delete.

❽ To add a divider line between items on the menu click Begin a Group and the line is added before the next addition.

CROSS-REFERENCE

See "Using the Menu Bar" in Chapter 1 for information about the default menu bar.

Once you create a new menu and drag it onto the menu bar, you drag items onto the menu list. Items to add include commands like print or copy, or a task information dialog box, or special items like a list of open project files or the most recently used files. Menu commands and toolbar commands are actually programming commands or macros. *Macros* are a recorded series of keystrokes that play back as you click the button or select an item from a menu. The macros for toolbars and menus in Project 2000 use Visual Basic as the programming language. You may add any command available in Project 2000 to your new menu. You may even add dividing lines in the menu to separate categories or groups of commands.

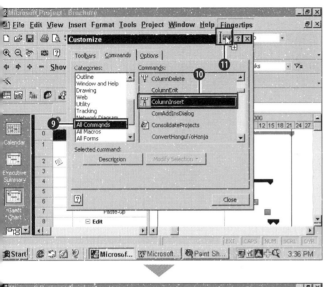

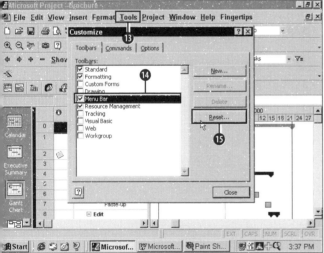

TAKE NOTE

RESTORING THE DEFAULT MENU BAR

If, after much customization and creativity, you have completely destroyed the functionality of Project 2000, the good news is that you can reinstate all the menu bar defaults, although you do need access to the Tools menu. To reinstate the defaults, choose Tools ➪ Customize ➪ Toolbars. Choose the Toolbars tab, select Menu Bar from the list, and click the reset button.

⑨ To insert commands onto the menu, select All Commands from the Categories list on the Commands tab.

⑩ Select a command such as ColumnInsert.

⑪ Drag the selection to the menu until the I-beam is displayed below the menu name.

⑫ Release to add the item to the menu.

⑬ To reset the default menu bar, choose Tools ➪ Customize ➪ Toolbars.

⑭ Select Menu Bar from the list of toolbars.

⑮ Click the Reset button.

FIND IT ONLINE

For a free weekly Microsoft Project tip in your e-mail, see **http://www.zdtips.com/imp/hpc-f.htm**.

Customizing Toolbars

The capability to modify and create custom tool-bars truly allows end users to take an "out of the box" software application like Project 2000 and feel like a software developer. For example, you might decide to add the bar styles and gridline commands to the Formatting toolbar, or design a toolbar to handle routine reporting functions, or condense existing toolbars to only the functions you use often. In this section you'll explore modifying and creating toolbars and buttons.

Working with toolbars is very similar to your earlier work with the menu bar. You'll use the same Customize dialog box as you design and edit toolbars.

As you already know, toolbars offer commands in the form of buttons. Clicking one of these buttons executes the programming for the button. The programming is called a macro. Later in this chapter you'll practice making simple macros that can then be attached to custom buttons as commands.

Many options exist for changing toolbars. For example, you can choose to simply add and delete buttons from existing toolbars, or create new toolbars and add command buttons to them. You can also modify buttons by changing the image of an existing button, editing the image with new colors, or creating new buttons and applying new commands or macros to them. Creating toolbars to handle routine commands for infrequent users is another great use of Project 2000's capabilities.

As you create your first new toolbar, it appears containing nothing but the toolbar name. At this point, you simply drag items from the list onto the toolbar. The toolbar automatically expands as you add more items. When appropriate, add divider lines to separate groups of buttons. When complete, drag the toolbar to a location at the side or bottom of the screen, dock it at the top, or simple let it float.

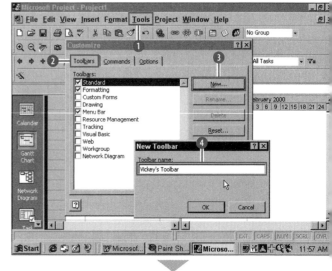

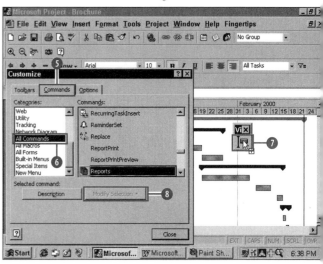

① To create a new toolbar, choose Tools ⇨ Customize ⇨ Toolbars.

② Select the Toolbars tab.

③ Click the New button.

④ Type the name of your new toolbar.

⑤ Click the Commands tab.

⑥ Select a category of items to place on the toolbar.

⑦ Select an item under Commands and drag it onto the new toolbar.

⑧ To modify any item, select it and click the Modify Selection button.

CROSS-REFERENCE

See Chapter 10 to get some grouping, filtering, and sorting button ideas for creating a new toolbar.

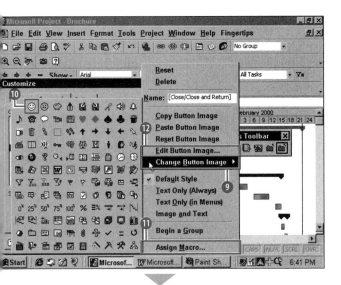

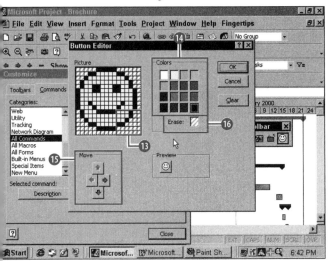

After dragging buttons onto your new toolbar, click any one of the buttons and click the Modify Selection button to further customize. If you choose to change the image, a box opens containing many sample images like smiling faces, piggy banks, musical notes, and clocks. If, on the other hand, you choose to edit the image, a button editor opens showing the button pixel by pixel. A *pixel* is a tiny square of color that can be modified using the provided color palette. Or, you can also change the command assigned to the button by choosing Assign Macro. A list of macros, both predefined and custom, is available.

TAKE NOTE

► USE CAUTION WHEN EDITING TOOLBARS

You can edit any toolbar whenever the Customize dialog box is open, so be careful when experimenting. For example, you can drag buttons off any toolbar that is currently showing. If you change an item unintentionally, open the Customize box again, choose the changed toolbar, and click the reset button.

⑨ On the Modify Selection list, select Change Button Image.

⑩ Click any image on the sheet and it will become the replacement image.

⑪ To change the command associated with the button, click Assign Macro.

⑫ To alter the appearance of the button, select Edit Button Image.

⑬ To alter the image, select any or several pixels.

⑭ Choose a color for the selected pixels.

⑮ Click the Move arrows to treat the pointer as a paintbrush moving across the pixels.

⑯ To remove a pixel color, select the pixel and click Erase.

FIND IT ONLINE

For a list of Microsoft Project companion products, see
http://www.projectmanagement.com/tools.htm.

Creating Custom Fields

In previous versions of Microsoft Project, users could only store custom data in static fields, not manipulate the data once entered. That has all changed with the release of Project 2000. In Chapter 10, you practiced developing custom grouping codes and assigning them to tasks using pick-lists. This is one example of the power of the new features for working with custom data. In this task, you'll explore two other features associated with custom fields, features that enable users to establish user-defined formulas to perform calculations using custom data and to use graphical indicators to represent data in a custom field.

Custom formulas are very common in financial calculations. For example, your company may have a burdened rate for resource usage that needs to be applied to your project costs. If your project includes multinational work, you may need to apply exchange rates to some of your cost fields. After performing risk analysis, as another example, you may add a contingency fund percentage to cover unplanned events.

Creating a custom field with a formula is best accomplished in a sequential fashion:

1. Begin your work with custom fields on the Customize Fields dialog box. Users first select which group, task, or resource to work with.
2. Select the type of field you wish to customize. Cost, Date, Duration, Finish, Flag, Number, Outline Code, Start, and Text are all available as field types.
3. Select the specific field from the list to customize. For example, ten cost fields appear on the list as Cost1 through Cost10. Simply choose one of these and rename it.

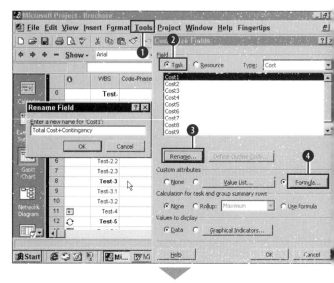

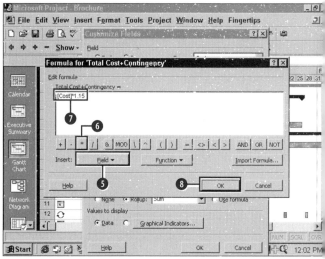

① To create a custom field using a formula, choose Tools ⇨ Customize ⇨ Fields.

② Select Task for the field; select Cost as the type and Cost1 for the new field.

③ Click Rename, and name the field using the dialog box.

④ Click the Formula button to establish the formula to calculate the new budget.

⑤ In the Formula dialog box, click Field; select Cost twice to insert the total cost field.

⑥ Click multiplication.

⑦ Click in the Edit field; enter contingency fund multiplier.

⑧ Click OK and OK again if you see a warning that any data in the field will be replaced with the formula-generated data.

CROSS-REFERENCE

See "Developing Custom Grouping Codes" in Chapter 10 for more about a different type of custom field.

4. Instead of using a value or pick-list, choose Formula, which opens a Formula dialog box. The formula that you create will return a value in the custom field as shown on a task or resource table. Due to the large number of fields and functions available in Project 2000, a complete listing of them here is not practical.

5. After entering the formula and returning to the Customize dialog box, establish the rollup calculation behavior for this field for summary tasks or group summaries.

For example, suppose a summary task has four subtasks with data in the custom field. When the data rolls up to the summary level, the summary task needs to know whether to average the four numbers, take a maximum or a minimum, find the standard deviation, sum the four numbers together, or simply apply the same formula you supplied for the custom field.

TAKE NOTE

USING GRAPHICAL INDICATORS

You can display field values as either data or graphical indicators. Graphical indicators are graphics that display showing whether a field's value is within a certain range, or above or below the range.

In the Customize Fields dialog box, click the calculation for Rollup summary tasks.

Choose a sum so that the total numbers for the subtasks will sum together for the summary total.

Under Values to display, choose Data to display numbers in the column.

To check the column, insert a Cost column on your Gantt Chart table.

Insert the Total Cost+Contingency (Cost1) column.

Using the Column Definition dialog box rename the column if you like.

▶ Compare the values to see the 15 percent increase.

FIND IT ONLINE

Find procedures for government use of earned value at www.acq.osd.mil/pm/currentpolicy/jig/evmig4.htm.

Creating Custom Forms

A s you saw in Chapter 14, forms can be a useful and safe method of entering project information. For example, it is common practice for members of the project team to update resource and cost information after the project starts. It is far easier, less time-consuming, and therefore less costly, to ask them to enter data into a custom form that contains just the fields for updating than to teach them how to use Project 2000 effectively.

Custom forms are accessible from the Forms button on the Custom Forms toolbar. Also, now that you are familiar with creating toolbars and toolbar buttons, consider making form buttons and either adding them to the existing Custom Forms toolbar or creating a new toolbar to hold them.

Use the Customize Forms dialog box to begin a new form. Use either the copy command to begin with a template of an existing form or click New to begin with an empty form. Since forms are saved in the file in which they are created, the Organizer (Forms tab) is available to copy forms to other files.

Clicking the New button automatically opens the Custom Form Editor with an empty form displayed. The Form Editor is like a program within a program in that you are creating a form file that you will save and exit from in order to return to Project 2000.

Onto your empty form, you drag text for explanation or field names, group boxes to create sections on your form, or drag fields into which entries are typed. You can also add OK and Cancel buttons although they appear by default on each new form. You can add a field as read-only so that a user may see the data but not edit it.

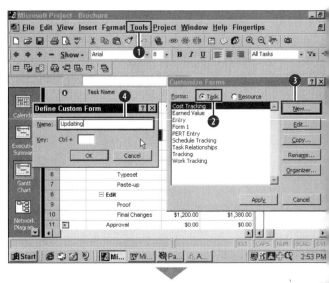

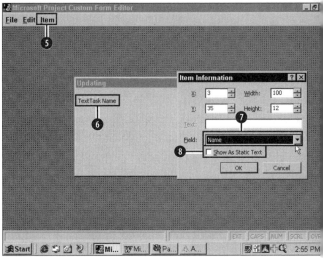

❶ To create a custom form, choose Tools ➪ Customize ➪ Forms.

❷ Click the radio button to create a Task form.

❸ Click the New button.

❹ Name the form in the Define Custom Form dialog box that opens.

❺ In the Custom Form Editor that opens, select Item ➪ Text.

❻ Enter the field entry text next to the placeholder word.

❼ Choose Item ➪ Field and the Item Information dialog box opens. Select Name from the Field drop-down list.

❽ Click to make the field data read-only, if desired.

CROSS-REFERENCE

See "Using the Tracking and Forms Toolbars" in Chapter 14 for more information about forms.

Use the Form Information dialog box to set the width and height of your form. You may also use X and Y co-ordinates to place the form on the screen or check the Auto box to ask Project to center the form on the screen for you. The coordinates refer to the starting position of the form. The X entry refers to the number of pixels from the left and Y the number of pixels from the top.

TAKE NOTE

▶ SHORTCUT KEYS IN USE BY PROJECT

When assigning optional shortcut keys to custom forms, remember that these are already in use by Project: B (Bold); N (File New); V (Edit Paste); C (Edit Copy); O (File Open); X (Edit Cut); D (Fill Down); P (File Print); Z (Edit Undo); F (Edit Find); S (File Save); I (Italics); U (Underline).

---

⑨ Drag the field entry box into position by the Task Name text.

⑩ Select Item ⇨ Group Box to add a form section or box within the form.

⑪ Use items from the Item menu to complete the form design.

⑫ When complete choose, File ⇨ Save.

⑬ To return to Project 2000 and close the Editor, choose File ⇨ Exit.

FIND IT ONLINE

For information about Project 2000 add-ons, see
http://www.genisystems.com.

Developing Macros

Macros are actually programs that carry out tasks whenever they are invoked. They are useful for doing those repeatable keystrokes or actions that you take in Project 2000. For example, use macros to display tables or views that you use often. Or, try running weekly status reports from a macro. By adding your macro as a button on a toolbar or to the menu bar, you can display the view, table, or report with one click of the mouse.

Macros are available in many software applications so you may already be familiar with them and their use. In Project 2000, macros are stored in the Visual Basic for Applications programming language. If you are a programmer, or aspire to be, you can write your macro directly in Visual Basic. For the rest of us, we'll use the macro recorder available in Project 2000 to accomplish the same programming goal.

The macro recorder acts like a music or sound recorder. You turn it on, record the keystrokes necessary to perform the task, and turn the recorder off. Project turns the recorded keystrokes into Visual Basic programming code. You can then edit the macro recording to "clean up" mistakes or play it back. The playback portion of the macro is what is attached to a toolbar button or the menu.

Keep the following tips in mind when working with macros:

▶ Macro names cannot contain spaces and the first character must be a letter. Consider using an underscore between words or capitalizing the first letter of each new word. For example, the custom report named "Resource X Remaining Availability" might become the macro name of "Resource_X_Remaining_Availability."

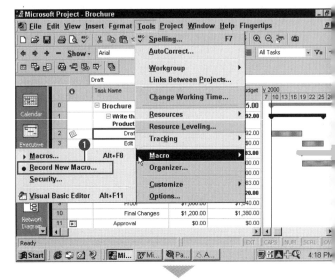

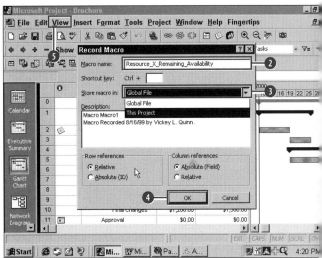

① To record a macro to print a custom report, choose *Tools ⇨ Macro ⇨ Record New Macro.*

② Type a macro name.

③ Choose a storage place for your macro.

④ Click OK. The macro will now record your keystrokes.

⑤ Execute the keystrokes to print the report (for example, *View ⇨ Reports).*

CROSS-REFERENCE

See "Customizing Toolbars" earlier in this chapter for more on assigning macro commands to toolbar buttons.

▶ If using optional shortcut keys, remember that some are already reserved for use by Project 2000.

▶ Consider the starting point of the macro. For example, if your macro displays a custom table, do you want to manually make sure you are displaying a Gantt Chart each time before you start the macro playback? Probably not. An easier solution is to assume you will be displaying a different view than the one you want for the macro and begin the macro recording by clicking the Gantt Chart button on the View Bar. When the macro plays back, even if the Gantt Chart is already displayed, clicking the Gantt Chart button again causes no harm.

▶ When defining the macro, if the active cell position is important to you, select absolute row position based on task ID and absolute column position based on column field name.

TAKE NOTE

▶ **MACRO VIRUSES**

Since macros are actually programs, it is a good idea to allow your antivirus program to scan for viruses if you share macros in your organization. With a macro, the virus "infects" the host computer when the infected macro opens.

⑤ When finished, stop recording by selecting Tools ⇨ Macro ⇨ Stop Recorder.

⑦ To test your macro, select Tools ⇨ Macro ⇨ Macros. Select your macro by name and click Run.

⑧ If you detect an error during playback, select Tools ⇨ Macro ⇨ Visual Basic Editor or rerecord the macro.

⑨ To assign a macro to a toolbar button, select Tools ⇨ Customize ⇨ Toolbars, and select the Commands tab.

⑩ Select All Macros.

⑪ Select the specific macro.

⑫ Drag the specific macro name from the Customize box onto the toolbar button.

FIND IT ONLINE

For more on free anti-virus software, see
http://www.thefreesite.com/antivirus.htm.

Personal Workbook

Q&A

1 When creating a table, what does *lock the first column* mean?

_____

_____

_____

2 What character do you place directly in front of a letter in a view name on the menu to create a shortcut?

_____

_____

_____

3 How do you restore the default menu bar?

_____

_____

_____

4 What dialog box must be open before you can drag a button off a toolbar?

_____

_____

_____

5 When creating a custom field, what is a *pick list*?

_____

_____

_____

6 What is the name of the program within a program used to create forms?

_____

_____

_____

7 What is a *macro?*

_____

_____

_____

8 What programming language is used for macros in Project 2000?

_____

_____

_____

ANSWERS: PAGE 328

EXTRA PRACTICE

1 Create a custom table that displays the WBS column to the left of the Task Name column.

2 Create a toolbar and add the Organizer command and three other commands to it.

3 Create one new custom field that uses a formula.

4 Create a macro that runs a report.

5 Create a macro that prints a view.

6 Attach a macro to a toolbar button.

REAL-WORLD APPLICATIONS

✔ In an effort to make Project 2000 easier to use for your new users, you create a toolbar that contains the most common commands.

✔ To assist your project coordinator during status tracking, you create a custom form containing tracking information fields.

✔ To save time, you create macros to print weekly reports and views and attach them to toolbars.

✔ To add a little humor into project management, you change some of the toolbar button images to something "not so serious."

Visual Quiz

How do you display this small blank toolbar? How do you position it at the top of the pane with the other toolbars?

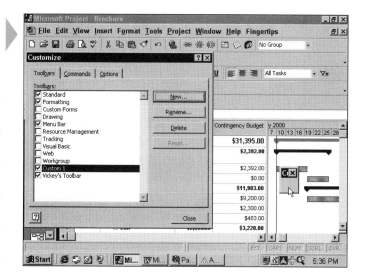

_____

_____

_____

_____

_____

Personal Workbook
Answers

Chapter 1

see page 22

1 **What are two ways to exit Project 2000?**

A: Close Project 2000 by choosing Exit from the File menu, clicking the Close button, or using Alt + F4.

2 **What is the Help Home Page?**

A: The Help Home Page lists the sources of help available in Project 2000.

3 **What is the purpose of a project binder?**

A: A project binder is an electronic folder that stores all relevant project documents and reports.

4 **What is a *hotkey*?**

A: A hotkey is a keyboard shortcut command that substitutes for a mouse click.

5 **In Project 2000, what is an *Office Assistant*?**

A: An Office Assistant is a form of online help that responds to user-entered commands.

6 **What are three ways to start Project 2000?**

A: You can start Project 2000 using the Windows Start command, clicking the Microsoft Project 2000 icon on the desktop, or clicking Project 2000 on the Quick Launch toolbar.

7 **What does an arrow to the right of a menu command indicate?**

A: An arrow to the right of a menu command indicates that an additional cascading or hierarchical menu is available.

8 **What are four toolbars available for display in Project 2000?**

A: The list of default toolbars includes Standard, Formatting, Custom Forms, Drawings, Tracking, Web, Visual Basic, Resource Management, Network Diagram, and Workgroup.

Visual Quiz

Q: **How do you change the appearance of the Office Assistant from Clippit (the paperclip) to The Genius?**

A: To change the appearance of the Office Assistant from Clippit to The Genius, right-click on Clippit, choose Assistant from the shortcut menu, choose the Gallery tab in the Options dialog box that opens, and select The Genius.

Personal Workbook Answers

Chapter 2

see page 38

1 What are the two main components that display as part of a Gantt Chart window?

A: The two main components are a spreadsheet (or table) and a chart.

2 What is a *combination view?*

A: A combination (or split) view displays two window panes, each containing a view.

3 Name one icon that displays in an Indicators column?

A: Indicator column icons include inserted project, unconfirmed assignments, hyperlinks, resource notes, resource overallocations, task notes, constraints, recurring tasks, completed tasks, and resource contours.

4 What are the three main types of views available in Microsoft Project 2000?

A: The three main types of views are graphical, sheet, and form.

5 What is the purpose of a table in a view?

A: A table displays columns of data using a spreadsheet format.

6 How do you change the default startup view?

A: To change the default startup view, choose Tools ⇨ Options, select the View tab, and select another view from the drop-down list.

7 What are two ways to adjust the width of a column?

A: To adjust column width either click and drag the column header divider, double-click the column header divider, or choose Best Fit from the Column Definition dialog box.

8 What is the purpose of the View Bar?

A: The View Bar is a quick and easy way to switch between commonly used views.

Visual Quiz

Q: How can you re-create this split window? (Hint: Use a Gantt Chart with the Schedule table on the top and a Task Form on the bottom pane.)

A: To re-create the window, choose Views ⇨ More Views, select the Task Entry view, and click the Apply button. Then, activate the top pane and select View ⇨ Table, and select the Schedule table.

Chapter 3

see page 54

1 Describe two techniques to create a new project file.

A: To create a new project file either choose File ⇨ New from the menu or click the New Project button on the Standard toolbar.

2 Under what conditions or constraints would you schedule the project from the finish date rather than from the start date?

A: Schedule from the finish date if the project has a "hard" deadline.

3 When is it reasonable for the Status Date to be different from the Current Date?

A: These two dates can be different if you are reporting progress as of a "frozen" status date that may be different from the current date.

4 On which Options tab is the date format choice found?

A: The date format is selected on the View tab.

Personal Workbook Answers

⑤ When would you use manual rather than automatic recalculation?

A: Use manual recalculation if you want to enter large quantities of data before seeing the impact of each entry to save time between recalculations.

⑥ What technique can you use to copy a calendar from one project to another?

A: Use the Organizer to copy a calendar from one project to another.

⑦ Describe the function of a project calendar.

A: All project tasks are initially scheduled based on a project calendar.

⑧ Describe what is meant by the calendar term "Non-default working hours."

A: Non-default working hours refer to user-defined work hours that are "outside" the work hours set on the default standard calendar.

Visual Quiz

Q: How do you select this noncontiguous group of dates in May, 2000?

A: To select noncontiguous dates, click the first date, and CTRL+click for all subsequent dates.

Chapter 4

see page 68

① What is the file extension for a standard Microsoft Project 2000 file?

A: The file extension for a standard Project 2000 file is .mpp.

② The mpt file extension is for what file type?

A: The mpt extension is for template files.

③ What is the function of a write reservation password when working with project files?

A: The function of a write reservation password is to ensure that only authorized users can edit information contained in the file.

④ Where can you see a list of your four most recently used files?

A: You can see a list of your four most recently used files on the bottom of the File menu.

⑤ How do you access the shortcut menu to rename a file?

A: To access a shortcut menu to rename a file, right-click the filename in the Save As dialog box or in the Open dialog box.

⑥ What is the function of the Global.mpt file?

A: The Global.mpt file stores elements common to all projects and opens each time you start Project 2000.

⑦ What are four types of information found in the Global.mpt file?

A: The Global.mpt file contains fields, calendars, forms, views, groups, toolbars, tables, reports, maps, filters, and modules.

⑧ What format should you use when sharing data with Microsoft Access?

A: To share data with Access, use the Microsoft Access Database file format.

Visual Quiz

Q: How do you establish password protection for a project file?

A: To establish password protection, choose File ⇨ Save As. Click the drop-down arrow on the Tools button and select General Options. Set password protection using the Save Options dialog box that opens.

Personal Workbook Answers

Chapter 5

see page 86

1 **What are two ways to open the Task Information dialog box?**

A: To open the Task Information dialog box, Choose Project ⇨ Task Information, or click the Task Information button on the Standard toolbar.

2 **What is the procedure for inserting a task between two other tasks?**

A: To insert a task, select a task that will be directly below the inserted task and choose Insert ⇨ New Task.

3 **Which dialog box is used to edit several tasks at once?**

A: The Multiple Task Information dialog box is used to edit several tasks at once.

4 **What is the difference between cutting a task from the list and copying the task?**

A: Cutting a task from the list actually deletes it onto the Clipboard whereas copying a task leaves the original and sends a copy to the Clipboard.

5 **What does the minus button on the Formatting toolbar do?**

A: The minus button hides subtasks of the selected task(s).

6 **What benefits can be gained from using custom WBS codes?**

A: Custom WBS codes are used to indicate a phase or related group of tasks.

7 **What is the purpose of a milestone task?**

A: A milestone task usually represents a flag, a completion, or an approval in a project.

8 **Where (on the menu) is the Recurring Task dialog box found?**

A: On the Insert menu. (Select Insert ⇨ Recurring Task)

Visual Quiz

Q: **Name the function of each of these buttons from the Formatting toolbar.**

A: From left to right, the buttons on the Formatting toolbar are Outdent, Indent, Show Subtasks, Hide Subtasks, Show (to an outline level), Font, Font Size, Bold, Italic, Underline, Align Left, Center, Align Right, Filter, Auto Filter, and GanttChartWizard.

Chapter 6

see page 104

1 **What three task types are available in Project 2000?**

A: The three task types are Fixed Duration, Fixed Work, and Fixed Units.

2 **What is the formula that Project 2000 uses to calculate duration?**

A: The formula Project 2000 uses to calculate duration is Duration = Work/Units.

3 **What are acceptable increments for duration estimates?**

A: Project 2000 accepts duration estimates in minutes, hours, days, weeks, and months.

4 **What is the definition of an *estimate?***

A: An estimate is, in simple terms, a rough or approximate calculation.

5 **Which estimating technique mentioned utilizes subject matter experts who independently estimate durations and record their assumptions?**

A: The Delphi technique utilizes subject matter experts.

Personal Workbook Answers

6 **What is a *predecessor task?***

A: In a Network Diagram, a predecessor task is a task whose scheduled timing determines the timing of another task.

7 **What is the difference between *lead* and *lag?***

A: In critical path calculations, lead time is time subtracted from a dependency relationship, whereas lag is time added to the relationship.

8 **When would you use a Network Diagram?**

A: You would use a Network Diagram to establish or view the logical flow of work through your project.

Visual Quiz

Q: **How do you display this dialog box? Which selection places a "?" after an estimated duration? Which selection sets a default duration unit for new tasks?**

A: To display this dialog box, choose Tools ⇨ Options. To indicate a task has an estimated duration, check the box for "Show that tasks have estimated durations" on the Schedule tab. To set a default duration unit for new tasks, choose a unit (minutes, hours, days, weeks, months) from the drop-down list for the "Duration is entered in" field on the Schedule tab.

Chapter 7

see page 116

1 **What information does Project 2000 use to calculate a schedule?**

A: To calculate a schedule Project 2000 uses information such as the project calendar, task type, estimates, resource calendars, constraints, and dependency relationships.

2 **When would you apply the Must Start On constraint type?**

A: Apply the Must Start On constraint when you want a task to begin on a specific date.

3 **What are the two constraint types that don't require a corresponding date entry?**

A: Neither As Soon As Possible or As Late As Possible require a date entry.

4 **What is the definition of *critical path?***

A: Critical path is defined as the longest sequence of tasks in a project.

5 **How is total slack calculated?**

A: The formula for calculating total slack is the Late Finish date minus the Finish date for a task.

6 **What are four ways to compress the critical path?**

A: Common techniques to compress the critical path include adding resources to critical tasks, working overtime to complete critical tasks sooner, contracting out deliverable production, reducing the project scope, and reducing the quality of the deliverables.

7 **What is the difference between setting a deadline date and establishing a constraint?**

A: A constraint date is used by Project 2000 to calculate the project schedule but a deadline date is not. However, a deadline date can act like a Finish No Later Than flag.

8 **When would you roll up task bars?**

A: You may roll up task bars when you wish to see individual subtask bars overlaid on top of the summary bar, typically to save space or report only at the summary task level.

Personal Workbook Answers

Visual Quiz

Q: How do you display these two icons in the Indicators column?

A: The small square icon represents a task that is constrained while the exclamation point represents a situation in which the scheduled date of the task is later than the deadline date.

Chapter 8

see page 128

 1 Where can you select the "Automatically add new resources" checkbox?

A: The checkbox to "Automatically add new resources" is located on the General tab of the Options dialog box.

2 What is a *material resource?*

A: A material resource is a consumable resource.

3 How many "full-time equivalent" writers are available if the maximum units is 250 percent?

A: If the maximum units available for writers is 250%, the "full-time equivalent" or FTE is 2.5 people.

4 How does a prorated cost accrual operate?

A: A prorated cost spreads the cost evenly across the task duration.

5 What is the purpose of a base calendar?

A: A base calendar acts as a starting point for a resource calendar.

6 What are the four main definition tabs of the Resource Information dialog box?

A: The four tabs in the Resource Information dialog box are General, Working Time, Costs, and Notes.

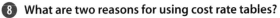 **7** What are two ways to access the Resource Information dialog box?

A: To access the Resource Information dialog box either right-click on a resource name in any resource view and choose Resource Information from the shortcut menu, or choose Project ⇨ Resource Information.

8 What are two reasons for using cost rate tables?

A: Two common reasons to use cost rate tables are to account for changes over time in standard pay rates or to charge different rates depending on work performed by resources.

Visual Quiz

Q: How do you display this dialog box? What do the two resource availability entries mean? What does *Resource Type* mean?

A: To display this dialog box, either right-click on a resource name in a resource view and select Resource Information from the shortcut menu or choose Project ⇨ Resource Information. The two resource availability entries mean that the available units of this resource vary over time. The Resource Type distinguishes between work and material resources.

Chapter 9

see page 148

1 What are the three task types?

A: Fixed duration, fixed units, and fixed work.

2 What is a *fixed duration* task?

A: For a fixed duration task, the user enters the duration and either units or work, and Project 2000 calculates the non-user entered number.

Personal Workbook Answers

3 **What is an advantage to using the Assign Resources dialog box?**

A: Using the Assign Resources dialog box, you can easily assign multiple resources to multiple tasks or a single resource to multiple tasks.

4 **What are three ways to assign resources to tasks?**

A: You can assign resources to tasks using the Assign Resources dialog box, the Task Information dialog box, or the resource Name column on a table.

5 **What is the primary difference between the Resource Usage and Task Usage views?**

A: The Task Usage view lists tasks with assigned resources while the Resource Usage view lists resources with task assignments.

6 **What are four kinds of resource contour patterns?**

A: The eight resource contour patterns are Flat, Back Loaded, Front Loaded, Double Peak, Early Peak, Late Peak, Bell, and Turtle.

7 **What are *fixed costs*?**

A: Fixed costs are direct user-entered cost entries.

8 **What are the two kinds of consumption of material resources?**

A: The two types of consumption of material resources are fixed and variable.

Visual Quiz

Q: **How do you access the Assignment Information dialog box?**

A: To access the Assignment Information dialog box either right-click a resource name and choose Assignment Information from the shortcut menu, or click the Assignment Information button on the Standard toolbar.

Chapter 10

see page 164

1 **What is the purpose of grouping?**

A: Grouping allows you to band tasks in meaningful groups based on user-defined criteria.

2 **How do you make custom group definitions available to other projects?**

A: Use the Organizer, Groups tab, to make group definitions available to other projects.

3 **What are the five steps needed to group tasks using a custom field?**

A: To group tasks using a custom field, (1) create a custom field, (2) define values for the field, (3) choose a view and include the field as a column on the table, (4) enter data or use the pick-list, and (5) create the group definition.

4 **What is a *Display only* filter?**

A: When using a Display only filter, the tasks that match the filter criteria display on the screen, whereas tasks that don't match, don't show.

5 **What is a *Highlight* filter?**

A: When using a Highlight filter, all tasks display onscreen but those tasks that match the filter criteria display using a different color or font.

6 **What is an *Interactive* filter?**

A: An Interactive filter is one that asks the user to enter specific criteria prior to "running" the filter.

7 **What are four views that cannot be sorted?**

A: The four views that cannot be sorted are the Calendar, Network Diagram, Resource Graph, and the Relationship Diagram.

Personal Workbook Answers

⑧ How do you return to an "unfiltered" view?

A: To return to an "unfiltered" view, choose All Tasks from the filter list.

Visual Quiz

Q: How do you complete this dialog box to group by resource group (primary) and then by standard pay rate?

A: To complete the dialog box, select Resource Group as the first row under the Field Name column and select Standard Rate as the second row field name.

Chapter 11

see page 182

① How do you jump from the beginning to the end of the project in the Calendar view?

A: Use Alt+Home and Alt+End to jump from the beginning to the end of the Calendar view.

② How do you access the Go To command in a Calendar view?

A: To access the Go To command in a Calendar view, choose Edit ➪ Go To, or right-click on the Calendar and choose Go To from the shortcut menu.

③ What is an *overflow indicator* on a Calendar view?

A: An overflow indicator is a small arrow that indicates that more tasks are scheduled for the date shown than can fit in the calendar date box.

④ What are three different techniques for identifying resource overallocation conflicts?

A: Identify resource overallocation conflicts by filtering for overallocations, looking for the overallocation icon in the Indicators column, looking at the Resource Sheet for names in red (default), or viewing the overallocated resources report.

⑤ Name three buttons found on the Resource Management toolbar?

A: The buttons found on the Resource Management toolbar include Resource Allocation View, Task Entry View, Go To Next Overallocation, Assign, Share Resources, Update Resource Pool, Refresh Resource Pool, Address Book, Resource Details, NT Account, Using Resource (filter), and Leveling Help.

⑥ What are two manual techniques for resolving resource conflicts?

A: To resolve resource conflicts consider substituting resources for the overallocated resource, delaying the start of the task until the resource is available, asking the resource to work overtime, or reducing the allocation percentage of the resource on tasks.

⑦ What is the drawback to using automatic resource leveling?

A: The main drawback to automatic leveling is that it uses a delay algorithm rather than optimizing your schedule.

⑧ Where do you establish the first day of the week as shown on the Calendar view?

A: Establish the first day of the calendar week on the Calendar tab of the Options dialog box.

Visual Quiz

Q: How do you display slack lines on your task bars?

A: Probably the easiest way to display slack lines is to use the GanttChartWizard. Instruct the Wizard to create a custom Gantt Chart and when asked about additional bars to display, click the radio button for Total Slack.

Personal Workbook Answers

Chapter 12

see page 212

1 **How do you add words to your custom dictionary for use with the spell checker?**

A: To add words to your custom dictionary, open the dictionary file (CUSTOM.DIC) from a text editor and type in custom words.

2 **How do you set a variable row height?**

A: To set variable row height, drag the bottom row divider line to the desired height.

3 **What is the difference between Format ⇨ Bar and Format ⇨ Bar Styles?**

A: The Format ⇨ Bar command sets formatting options for the task(s) selected while the Format ⇨ Bar Styles command formats by task category.

4 **What are three buttons found on the Drawing toolbar?**

A: Buttons on the Drawing toolbar include Draw, Line, Arrow, Rectangle, Oval, Arc, Polygon, Text Box, Cycle Fill Color, and Attach to Task.

5 **What is the primary difference between printing a view and printing reports?**

A: A view is a graphic printout and a report is a text printout.

6 **What are the two scaling options available when resizing output?**

A: When resizing output, the two scaling options available are to adjust to a user-specified percentage of normal or to fit to a user-specified number of pages wide and tall.

7 **How do you add a company logo to a view's footer printout?**

A: To add a company logo, click the Insert Picture button and select the logo file.

8 **What are the five categories of standard report groups?**

A: The five categories of report groups are Overview, Current Activities, Costs, Assignments, and Workload.

Visual Quiz

Q: How do you display this dialog box? What purpose does it serve?

A: To display the Page Setup dialog box, choose File ⇨ Page Setup or click the Page Setup button from Print Preview.

Chapter 13

see page 226

1 **What is a *URL?***

A: A URL (Uniform Resource Locator) is a Web address.

2 **What is an *HTML document?***

A: An HTML (Hypertext Markup Language) file contains the formatting codes necessary for Web page display.

3 **What is the purpose of an Import/Export map?**

A: An Import/Export Map allows the selection of task, resource, and assignment to be included in the HTML document.

4 **What is a *hyperlink?***

A: A hyperlink is an icon or underlined word or phrase that allows you to quickly jump from Web page to Web page or to another location on the current page.

Personal Workbook Answers

5 How do you save a Project 2000 project as a Web page?

A: To save a Project 2000 project as a Web page, choose File ⇨ Save As Web Page.

6 What is the name of the default HTML document template that comes with Project 2000?

A: The default HTML template that comes with Project 2000 is Standard Export.html.

7 What are the four tabs in the Define Import/Export Map dialog box?

A: The four tabs are Options, Task Mapping, Resource Mapping, and Assignment Mapping.

8 What is a *Web browser*?

A: A Web browser is an application such as Netscape Communicator or Microsoft Internet Explorer that allows you to view pages on the Internet.

Visual Quiz

Q: How do you access this dialog box?

A: To access the dialog box, either click the Insert Hyperlink button on the Standard toolbar or choose Insert ⇨ Hyperlink.

Chapter 14

see page 252

1 How do you save a baseline?

A: To save a baseline, choose that option through the Planning Wizard when you save the file or choose Tools ⇨ Tracking ⇨ Save Baseline.

2 What is a *progress line*?

A: A progress line connects progress indicators on each task bar.

3 What is the difference between Start date and Actual Start date?

A: A Start date is the currently scheduled start date while the Actual Start Date is the date the task physically starts.

4 What are three useful tracking buttons on the Tracking toolbar?

A: Buttons on the Tracking toolbar include Project Statistics, Update as Schedules, Reschedule Work, Add Progress Line, 0%, 25%, 50%, 75%, 100%, Update Tasks, and Workgroup Toolbar.

5 What are two places to enter actual schedule data into Project 2000?

A: You may enter actual schedule data using the tracking table, the Task Information dialog box, the Multiple Task Information dialog box, the Update Tasks dialog box, or by using the Tracking form.

6 What does *BCWP* mean?

A: BCWP is an earned value term which means Budgeted Cost of Work Performed.

7 How do you save an interim plan?

A: To save an interim plan, choose Tools ⇨ Tracking ⇨ Save Baseline, and click the "Save interim plan" radio button.

8 What does the Copy Picture button do?

A: The Copy Picture button makes a screen "snapshot" and converts the "snapshot" into a file for placement in an application.

Visual Quiz

Q: How do you access this dialog box? What purpose(s) does it serve?

A: To access the Update Project dialog box, choose Tools ⇨ Tracking ⇨ Update Project. Use this dialog box to automatically update tasks based on the status date.

Personal Workbook Answers

Chapter 15

see page 276

1 **What are two workgroup communication options?**

A: Two forms of communication are e-mail and the World Wide Web.

2 **Web-based messaging in Project 2000 consists of what two major components?**

A: Web-based messaging consists of a server and a client.

3 **What three database types are supported with Web-based messaging in Project 2000?**

A: The three database types are Oracle, SQL Server, and Microsoft Database Engine (MSDE).

4 **What is the name of the Microsoft Project Web Client?**

A: The name of the Web Client is ProjectCentral.

5 **What should you do if your name does not appear in the list of users eligible to log on to ProjectCentral?**

A: Click the hyperlink Setting up a Web Client Account.

6 **What does the acronym MAPI mean, as in MAPI-compliant, 32-bit e-mail system?**

A: MAPI means Messaging Application Programming Interface.

7 **What is the name of the Web server included on the Project 2000 CD-ROM?**

A: The name of the Web server is Internet Information Server (IIS) or Microsoft Project Central Server.

8 **Which tab in the Options dialog box is used to establish the Web Client Server URL for use by the Web Client?**

A: The Workgroup tab is used to establish a server URL.

Visual Quiz

Q: **Where do you enter the default workgroup messaging options and establish the Web Client Server URL? How do you access this dialog box?**

A: Choose Tools ⇨ Options and select the Workgroup tab. Here you can enter the default workgroup messaging options.

Chapter 16

see page 296

1 **What are three techniques for working with multiple project files?**

A: To create a multiple project file, use New Window, Insert Projects, or Save a Workspace.

2 **What is the function of the Window ⇨ Arrange All command?**

A: The Arrange All command resizes and tiles all open windows for display.

3 **What are two project consolidation techniques that produce the inserted projects icon in the Indicators column?**

A: The two consolidation techniques that produce inserted projects icons are the New Window command and the Insert Project command.

4 **What is the purpose of saving a workspace?**

A: Save a workspace to save time in opening multiple files together rather than one by one.

5 **How do you set a dependency link between tasks in different project files?**

A: To set dependency links between tasks in different project files, type the complete path to the external predecessor in the predecessor field for the successor task (or follow the same technique for a successor task).

Personal Workbook Answers

6 **What is an *external* task?**

A: An external task is a task representing an external dependency link.

7 **How do you discontinue using a shared resource pool?**

A: For a sharing file to discontinue sharing resources, choose Tools ⇨ Resources ⇨ Share Resources and click the Use own resources radio button. To discontinue sharing from the Resource Pool file, choose Tools ⇨ Resources ⇨ Share Resources, select the file(s) that will no longer share, and click the Discontinue sharing button.

8 **What does the exclamation point next to the inserted projects icon in the Indicators column indicate?**

A: The exclamation symbol represents that the inserted project is read-only.

Visual Quiz

Q: What is the purpose of this dialog box? How do you access it?

A: The purpose of the New Window dialog box is to insert open project files into a new multi-project window. To access it, choose Window ⇨ New Window.

Chapter 17

see page 314

1 **When creating a table, what does *lock the first column* mean?**

A: When scrolling through columns, a locked column will not scroll off the screen.

2 **What character do you place directly in front of a letter in a view name on the menu to create a shortcut?**

A: Place an ampersand (&) symbol directly in front of the intended shortcut letter.

3 **How do you restore the default menu bar?**

A: To restore the default menu, choose Tools ⇨ Customize ⇨ Toolbars. Then, select the Toolbars tab, select the menu bar, and click the reset button.

4 **What dialog box must be open before you can drag a button off a toolbar?**

A: The Customize dialog box must be open before you can drag a button from a toolbar.

5 **When creating a custom field, what is a *pick-list*?**

A: A pick-list is a user-defined list of values that appear as a pick-list for data entry.

6 **What is the name of the program within a program used to create forms?**

A: The Custom Form Editor is the program within a program used to create forms.

7 **What is a *macro?***

A: A macro is a recorded set of keystrokes and mouse clicks.

8 **What programming language is used for macros in Project 2000?**

A: Visual Basic is the macro programming language for Project 2000.

Visual Quiz

Q: How do you display this small blank toolbar? How do you position it at the top of the pane with the other toolbars?

A: To create a new toolbar, choose Tools ⇨ Customize ⇨ Toolbars. Then select the Toolbars tab and click the New button. To position the new toolbar at the top, simply drag it to the top and, when released, it will "anchor" with the other toolbars.

Appendix B:
Installing Microsoft Project 2000

Before You Install

Prior to installing Microsoft Project 2000, consider the programs discussed below.

Internet Explorer

If you have Internet Explorer 5.0 already installed, setup for Project 2000 may update it to a newer version. If you have Internet Explorer 4.*x* installed and you do not want Project 2000 setup to install Internet Explorer 5.0, choose the "Do not upgrade Microsoft Internet Explorer" option. If you use Netscape Navigator or another browser and you don't want to install Internet Explorer at all, choose "Windows Web Browsing Components Only."

Web Server and Client Installation

For information about installing the new Web server and client components, see the document Websetup.doc in the Docs folder on your installation CD-ROM.

Installation

To install Project 2000, insert your CD-ROM and click the "Install Microsoft Project 2000" link when the install shield screen automatically displays.

Alternatively, if the install shield screen does not appear, run the Setup.exe file.

For either of the previous setup options, follow the instructions on the screen.

You can install Project 2000 in one of three ways:

► Follow a traditional install and install all components on your local hard drive or network server.
► Install components on an "as needed" basis. Keep your CD-ROM handy so that you can install components when the need arises.
► Run Project 2000 from the CD-ROM. In other words, do not install it to a hard drive or server.

If you want to install to a folder other than the default folder, click the Customize button during the "Ready to Install" setup step.

If you want to keep a previous version of Microsoft Project along with the new installation of Project 2000, click "Keep these programs" at the "Remove Previous Versions" setup step.

Appendix C:
Project Management Web Sites

Here are just a few of the many project management (and related) Web sites. For other sites, try searching the Web for "project management associations" or "project management organizations."

Site Name	Web Address
American Society for Quality Control	**http://www.asq.org**
Architecture, Engineering, Construction Business Center	**http://www.aecinfo.com**
Asociación Española de Project Management (AEPM)	**http://www.aepm.org**
Association for Project Management — United Kingdom	**http://www.apm.org.uk/**
Association Francophone de Management de Projet (AFITEP)	**http://www.afitep.fr/**
Australian Institute of Project Management	**http://www.aipm.com.au/**
Building Industry Exchange	**http://www.building.org**
GPM International Project Management Association (Germany)	**http://www.gpm-ipma.de/start.html**
International Cost Engineering Council	**http://www.icoste.org/**
International Project Management Association	**http://www.ipma.ch/**
Japan Project Management Forum	**http://www.enaa.or.jp/JPMF/**
National Contract Management Association	**http://www.ncmahq.org/**
National Society of Professional Engineers	**http://www.nspe.org**
Project Management Institute Canada	**http://www.pmicanada.org/**
Project Management Institute United States	**http://www.pmi.org**
Software Program Managers Network	**http://www.icompe.com/**
Swiss Society for Project Management	**http://www.spm.ch/**
The Institute of Project Management of Ireland	**http://www.projectmanagement.ie/**
The Project Management Association of Iceland (VSF)	**http://www.skima.is/vsf/**
Risk Management Interest Group	**http://www.risksig.com/index.htm**

Glossary

actual
An amount of time, work, or cost that has already been spent.

Actual Start Date
The date the task physically starts.

ACWP
Actual Cost of Work Performed is the total amount spent on a task to date.

ALAP
An "as late as possible" task constraint that causes the task to finish just before the start of its successor task.

ASAP
An "as soon as possible" task constraint that causes the task to start as soon as its dependency criteria with predecessor tasks is met.

ASCII
American Standard Code for Information Interchange.

BAC (Budgeted at Completion)
A task's total baseline cost.

baseline
A "snapshot" or record of the planned start and finish dates, duration estimates, work, and cost information for each task and resource.

BCWP (Budgeted Cost of Work Performed)
The achieved cost of the task, calculated as Baseline Cost × Percent Complete.

BCWS (Budgeted Cost of Work Scheduled)
The baseline cost multiplied by the planned completion percentage (by the reporting date) or how much of the budget should have been spent by this date.

binder
An electronic folder that stores all relevant project documents and reports.

bitmap
A format that stores graphic images using the extension .BMP.

bottom-up calculations
Calculations that result from summarizing all lowest-level task information.

calendar
A record of working time and nonworking time for a project.

Glossary

cascading menu
A menu that opens from a higher-level menu. Also known as a hierarchical menu.

chevrons
Downward pointing menu arrows that indicate additional options. When your cursor passes over these arrows the additional menu displays, cascading downward.

clients
The group (or individual) that accesses a server in a networked environment.

clipboard
The Windows temporary storage location for items held during cut, copy, and paste operations.

collapse
To hide a task's subtasks in an outline view.

combination view
A combination (or split) view displays two window panes each containing a view.

consolidated project
A project file that contains multiple projects.

constraint
A restriction or boundary applied to the project schedule, budget, scope, or resources.

critical path
The longest sequence of tasks in the project.

critical task
A task that has no slack or float.

CV (Cost Variance)
BCWP minus ACWP.

default
The initial setting for an entry field.

deliverables
Tangible end results of a phase or project.

Delphi
An estimating technique that asks subject matter experts to independently develop estimates and list assumptions for a given task.

Display Only filter
The tasks that match the filter criteria display on the screen, whereas tasks that don't match, don't show.

duration
The elapsed time from the start to the finish of a task.

EAC (Estimated at Completion)
A task's total cost.

earned value
A technique used to objectively demonstrate project progress using monetary calculations.

elapsed time
An estimate of duration based on a 24-hour, 7-day week calendar.

estimate
An approximate calculation or forecast.

Glossary

expand
To show the subtasks in an outline view.

external task
A task representing an external dependency link.

fixed costs
Direct user-entered cost entries.

forecasting
An estimating technique that looks at past historical information, compares the historical actuals to the current task, considering the variables that are different, and then forecasts what is likely.

free slack
Amount of time a task can slip without affecting its next successor task.

FTE
Full-time equivalent is a means of estimating or calculating resource needs.

Gantt Chart
A well-known project management visual tool to display task bars on a time grid.

Global template file
The Global.mpt file contains elements common to all project files.

gridlines
Horizontal and vertical lines that separate rows and columns in a table or graph, or on a timescale.

grouping
Allows you to band tasks in a view in meaningful groups based on user-defined criteria.

highlight filter
A filter technique whereby all tasks display onscreen, but those tasks that match the filter criteria display using a different color or font.

home page
The first page of a Web site.

hotkeys
Shortcut commands that substitute for mouse clicks as a method of selection.

HTML
HyperText Markup Language is the format used for Web pages or documents.

hyperlink
A link between Web addresses that allows you to jump from location to location, usually by clicking a graphic or icon or by clicking underlined words.

I

interactive filter
A filter technique that asks the user to enter specific criteria prior to "running" the filter.

Glossary

J

Java
A programming language that is popular for Web-based applications.

L

lag
In a dependency relationship, lag is time added to the dependency link.

LAN
Local Area Network.

lead
In a dependency relationship, lead is time subtracted from the dependency link.

M

macro
A recorded set of keystrokes and mouse clicks.

MAPI
Messaging Application Programming Interface.

material resource
A consumable resource such as gasoline, lumber, paper, silk, or irrigation line.

milestone tasks
Zero duration tasks that represent points in time.

N

Network Diagram (aka PERT diagram)
A project management tool that displays the flow of work through a project.

nondefault working hours
User-defined work hours that are "outside" the work hours set on the default standard calendar.

O

Office Assistant
A form of online help that responds to user-entered commands.

OLE
Object Linking and Embedding. A tool for sharing information between applications.

overallocation
Refers to the situation in which a resource is assigned for more work in a time period than the resource has available.

overflow indicator
A small arrow that indicates that more tasks are scheduled for the shown date than can fit in the calendar date box.

P

pane
A section of a window that contains a view.

Glossary

PERT analysis
An estimating technique that looks at risk factors and their relationships to duration estimates and then uses a weighted average to predict task duration.

PERT chart
Program Evaluation and Review Technique chart used as a project management tool to show task dependencies.

phase exit
In project management terms, a phase exit is a review held at the end of a phase.

pick-list
A user-defined list of values that appear as a pick-list for data entry.

predecessor
In a dependency relationship, the task that determines the timing of another task.

program
A collection of related projects.

progress lines
Lines that connect the progress indicators on each task for a visual reference.

project
A temporary endeavor undertaken to create a unique product or service.

project life cycle
Identifies the process or steps of managing projects from concept to close-out.

project management
The application of knowledge, skills, techniques, and tools in order to meet or exceed stakeholder expectations.

prorated cost
A prorated cost spreads the cost evenly across the task duration.

recurring task
A task that repeats throughout the life of a project.

resource
People, equipment, or material necessary to complete a task.

resource-driven
A task whose duration and scheduling is determined by the number of resources assigned.

resource group
A single resource definition that refers to a group of people (a team).

resource pool
A list of shared resources available to one or more projects.

schedule crashing
A term used to describe techniques for compressing the critical path.

server
The hardware and software controlling the accessibility of information in a networked environment.

Slack
Amount of flexibility that noncritical path tasks have in their scheduling. Also called *float*.

Glossary

SME
Subject matter expert.

Start Date
The currently scheduled start date.

successor
In a dependency relationship, the task whose timing is determined by another task.

summary tasks
A task that summarizes information for all the tasks indented underneath it, such as duration, work, and cost.

SV (Schedule Variance)
Calculated as BCWP minus BCWS. A negative amount indicates the task is ahead of schedule.

table
A predetermined set of columns typically chosen for a particular project management purpose.

task
A single project element or activity.

task nodes
Boxes that represent tasks in a Network Diagram.

Total Slack
Amount of time a task can slip without affecting the end date of the project.

tracking
The techniques used to record, enter, and analyze actual project progress information.

units
The percentage of time a resource is assigned to a task.

URL
Uniform Resource Locator is an address of a Web site.

VAC (Variance at Completion)
BAC minus EAC. A negative number indicates overbudget.

Visual Basic
The macro programming language for Project 2000.

W

wallpaper
A Windows-supplied bitmap pattern that displays on the desktop.

WBS chart
A Work Breakdown Structure chart is a hierarchical chart, like an organizational chart or tree chart, whose purpose is to assist in the organization of the project from a conceptual level down to the task level.

Web browser
An application, such as Microsoft Internet Explorer or Netscape Communicator, that allows you to access Web pages.

work
The amount of effort or billable time a resource is assigned to the task.

Index

Index

Index

Index

Index

Index

I

icon
    Indicators, 36–37
    Microsoft Project 2000, 8
    View Bar, 30
ID column, 288
ID number, 163, 289
ID order, 162
IDG Books Worldwide, 216
IIS. *See* Internet Information
        Server
illustrations, 197
Import/Export map, 217,
        218–219
Incomplete Tasks filter, 159
indent, report style, 79, 80
Indicators column
    close-out feature, 275
    described, 36–37
    optimizing, 112
    reviewing, 168
industry standard earned value
        results, 246–247
information. *See also* data
    adding to projects, 17
    post-project close-out,
        274–275
    sharing, 179
    sorting and filtering, 17
Information Technology, 256
initials, 121
Insert menu
    described, 17
    hyperlink, 225
    Page Break, 198

Project, 286
    Recurring Task, 83
inserting
    drawings, 196–197
    objects, 196–197
    projects, 286–287
    rows, 219
    tasks into the current list, 76
    working with inserted
        projects, 288–289
installing, Microsoft Project
        2000, 8
interactive filter, 158–159
Internet, 215
Internet Explorer, 216, 222, 256
Internet Information Server
        (IIS), 264
Internet Service Provider
        (ISP), 256
interval, 155
intranet
    Executive Information
        System, 215
    saving files to, 59
    workgroups, 256
irrigation line, 120
ISP. *See* Internet Service
        Provider
IT/IS department, 256

J

job category, 120

K

kill points, 6

L

lags, 96–97
LAN administrators, 59
landscape print orientation, 200
Late Finish, 110
Late Peak resource contour, 143
Late Start, 110
Late/Overbudget Tasks
        Assigned To filter, 245
Layout dialog box
    described, 175
    roll up Gantt bars, 114
lead, 96–97
legends
    graphics, 197
    report, 202–203
length, 85
lessons, 5
lettering, WBS code, 84
letters, menu, 16
Leveling Help button, 179
life cycle, 6–7
light blue, 223
lines
    separate timescale sections, 95
    tables, 191
links, *See also* hyperlinks
    Assistant character named, 15
    outlined tasks, 103

Index

Index

Index

Index

Index

Index

Index

Index

Index

my2cents.idgbooks.com

Register This Book — And Win!

Visit **http://my2cents.idgbooks.com** to register this book and we'll automatically enter you in our fantastic monthly prize giveaway. It's also your opportunity to give us feedback: let us know what you thought of this book and how you would like to see other topics covered.

Discover IDG Books Online!

The IDG Books Online Web site is your online resource for tackling technology — at home and at the office. Frequently updated, the IDG Books Online Web site features exclusive software, insider information, online books, and live events!

10 Productive & Career-Enhancing Things You Can Do at www.idgbooks.com

- Nab source code for your own programming projects.

- Download software.

- Read Web exclusives: special articles and book excerpts by IDG Books Worldwide authors.

- Take advantage of resources to help you advance your career as a Novell or Microsoft professional.

- Buy IDG Books Worldwide titles or find a convenient bookstore that carries them.

- Register your book and win a prize.

- Chat live online with authors.

- Sign up for regular e-mail updates about our latest books.

- Suggest a book you'd like to read or write.

- Give us your 2¢ about our books and about our Web site.

You say you're not on the Web yet? It's easy to get started with IDG Books' *Discover the Internet*, available at local retailers everywhere.